For Reference

Not to be taken from this room

HISTORICAL ATLAS OF
U.S. PRESIDENTIAL ELECTIONS
1788–2004

J. Clark Archer, Stephen J. Lavin, Kenneth C. Martis, and Fred M. Shelley

CQ PRESS

A DIVISION OF CONGRESSIONAL QUARTERLY INC.
WASHINGTON, D.C.

10-17-2006
WW
$150

CQ Press
1255 22nd Street, NW, Suite 400
Washington, DC 20037

Phone: 202-729-1900; toll-free, 1-866-4CQ-PRESS (1-866-427-7737)

Web: www.cqpress.com

Interior design: Judy Myers
Cover design: TGD

Cover photos: *left,* Lincoln-Hamlin 1860 campaign poster, Library of Congress; *center,* Harry S Truman in 1948, St. Louis Globe-Democrat Archives of the St. Louis Mercantile Library, University of Missouri, St. Louis; *right,* 2004 election supporters, Bob Mack/Associated Press.

Table 2, page 7: Reprinted by permission of Sage Publications Inc.

∞ The paper used in this publication exceeds the requirements of the American National Standard for Information Sciences—Permanence of Paper for Printed Library Materials, ANSI Z39.48-1992.

Printed and bound in Canada

10   09   08   07   06   1   2   3   4   5

ISBN-10: 1-56802-955-1
ISBN-13: 978-1-56802-955-9
LCCN: 2006049280

~

In grateful recognition of our life partners

Jill A. Archer

Ruth Schmidle Lavin

Myra Nicholas Lowe

Arlene Shelley

CONTENTS

LIST OF MAPS

PREFACE

In December 1788, the eligible male citizens of Massachusetts and New Hampshire became the first Americans to vote in a U.S. presidential election. In compliance with the Constitution, the second presidential election took place four years later, in 1792, with electors from each state selecting the president through the electoral college system. Presidential elections have been held every four years since for more than two centuries. These elections represent one of the longest continuous sequences of recorded, broad-based democratic balloting for a national leader.

In virtually all of the states, counties (called parishes in Louisiana) have been the local administrative authorities in the organization, management, counting, and reporting of presidential voting. In the U.S. system of government, counties play a critical role in the states, as the states do in the nation. In recent presidential elections, more than 3,000 counties reported voting results, producing a large national database. The assembly of votes at the county level allows for detailed differential illustration and analysis of presidential balloting within states, between neighboring states, and across the nation as a whole. Throughout U.S. history, regional and sectional coalitions have been central to the electoral process, so documented geographical aspects of the presidential vote are quite revealing if one seeks to understand the totality of the democratic process and the cultural and social milieu of the nation. The *Historical Atlas of U.S. Presidential Elections, 1788–2004* improves understanding of U.S. political history in a new way—the comprehensive mapping of presidential elections at the county level.

The *Atlas* represents a number of firsts in U.S. political history. It is the first reference book to map election outcomes for all the counties in every presidential election, through 2004. Its four-color, national popular vote map for each election depicts the winning candidate and party affiliation in each county, allowing for longitudinal analysis of electoral patterns for every county, state, region, and section throughout U.S. history. These maps use two different color intensities to designate plurality and majority levels of support for the winning candidates from each major party and third party receiving more than 2 percent of the national vote. In addition, maps for each of these leading candidates depict their strength in every county using five levels of color variations and allow for analysis of party voting patterns. The county boundaries on all maps appear as they were drawn at the time of each election.

The mapping of every presidential election required the creation of a unique database of election statistics and county boundaries. County presidential election statistics were compiled from numerous electronic, print, and unpublished sources. These statistics were then organized in a geographic information science (GIS) system to produce a corrected, refined, and accurate electoral database unparalleled in U.S. political studies. In a similar manner, information on county boundaries over the years was collected and combined in the same GIS process to produce a graphical display of unmatched precision.

ORGANIZATION

Creation of the *Atlas* took decades of discussion and planning and more than three years of research, compilation, and writing. Its organization is designed to facilitate its use as an atlas as well as a general reference. It is divided into three major parts: the introduction, which provides an overview of presidential election history and the electoral process, as well as details on political cartography and the construction of the election maps; two sets of four-color maps illustrating the distribution of presidential votes at the county level; and election "vignettes" examining the candidates and issues in each of the fifty-five elections from 1788 to 2004.

The introduction notes that in early U.S. history, many of the states did not hold popular elections for president or for presidential electors. Instead, their legislatures selected electors who then cast ballots for president in the electoral college. It also addresses the issue of political parties and presidential elections, discussing in detail political party nomenclature, particularly with respect to the changes in parties and party names, all of which is reflected in the maps. Political scientists and historians have identified at least six different "party systems," or political party eras, in U.S. history thus far. Discussion of the critical elections that signal the advent of each system and of the eras themselves provide insight into the nation's political evolution, clarifying such matters as the differences between the Republican Party of the 1860s and the Republican Party of the 1980s. The maps' presentation of the geography of presidential elections over the centuries calls into question some of the accepted analyses and theories of several critical elections and political eras.

The section "Changes in the Electorate" examines voter eligibility and who voted over the years. The popular electorate of 2004 differed fundamentally from the popular electorate of 1788. The discussion on eligible voters covers the gamut, from the white male franchise to African American voting rights to women's suffrage to age restrictions and residency requirements. The political geography of the U.S. electorate is illustrated in the four-color maps, mirroring population geography and population expansion. The geography of frontier expansion is discussed, along with urbanization and suburbanization, which have enormous import on understanding and interpreting modern election maps. Population growth since the 1790 census is also explored to provide context for understanding the voting maps. Comparisons between the actual vote numbers and the percentage of voter turnout over the various political eras help in gauging changing levels of voter participation. This section concludes with a unique cartographic depiction of voter participation comparing the 1848, 1900, 1948, and 2000 elections and detailed analysis to explain changes in the geography of voter participation.

There is a rich intellectual history with respect to the need, theory, and practicality of mapping presidential elections by county, yet the fact remains that until now there was no such comprehensive reference. The section "Previous Works in Mapping U.S. Presidential Elections" opens with the development of the cartographic art and the techniques of depicting human data on maps. In the late 1800s, the technology of cartography and presidential vote data were married to produce maps of individual elections. Intellectual leaders, among them historian Frederick Jackson Turner, promoted vote mapping as a way to better understand U.S. history. The only other attempt to map the entire series of presidential elections appeared in Charles O. Paullin and John K. Wright's *Atlas of the Historical Geography of the United States* (1932), which does not show all the county boundaries and has numerous other cartographic display problems. In the late twentieth century, the advancements of GIS technology and the World Wide Web facilitated the comprehensive compilation of recent voting data and county boundaries to allow the construction of modern election maps.

"Construction of the Presidential Elections Maps," the final section of the introduction, outlines in detail the vote data sources and the methodology of data refinement, procedures for ensuring accuracy, and the organization of the final maps. The accuracy and origins of county boundary data are also discussed. In the end, a unique data set of votes and state and county boundaries were combined in a GIS system and enhanced to produce publication-quality maps.

The maps depicting the fifty-five presidential elections constitute the centerpiece of the *Atlas*. On right-hand pages, a large map illustrates the popular vote winner and party affiliation in each county and indicates whether victory was by majority or plurality. In the lower right-hand corner, a map illustrates electoral college voting. In the lower left-hand corner, two pie charts depict popular vote and electoral college percentages. The latter allow for quick visual comparisons between popular votes received and the electoral college margin.

On the left-hand pages, unique maps illustrate the level of support in each county for the leading candidates. Their popular vote strength is represented by five levels of support. For example, in 1912 three major candidates—Republican William Howard Taft, Democrat Woodrow Wilson, and Progressive Theodore Roosevelt—have individual maps along with Socialist Eugene V. Debs, who received 6 percent of the national vote. Each candidate's map shows the same 2,965 counties and uses five hues of a color to indicate levels of support. This page alone contains 11,860 counties with more than 59,300 possible voting support categories. On the facing page, the 1912 popular vote map depicts the 2,965 counties and the four candidates represented by two hues of intensity each, for a total of 23,720 possible results. The cartography for the 1912 election presents a total of 14,825 counties with 83,020 intensity hue options.

Vignettes of each of the fifty-five presidential elections provide a review of the candidates, major issues, and geographic aspects of the electoral and popular votes. These vignettes make the *Atlas* a stand-alone reference with respect to presidential elections. Every narrative begins with a list of the presidential and vice presidential candidates from each of the major parties and includes their home states, because geography was and remains an important consideration in constructing tickets. The listings also include third-party candidates who received more than 2 percent of the national vote. The final electoral vote count is provided, along with percentages for the electoral and popular votes. Each vignette begins with a review of the major issues of the preceding four years and goes on to cover candidate selection, including the political and geographic considerations inherent in these choices. The campaigns are covered in depth only if overwhelmingly regional or sectional issues were paramount.

In most elections, regional and sectional groupings became evident in the final electoral college vote. This was as obvious and critical in 2004 as it was in 1796, 1860, and 1896. Detailed review is provided for the popular vote map for each campaign. Vote patterns more often than not spill over state boundaries, so the maps provide exacting evidence of the geographic extent of political sentiment and political regions. Some patterns repeat themselves through a political party era or even the course of a century. If a particular election is of interest, the reader is advised to examine the several previous and subsequent election vignettes for comprehensive understanding. For example, if a researcher wants to examine the geographic aspects of the 1848 presidential vote, that particular vignette offers sufficient coverage, but additional information on voting patterns during the Whig-Democrat era is also found in the vignettes for 1836 to 1852. Numerous vignettes highlight patterns on the individual candidate maps that may not be obvious on the primary, popular vote map. Vignettes usually conclude by identifying important post-election and post-inaugural issues that affect the next election.

The division of labor in the research, compilation, and final construction of the *Atlas* rested upon the expertise of each author. J. Clark Archer assumed the enormous task of assembling voting and county boundary data. This process included some original research by Archer and Kenneth C. Martis and took several years. Once the election and geographical boundary data were assembled and correlated, draft display maps were produced. These maps were then checked and double checked for accuracy over a one-year period by Martis and Deva Solomon at West Virginia University and Fred M. Shelley, Adrienne Proffer, and Kimberly Zerr at the University of Oklahoma. Stephen J. Lavin then created print-quality maps. Archer, Martis, and Shelley provided the text of the *Atlas*. Martis wrote the first draft of the preface and the acknowledgments and edited the bibliography. He also penned the initial drafts of the presidential election vignettes from 1788–1789 through 1876, and Shelley took responsibility for writing those for 1880 through 2004. Archer, Martis, and Shelley shared in the writing of the introduction: presidential elections (Martis); political party nomenclature (Martis); critical elections and political party eras (Martis); geographic voting patterns and critical election theory (Martis); nomination process (Shelley); eligible voters (Martis); political geography of settlement (Archer); historical trends in suffrage and voter participation (Archer); geography of voter participation in 1848, 1900, 1948, and 2000 (Archer); previous works in mapping presidential elections (Martis); construction of presidential election maps (Archer).

The *Atlas* combines geography, history, and politics in a unique reference with the goal of examining, expanding, advancing, and encouraging the geographic understanding of U.S. political history. It is hoped that the *Atlas* will become a standard source that not only answers questions about presidential elections, but elicits many more.

ACKNOWLEDGMENTS

The *Historical Atlas of U.S. Presidential Elections, 1788–2004* evolved from decades of discussions and proposals and more than three years of labor. For more than a quarter century, we reflected on the comprehensive mapping of presidential votes by county, which had never been done. Many people have provided ideas and support in our effort to fill this enormous gap in U.S. political history.

A work of this kind could not have been accomplished without previous decades of effort by scholars collecting presidential voting data and researching county boundaries. In the early twentieth century, researchers compiled historical election data as written sources, and in the 1960s and 1970s, these and other sources were put into machine-readable formats, stored, and made available at the Inter-University Consortium for Political and Social Research. Many geographers and historians have worked on the reconstruction of county boundaries over time, and we greatly appreciate their vision and contributions as well as those of earlier schol-

ars whose works facilitated our use of a GIS system of data organization and visualization. The data sets drawn upon in constructing the maps presented here are detailed in the introduction. In addition, bibliographic entries provide full citations to these sources along with the many scholarly articles addressing the practical and theoretical questions of using interlinked electoral and cartographic data.

This *Atlas* was developed and finalized at the geography departments of J. Clark Archer and Stephen J. Lavin at the University of Nebraska–Lincoln, Kenneth C. Martis at West Virginia University, and Fred M. Shelley at the University of Oklahoma. The laboratories and computer facilities of these departments were essential in organizing, constructing, and editing the *Atlas*. We thank our departments and colleagues for their support, especially department chairs Trevor Harris at West Virginia and David Wishart at Nebraska for cultivating an academic milieu that promotes and values long-term scholarly research. The historical research entailed in a work of this scope required the patient assistance of several library research staffs and reference librarians, so for their assistance we thank all at West Virginia's Wise Library, Nebraska's Love Library, and Oklahoma's Bizzell Memorial Library.

At West Virginia University, geography undergraduate students Jeff Rogers and Christopher Stewart provided us valuable research assistance. Deva Solomon spent more than a year as a research assistant on the project and contributed significantly to checking voting and boundary data. Several of his ideas made the research process much more efficient and revealed errors in the standard electronic vote and boundary data sets. The *Atlas* is much more precise because of his participation. At the University of Oklahoma, graduate assistants Adrienne Proffer and Kimberly Zerr and undergraduate assistant Emily Duda also provided essential support with background research and checking of final data and maps.

In closing we thank the staff at CQ Press, without whose backing this book would not have been possible. The publication of an oversized, four-color atlas is a substantial financial and editorial commitment. Mary Carpenter, our principal editor and contact throughout this process, guided us through constructing the book and editorial issues. We thank Robin Surratt, our copyeditor, for improving the clarity of our writing. We also extend our gratitude to Inge Lockwood for proofreading the pages and to Sally Ryman for compiling the index. In 2002 we published the *Atlas of American Politics, 1960–2000* with CQ Press. Mary and development editor David Arthur recognized the value of such publications and encouraged and supported us in the proposal and production of this presidential atlas.

J. Clark Archer
Stephen J. Lavin
Kenneth C. Martis
Fred M. Shelley

INTRODUCTION

PRESIDENTIAL ELECTIONS

THE PRESIDENT AND THE ELECTORAL COLLEGE

The U.S. Constitution created three separate and equal branches of the federal government: the executive, judiciary, and legislature. Article 2, section 1, established the executive office of the president. Some of the proposals put forth at the Constitutional Convention would have had the president elected by Congress, but the delegates rejected these based on the belief that such an arrangement would make the chief executive beholden to the legislative branch. According to the founders' governing philosophy of checks and balances, the president needed to be independent. The convention also rejected proposals to have the president popularly elected on the ground that it would leave too much power in the hands of the masses. Instead, the founders settled on a unique presidential elector system that in a nod to republicanism (independence and rule of the people through indirect governance) inserted a barrier of elites—state electors—between the mass vote and the final vote for the president. Allocating this voting power to the states represented a nod to federalism (decentralization of political power). Under this system, when individuals cast their vote for a presidential candidate, they are in reality casting a vote for an elector who has "pledged" to cast his or her vote in the electoral college for their mutual candidate. The term *electoral college* to identify the collective body of electors became common in the early nineteenth century and does not appear in the Constitution.

In the electoral college, each state has a vote equal to the number of its members in the House of Representatives plus its two senators.[1] Because each state elects two senators regardless of the size of its population, states with relatively smaller populations would appear to have an advantage in Senate and electoral college representation. Most states, however, employ a winner-take-all system for selecting their electoral college representatives. Mathematical analysis illustrates that voters in larger states actually hold the advantage over those in smaller states in determining the outcome of the presidency.

This tendency is illustrated by examining those states most crucial in determining election outcomes. For example, in the tight election of 2000, the popular vote in Florida, Iowa, Oregon, and New Mexico was closely contested. Democratic candidate Al Gore won Iowa by only 4,144 popular votes, Oregon by 6,765, and New Mexico by 366. Republican candidate George W. Bush won Florida by 537 votes. Because the number of electoral votes in Florida exceeds the combined total for Iowa, Oregon, and New Mexico, Bush won a majority in the electoral college. Had Gore won Florida, he would have won the election regardless of who won Iowa, Oregon, or New Mexico. Thus the result in Florida, the key swing state, determined the national outcome. In other recent close elections, such key states have also been large—Ohio in 2004 and in 1976 (along with smaller Mississippi) and Illinois and Texas in 1960. The electoral college is somewhat undemocratic not only in its allocation of political power, but also in its potential contradiction of the national plurality of popular votes. Four times in U.S. history, the candidate receiving the most popular votes was not elected president: 1824 (Jackson), 1876 (Tilden), 1888 (Cleveland), and 2000 (Gore).

SELECTING ELECTORS

The Constitution leaves it to the individual states to select a method for choosing its presidential electors. In the young, undeveloped democracy of the United States, and with states and regions of a variety of political cultures, the states devised a number of electoral systems in the country's first forty years. The early selection systems for electors are divided in the *Atlas* into three general categories: election by state legislature, winner-take-all election by popular vote statewide, and election by popular vote in districts. Table 1 lists the states participating in presidential votes from the first election in 1788–1789 through the twelfth election in 1832 and their method of choosing electors.

1

TABLE 1   Methods of Selecting Presidential Electors, 1788–1789 to 1832

STATE	1788–1789	1792	1796	1800	1804	1808	1812	1816	1820	1824	1828	1832
Connecticut	LEG	LEG	LEG	LEG	LEG	LEG	LEG	LEG	POP	POP	POP	POP
Delaware	POP (d)	LEG	LEG	LEG	LEG	LEG	LEG	LEG	LEG	LEG	LEG	POP
Georgia	LEG	LEG	POP	LEG	LEG	LEG	LEG	LEG	LEG	LEG	POP	POP
Maryland	POP	POP	POP (d)	POP (d)	POP (d)	POP (d)	POP (d)	POP (d)	POP (d)	POP (d)	POP (d)	POP (d)
Massachusetts	POP (d) + LEG[a]	POP (d) + LEG[b]	POP + LEG[c]	LEG	POP (d)[d]	LEG	POP (d)	LEG	POP (d)[d]	POP	POP	POP
New Hampshire	POP[b]	POP	POP[b]	LEG	POP	POP	POP	POP	POP	POP	POP	POP
New Jersey	LEG	LEG	LEG	LEG	POP	POP	LEG	POP	POP	POP	POP	POP
Pennsylvania	POP	POP	POP	LEG	POP	POP	POP	POP	POP	POP	POP	POP
South Carolina	LEG	LEG	LEG	LEG	LEG	LEG	LEG	LEG	LEG	LEG	LEG	LEG
Virginia	POP (d)	POP (d)	POP (d)	POP	POP	POP	POP	POP	POP	POP	POP	POP
New York		LEG	LEG	LEG	LEG	LEG	LEG	LEG	LEG	LEG	POP (d)[e]	POP
North Carolina		LEG	POP (d)	POP (d)	POP (d)	POP (d)	LEG	POP	POP	POP	POP	POP
Rhode Island		LEG	LEG	POP	POP	POP	POP	POP	POP	POP	POP	POP
Vermont		LEG	LEG	LEG	LEG	LEG	LEG	LEG	LEG	LEG	POP	POP
Kentucky		POP (d)	POP (d)	POP (d)	POP (d)	POP (d)	POP (d)	POP (d)	POP (d)	POP (d)	POP	POP
Tennessee			LEG	LEG	POP (d)	POP (d)	POP (d)	POP (d)	POP (d)	POP (d)	POP (d)	POP
Ohio					POP	POP	POP	POP	POP	POP	POP	POP
Louisiana							LEG	LEG	LEG	LEG	POP	POP
Indiana								LEG	LEG	POP	POP	POP
Alabama									LEG	POP	POP	POP
Illinois									POP (d)	POP (d)	POP	POP
Maine									POP (d)[d]	POP (d)[d]	POP (d)[d]	POP
Mississippi									POP	POP	POP	POP
Missouri									LEG	POP (d)	POP	POP
Popular election	6	6	8	5	11	10	9	10	15	18	22	23
Legislative election	4	9	8	11	6	7	9	9	9	6	2	1

LEG   Presidential electors chosen by state legislature
POP   Presidential electors chosen by popular vote in statewide election
POP (d)   Presidential electors chosen by popular vote in districts

Note: The original thirteen states appear in italics. New York did not participate in the 1788–1789 election because its legislature could not decide on a final list of electors. North Carolina and Rhode Island did not participate because they had not ratified the Constitution.

[a] Popularly elected electors at the district level, after which the legislature chooses one elector from the top two candidates.
[b] Legislature makes final choice when there is no majority.
[c] Legislature makes final choice when there is no majority and also selects two additional electors.
[d] Popular election of two additional presidential electors in statewide vote.
[e] Popularly elected presidential electors, then popularly elected electors choose two additional electors.

Allowing the state legislature to select presidential electors was a common early method. The actual power to choose electors using this method rested with the political party in the majority in the legislature. Some states preferred this method not only to ensure control of the dominant party, but also to keep the choice of the president from the masses. Legislative selection of presidential electors peaked in the 1800 election, when eleven of the sixteen states used this method.

In the early nineteenth century, legislative selection of electors gave way to statewide popular election (which at the time meant by the eligible white male population) in a winner-take-all format. Although popular election gained strength throughout this period, it rapidly became the generally accepted method during the rise of Jacksonian Democracy—the mid-1820s through the mid-1830s. By the 1832 election, South Carolina was the only state in which the legislature continued to select electors, a method it retained until 1868.[2]

The most widely used popular election method in U.S. history is the statewide vote. Electors associated with the majority or plurality ticket or candidate receive all of a state's electoral votes (though technically electors are not required to vote in accordance with the popular mandate). There have been numerous instances in which a candidate has only barely exceeded half the popular vote in a two-way race and won the entire electoral vote of a state. Furthermore, there have been many other instances of a candidate in three-way or four-way races winning all of a state's electoral votes with a 30 or 40 percent plurality of the popular vote. A recent and pivotal example of the latter occurred in the 2000 election, when George W. Bush received 2,912,790 popular votes in Florida (48.85 percent) and Al Gore won 2,912,153 (48.84 percent). Bush therefore won all of Florida's twenty-five electoral votes and consequently the presidency.

Popular voting by district is a variation of presidential elector selection based on the philosophy that different regions within a state have different political interests and ideologies that should be accommodated. In addition, it derives from the general unfairness of giving 100 percent of the electoral vote to 50 percent of the voters. Delaware, Massachusetts, and Virginia used versions of district-chosen electors in the first presidential election; the method was employed frequently in the first forty years of U.S. history. Various adaptations of the district vote evolved, the two most common being creating districts equal in number to the number of electors or electing one elector from each congressional district with the remaining two elected statewide or by the legislature. Maryland was the most consistent early user of district presidential elections, employing it from 1796 through 1832. In all but the two uncontested Monroe elections, in 1816 and 1820, Maryland cast electoral votes split between two candidates, reflecting state regional and political differences. As Table 1 indicates, the district method peaked in the 1820 election, when six out of twenty-four states used this variation. It ended with Maryland's last use of it in 1832.[3]

In the late twentieth century, democratic reformers resurrected the district system as a more equitable method of allocating state electoral votes, suggesting that it would (among other things) generally reflect the popular vote. In 1972 Maine became the first state to reintroduce district voting, giving one electoral vote to the winner in each congressional district and assigning two to the statewide winner. Nebraska instituted a similar system in the 1992 election. As of 2004, Maine and Nebraska were the only two states using a district allocation method, with all other states and the District of Columbia using the winner-take-all method.

THE ELECTORAL COLLEGE VOTE

Presidential electors in each state are selected on election day. In early popular elections, the voters actually cast ballots for the electoral college aspirants, who were sometimes listed on a slate pledged to a certain presidential candidate. There were numerous perplexing instances of electors being listed without a political party or even a candidate indicated on the ballot.[4] In the contemporary United States, voters select a presidential candidate on the ballot with their vote implicitly going to a slate of electors who pledge to vote for that candidate. Political parties in each state choose the individual electors, usually based on loyal party membership. Although the overwhelming majority of electors have cast their ballots for the candidate the voters selected, the occasional "faithless electors" have strayed from their popular ballot pledges to support a different party or candidate. In 2004, for example, one Democratic elector in Minnesota cast his presidential ballot for John Edwards instead of John Kerry. In no case, however, has the activity of a faithless elector affected the outcome of an election.

The founders decided that direct elections for the House of Representatives be held every two years, indirect elections for the presidency every four years, and indirect elections for each seat in the Senate every six years. After formal ratification of the Constitution in 1788, the first presidential and congressional elections got under way later that year and concluded in early 1789. With a four-year presidential term mandated by the Constitution, the second presidential election took place in 1792. Presidential elections have been held every four years since.

The Constitution does not provide specific instructions for the dates, times, places, and method of presidential elections. The founders had instead chosen to leave such matters to the states. The Constitution does, however, state, "The Congress may determine the time of choosing the electors, and the day on which they shall give their votes; which day shall be the same throughout the United States." In 1792 Congress passed a law mandating the selection of electors within thirty-four days of the first Wednesday in December. In the first fifty years of presidential elections, the states not only adopted various methods of presidential elector selection, but also had a wide variety of dates, times, places, and voter qualifications with respect to elections.

In the mid-1840s, Congress passed a law mandating that presidential elections take place on "the Tuesday after the first Monday in November," a provision that still stands.[5] The national legislature has also mandated when state electors should meet and cast their votes. The date of the electoral college meeting has varied over the years, from the first law mentioned above, the first Wednesday in December, to the current provision passed in 1934—the first Monday after the second Wednesday in December. On this date the presidential electors meet in their various states and cast presidential ballots. At the time of the 2004 election, only about half of the states had statutes or other provisions requiring electors to cast their ballots for the popular vote winner (see Figure 1, Electoral Ballot Pledge Laws,

November 2000). The Constitution imposes no such restriction on electors, and faithless electors have rarely, if ever, been penalized.

The final stage in the presidential election process is certification by Congress. The Constitution asserts that each state must make a list of votes for president and vice president and "sign and certify, and transmit sealed to the seat of government of the United States, directed to the President of the Senate; – the President of the Senate shall, in the presence of the Senate and House of Representatives, open all the certificates and the votes shall be counted." Presidential inaugurations had been held on March 4 until the Twentieth Amendment in 1933 changed the date to January 20. In 1934 Congress determined the date of vote certification to be January 6.

FIGURE 1

Electoral Ballot Pledge Laws, November 2000

Electors Bound by State Law and Pledges (27 States)

Alabama	Maryland	Ohio
Alaska	Massachusetts	Oklahoma
California	Michigan	Oregon
Colorado	Mississippi	South Carolina
Connecticut	Montana	Vermont
District of Columbia	Nebraska	Virginia
Florida	Nevada	Washington
Hawaii	New Mexico	Wisconsin
Maine	North Carolina	Wyoming

Electors Not Bound (24 States)

Arizona	Kansas	North Dakota
Arkansas	Kentucky	Pennsylvania
Delaware	Louisiana	Rhode Island
Georgia	Minnesota	South Dakota
Idaho	Missouri	Tennessee
Illinois	New Hampshire	Texas
Indiana	New Jersey	Utah
Iowa	New York	West Virginia

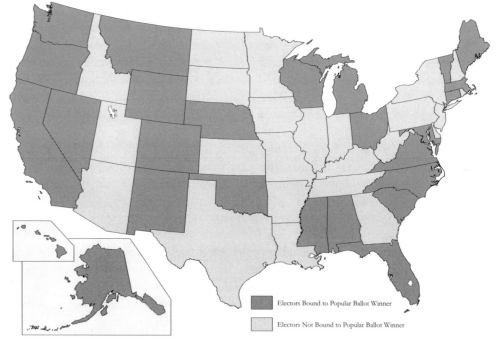

Electors Bound to Popular Ballot Winner

Electors Not Bound to Popular Ballot Winner

Source: National Archives and Records Administration, "What Is the Electoral College? State Laws and Requirements: List of Electors Bound by State Law and Pledges, as of November 2000," www.archives.gov/federal-register/electoral-college/laws.html.

POLITICAL PARTIES AND PRESIDENTIAL ELECTIONS

PARTY NOMENCLATURE

GEORGE WASHINGTON ELECTIONS, 1788–1789 AND 1792

George Washington received the unanimous support of the founders to become the first U.S. president, and he was the favorite among people from all regions and political philosophies. Because of this unanimity, Washington ran largely unopposed in the first and second presidential elections. No formal political parties existed at the time.

THE FEDERALIST AND REPUBLICAN ERA, 1796–1824

The period 1788–1824 coincides with what modern political historians regard as the First Party System of U.S. politics, with voting blocs emerging in Congress during the eight years of the Washington administration. These blocs generally consisted of those who wanted restricted federal government and those who believed that the country needed a strong federal government, especially with respect to developing the national economy. Leaders in favor of limited government and states' rights included Thomas Jefferson and James Madison. Those wanting a strong federal government counted among themselves George Washington, Alexander Hamilton, and John Adams. By the mid-to-late 1790s, increasing numbers of state and local political leaders fell into one camp or the other. In Congress, most senators and representatives tended to align in either a pro-administration Washington-Hamilton bloc or an anti-administration Jefferson-Madison bloc.

The 1796 election—the first contested presidential election—featured two candidates with distinct opposing political viewpoints. John Adams, Washington's vice president, promoted an expanded federal power, and his followers were called Federalists. Thomas Jefferson advocated a more limited federal power, and his followers were called Republicans. Among the Republicans in the 1790s, a "democratic" faction favored the radicalism of the French Revolution. During this period, Federalists sometimes derisively called all Republicans "democrats." Some historians use the nomenclature "Democrat-Republican" to identify the party in recognition of this usage and to conveniently distinguish it from the modern Republican Party, which was founded in the mid-1850s. The terms *Democrat* and *Republican*, however, were rarely used together in the late eighteenth and early nineteenth centuries. The *Atlas* uses the term *Republican* to more accurately reflect the label employed in descriptions of that day.

JOHN QUINCY ADAMS VERSUS ANDREW JACKSON, 1828

In the late 1810s and early 1820s, the Federalist Party declined as a national force, remaining competitive only in New England and a few scattered localities. The Republican Party grew in dominance, but split into factions during and after the election of 1824. One faction, led by John Quincy Adams and Henry Clay, favored continued expansion of the power of the federal government. This bloc pursued such policies as a national bank, a tariff to protect emerging U.S. manufacturing, and federally sponsored internal development projects, such as canals, river improvements, harbors, and road construction. The opposing bloc—led by "Old" Republicans like William H. Crawford, Martin Van Buren, and eventually Andrew Jackson—were strict constitutional constructionists, who advocated limiting federal powers. The constitutional constructionists supported the states' rights philosophy of Jefferson and thus saw no constitutional authority for the federal government to establish such institutions as a national bank or to appropriate funds for internal improvements, which they deemed to be matters of state or local rather than federal responsibility.

The 1828 ballot represents a transition election in terms of political party nomenclature. The John Quincy Adams and Andrew Jackson groups both traced their political lineage to the Republican Party and Jefferson. The terms for identifying political affiliation varied widely from region to region, state to state, district to district, and county to county. The followers of Adams were sometimes called Republicans, Federalists, Federalist Republicans, Adams, Adams men, administration party, or national Republicans. The followers of Andrew Jackson were called Republicans, Jacksonians, Jackson men, anti-administration, democrats, or Democrat Republican. No nationally uniform labels existed. Furthermore, in this election year, local rather than national nomenclatures prevailed because caucuses and national nominating conventions had yet to evolve. Many modern textbooks, popular publications, and even scholarly works casually use the term *Democrat* to describe the Jackson coalition and *National Republican* (or even *Whig*) to describe the Adams coalition. A careful study of congressional election nomenclature during this period found no common, national political party terminology, but did reveal the publications of the day describing candidates commonly as "Jackson" or "Adams" (or "anti-Jackson") in most districts. A study of the 1828 election in Pennsylvania summarizes what probably was the case in most places.

> It was not until the spring of 1828 that the people of Pennsylvania finally relinquished all formal partisan affiliations and took their places under the standards of Jackson and Adams. It was only then that county politicians generally adopted the presidential issue as the bases of their local division. Announcements of local nominating conventions

were now worded: "Resolved: That the county meeting to be held on . . . the delegates be requested to nominate and settle such ticket, as will give a general satisfaction as possible to the friends of [Andrew Jackson or John Quincy Adams] throughout the county & district, without reference to political distinctions which have heretofore divided us."[6]

The best political identifiers for the 1828 presidential election are simply "Adams" and "Jackson." In retrospect, the 1828 election often is regarded as a partisan realignment election leading to the emergence of the Second Party System, which lasted until the mid-1850s.

NATIONAL REPUBLICAN AND DEMOCRAT REPUBLICAN, 1832

The presidential election of 1832 was also a transition election. During the first Jackson administration (1829–1833), the two rival political groups had grown in distinction. Of importance in understanding the election of 1832 is the fact that the first national presidential nominating conventions were held in 1831 and 1832. These conventions traditionally represent the beginning of formal, self-identifying, nationally accepted political party terminology. A small third party, the Anti-Masonic Party, reported the proceedings of their national, state, and local conventions in 1831. A national gathering of anti-Jackson forces called itself the National Republican Convention. The original resolution by a New Hampshire legislative caucus calling for a Jacksonian national convention appealed for a meeting of "fellow republican brethren in other states, friendly to the re-election of Andrew Jackson."[7] The Jacksonian convention produced the 1832 publication "Summary of the Proceedings of a Convention of Republican Delegates, From the Several States in the Union, for the Purpose of Nominating a Candidate for the Office of Vice-President of the United States; Held at Baltimore, in the State of Maryland, May, 1832."[8]

Nevertheless, many Jacksonians and state and local party organizations came to adopt the name Democrat, or Democrat Republican, to distinguish themselves from rival National Republicans. The anti-Jackson and Jackson coalitions both continued to use the Republican label as popular signals of their origins in the earlier Jeffersonian Republican Party. During this period, congressional candidates usually did not contest elections under party names, though House candidates normally made known their personal preferences for policies describable as either Jackson, Jacksonian, administration (pro-Jackson), anti-administration (anti-Jackson), or as Opposition (anti-Jackson), depending on the region, state, district, or county. "National Republican" was increasing in usage, mainly in New England. One classic study of this era summarizes the emerging nature of party labels:

> Party nomenclature in this election was still unsettled, varying in different sections. Even in 1832 the followers of Jackson officially called themselves the "Republican party," while the Clay men sometimes used the

same name and sometimes were dubbed by their opponents the "Federalists." But the Baltimore convention that nominated Clay, the designation "National Republican party" was formally used. By 1832 the press was calling the president's supporters "Democratic Republicans."[9]

The 1832 *Atlas* maps use the labels National Republican for Clay and Democrat Republican for Jackson.

THE WHIG AND DEMOCRAT ERA, 1836–1856

By the mid-1830s, the Jacksonian Democratic Republican Party was increasingly identified simply as the Democratic Party. After the 1832 election, the anti-Jackson National Republican coalition reformulated itself as the Whig Party. The term *Whig* emerged in 1834 and by the 1836 election had become common. The *Atlas* recognizes the 1836 election as transitional in two respects: in the shift from local and state party affiliations and party labels toward nationwide two-party competition and as the final phase in the transition from individual, personality-dominated political coalitions to formal party organizations maintained between as well as during election campaigns. The period between the 1828 election and the mid-1850s coincides with the historical stage of the Second Party System.

REPUBLICAN AND DEMOCRAT ERA, 1856–2004

The modern Republican Party, born in the mid-1850s, is not to be confused with the Jeffersonian Republican Party of early U.S. history. In 1856 the Republican Party held its first national presidential nominating convention and appeared on the ballot in all the northern states. Also in 1856, the Whig Party held its last presidential nominating convention, at which delegates voted to endorse the American Party candidates and platform. The 1856 presidential election represented the transition election from the Whig-Democrat era to the Republican-Democrat era. In addition, the 1856 and 1860 elections were realignment elections heralding the start of the Third Party System, which lasted until the mid-1890s. Although the names of the Democratic Party and the Republican Party have remained the same for the last one hundred fifty years, they have experienced significant and numerous changes in party philosophies and voter support structures. Particularly noteworthy changes involved national, state, and local politics in party realignments in the mid-1890s, early 1930s, and mid-1960s.

CRITICAL ELECTIONS AND POLITICAL PARTY ERAS

The election maps in the *Atlas* illustrate American political history in a continuous flow. Other researchers of electoral history have, however, divided the more than 200 years of democratic balloting into a number of eras or systems based on periods

TABLE 2   Widely Acknowledged Political Party Systems

Party System	Partisan Realignment	Stable Phase	Mid-sequence Adjustment	Decay Phase
I				
II	1828	1830–1840	1842	1844–1858
III	1860	1862–1874	1876	1878–1894
IV	1896	1898–1910	1912	1914–1930
V	1932	1934–1946	1948	1950–

Source: Jerome M. Clubb, William H. Flanigan, and Nancy H. Zingale, *Partisan Realignment: Voters, Parties, and Government in American History* (Beverly Hills, Calif.: Sage Publications, 1980).
Note: Political parties did not exist at the beginning of the U.S. electoral democracy, therefore no partisan phases or adjustments are provided for the First Party System.

TABLE 3   Political Party Eras

Party System	Era	Partisan Realignment/ Critical Election	Stable Phase	Mid-sequence Adjustment	Decay Phase
First	Pre-party/Experimental				1820–1826
Second	Democratizing	1828	1830–1840	1842	1844–1858
Third	Civil War	1860	1862–1874	1876	1878–1894
Fourth	Industrialist	1896	1898–1910	1912	1914–1930
Fifth	New Deal	1932	1934–1946	1948	1950–1966
Sixth	De-alignment	1968	1970–	1976, 1992, 1996	

Note: Some political scientists contend that a critical election and realignment occurred in 1994, signaling the start of the Seventh Party System. That year the Republican Party captured the U.S. House of Representatives for the first time since 1952 while also winning numerous governorships, state legislative seats, and other state and local offices.

when voting behavior and political party support held somewhat steady. Each era begins and ends with a critical election, in which a large segment of the electorate realigns or changes its partisan affiliation. Such elections usually follow major political or economic crises. Political scientist V. O. Key Jr., in "A Theory of Critical Elections" (1955), was one of the first scholars to examine possible electoral periodization.

Table 2 outlines a widely accepted version of political party systems based on critical elections and partisan realignments for the United States' first 175 years or so, until the 1950s. Based on twenty-five years of debate and refinement of the concept of periodization, the table provides dates for the four historical critical elections indicating party realignments, identifies periods of voting stability after these elections, gives dates of mid-sequence adjustments, and identifies periods of decay before the next critical election. The identification of modern critical elections is more problematic, because political party eras are best determined after long periods of voting. Thus contemporary realignment and eras remain somewhat speculative. Two tables are presented here: Table 2 cites a widely accepted version of historical party systems, and Table 3 brings these systems up to date and provides the common names given to each era. Other versions in critical election literature vary somewhat in their calculation of electoral eras and start and end dates. In addition, some revisionist historians have very different versions, such as dating the Civil War period as beginning in the 1830s and ending with the congressional election of 1874 (or in the mid-1890s). The following discussion references Table 3.

FIRST PARTY/EXPERIMENTAL SYSTEM, 1788–1824: PRE-PARTY ERA

The First Party System is called the Pre-party or Experimental Era because modern political parties had not yet formed, and state and congressional parties fashioned loose alliances (especially in presidential election years). Ten elections were held during this era. Pre-revolutionary colonial legislatures had featured factions representing various economic, religious, social, and regional interests. During the congresses of the confederation and the drafting and final approval of the Constitution, political differences arose over the role, strength, and power of the central government. On the one hand, the Federalists supported a strong central government, while on the other hand, the Anti-Federalists supported more limited constitutional powers for the federal government and strong states' rights. Out of this conflict, the Federalist and Republican "parties" arose in the 1790s. The Federalists enthusiastically supported the Constitution; many Republicans were initially Anti-Federalist supporters of strict limits on federal power. Political parties in the modern sense—having such characteristics as quadrennial conventions, formal platforms, and a national party structure—did not begin to develop until the 1830s.

SECOND PARTY SYSTEM, 1828–1858: DEMOCRATIZING ERA

In the Democratizing Era, the white male franchise expanded and popular voting emerged as a standard selection process for presidential electors. In addition, such institutions as state party conventions and quadrennial national presidential nominating conventions emerged. The presidential election of 1828 represented a significant departure from previous elections. The Federalist Party had almost disappeared during the Era of Good Feeling (generally from around 1815 to 1825), and the Republicans emerged as the only true national political faction. In 1820 President James Monroe had been reelected essentially without opposition. In 1824, however, the dominant Republican Party of the First Party System fielded four candidates for the presidency. Each candidate represented different philosophies of governance, political ideologies, and regional concerns. After the popular election, the electoral college deadlock, and the final presidential ballot by state in the House of Representatives in 1825, two general groups coalesced around the competing government philosophies and dominant political figures of the time: John Quincy Adams, the victor in the 1824 election, and Andrew Jackson, who would succeed him. In the 1830s, the Jackson faction emerged as the Democratic Party, and the Adams grouping became the National Republican Party, which eventually came to be known as the Whig Party. These parties characterize the Second Party System.

THIRD PARTY SYSTEM, 1860–1894: CIVIL WAR ERA

The 1860 presidential election was one of the most contested, contentious, and critical in U.S. history: The results led directly to secession by the South and the Civil War. The war, the country's bloodiest, produced consequences for the geography of political party support that lasted at least a hundred years, through two subsequent realignments. Political party support during the Second Party System had not been sectional. Rather, Democrats and Whigs had backers in all parts of the nation. Political party support characteristic of the Third Party System was eventually solidly sectional, with the Republicans dominating the Deep North—those counties farthest north in New England, New York, and the Midwest—and the Democrats dominating the Deep South. The nine elections of the period witnessed the extension and then the deprivation of African American male voting in the South and the reemergence of white voting power after Reconstruction and resulting strong sectional divisions and electoral geography. The Republican Party dominated politics from 1862 to 1874, the stable phase of the Third Party System. After Reconstruction and the return of the solid southern Democratic base and its alliance with some northern native and immigrant voters, the two parties became highly competitive in the decay phase of 1878 to 1894.

FOURTH PARTY SYSTEM, 1896–1930: INDUSTRIALIST ERA

The Fourth Party System is sometimes called the Industrialist Era because industrial and financial interests were extremely influential in both parties, especially the northern-based Republicans. The Panic of 1893 was the worst economic depression in U.S. history up to that time. The Democrats controlled the presidency and both chambers of Congress during the crisis, and in the critical presidential election of 1896, the voters, including many members of the northern, urban working class, blamed the Democrats, turning the next period in U.S. politics into a Republican-dominated one. The solid Republican North was not only extended along the northern tier of states, but also increased in population and electoral votes as urban industrial development resulted in the manufacturing belt. A Republican Party ideological split in 1912 produced eight years of Democratic presidents during the Fourth Party System.

In the previous political eras, political parties disbanded while others organized, highlighting the change in systems. For example, the Federalists characterized the First Party System and the Whigs the Second Party System. The Republican Party emerged at the beginning of the Third Party System. In the 1896 realignment, however, the political party names and structures remained the same, but the voting allegiances of the population changed enough to suggest a new party era. This change in partisan allegiance is the essence of all new party eras.

FIFTH PARTY SYSTEM, 1932–1966: NEW DEAL ERA

The October 1929 stock market crash led to the Great Depression and the worst economic crisis in U.S. free-market capitalism. As in 1896, the electorate blamed the party in power, but this time the Republicans controlled all the branches of the federal government. The Democratic landslide in the 1932 presidential election resulted from a coalition that would last for more than thirty years; some aspects of it persist to the present. Northern working-class whites, many of them immigrants and labor union members, became fully ensconced in the Democratic Party. In addition, African Americans in the North began leaving the party of Lincoln and joining the Democrats, while the southern base of the Democratic Party remained loyal and was especially pleased with the New Deal social programs that aided rural poor whites. The Democratic Party contained a coalition of all classes, immigrant and native born, Catholic, Jew, black, and white with an urban North and rural South base. This coalition began to decay in 1948 and into the 1950s and finally ruptured in the 1960s. John F. Kennedy, running in 1960, is (thus far) the last Democratic presidential candidate from the North to be elected. His election represents the last in which the grand coalition of the New Deal era held together.

SIXTH PARTY SYSTEM, 1968–: DE-ALIGNMENT ERA

The Sixth Party System is called the De-alignment Era because political party registration and strict loyalties lessened and the population became more willing to split tickets and to vote for candidates after considering not only their economic interests, but also a wide variety of social and cultural issues, such as civil rights, gun control, abortion, same-sex marriage, and so-called family values. Republican Richard Nixon won the presidency in 1968. From 1968 to 2004, the Democrats won only three of the ten presidential elections held. In each of these victories, the winning candidate was a moderate from the South, and the elections can probably be described in critical election terminology as "mid-adjustment" or "deviating" elections. Many political scientists and historians believe that a new Republican-dominated Sixth Party System emerged in 1968 with a strong geographical component.

The Republican Party has dominated the South in recent elections. Beginning abruptly in 1964, the South switched from being solidly Democratic to voting solidly Republican, in part as a result of civil rights and racial politics. The South has a strong conservative, traditionalist political culture, and in the contemporary United States, the conservative wing has dominated the Republican Party while the liberal wing has dominated the Democratic Party. In addition to holding the South, the Republicans have consistently dominated the Great Plains and interior western regions. The Democrats on the other hand emerged in this era to dominate the Northeast, several midwestern states, and the Pacific Coast. Many of the states in these regions have a strong progressive, moralistic political culture. This voting pattern is almost a complete switch from the post–Civil War North-South pattern. In close elections in this era, the swing of a few southern states—for example, Florida—for the Democrats or the swing of a few northern states—such as Ohio—to the Republicans, has made the difference.

In 1994 the Republicans extended their electoral dominance to Congress, capturing the House of Representatives for the first time since 1952. (Some political scientists contend that this event heralded the beginning of a new era and Seventh Party System, but it is too soon to make this claim definitely.) The Republican presidential victories in 2000 and 2004 geographically mirrored the Republican presidential sweeps in 1972 and 1984. In these elections, the vast majority of the 3,000 plus counties, mostly representing rural America, voted Republican, while the Democrats carried a few hundred urban counties and a few outliers dominated by minority or academic communities. Excepting the elections of Democratic southerners Jimmy Carter in 1976 and Bill Clinton in 1992 and 1996, there appears to be a new urban versus suburban-exurban-rural configuration to electoral geography in the Sixth Party Era.

GEOGRAPHIC VOTING PATTERNS AND CRITICAL ELECTION THEORY

In contrast to the eras set out above, in *Section and Party* (1981), an analysis of state-level popular vote patterns, geographers J. Clark Archer and Peter J. Taylor argue that there may be only three major eras of presidential politics: politics of sectional compromise, from the Constitution to the Civil War; politics of sectional dominance, from the Civil War to the late 1940s; and politics of sectional volatility, from the late 1940s to the early 1980s. The authors also suggest that beginning in the 1960s a new geographic alliance emerged that normally pits the conservative and rural South, Great Plains, and interior West against the liberal and urban North and Pacific Coast.

The periodization of more than two hundred years of U.S. elections is obviously a complex task, especially as it concerns the last several decades. The realignment literature focuses on the multifaceted analysis of individual and group voting behavior. In advancing the understanding of U.S. history in general and electoral eras in particular, the *Atlas* presents four-color maps that for the first time detail all presidential elections from 1788 to 2004 at the county level. In some instances, the electoral eras put forward by political scientists and historians are not supported by the geographical voting patterns illustrated in the *Atlas*. In some cases, geographical patterns suggest that political eras began sooner or lasted longer than generally accepted or did not exist at all. For instance, the Second Party System's Whig-Democrat era is recognizable by a definite and consistent geographical pattern. The Third Party System offers a contrasting example, in which the geographic pattern fails to correspond to the dates assigned to its start. Most literature suggests that the Third Party System begins in 1860. Because the presidential election of 1856 displays a geographical pattern unlike previous elections, one could argue that the Second Party System had sufficiently broken down and that a new party system had begun in the mid-1850s. Furthermore, when one adds to the analysis the party composition of Congress in 1854 and the geography of the congressional elections of 1856 and 1858, the result strongly suggests a new pattern before 1860.

The Republican North–Democratic South geographical pattern of presidential and congressional elections that emerged after Reconstruction is one of the starkest and longest lasting in U.S. history. It persisted from the 1870s through 1948 and perhaps into the 1960s, spanning three different conventional electoral eras. Although there was a purported realignment of northern urban workers (and some in the border states) in the 1890s, party support in the state-level popular vote remained somewhat consistent from the 1870s through the 1920s and later. As Archer and Taylor suggest in *Section and Party*, the geographical voting patterns in the 1896 and 1932 presidential votes may simply have been deviations and adjustments in a long post–Civil War pattern.

As Table 3 indicates, recent conventional thought holds that the New Deal Party Era ended in 1966 and a new era began in 1968. Although a Democrat won the presidential election of 1964, a new persistent geographical voting pattern emerged that year ending the New Deal coalition. In some respects the geographical end of the New Deal alignment had been heralded earlier, by the Dixiecrat revolt of 1948 in the Deep South and by Republican successes in the rim South during the Eisenhower elections of 1952 and 1956. For the first time since Reconstruction,

however, a huge bloc of counties in the Deep South voted Republican in 1964. In addition, many rural and farm counties in the North voted Republican, some for only the first or second time since the 1850s. In the South, Georgia had never given its electoral votes to a Republican in the history of the Republican Party, while in the North, Vermont had never given its electoral vote to a Democrat in the history of the Republican Party. Both situations changed in 1964. Elections on the congressional level also reflected a similar geographical realignment. Perhaps a new political era actually began in 1964.

The extensive literature on critical election theory addresses the difficult task of determining when political/electoral eras begin and end. In the end, critical elections and party systems as identified by geographical voting patterns may simply differ from those elections and systems discussed in the political science and history literature. It is hoped that the maps presented here, and the geo-coded quantitative data set developed in their production, will help further this discussion and future research.

THE NOMINATION PROCESS

The history of presidential candidate selection is a fascinating one, reflecting important changes in U.S. political history and geography. In the pre-party First Party System, the states employed a wide variety of methods for selecting candidates and slates of electors. These included selection by consensus among members of Congress and other party leaders, a congressional caucus, state legislatures, and meetings of local and state political organizations. Since the development of modern political parties early in the Second Party System, with few exceptions presidential elections have been contested between candidates endorsed by the major political parties—Whigs and Democrats before the Civil War and Republicans and Democrats since.

CANDIDATE SELECTION, 1788–1831

In 1789 George Washington was elected unanimously as the first U.S. president. He had been president of the Constitutional Convention and the fearless commander of the revolutionary forces during the War of Independence. He was widely considered the new nation's foremost citizen and universally regarded as the logical choice for the presidency. In 1796 Washington announced his intention to retire from office after completing his second term. His retirement after two terms set a precedent that would last nearly 150 years—until 1940—when Franklin Roosevelt sought and won a third term as president shortly before the outbreak of World War II.

Washington regarded the presidency as being above politics, but by the end of his second term, Federalist and Republican factions had emerged within his administration: Vice President John Adams, a Federalist, and Secretary of State Thomas Jefferson, a Republican, were the two leading figures in Washington's government. The Federalists held a narrow majority in the electoral college and in 1796 elected Adams over Jefferson to succeed Washington as president. Several other prominent members of each faction also received electoral college support.

In the electoral system established by the founders, electors cast two ballots, with the person getting the most votes becoming president and the runner-up the vice president. In 1796 Jefferson had come in second to Adams in the electoral college, so Jefferson became vice president. Political and personal disagreements between the two men, however, impeded the smooth functioning of Adams' administration. A tie between Republicans Jefferson and Aaron Burr in 1800 forced the House of Representatives to determine the winner, illustrating another pitfall in the original system and galvanizing support for reform. To avoid such situations in the future, Congress passed the Twelfth Amendment, ratified in 1804, requiring that separate electoral votes be cast for president and vice president. Also of significance is the Twelfth Amendment's implicit recognition of political parties. The separation of ballots for president and vice president meant that a political faction or party could select candidates for each office. In the early 1800s, the party or the faction's representatives in Congress usually caucused, identified candidates, and then made them known to local party officials and activists.

CANDIDATE SELECTION, 1831–2004

PRESIDENTIAL NOMINATING CONVENTIONS

In 1828 the Anti-Masonic Party, a small group, formed in upstate New York. As its name implies, the party opposed Freemasonry, with its members pledging not to vote for Masons running for public office. The party's significance today is chiefly as the first party to hold a national nominating convention. Party leaders invited Anti-Masons in each state to send representatives to Baltimore in 1831 for a national nominating convention. The delegates selected William Wirt, ironically a Mason, as its presidential nominee. The Anti-Masonic movement eventually dissolved, and many of its supporters joined the Whig Party. The Democrat Republicans (forerunner of the Democrats) and National Republicans (forerunner of the Whigs)—the two major factions in the early 1830s—copied the idea and held national conventions in 1832. Ever since, both major parties and many third parties have convened quadrennial national conventions to select their presidential nominees.

The shift from caucuses to conventions reflected several important trends. First, this shift coincided with the general adoption of universal white male suffrage. Many states had previously restricted the franchise to landowners, but property qualifications for voting had diminished by the 1820s. By 1828 almost every state allowed white male citizens to cast ballots for presidential electors to the electoral college. Conventions were seen as a means of allowing rank-and-file voters more direct input into the selection of their party's nominees, whereas the elite caucuses of elected officials were viewed as less willing to represent popular interests. Second, dramatic improvements in transportation facilitated the trend toward conventions. In George Washington's day, a trip of only a few hundred miles could take days or even weeks on horseback or by stagecoach over rough, unpaved roads that were often impassable in muddy or inclement weather. By the 1840s, travel by railroad had become common in the eastern United States, making it easier and more convenient for many delegates to travel quickly to a central location to participate in a convention.

The geography of convention locations has changed in interesting ways over the years. In the nineteenth century, parties selected locations primarily on the basis of facilitating travel given the primitive transportation technology at the time. The first six Democratic national conventions (1832 through 1852) all convened in Baltimore, which was easily accessible by sea and rail from throughout the eastern seaboard. After the Civil War, the parties chose midwestern cities for their conven-

tions. They were conveniently located relative to the national rail network and therefore easily accessible to delegates from throughout the country. Between 1876 and 1904, for example, the Democrats held three conventions in St. Louis, three in Chicago, and one each in Cincinnati and Kansas City. The Democrats held their first national convention on the West Coast in 1920, when they met in San Francisco, and their first post–Civil War convention in the South in 1928, when they met in Houston.

The Republicans also held most of their conventions during this period in the Midwest. Nine of their fifteen conventions between 1876 and 1932 were in Chicago, the country's leading rail center. The other six took place in Cincinnati, Cleveland, Kansas City, Minneapolis, Philadelphia, and St. Louis. The Republicans called their first convention in the South only in 1968, when they met in Miami Beach, no doubt a reflection of the party having made few inroads in the region prior to World War II. Since then, Republican national conventions have taken place in Dallas (1984), New Orleans (1988), and Houston (1992).

After World War II, developments in aviation lessened the importance of delegate convenience in selecting a location for the nominating convention. Delegates from throughout the country could travel easily to any other location by air. The parties then began choosing convention sites for symbolic purposes, because of the personal preferences of leading party figures, or after extensive outreach and marketing efforts by potential host cities. In 2004, for example, the Republicans met in New York City, because party leaders wanted to call attention to President George W. Bush's actions in response to the attacks of September 11, 2001, implying that the rival Democrats would be less successful in dealing with terrorism. Conventions are highly lucrative for the host cities, so city officials and business and civic promoters actively encourage party leaders to select their communities as convention sites. In 2004 the Democratic National Convention in Boston hosted 4,323 delegates and 611 alternates. Thousands of additional visitors—family members of the delegates, party officials, party activists, corporate and interest group lobbyists, journalists, and spectators—also attended the convention and associated activities. These thousands of visitors pumped large amounts of money into Boston's economy, spending tens of millions of dollars in hotels, restaurants, shops, and other venues.

The national conventions have had several purposes of varying importance over time. The two major purposes are the selection of candidates for president and vice president and the development of a party platform, the set of statements that articulate the party's views on major issues. In the nineteenth and early twentieth centuries, state and local party leaders selected most convention delegates, many of whom were unpledged and free to vote for whichever candidate they wished. Before the roll call of states began, many conventions were wide open, with no candidate clearly favored for the nomination. An incumbent president was more likely than not to be renominated by his party with little or no opposition, but some incumbents, including Franklin Pierce and Chester Arthur, were denied renomination at their national conventions. It was not unusual at the conventions for votes during the first or second ballots to be distributed among a dozen or more candidates, and thirty or forty or more ballots needed to select the nominee. The Democrats hold the record, set in 1924, for the most ballots. They required 103 ballots over nearly two weeks to select John W. Davis of West Virginia as their presidential candidate.

Given the earlier wide-open nature of many conventions, "dark horse" candidates such as Davis were often selected. Orators who gave particularly noteworthy performances at conventions sometimes won their party's nomination, as did James Garfield in 1880 and William Jennings Bryan in 1896. Others, including Davis, represented compromise candidates, selected when the convention proved unable to otherwise resolve deadlocks between leading contenders. In a few cases, spectators played important roles. Attendees seated in the galleries at the 1940 Republican convention repeatedly chanted "We Want Willkie!" Some of the delegates taking in these chants may have been convinced that Wendell Willkie was highly popular among the party's rank and file and that he deserved serious consideration for his party's nomination, which he won.

PRESIDENTIAL PRIMARIES

The nominating process began to change in the early twentieth century, when some states began to hold presidential primary elections. The purpose of the primaries was twofold: to provide information about the relative strength of the potential nominees among a state's electorate and to select delegates to the national conventions. In states without primary elections, state and local party officials generally chose delegates. In many states that held primaries, some or all members of the state's national party delegation were chosen in these elections. Slates of potential delegates pledged to particular candidates typically ran against one another in primary elections. Delegate seats tended to be apportioned among the candidates on the basis of primary election support, although in the early twentieth century some states selected their delegations on a winner-take-all basis. Party rules required delegates selected in primary elections to support the candidate with whom they were associated at the national convention, for at least one or two ballots.

The number of states holding primary elections has increased steadily, and today well more than half employ them. Others hold precinct caucuses, at which registered voters express preferences for potential nominees by electing delegates to higher-level meetings. Primary elections and caucuses frequently draw national attention and provide information to voters throughout the country about the popularity of prospective nominees. In 1960, for example, John Kennedy's victories over Hubert Humphrey in primary elections in Wisconsin and West Virginia proved critical to his success in winning the Democratic presidential nomination

and eventually the presidency. In 1968 Senator Eugene McCarthy's near-victory in the initial New Hampshire primary helped persuade President Lyndon Johnson to withdraw his name from consideration for a second full term in the White House. Eight years later, the previously unknown Jimmy Carter ran surprisingly well in Iowa's Democratic Party precinct caucuses, giving Carter national attention and helping propel the obscure former governor of Georgia toward his party's nomination and the White House.

The primary and caucus system has dramatically reduced the importance of the national convention in the selection of presidential nominees. Not since 1952 has a major party taken more than one ballot to determine its candidate. The identity of the nominee is usually known well in advance of the convention on the basis of primary and caucus results. The role of the convention has grown increasingly ceremonial, giving the party an opportunity to showcase its candidates and platforms. Speakers of national interest and "star power" deliver speeches in support of the party's positions and candidates on prime-time television, generating publicity for the nominees and the party. Public opinion polls usually show a slight increase, or "bump," in a candidate's popularity during and shortly after the party's convention.

The decreased importance of the convention in nominee selection has also increased the power of incumbency in the renomination process. Over the past century, incumbent presidents eligible for renomination who wanted to run again have without exception been renominated. A few were challenged for their party's nomination, notably Carter in 1980, who was challenged by Massachusetts senator Edward Kennedy, and Gerald Ford in 1976, who was challenged by former California governor (and future president) Ronald Reagan. Of note, both Carter and Ford survived their intraparty challenges but were beaten by their opponents in the general election.

SELECTION OF THE VICE PRESIDENTIAL NOMINEE

Another important function of the convention is the selection of a vice presidential nominee. Putting forward a geographically and ideologically "balanced" ticket is frequently a party objective. During the Third and Fourth Party Systems—between the Civil War and the Great Depression—the Deep North was heavily Republican, while the Deep South was heavily Democratic. Candidates won or lost in the populous swing states among the border states, Mid-Atlantic states, and the Great Lakes region. Thus, between 1860 and the mid-twentieth century, both major parties tended to select so-called balanced tickets, with one nominee from the Mid-Atlantic area (usually New Jersey, New York, or Pennsylvania) and a running mate from the Great Lakes region (usually Indiana, Illinois, or Ohio). For example, the 1880 election, which evolved as the closest popular vote ever, pitted major-party nominees James A. Garfield of Ohio and Chester A. Arthur of New York for the Republican Party against Winfield Scott Hancock of Pennsylvania and William

English of Indiana for the Democratic Party. In the 1916 election, another close race, Woodrow Wilson of New Jersey and Thomas Marshall of Indiana ran for the Democrats against Charles E. Hughes of New York and Charles Fairbanks of Indiana for the Republicans.

Although geographical balance has often been an important criterion in selecting a vice presidential nominee, other factors also matter. In some elections, a party has offered the vice presidential nomination to the candidate who finished second to the nominee in primary elections and caucuses. For example, in 2004 Democratic senator John Edwards of North Carolina finished second to the party's presidential nominee, Massachusetts senator John Kerry, in a number of primary elections, and Kerry selected Edwards as his running mate. Similar circumstances prevailed in the selection of Republican George H. W. Bush as Ronald Reagan's running mate in 1980. The vice presidential nomination is also sometimes offered to a representative of a rival faction within the party, in part to placate that bloc and generate support for the national ticket among that faction's ranks. Chester A. Arthur in 1880 and John Nance Garner for the Democrats in 1932 are examples of this tactic. Ideological balance is also sometimes considered, with a progressive candidate selecting a more conservative running mate or vice versa. In today's highly mobile society, geographic balance no longer stands out as paramount in the selection of a vice presidential nominee.

THIRD-PARTY CANDIDATES

In a number of elections, third-party candidates have challenged the two major political parties for the presidency. In some cases, third parties formed following splits within one of the two major parties. For example, Theodore Roosevelt ran for president in 1912 as a candidate of the Progressive, or "Bull Moose," Party, following a split within the Republican Party between Roosevelt's supporters and those of the more conservative incumbent, President William Howard Taft. In 1948 opponents of civil rights legislation in the South walked out of the Democratic National Convention and nominated Gov. Strom Thurmond of South Carolina as the candidate of the States' Rights Democratic Party.

Other third-party candidacies have originated outside the existing two-party system, often resulting from perceptions that neither major party would address certain matters of importance. The People's, or "Populist," Party arose in the 1890s in response to a common belief among midwestern and western farmers that neither the Republicans nor the Democrats cared about their concerns. In 1924 Progressive Robert LaFollette ran as a third-party candidate in the belief that both major parties were taking an excessively conservative approach to issues. Other such candidacies include the 1968 third-party effort of Alabama governor George Wallace—who remarked that there was "not a dime's worth of difference" between the two major parties—and that of Independent Ross Perot in 1992. The *Atlas*

includes maps showing popular vote percentages for these and other third-party candidates receiving 2 percent or more of the popular vote.

Since the Civil War, almost all states have chosen their electors through a winner-take-all system in which the electors chosen are those associated with the candidate who receives a majority or plurality of the popular vote. The winner-take-all system is not, however, a requirement. The Supreme Court, in *McPherson v. Blacker* (1893), upheld the freedom of each state to identify its own method of translating popular votes into representation in the electoral college. Virtually all of the states, however, have used this system for the past 150 years. Today only two states, Maine and Nebraska, use an alternative system, in which the winner in each House district gets one electoral vote and the statewide winner gets two electoral votes in addition to the votes he or she won in the districts. The forty-eight states using the winner-take-all system give established parties a highly significant advantage relative to third parties. Those who consider voting for an alternative contender are frequently admonished not to "waste their votes" by casting their ballots for a third-party candidate. Of course, this becomes a self-fulfilling prophecy, and third-party candidates seldom prove to be competitive at the national level. Since World War II, only two third-party candidates—Thurmond in 1948 and Wallace in 1968—have won electoral votes. Both of them were popular in the Deep South, but had little appeal outside that region.

Many third parties eventually merge into one of the major parties. The Populists merged with the Democrats in 1896, after William Jennings Bryan won both parties' nominations. In 1912 Progressive Theodore Roosevelt became the only third-party candidate in the twentieth century to take second place in the popular vote when he outpolled Republican William H. Taft but lost to Democrat Woodrow Wilson. Four years later, Republican leaders, anxious to defeat Wilson, worked to repair the split between the Progressives and Republicans. They did so by securing the nomination of Charles E. Hughes, whom both factions found acceptable; he lost to the incumbent Wilson in a close race. Some Progressives encouraged Roosevelt to run a second time as a third-party candidate, but he declined to do so and instead endorsed Hughes. The Progressive movement collapsed, and two-party competition between Democrats and Republicans resumed.

Most U.S. third parties have been short-lived, and few have had any meaningful impact on presidential politics beyond more than one or two elections. In contrast, the Democratic and Republican Parties—both being more than 150 years old—are among the longest-lived, most stable political institutions in the world. Even today, candidates and orators try to identify themselves with famous presidents and other prominent members of their party from the distant past who have emerged as mythic figures in the iconographies of the party and the nation. Republican candidates today identify themselves and their campaigns with Abraham Lincoln, Theodore Roosevelt, and Ronald Reagan, while Democrats associate their candidacies with Andrew Jackson, Franklin D. Roosevelt, Harry Truman, and John F. Kennedy.

CHANGES IN THE ELECTORATE

The *Atlas* maps every presidential election by county through 2004. Over more than two hundred years, vast changes have modified suffrage requirements and influenced voter participation patterns. To better understand presidential elections in general, and the election vote patterns illustrated and analyzed in the *Atlas* in particular, one must examine the composition of the electorate in each stage of U.S. history. Although the Constitution mandates presidential and congressional elections, the specific requirements regarding the manner, time, date, place, and voter qualifications surrounding presidential elections were initially matters left to the individual states.

WHITE MALE FRANCHISE

In early U.S. history, each state established its own qualifications for voter eligibility. In general, states restricted the franchise to males of Caucasian origin; women and non-whites generally could not vote. By no means, however, was suffrage universal even among white males, with most states imposing additional restrictions on the franchise. Property ownership—in most instances interpreted as payment of property taxes—represented the most common qualification in the majority of states, but not even all such taxpayers were deemed eligible to vote. The states varied in their requirements regarding the amount of property owned and taxes paid on a yearly basis. The Federalist Party took an elite view of democracy and governance, with Federalist officials and legislators usually favoring a restricted electorate. Thomas Jefferson's ideal of a yeoman democracy led Republican officials and legislators to pursue lesser requirements for property ownership. The first great increase in the white male franchise took place during the period of Jeffersonian democracy in the first decade of the 1800s. In general, most rural males owning some land gradually received the vote. Prohibitions still applied to paupers and the habitually unemployed. Also, many urban laborers without property had difficulty meeting some state franchise requirements.

A second great increase in the white male franchise took place during the era of Jacksonian democracy, approximately the mid-1820s to the mid-1830s. The number of voters almost doubled between the 1824 election (Jackson versus Adams versus Crawford versus Clay) and the 1828 election (Jackson versus Adams). Westerner Andrew Jackson's overwhelming victory over the incumbent New Englander John Quincy Adams in 1828 can be partly attributed to franchise expansion. Indeed, most of the new western states admitted to the Union during the nineteenth century included universal white male suffrage as part of their state constitutions, while most of the original states, with a heritage of voter restrictions going back to colonial days, retained some sort of franchise limitation.

Rhode Island was one of the last bastions of elite male franchise. It had such high property qualifications that nearly half of its male citizens were unqualified to vote. In the early 1840s, these voter restrictions led, in part, to the so-called Dorr Rebellion, a violent confrontation led by Thomas W. Dorr. The conservative Whig Party, which tended to support a restricted franchise, dominated Rhode Island, while the state's smaller Democratic Party, with its Jacksonian heritage, tended to support a more universal franchise. Most states moved eventually toward universal white male suffrage, but even in the early twentieth century, Pennsylvania, Rhode Island, and the eleven former Confederate states still retained some sort of property or taxpaying qualification. The eleven southern states used these qualifications mostly as a tool to prevent blacks from voting, although they also had some effect on voting by poor whites. It took until 1964—with ratification of the Twenty-fourth Amendment—to eliminate all tax and poll tax restrictions. Some franchise restrictions continue with respect to circumstances, such as a felony criminal conviction, imprisonment, and mental impairment.

AFRICAN AMERICAN VOTING RIGHTS

In 1860 more than 90 percent of African Americans living in the United States were enslaved in the South. Free black males living in the North had unrestricted voting privileges in a few states, but even in this region most states had a number of limitations on voter participation. After the Civil War and emancipation, southern Reconstruction states' constitutions generally allowed unrestricted black male franchise. The newly bestowed African American suffrage significantly affected the 1868 and 1872 elections. It was not, however, until the Fifteenth Amendment, ratified in 1870, that the Constitution banned racial voting discrimination in all the states. In the South, white-dominated post-Reconstruction state governments and state and local Democratic Party organizations then adopted "legal" mechanisms—such as poll taxes, literacy tests, minor criminal offenses, whites-only primaries, property requirements, and residency laws—to virtually eliminate black voting. Poor illiterate Southern white males were mostly exempt from these laws by way of grandfather clauses, which allowed their participation if an ancestor had participated in elections or other civil activities. Economic reprisals and electoral violence and intimidation by groups such as the Ku Klux Klan also reduced black voting.

The African Americans who joined the Great Migration from the South to the North that began during World War I and continued into mid-century settled primarily in urban industrial centers. They increasingly became a voting force in inner cities and urban counties. The civil rights movement of the 1950s and 1960s called for economic, social, and political equality, including full voting rights for African Americans everywhere. The Voting Rights Act of 1965, which has some provisions directed specifically at southern states, was a key piece of federal legislation affecting presidential voting patterns. As southern blacks registered and voted, they became a force in many rural counties in the South, especially where they formed the majority of the local population. These counties are conspicuous on late twentieth-century election maps, often revealing patterns similar to those of the 1868, 1872, and 1876 elections, in which southern blacks had been allowed to vote in large numbers. Since the beginning of the Fifth Party System in the 1930s, African Americans have voted overwhelmingly for the Democratic Party. Taking into consideration the residential geography of the African American population is thus key to understanding the electoral geography of support for contemporary Democratic presidential candidates.

WOMEN'S SUFFRAGE

Earlier restrictions on female voting derived from the economic, political, and social structure of late eighteenth-century society, not from the Constitution. The male vote purportedly represented the vote of the entire family. Upon the death of the male head of a family, however, women still faced outright denial of the franchise or severe voting restrictions, even if they owned property. The first national convention for women's voting rights met in 1848 at Seneca Falls, New York, and called for a constitutional amendment for women's suffrage. Suffragettes Susan B. Anthony, Elizabeth Cady Stanton, Lucy Stone, and others worked for legal reforms nationally and state by state, because although the Constitution did not explicitly prohibit women's suffrage, the issue was commonly regarded as a matter best left to the states.

In the mid- and late nineteenth century, women increasingly voted in some state, county, and municipal elections. For example, some states gave women "partial suffrage," allowing them to vote in board of education elections, because boards handled issues involving children. Wyoming became the first territory to grant universal women's franchise, in its 1869 territorial constitution. By the 1896 presidential election, women had full voting rights in Colorado, Idaho, Utah, and Wyoming. By the 1916 election, virtually all the states from the Rocky Mountains westward had full female franchise. Ratification of the Nineteenth Amendment in early 1920 made the November 1920 presidential election the first federal election in which all American women could vote. Slightly more than 18.5 million people had participated in the 1916 election, but almost 26.8 million voted in 1920.

AGE RESTRICTIONS

Age has always been one of the major qualifications for voting and holding office, as evidenced by relevant colonial and early U.S. electoral laws. The founders wrote age restrictions for officeholders into the Constitution: one must be thirty-five to become president, thirty to be a senator, and twenty-five to become a member of the House. Each state determined at what age a person reached the so-called age of majority and voting competency, partly based on earlier English common law. In general, the states early on established twenty-one years as the age of full political competency, although a few set requirements as high as twenty-four years. The Fourteenth Amendment, ratified in 1868 to ensure African American enfranchisement, also holds that voting rights would not be denied "to any male inhabitant of such state, being twenty-one years of age and citizens of the United States."

During World War II, a great portion of the armed services consisted of Americans ages eighteen to twenty-one years old. Many believed it hypocritical that persons in this age group could serve, be wounded, or die in service of their country but could not vote. In fact, Georgia lowered its voting-age qualification to eighteen in 1943, and Kentucky reduced its age requirement to eighteen in 1955. Alaska set its voting-age requirement at nineteen upon entering the Union in 1959, while Hawaii set its at twenty. Momentum grew in the 1960s to lower the nationwide federal franchise to persons eighteen years of age, with the youth movement and the Vietnam War giving further momentum to this proposal. The Voting Rights Act of 1970 attempted to lower the national voting age to eighteen, but the Supreme Court ruled that Congress could not apply this to state and local elections. It took the Twenty-sixth Amendment, ratified in 1971, to finalize the national voting age at eighteen. The amendment received widespread support and became the most quickly adopted amendment in U.S. history. Although voter participation is generally lowest among those eighteen to twenty-one years old, the number of voters in the 1972 presidential election totaled 77.7 million, substantially more than the 73.2 million in 1968. In the twenty-first century, there have been movements to lower the voting age even further, usually to sixteen. The voting age internationally is eighteen on average, but does range, for example, from fifteen in Iran to sixteen in some German states and cities and to twenty in Japan.

RESIDENCY REQUIREMENTS

Where a vote is considered cast in U.S. elections has historically been place bound. The location of principal legal residence determines not only the specific place where a vote is cast and counted, but also the choice of candidates, who run within the geographical boundaries of ward, city, township, borough, magisterial district, county, and state. In early U.S. history, counties established courthouses and city halls in part as places of voting. As populations grew, depending on the physical size of the city or county, they set up auxiliary voting places and required citizens on election day to vote at these sites based on their place of residence. In the late twentieth century, the phenomena of online voting and early voting became increasingly common. Some voters can now cast their ballots in cyberspace rather than at a physical polling station.

U.S. society has always been mobile, and as citizens moved and established new abodes, many cities, counties, and states established length-of-legal-residence qualifications before allowing people to vote. The logic in most cases held that it took a certain amount of time to know and understand local politics, issues, and candidates in order to cast an informed ballot. Length-of-residence requirements also prevented interlopers, temporary residents, and one-time out-of-state voters from affecting the election of local officials or passage of local ballot initiatives and referendums. Length of residence varied from state to state and locality to locality, with some places requiring residency of as much as a year before registering to vote. Democratic reformers who desired as broad a franchise as possible argued that although local issues may not be familiar to new residents, the knowledge of and familiarity with presidential parties and candidates was universal. In 1970 the revision of the original Voting Rights Act established a national thirty-day residency requirement for presidential elections. In *Dunn v. Blumstein* (1972), the Supreme Court determined as unconstitutional lengthy residence requirements for state and local elections. The Court suggested thirty days or less for residency and voter registration requirements, and virtually all states have adopted this time frame.

DISTRICT OF COLUMBIA VOTING RIGHTS

Article 1, section 8, of the Constitution gives Congress the power to establish a geographically separate "Seat of the Government of the United States" not to exceed ten miles square (that is, 100 square miles). The land for the national capital was to be ceded by states to the federal government. In 1790 Congress, in one of its first acts, authorized President Washington to purchase land somewhere along the Potomac River for this seat of government. Agreement was reached on this location by way of deals and compromises in Congress and with the intent to make the capital accessible from all sections of the country, including promised access into the west along the Potomac River. The original 100-square-mile capital district straddled the river along the communities of Georgetown, Maryland, and Alexandria, Virginia.

In 1800 the federal government moved from Philadelphia to the City of Washington in the District of Columbia. Shortly thereafter Congress passed a law establishing complete control over District affairs. During debate on this legislation, congressional members discussed the voting rights of Americans living in the District. Because the District was not a state or part of one, its residents never received congressional and presidential voting rights. The lack of representation in a state legislature and Congress prompted the Alexandria citizens of the District to petition for "retrocession," and in 1846 the portion of the city on the southern side of the Potomac was ceded back to Virginia, accounting for the District's current size of nearly sixty-eight square miles. The population of the District grew consistently, and the rapid expansion of the federal government during the administrations of Franklin Roosevelt propelled the District to one of the largest U.S. cities, which the founders never envisioned.

The contradiction of the residents of the national capital being required to pay federal taxes and serve in the armed forces but being denied the vote for president prompted the adoption of the Twenty-third Amendment in 1961, giving the District presidential electors equal in number as "if it were a state," with the number of electoral votes equal to the number of electoral votes held by the smallest state in population. The *Atlas* first shows the District boundaries in the 1792 elections map, notes the change in the size of the District in the 1848 election after the Virginia retrocession, and designates it as not voting in presidential elections until 1964. Since 1964 the District has had three presidential electors, and they have voted Democratic every time, in part because a majority of voters in the District have been African Americans. In 1978 Congress passed a constitutional amendment conveying full statehood on the District of Columbia, but the required number of states failed to ratify it. In 2000 one Democratic elector from the District declined to vote in the electoral college to protest the District's lack of congressional representation.

POLITICAL GEOGRAPHY OF SETTLEMENT

Understanding the political forces that created the geographical patterns depicted by the *Atlas* election maps requires an underlying knowledge of the spatial aspects of U.S. settlement history. Indeed, among the most conspicuous differences between the first and the last election map is that the United States of 1788–1789 was bounded on the west by the Mississippi River and was largely unorganized beyond the crest of the Appalachian Mountains, whereas the United States of 2004 extends across the North American continent, from the shores of the Atlantic Ocean to the shores of the Pacific Ocean and the coasts of Alaska and Hawaii.

Despite this dramatic increase in physical size, advances in transportation and communication have made the United States in effect smaller. In the late eighteenth century, news traveled slowly; weeks and months elapsed as news spread throughout the country, in letters and journals, of the size and geographical extent of George Washington's popular mandate. In contrast, by the early twenty-first century, rapid computer-based tabulations of votes and virtually instantaneous telecommunications disseminated news of the razor-thin margins that separated Republican George W. Bush from Democratic rivals Al Gore in 2000 and John

Kerry in 2004 to people living thousands of miles apart within moments of poll closings in successively more western time zones.

FRONTIER EXPANSION WEST

A detailed tracing of U.S. territorial expansion and settlement exceeds the scope of this *Atlas,* but it is helpful to highlight a few benchmarks of U.S settlement history using the census years 1790, 1850, 1900, 1950, and 2000 as foci. The first census—conducted in 1790 to apportion seats in the U.S. House of Representatives and electoral votes among the states—recorded a population of slightly more than 3.9 million. Settlement was overwhelmingly rural, with a mere 201,655 people, or 5.1 percent of the population, living in twenty-four urban areas of 2,500 or more. The center of population—the mean geographical balance point for the population distribution of the entire United States—in 1790 was later calculated to be about twenty-three miles east of Baltimore, Maryland, near the northern end of the Chesapeake Bay. This meant that the District of Columbia was indeed somewhere near to the U.S. population center when Congress agreed to make it the site of the federal capital. Although the tidewater setting of the population center at the first census may seem somewhat surprising, it should be recalled that most Euro-Americans lived east of the Appalachians and that "Indians not taxed" were not enumerated by the census before the early twentieth century.

The first half of the nineteenth century witnessed an enormous expansion of the territory under U.S. sovereignty, involving most notably the Louisiana Purchase (1803), the Florida Treaty (1819), annexation of Texas (1845), the Oregon Territory (1846), and the Mexican Cession (1848). The population also grew rapidly—in part because of a high birthrate, large family size, and immigration—reaching 23.2 million by the time of the seventh census in 1850. The 1803 acquisition of the drainage basin of the Mississippi River and several of its tributaries, coupled with the opening of the Erie Canal in 1825, had greatly facilitated water-borne transport, enabling expanded commerce between the developing interior's agrarian frontier and growing industrial port centers in the east and abroad. By 1850 New York City's population had surpassed 500,000, and slightly more than 3.5 million people, or 15.2 percent of the total population, lived in 236 urban areas. The center of population had crossed the crest of the Appalachians to a point about twenty-three miles southeast of Parkersburg, Virginia (now West Virginia).

Further territorial expansion occurred after the Civil War, with the acquisition of the territories of Alaska in 1867 and Hawaii in 1898. One of the most notable settlement transformations of the second half of the nineteenth century involved the immense agrarian frontier development spurred by the Homestead Act of 1862 and its many legislative successors, including the Timber Culture Act of 1873, the Desert Land Act of 1877, and the Enlarged Homestead Act of 1909. In addition, populations moved farther west with the expanding railway network—which had become transcontinental with the linking of the eastern and western sections of the Union Pacific at Promontory, Utah, in 1869—and intensifying farm mechanization using draft animals and then steam traction by the end of the nineteenth century. These and other changes in agricultural technology influenced farm employment, which in turn influenced farm population and also nearby town population. Historian Frederick Jackson Turner examined the results of the 1890 census and then famously announced that the American frontier had closed, but an even more important though less heralded threshold had been crossed a decade earlier: the 1880 census revealed that for the first time slightly more than one-half of the U.S. labor force did not work on farms. This transition meant that the Jeffersonian ideal of agrarian freeholding no longer represented a realistic aspiration for a majority of Americans. Instead, employment opportunities were found in growing urban centers, where migrants from rural areas and growing numbers of immigrants from abroad toiled in smelters and factories to manufacture locomotives, steamboats, tractors, elevator cars, light bulbs, repeating rifles, and countless other products demanded by producers, consumers, and governments at home and abroad. The Populist Revolt of the 1890s and the Pullman strike of 1894 serve as reminders that the agrarian to industrial transition was not always smooth.

The U.S. population continued to grow rapidly, reaching 76.1 million by the twelfth census in 1900. Although no longer predominately agrarian, the United States was not yet predominately urban in 1900, when 30.2 million people, or 39.6 percent of the total population, lived in 1,737 urban areas. The center of population had reached a point six miles southeast of Columbus, Indiana, placing it toward the south-central edge of what was becoming known as the manufacturing belt.

URBANIZATION OF THE ELECTORATE

The first half of the twentieth century was a remarkable period of two bloody world wars (1914–1918 and 1939–1945) separated by an intervening depression that followed the stock market crash of 1929. Millions of Americans were either under arms or out of work. During this period, the United States became a nation of predominantly city dwellers. Indeed, the census of 1920 records this critical threshold, revealing that the nation's 2,722 urban areas with populations of 2,500 or more had 54.1 million residents, or 50.9 percent of a total population of 106.5 million. The emergence of an urban majority sent shockwaves through the body politic. U.S. senators and representatives from rural states and rural districts put aside their partisan differences to effectively thwart all efforts to reapportion the House of Representatives based on the results of the 1920 census. The decade of the 1920s became the only one during which seats in the House and in the electoral college failed to be redistributed to reflect population changes.

The 1920 census also showed that most foreign immigrants were choosing to settle in urban areas, particularly in large and industrial urban locations. Anti-city and anti-immigration sentiments joined to fuel passage of immigration acts establishing quotas and other restrictions on immigration, effectively ending by the mid-1920s the late nineteenth- and early twentieth-century era of mass immigration. The United States' foreign-born population, which had reached 13.1 percent in 1920, fell by almost half, to 6.9 percent, at mid-century. Although immigration restrictions and declining birthrates slowed population expansion, the total population had grown to 151.7 million by the seventeenth census, in 1950. The Great Depression temporarily slowed urban expansion, but 96.5 million Americans, or 63.6 percent of the total population, lived in urban areas by 1950. The census that year showed that the center of population had crossed the southwestern Wabash River border of Indiana to a point eight miles northwest of Olney, Illinois.

SUBURBANIZATION OF THE ELECTORATE

If the first half of the twentieth century can be regarded as the era during which the United States became predominately urban, the second half of the twentieth century is the era during which it became predominately suburban, exurban, and metropolitan. The second half of the century is also a period in which the center of population continued to progress westward, crossing the Mississippi River in 1980 to a point less than one mile west of De Soto, Missouri, a small town less than an hour's

drive from St. Louis. Perhaps fittingly (or maybe just coincidentally), the 1980 presidential election transferred power from southerner Jimmy Carter, a Georgia Democrat, to westerner Ronald Reagan, a California Republican.

The most important settlement story of the last half of the twentieth century was the population shift from rural areas, small towns, and central cities toward large metropolitan suburbs. This shift flowed from rubber-tired, petroleum-powered motor vehicles traveling broad ribbons of concrete built with federal funds under the provisions of President Dwight Eisenhower's most important piece of domestic legislation—the Interstate Highway Act of 1958. In addition, significant federal income tax deductions for home ownership affected patterns of settlement to an extent rivaled or surpassed only by the Northwest Ordinances of the late eighteenth century and the homestead and railroad acts of the mid-nineteenth century. By the time of the twenty-second census, in 2000, 226 million people, or 80.3 percent of the total U.S. population of 281.4 million, lived in census-defined metropolitan areas. Moreover, 161.5 million, or 57.4 percent of the total U.S. population, lived in metropolitan areas with populations of 1 million or more. In short, from the time of the first census, in 1790, to the time of the most recent census, in 2000, the United States went from being predominantly rural to predominantly urban to predominantly metropolitan, with its total population growing from less than 4 million people to more than 280 million.

HISTORICAL TRENDS IN SUFFRAGE AND VOTER PARTICIPATION

SIZE OF THE ELECTORATE

In the *Atlas,* the discussions of each election contain explanations of linkages between the changing geography of settlement and the changing geography of election outcomes. That said, however, it deserves reiterating that the total numbers and the geographical distributions of votes cast in each election vary in some obvious ways in relation to population size and population distribution. Although suffrage, racial, and age restrictions have certainly played roles in determining the total number of popular votes cast, the growth in population has been the most apparent underlying determinant in each successive presidential election. As Figure 2 shows, the total number of popular votes cast from 1788–1789 to 2004 rose from just a few thousand in early elections, when the nation's population was quite small, to tens of millions by the late nineteenth century.

The 1828 presidential election was the first to involve more than 1 million popular ballots. The 3 million threshold was passed for the first time in 1852, and in 1896 Americans cast nearly 14 million votes. The dominant trend of the last century was one of great expansion in the size of the electorate, despite several brief periods of near stability or even election-to-election decline in total voting numbers after the end of the nineteenth century, such as a plateau period in the early years of the twentieth century and a brief dip during World War II. Citizen participation in presidential elections roughly doubled from 14 million votes in 1900 to 29 million in 1924, primarily because of the extension of the full franchise to women. It doubled again, to 62 million votes, in 1952 and nearly doubled yet again, to 122 million popular votes, in 2004, partially because of the extension of the franchise to eighteen-year-olds. Indeed, many more popular presidential votes were cast in the diminutive state of Rhode Island in 2004 as in all of the United States in the first presidential election of 1788–1789.

VOTER PARTICIPATION

Although changes in population size trump all other factors when considering only vote totals, other factors come into play when attention shifts to voter participation. Proportions of voter participation can be calculated using as a base figures for registered eligible voters or for the relevant voting-age population. In either case, vot-

FIGURE 2 — Popular Vote and Voter Turnout in U.S. Presidential Elections, 1788–2004

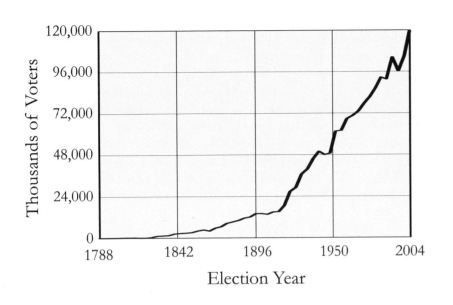

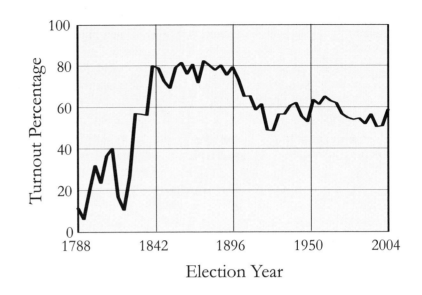

Source: Voters: for 1788–1820, various sources, including Michael J. Dubin, *United States Presidential Elections, 1788–1860: The Official Results by County and State* (Jefferson, N.C.: McFarland, 2002); Inter-University Consortium for Political and Social Research, "United States Historical Election Returns, 1788–1823," ICPSR#79 [computer file], 5th ed., Ann Arbor, Mich., updated February 16, 1992; Philip J. Lampi, personal correspondence, American Antiquarian Society, Worcester, Mass., 2005; for 1824 to 1996, *Presidential Elections, 1789–1996* (Washington, D.C.: CQ Press, 1997); for 2000, Federal Election Commission, "2000 Presidential Popular Vote Summary for All Candidates Listed on At Least One State Ballot" (updated December 2001), www.fec.gov (accessed September 1, 2005); for 2004, Federal Election Commission, "2004 Presidential Popular Vote Summary for All Candidates Listed on At Least One State Ballot" (updated May 2005), www.fec.gov (accessed September 1, 2005); and original research by the authors.

Source: Turnout percentage: for 1788–1996, Harold W. Stanley and Richard G. Niemi, *Vital Statistics on American Politics, 1999–2000* (Washington, D.C.: CQ Press, 2000), table 1-1, pp. 12–13; for 2000, the figure was calculated from voting-age population data at www.census.gov; for 2004, "Turnout at Record High," *USA Today,* November 5, 2004, p. 7A.

ing participation proportions in effect control for changes over time in population size, and thus allow for consideration of other influences, such as suffrage requirements or electoral mobilization. Because most states only formalized voter registration in the late nineteenth or early twentieth centuries, voting-age population is the more useful base when considering voting across historical periods. Measures of the relevant voting-age population can, however, present challenges, especially in earlier elections. For instance, population figures for elections in non-census years are necessarily estimates or projections, which can be quite unreliable, especially for smaller areas, such as counties, whose populations can change rapidly through in- or out-migration. In addition, census tabulation categories have varied over the

years, so reports of numbers of persons in appropriate age, gender, citizenship, wealth, property ownership, literacy, or other suffrage-relevant categories may not be consistently available for a particular period.

Such data problems are especially acute for elections in the late eighteenth and early nineteenth centuries and are not entirely irrelevant for the modern era. Although the government did not count most Native Americans before the early twentieth century, other categories of non-citizens usually were included in census enumerations. All modern U.S. census data report total resident populations, regardless of citizenship status. Resident adult non-citizens have been ineligible to vote in the United States since the 1920s. Census voting-age population data consequently lead to turnout percentages being underestimated by as much as 10 percent or more in areas with high concentrations of non-citizens. To further complicate matters, nearly two dozen states in the Midwest, South, and West once permitted immigrant non-citizens to vote upon declaration of their intent to become U.S. citizens. In 1926 Arkansas became the last state to terminate alien voting rights.

Figure 2 also presents percentages of voter turnout nationwide for presidential elections from 1788–1789 to 2004. Although the record is fragmentary, it appears that barely one-tenth of potentially eligible voters cast ballots in the 1788–1789 election. Although the Constitution had just been ratified, many states retained tight restrictions on the franchise, giving the vote only to male property owners paying substantial taxes. Also, in several participating states, the legislatures appointed electors, as opposed to their being popularly elected (see Table 1).

Political circumstances and the competitiveness of elections varied greatly from one contest to the next during the nation's formative era up to 1824. Selection methods differed from state to state and even from election to election, as electors were variously appointed, popularly elected by district, or popularly elected at-large. Policy issues or party differences drew voters to the polls in some elections, while in others minor personality differences between candidates with similar views on important issues failed to excite the electorate. Turnout fluctuated considerably, reaching nearly one-third in the pivotal election of 1800, dropping to one-fourth in 1804, rising appreciably to four-tenths in 1812 (in response to the War of 1812), plummeting to barely one-tenth in the uncontested 1820 election, but then rising again to one-quarter in the four-way race of 1824. Although the presidential and congressional election records remain incomplete, nearly twice as many votes were cast in congressional elections than in most presidential elections held before 1828. In other words, legislative elections seem to have outweighed executive elections in popular importance during the formative period.

With progressively fewer restrictions on the white male franchise, turnout increased substantially to more than half of the eligible electorate in the presidential elections of 1828, 1832, and 1836 and then jumped to even higher levels from 1840 through the late nineteenth century. Several elections, including those of 1860, 1876, and 1888, produced extraordinary turnouts in which more than four-fifths of potentially eligible voters cast ballots. Higher participation in part reflected nearly universal acceptance of the practice of choosing electors through popular voting rather than legislative appointment. Another important change was the emergence of the president as the leading political figure. Although Americans cast more votes in congressional elections than in early presidential elections, there appears to have been a notable transition in the second and third decades of the nineteenth century, when voter attention shifted from greater interest in legislative elections to greater interest in selecting the chief executive. Indeed, in several critical elections, such as those of 1828 and 1860, popular presidential ballots outnumbered congres-

sional ballots by one-fourth or more. The now familiar pattern of considerably greater participation in presidential election years than in "off-year," or midterm, state or national legislative election years became especially pronounced during the last half of the twentieth century, but can be seen to have emerged during the second third of the nineteenth century.

In retrospect, the election of 1896 represents the end of a half-century of high voter turnout for presidential elections. Although turnout fell in most areas of the nation after 1896, the greatest declines concentrated in the Old Confederacy. In the South, the decline in voter turnout was precipitous, falling from nearly 58 percent in 1896 to just 19 percent in 1924. The almost total elimination of the black male vote because of Jim Crow laws, intimidation, poll taxes, and the almost total domination of one political party, the Democrats, greatly suppressed southern voter turnout. Outside the South, voter turnout declined from more than 80 percent in elections held between 1876 and 1896 to slightly less than 60 percent for those held during the early 1900s. Also outside the South, the widespread adoption of more formalized residency and voter registration requirements early in the twentieth century seems to have been undertaken in part to diminish voting fraud and the influence of foreign-born immigrants in city, state, or national elections. In the South, which attracted relatively few foreign immigrants from the mid-nineteenth to the mid-twentieth centuries, the aim was clearly to dilute the influence of black voters, especially after fusion Republican-Populist legislators who had been elected in several southern states suffered defeat in the wake of William Jennings Bryan's unsuccessful fusion Democrat-Populist presidential candidacy in 1896. Literacy tests, grandfather clauses, and outright physical violence count among the measures used to discourage minority voters from attempting to cast ballots.

As a result of precipitous declines in turnout in the South and slight declines elsewhere, the aggregate national rate fell from about four-fifths in the late nineteenth century to just half of the potential electorate in the early twentieth century. The lowest levels occurred in the elections of 1920 and 1924, when just 49 percent of potentially eligible voters cast ballots. The Progressive Era adoption of more stringent residency or voter registration requirements as well as the "southern system" of anti-minority voting rights restrictions contributed to the decline, but the success of the women's suffrage movement also seems to have played a role in the decline. Several western states that gained statehood in the late nineteenth century had entered the Union without gender-linked suffrage restrictions. State-level relaxation of such restrictions gained momentum in the first and second decades of the twentieth century, so that by 1919 statutes had been passed in about half of the states to allow women to vote. State-level turnout comparisons of elections before and after adoption of women's suffrage laws suggest that a roughly 5 percentage point decline in voter turnout often coincided with the doubling of the potential electorate to include both women and men. Ratification of the Nineteenth

Amendment in 1920 universalized women's suffrage in federal elections. Male and female turnout rates are now about the same, but the convergence required a span of several decades.

After declining until the early 1920s, voter turnout rebounded during much of the remainder of the twentieth century, though never again to the levels of the late nineteenth century. From around 1940 to 1968, voter turnout in presidential elections rose or fell within a relatively narrow band centered around 60 percent of potentially eligible voters. From the Great Depression into the New Deal era, mobilization of voters among newer immigrant groups probably played a role in higher turnouts. Turnout declined somewhat after World War II to only 53 percent in 1948, when Democrat Harry Truman surprised contemporary analysts to edge Republican Thomas Dewey in a close contest. Turnouts then returned to above 60 percent in all the presidential elections held from 1952 through 1968.

Controversy surrounds the explanations put forth for the decline in voter turnout after 1968 to near the end of the twentieth century, especially because the trend occurred during the South's so-called Second Reconstruction. Among the more important levers used to dismantle the minority suffrage discrimination in the South were ratification of the Twenty-fourth Amendment in 1964, outlawing poll tax barriers in federal elections, and passage of the Voting Rights Act in 1965, banning literacy tests and strengthening federal supervision of voting practices. Voter turnout among the potential electorate rose in the South from roughly one-quarter, the level that had prevailed since the early 1920s, to nearly or slightly more than one-half in all subsequent presidential elections. Most of the increase, of course, reflected the participation of re-enfranchised minority citizens. Although voter turnout in the South continues to lag behind that of the rest of the nation by several percentage points, the size of the difference in the early twenty-first century is dramatically less than it was in the mid-twentieth century.

Three factors appear to be the most plausible in explaining the overall decline in voter turnout in the late twentieth century: the enfranchisement of younger people, increases in documented and undocumented foreign immigration, and an attenuation of party organization and party identification. In 1971 the Twenty-sixth Amendment lowered the age of majority for participation in federal elections from twenty-one years to eighteen years. Younger people continue to vote at lower rates than do older people, perhaps in part because they are less interested in politics and because their greater geographical mobility makes it harder for them to satisfy length-of-residency requirements. Higher incarceration rates may also be a factor, given that convicted felons lose their voting eligibility in many jurisdictions. Immigration to the United States surged during the last half of the twentieth century to levels rivaling those at the end of the nineteenth century. The census counts all residents regardless of citizenship status, but undercounting of undocumented persons fearful of contacts with officialdom cannot be ignored.

According to the Census Bureau, as of 2004 the U.S. resident population of 288 million consisted of 88.1 percent native-born citizens, 4.6 percent naturalized citizens, and 7.3 percent foreign-born non-citizens. The overall foreign-born proportion of 11.9 percent in 2004 was more than twice the corresponding figure of 4.7 percent in 1970. Higher proportions of non-citizens who are ineligible to vote tend to lower measures of voter turnout, especially in states where larger numbers of undocumented aliens reside.

Most commentators have observed that voter participation rates tend to be highest among potential voters who have the greatest personal interest in politics and that the degree of personal interest in politics tends in turn to correspond with the intensity of personal identification with an organized political party. National time-series data collected through survey research to measure party commitment became common from the early 1950s onward. These surveys indicate that the number of people who identify as "independent," having no or only very weak commitments to major parties, edged up from roughly one-fifth of survey respondents in the 1950s to roughly one-third by the end of the twentieth century. Related trends include exit poll–based indications of increases in split-ticket voting (for candidates of more than one party) and diminutions in the formal candidate selection roles of national party organizations as larger proportions of nomination convention delegates came to be selected through primary elections. After declining for more than two decades, proportions of "strong" party identifiers showed some tendency to rise very late in the twentieth and early in the twenty-first centuries. The implied resurgence of interest in politics may have been one of the factors underlying the coincident increase in voter turnout in presidential elections, which reached approximately 59 percent in 2004.

GEOGRAPHY OF VOTER PARTICIPATION: 1848, 1900, 1948, AND 2000

Considerable understanding of geographical variations can be gleaned from patterns of voter participation based on total numbers of votes cast for presidential electors in each county for selected elections. The maps in Figure 3 depict the total numbers of popular votes cast for all candidates in each county for the presidential elections of 1848, 1900, 1948, and 2000.

Because of the wide range in the popular votes cast in these elections—2.9 million in 1848, 14 million in 1900, 48.8 million in 1948, and 105.4 million in 2000—the size of map symbols have been scaled logarithmically. The area of the circle that appears within each county is proportional to the logarithm of the total number of votes cast in that county. Such scaling has the effect of increasing the visual prominence of counties where fewer votes were cast in a given election while preserving the visual evidence of relative geographical patterns within and between elections. Without such scaling, the symbols for less populous counties in earlier elections

FIGURE 3   **Patterns of Voter Participation: The Elections of 1848, 1900, 1948, and 2000**

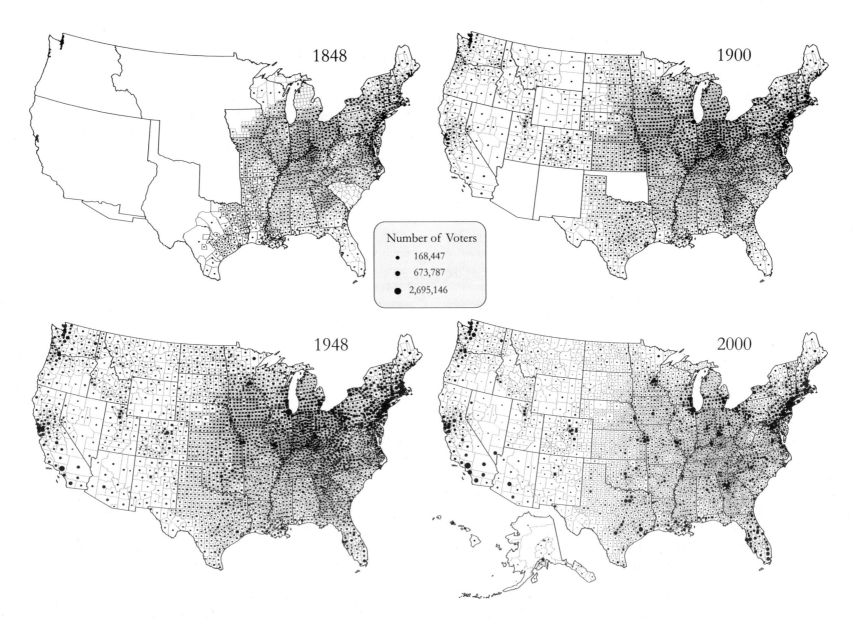

These maps depict the total popular votes by county in the presidential elections of 1848, 1900, 1948, and 2000. The symbol in each county is proportional to the logarithm of the total number of votes cast for all presidential candidates in that county at each election.

would be so small as to be invisible, while the symbols for populous counties in later elections would appear as enormous, merging globs. Counties in states where legislatures selected electors, territories or counties not yet settled, and counties for which data are missing are represented by the absence of a map symbol.

Two sets of considerations underpin interpretations of the patterns on the four maps. The first involves the settlement processes that determined the size and composition of the population of each county. As described above, distinct rates of natural population growth or decline, domestic and international migration, urbanization, agricultural and industrial development, employment opportunities, living standards, and other relevant measures differentiated counties at the time of each of the elections represented. The second consideration is the suffrage rights of citizens and their interest in exercising those rights by voting. Different formal suffrage provisions involving age, gender, race, ethnic status, and other population characteristics prevailed in geographically varying ways at the time of each election, as did politically charged policy-relevant issues, party structures, and candidate personalities.

The position of the western settlement frontier at about the 100th meridian in 1848, the subsequent sequence of statehood admission, and the overall growth of the total U.S. population from about 20 million in 1848, 76 million in 1900, some 148 million in 1948, and 281 million in 2000 are the most conspicuous underpinnings of the four maps' patterns. The expansion of suffrage rights from roughly the white male one-third of the population in 1848 to nearly all non-incarcerated adult citizens by 2000 coupled with significant changes in the American polity during the same interval of time also influenced the sizes of the circles representing the total numbers of votes cast. Approximately two-thirds of the visual variation in circle size can be considered a function of geo-demographic changes, and the remaining one-third can be considered a function of changes in suffrage and political structure.

The map of voter participation in the election of 1848 exhibits a predominant pattern of relative uniformity in the total numbers of votes cast in each county. Careful inspection shows that some symbols are larger than others, especially in southern New England or along the Mid-Atlantic seaboard, but the overall impression is one of a fairly regular intensity of voter participation in the 1848 election. This uniformity, of course, reflects a predominantly agrarian pattern of settlement at a time when agriculture involved the muscle power of humans and draft animals, and barely one American in seven lived in an urban center. Somewhat surprisingly from a modern perspective, the symbols visible in many counties in southern states are not as inconspicuous as might have been expected. A glance at turnout rates, however, supports the visual impression, for while about 74 percent of potentially eligible voters cast ballots in non-southern states in 1848, the corresponding proportion of 68 percent for southern states was not appreciably lower. In other words, nearly the same proportions of adult white males voted in the South and non-South in the presidential election of 1848.

The map of voter participation in the 1900 election exhibits a predominate pattern of geographical uniformity, but regional differences are more pronounced than in 1848. Large urban centers, such as New York, Chicago, and San Francisco, stand out. The large industrial region east of the Mississippi and north of the Ohio Rivers also is prominent. This region would soon be known among geographers as the manufacturing belt, an area at the time already among the leading industrial zones in the world. About half of the population lived and worked within this manufacturing belt in 1900. Sparser settlement prevailed west of the 100th meridian, but rural population densities remained relatively uniform, reflecting the continued reliance of farm production on human and animal power. Smaller circles appear in counties in southern states, which were less urbanized than the rest of the nation and where restrictions on voting rights were taking hold. Turnout in the South in 1900 fell to 44 percent, compared with 83 percent in the rest of the country.

The map of voter participation in 1948 exhibits an intensification of several trends apparent a half-century earlier. The manufacturing belt and the adjacent western corn belt are especially conspicuous as areas where substantial numbers of votes were cast in most counties in the 1948 presidential election. High levels of agricultural as well as industrial production had proved important to the national effort in World War II, and blue-collar jobs continued to be well compensated in the factories that had turned to the production of automobiles, televisions, and other consumer durables as household formation and higher living standards took hold, leading, among other effects, to the postwar baby boom. Large cities—New York, Philadelphia, Chicago, Minneapolis, St. Louis, Kansas City, San Francisco, and Los Angeles—as well are clearly represented by large map symbols, indicating large numbers of voters. Although the "farm vote" continued to be of vital importance to candidates interested in garnering support from the midsection of the nation, nearly two out of three Americans lived in urban centers according to the census of 1950.

Many of the symbols for counties in southern states are, not surprisingly, much smaller than a glance at a map of population alone might imply, as southern turnout was a mere 25 percent, while turnout in the rest of the nation stood at 62 percent in 1948. Of pertinence, political scientist V. O. Key published *Southern Politics* just one year later. He predicated his careful empirical analysis on his "belief that southerners possess as great a capacity for self-government as do citizens elsewhere in the country."

Settlement processes during the last half of the twentieth century strongly influenced the map of voter participation in the 2000 election. The important components included the Interstate Highway Act of 1958, which effected an opening of expanding zones of suburban and exurban residential and commercial development around central city cores; the gradual "rusting" of the once great manufacturing belt as U.S. industry attempted to adjust to globalized production systems; and ongoing agricultural mechanization, which led to labor redundancy, out-migration, and population aging in place in many rural sections of the nation. As a result, although the same symbol size sequence appears on all four maps, the depiction of numbers of votes cast in more rural settings is conspicuously lower in density on the map for 2000 than on the maps for the earlier elections, despite more than twice as many popular votes (105.4 million) being cast in the 2000 election than had been cast a half-century earlier in the 1948 election (48.8 million). In addition to the large industrial cities clearly evident as early as 1900, many southern and western cities—including Miami, Atlanta, Memphis, Houston, Dallas–Fort Worth, Austin–San Antonio, Denver, Portland, and Seattle—now stand out on the map. The dominant message of the 2000 map, therefore, can be summarized as increasing metropolitan votes, but decreasing rural votes.

At the time of the 2000 census, 844 county and county-equivalent areas out of a total of 3,141 fell within the boundaries of census-defined metropolitan statistical areas (MSAs). Use of computer-based GIS technology to aggregate popular votes cast in the 2000 election across the nation according to MSA boundaries shows that about 83.3 million of the total 105.4 million votes were cast in counties within metropolitan areas. So, about 79 percent of all popular votes were cast by voters who lived within the roughly 20 percent of land located within MSA boundaries. This fact is extremely important in interpreting recent election maps. By implication, the 19.7 percent of residents who lived outside of MSAs were slightly more likely to vote than were the 80.3 percent of residents who lived within MSAs, but the difference between MSA versus non-MSA voter participation rates clearly was quite small. Still, about four out of five popular votes in the 2000 election were cast by voters who lived in metropolitan areas. In 2000 Democratic candidate Al Gore tended to run more strongly in large metropolitan areas than in rural and small-town settings, while Republican George W. Bush tended to run more strongly in rural counties and smaller metropolitan areas than in major metropolitan settings. Gore received about half a million more popular votes than Bush did, but according to the calculus of the electoral college, Bush won the federal election and therefore captured the White House.

PREVIOUS WORKS IN MAPPING U.S. PRESIDENTIAL ELECTIONS

EARLY STATISTICAL CARTOGRAPHY

The art and science of statistical cartography had developed in Austria, France, Prussia, and the United States by the mid-nineteenth century to the point of portraying human phenomena on maps. The earliest thematic statistical maps dealt with population characteristics from census counts and displayed such phenomena as agriculture, industry, diseases and their spread, as well as election results. The *Statistical Atlas of the United States based upon the Results of the Ninth Census, 1870* was the first major effort at mapping census data in the United States. Among the many other topical maps in the census atlas was a series on population density, illustrating the spread of population westward from the first 1790 census to 1870.

The 1870 census maps provided the techniques, inspiration, and data for the production of maps in privately published atlases and books. Previously, political almanacs, such as the *Tribune Almanac,* had published detailed tables of county-level presidential election returns since the 1840s. Advances in cartographic capabilities and available voting data were married by Fletcher W. Hewes and Henry Gannett in *Scribner's Statistical Atlas of the United States, Showing Their Present Condition and Their Political, Social and Industrial Development* (1883). A few years later, Hewes published *The Citizen's Atlas of American Elections* (1888), an entire volume devoted to elections. These two works are considered the first U.S. publications to present large, professionally designed, detailed county-level maps of presidential elections.

FREDERICK JACKSON TURNER AND THE ORIGINS OF QUANTITATIVE HISTORY

Frederick Jackson Turner, one of the most noted American historians, is most famous for his frontier and sectional theories of U.S. history. Turner, a friend and graduate school classmate of future president Woodrow Wilson, was trained as a historian in the 1880s and began writing in the 1890s. The explosion of census maps and statistical atlases during this time period clearly influenced Turner, as is unmistakably evident in his academic writing and his work in later years. In one of his seminal books, *Significance of Sections in American History* (1933), Turner used five county presidential election maps as critical pieces of evidence for his sectional theory, which proposes that U.S. history is best explained by the different economic and political interests of three great sections—the North, South, and West. In this work, he also employs an additional series of county maps of Illinois, Indiana, and Ohio voting patterns for comparison to settlement migration and physical geography. In the posthumously published *United States, 1830–1850*

(1935), Turner used ten different county presidential election maps to illustrate his points and to compare political patterns with numerous other map patterns, such as internal migration and agricultural products. Turner emerged as one of the leaders in the "quantitative history revolution" that became a powerful force in the first half of twentieth-century U.S. historiography.

ATLAS OF THE HISTORICAL GEOGRAPHY OF THE UNITED STATES

Frederick Jackson Turner and others in the Turnerian school of quantitative history worked toward producing a comprehensive scholarly atlas of U.S. history. Work on such an atlas began in 1912 and eventually received sponsorship from the American Geographical Society and Carnegie Institution. Historian Charles O. Paullin and geographer John K. Wright led the project. The final product, *Atlas of the Historical Geography of the United States,* appeared in 1932. The centerpiece of the section "Political Parties and Opinion, 1788–1930" is seventy-two political maps equally divided between critical congressional roll-call votes and presidential elections. The presidential election maps—four-color and county based—begin with the 1788–1789 election and go through the 1928 contest. This is the first complete series of presidential maps in this format. Because of the lack of early historical voting data at the time, Paullin and Wright used the electoral college vote for the first three elections and a mix of votes for president, Congress, governor, and other votes to "represent" political sentiment for the presidential maps covering 1800 to 1816. The Paullin and Wright maps regrettably do none of the following: show most county boundary lines, segregate the vote for individual major candidates, differentiate counties with respect to the intensity of the vote, or illustrate the extent of third- and fourth-party votes. The

maps are also small in size. The *Atlas of the Historical Geography of the United States* is nonetheless an epistemological and historical breakthrough in U.S. electoral cartography.

NATIONAL ATLAS PROJECT AND THE WORLD WIDE WEB

In the latter half of the twentieth century, presidential election mapping became increasingly common. A plethora of books appeared with the phrase "presidential atlas" in their title, but most merely mapped and reiterated the state-level electoral college results. *Electing the President, 1789–1988* published by the federal government's National Atlas Project in 1989, represents a notable exception. This work contains four-color intensity-based county-level presidential election maps for the five contests from 1972 to 1988. Additional National Atlas Project maps are available electronically via the World Wide Web through the 2004 election.

With the advent of computer-driven geographic information science (GIS) technology and digital cartography in the 1990s, a proliferation of private consulting firms and individuals produced county-level color maps for the 1996, 2000, and 2004 elections. News organizations produced many of these maps, and they are readily available on the Web. In addition, private Web sites have produced undocumented county election maps, some going back as far as 1960. These sites present one map showing the winner of each county, but without such variables as intensity of the vote, individual candidate vote patterns, or third-party trends and intensity. A significant gap exists between the last Paullin and Wright presidential map (1928) and the oldest National Atlas Project map (1972). Scholarly county-level maps for the ten elections between 1932 and 1968 have never been published in print or are not in wide circulation.

CONSTRUCTION OF THE PRESIDENTIAL ELECTIONS MAPS

Production of the *Historical Atlas of U.S. Presidential Elections, 1788–2004* required the assembly of a large database of election statistics and county boundaries unique in U.S. historical election research. The county-level statistics were compiled from numerous electronic, print, and unpublished sources. The combined statistics were analyzed using GIS technology to produce a corrected, refined, and accurate political database unparalleled in U.S. election studies. In a similar manner, county boundary information from various sources was combined to produce cartographic displays of geographical precision previously unmatched in election research.

VOTING DATA SOURCES

Creating the maps presented in the *Atlas* required assembling two distinct but related types of information from many different sources. The first involves cartographic attributes and addresses the question What qualities or quantities about elections need to be represented on the map? The second type of information involves cartographic locations and addresses the question Where should these qualities or quantities be positioned on the map? Uncertainties or errors involving cartographic attributes or cartographic locations can yield misleading or deceptive maps. In the past, cartographers would draw formal arrangements of flowers or menacing dragons on their cartographic creations to obscure the less well known regions where geographical knowledge faded into geographical fantasy. Cartographers still grapple with the omnipresent issue of how to honestly convey cartographic uncertainties on modern computer-produced maps.

PRESIDENTIAL ELECTOR DATA

Addressing the cartographic attribute question of what quantities or qualities need to be represented involved collecting data on the popular and electoral college outcomes of all U.S. presidential elections. Electoral college outcomes have been officially recorded and well documented from the outset. The number of electors apportioned to each state and the division of their vote at each presidential contest are among the most readily retrievable and indisputable facts. Division of the popular vote can, however, be much less certain, especially at small geographical scales and further in the past. Indeed, the votes of citizens are not now and never have been explicitly mandated components of the electoral college framework established by the Constitution.

Article 2, section 1, of the Constitution and the Twelfth Amendment, ratified in 1804, set out in considerable detail the procedures that must be followed as electoral votes are cast in each state and then transmitted and counted before a joint session of the two houses of Congress. The votes cast by the electors of each state at each presidential election thus become formal records of Congress. These include the ballots from 1800 and 1824, when no presidential candidate achieved an absolute majority and therefore left the final decision to a vote of state delegations in the House of Representatives.

NATIONAL VOTING DATA

Although the Constitution's explicit provisions for selecting a president through the indirect democracy mechanisms of the electoral college have led to well-documented electoral outcomes, no similar constitutional authority requires recording the votes cast by citizens in choosing presidential electors. Indeed, Article 2, section 1, of the Constitution evades specificity on the details of how electors should be chosen, instead merely stipulating, "Each State shall appoint, in such Manner as the Legislature thereof may direct, a Number of Electors, equal to the whole Number of Senators and Representatives to which the State may be entitled." As noted above, state legislatures have used a variety of different methods for selecting electors, especially early in the nation's history. In practice, the electors of all states have been chosen by popular vote since the mid-nineteenth century. Several constitutional amendments—including the Fourteenth, Fifteenth, Nineteenth, Twenty-fourth, and Twenty-sixth Amendments—and numerous legislatively enacted provisions of the U.S. Code, concern the rights of citizens to vote in federal elections to choose

members of the House of Representatives, the Senate, and the electoral college. There remains, however, no presidential selection equivalent to the Seventeenth Amendment, ratified in 1913, which requires that U.S. senators be elected by direct popular vote.

Recent presidential elections have been conducted under federal statutes requiring that the governor of each state send by registered mail to the archivist of the United States a "certificate of ascertainment" listing the names and popular votes received by persons appointed as electors "as soon as possible" after a general election. The legal staff of the Office of the Federal Register holds the responsibility of examining each certificate for "legal sufficiency" to ensure, for example, that no one appointed as an elector is a "Senator or Representative, or Person holding an Office of Trust or Profit under the United States" (specifically excluded under the Constitution's Article 2, section 1). In the presidential 2004 contest, the certificates of ascertainment were required to be submitted to the archivist no later than December 14, 2004, and to contain in addition to the names and votes received by winning electors, the names and votes received by all other candidates for elector in a state.

The certificates of ascertainment for recent elections have been deposited in the National Archives as formal records of the popular votes received by candidate electors in each state. Citizens interested in seeing the certificate for any state can view facsimiles at the National Archives' Web site, at http://archives.gov/federal-register/electoral-college. The Federal Election Commission's Web site, www.fec.gov, also offers "Presidential Electoral and Popular Vote," tables of recent elections by state. For state-level popular vote totals for pre-1990 elections, the National Archives' Web site relies on non-federal records. For example, for elections from 1824 to 1988, it cites "Source for Popular Vote Totals" from *Presidential Elections, 1789–1996* (1997), published by CQ Press. State-level presidential election data are also available from the Office of the Clerk of the U.S. House of Representatives, which provides facsimile copies of the biennial series "Statistics of the Congressional and Presidential Election" at http://clerk.house.gov/members/electionInfo/elections.html. Volumes from this series are available for presidential and congressional elections from 1920 to the present.

For elections after 1820, the state and national popular vote figures published in various works by Congressional Quarterly are generally regarded as among the most accurate. See, for example, *Presidential Elections, 1789–1996* (1997), *America Votes* (various years), and *Congressional Quarterly's Guide to U.S. Elections*, 5th ed. (2005). For elections from 1824 to 1996, the popular vote numbers and percentages reported in this *Atlas* for the nation as a whole are from Congressional Quarterly's *Presidential Elections, 1789–1996* (1997). For elections from 1788–1789 to 1820, Michael J. Dubin's *United States Presidential Elections, 1788–1860* (2002) was the main source for national-level popular vote numbers and proportions, with additional information from the work of Philip J. Lampi of the American Antiquarian

Society in Worcester, Massachusetts. National-level popular vote figures for the 2000 and 2004 elections are from *America Votes, 24,* published by CQ Press, and from the Web site of the Federal Election Commission.

COUNTY VOTING DATA

Although state-level and national-level data on popular voting for presidential electors can be found in numerous reference works, county-level voting data are considerably scarcer. Indeed, the problem of assembling data on popular votes cast at the geographical scale of the county (or occasionally the district) posed one of the greatest challenges to producing the *Atlas.* A similarly difficult problem involved tracing changes of county (and district) boundaries over time.

County-level popular election returns sit, of course, rather far back in the chain of popular vote aggregation that leads, according to the long prevailing winner-take-all custom, to slates of electoral candidates at the state level. Out of federal deference or neglect or both, the archival responsibilities have generally been left to the states or their administrative subdivisions for maintaining records of popular votes cast in presidential elections at the county level or lower. County-level election data are therefore generally unavailable from federal data providers. Investigators interested in fine-grained study of elections at substate geographical scales must turn to the archives of each state or to published compilations assembled by private or academic researchers. The only known exception involves county-level data for five presidential elections held in the late twentieth century that were included, along with many demographic or economic variables, on "USA Counties," CD-ROMs published by the Census Bureau (May 1999). Even this exception serves to prove the rule, because its county-level voting data for presidential elections from 1980 to 1996 turn out, on closer inspection, to have been adopted from the *America Votes* series rather than collected by bureau employees.

A large proportion of all of the county-level data assembled for the *Atlas* was drawn from one or more of four computer-readable compilations available from the Inter-University Consortium for Political and Social Research (ICPSR) in Ann Arbor, Michigan. These include ICPSR Study no. 1, "United States Historical Election Returns, 1824–1968" (updated April 26, 1999); ICPSR Study no. 13, "General Election Data for the United States, 1950–1990" (updated June 6, 1995); ICPSR Study no. 79, "United States Historical Election Returns, 1788–1823" (updated February 16, 1992); and ICPSR Study no. 8611, "Electoral Data for Counties in the United States: Presidential and Congressional Races, 1840–1972" (updated February 19, 1992). These data files include information for other elections, such as House and Senate races, and were designed for compatibility with the computer-input format requirements of major statistical packages, such as SAS (SAS Institute, 1999) and SPSS (SPSS Inc., 1998). Computer preprocessing, including the creation of several small computer programs in BASIC, was necessary to

extract data on presidential elections alone and also to reformat data structures to ASCII or DBASE formats compatible with Atlas*GIS, Strategic Mapping's geographic information science software used to produce the base maps for the *Atlas.*

Several printed reference works also were consulted to supplement and extend the county-level data obtained from the ICPSR files because returns for some counties in some elections are coded as "missing" in the ICPSR data files, a common occurrence, especially for nineteenth- and eighteenth-century elections. With the goal of minimizing the figurative use of flowers and dragons on the *Atlas*'s maps, each missing data field prompted serious efforts to fill in dreaded blank spaces. On occasion, these efforts went so far as the inclusion of late voting returns filed from counties that had reported too late to affect the selection of electors in their state at a particular election.

Another reason for consulting printed reference works is that the seemingly straightforward question of how many popular votes were cast for a specific presidential candidate in a particular county does not always produce a simple answer. The complexity of answers tends to be greater for earlier elections than for later ones. Answers generally become simpler for those starting at the end of the nineteenth century, owing to the widespread adoption of the secret, or "Australian," ballot coupled with the increasingly prevalent custom of presenting winner-take-all party slates of electors, whose names were increasingly replaced on ballots by the names of the presidential candidates to whom they were pledged. Earlier, different states followed different balloting practices, but it was not uncommon for voters to be able to cast several "presidential" votes, while picking and choosing among the individual names of many candidates for the electoral college. For example, if a state had five electoral votes then each voter might be required to choose five names from a long list of candidate electors.

Even today, although the predominant practice is for each voter to cast one presidential vote for a single slate of electors, it is not unknown for more than one slate of electors to be pledged to a particular presidential candidate. In New York in 2004, for example, the Bush-Cheney ticket received 2,806,993 popular votes under the Republican Party label and an additional 155,574 votes under the Conservative Party label, and the Kerry-Edwards ticket received 4,180,755 votes under the Democratic Party label and an additional 133,525 votes under the Working Families Party label. For the *Atlas,* votes cast for a particular candidate who appeared under such separate joint endorsements within a state or county have been added together before calculating vote proportions. Votes cast for a presidential candidate listed on ballots in different states under different party labels—as was the case of schismatic southern Democratic candidate Strom Thurmond in 1948 for example—are similarly given a single, common designation in the volume. Such ballot-linked complexities have become relatively rare, but they were more common before the late nineteenth century.

One of the more important print sources consulted in efforts to supplement and extend the county-level data drawn from ICPSR files was Richard M. Scammon's *America at the Polls* (1965), which contains carefully researched county-level returns for elections from 1920 to 1964. For elections from 1968 to 2000, quadrennial editions of *America Votes,* by Scammon and others, have been given much attention. Edgar Eugene Robinson's *Presidential Vote, 1896–1932* (1970) is an important source for late nineteenth- and early twentieth-century elections. For the mid- to late nineteenth century, the main print source consulted is Walter Dean Burnham's *Presidential Ballots, 1836–1892* (1955). In addition to recording voting returns, it also contains helpful material on county formation and boundary changes. For elections in the late eighteenth and early nineteenth centuries, Dubin's *United States Presidential Elections, 1788–1860* provides considerable early county-level election data previously unknown or unavailable to most interested scholars.

The tasks of vote data assembly and map compilation were undertaken more or less simultaneously. Computer technology allowed for sophisticated analyses and creation of preliminary maps for joint research purposes relatively effortlessly at intermediate stages of work on the *Atlas.* Many data gaps or clerical errors in keyboard data entry came to light through the GIS techniques used in creating temporary onscreen map displays and comparing sets of data values compiled from different sources. Presumably coincidental county-level data values that differed by more than 2 percent in magnitude were closely inspected as potential evidence of data-entry errors or of inconsistent interpretations of the party affiliations of electors or presidential candidates. The gaps and inconsistencies uncovered generated efforts to find additional sources of relevant voting data. In some cases this meant combing through footnotes in the compilations cited in the preceding paragraph for material on late-reporting counties whose unofficial returns had been excluded from the main data presentations. In other cases, such errors or omissions were found to be linked to changes in county names or demarcations or minor spelling inconsistencies between or among data sources. Yet in other cases, efforts turned toward an examination of county-level voting data found in almanacs published shortly after an election. These included various volumes of the *Tribune Almanac,* the *Chicago Daily News Almanac,* and the New York World's *World Almanac and Book of Facts.* In addition, the *Atlas* benefits from information on previously unknown returns for several counties in New Jersey and Virginia for very early elections from personal correspondence with Philip J. Lampi of the American Antiquarian Society.

CARTOGRAPHIC DATA SOURCES

Statistical-numerical or perhaps even historical-narrative research on the correlates or consequences of popular voting for presidential electors can be undertaken rewardingly using vague locational referents, such as "Observation x" or "County y."

Maps, however, are geographically less forgiving tools of information analysis and communication than are statistical coefficients or verbal narratives. On a map, it would be equally as grave an error to locate Suffolk County, Massachusetts, along the shores of the Chesapeake Bay as it would be to shade Suffolk County using a hue representing victory by the Virginian Thomas Jefferson in the critical election of 1800.

During the more than two hundred years covered in the *Atlas,* the United States expanded westward from an initial set of newly federated independent former colonies concentrated along the coast of the Atlantic Ocean to territorial sovereignty over the Pacific Coast of North America and beyond to Alaska and the Hawaiian Islands. Lands to the south and west that were little more than mythical when George Washington became president were captured or purchased from foreign powers, partitioned into provisional territories, surveyed into administrative subdivisions under the guidance of the Northwest Ordinances, and in due time organized and admitted to the Union as full-fledged states under the terms of Article 4 of the Constitution. With the same guarantee of "a Republican Form of Government" enjoyed by the citizens of all previously admitted states, the citizens of each newly admitted state also received representation in Congress and in the electoral college.

From an uncertainly bounded aggregate territory of about 865,000 square miles following the 1783 Treaty of Paris concluding the Revolutionary War, the land area of the United States had quadrupled to slightly more than 3.5 million square miles by the end of the nineteenth century. Limited geographical knowledge coupled with vague, overlapping, and conflicting territorial claims among France, Great Britain, Spain, Mexico, Russia, and the United States led to cartographic uncertainties in depicting North American national boundaries in the late eighteenth and early to mid-nineteenth centuries. Since the brief and bloody interlude of the Civil War, no state has changed its name or identity subsequent to statehood. State boundaries have, however, been altered on various occasions. For example, early states ceded their western claims to the Union, and adjacent states adjusted their boundaries in acknowledgment of natural changes in the course of rivers or following improvements in surveying technologies. The constitutional requirement of Article 4, section 3—that any changes in the territorial jurisdictions of States require the "Consent of the Legislatures of the States concerned as well as of the Congress"—has tended to restrict the extent and frequency of changes to state boundaries.

The internal subdivisions of states, such as counties, parishes, municipalities, or townships, do not enjoy the protections given to states in the Constitution. Governmental custom and in some instances formal provisions of state constitutions or statutes have provided considerable durability for county or parish boundaries, especially since the early twentieth century. The identities, names, and boundaries of counties and parishes were, however, sometimes greatly altered as the frontiers of settlement and political integration progressed westward. County boundaries remain subject to alteration, as illustrated by the dissolution and merger of Clifton Forge City into Alleghany County, Virginia, in July 2001 and the formation of Broomfield County, Colorado, from pieces taken from four older counties in November 2001. Other changes between the 2000 and 2004 elections included the wholesale revision of Alaska's state senate districts, which are used for purposes of mapping in the *Atlas* because Alaska lacks county divisions. All told, several thousand such boundary changes are reflected in the maps produced here.

Determining the geographical alignments of national, state, and county or parish boundaries at the time of each presidential election required consulting a large number of sources. The sometimes uncertain or contested boundaries between the United States and foreign jurisdictions, such as Canada or New Spain, were traced through various documents, particularly ones published by Henry Gannett, Franklin K. Van Zandt and the U.S. Geological Survey, Wilbur E. Garrett and Ronald M. Fisher and the National Geographic Society, and Charles O. Paullin and John K. Wright and the American Geographical Society.

Additional larger-scale cartographic and geographically detailed sources were necessary for tracing the alignments of state, county and parish, and territorial boundaries over time. After conversion from the ArcView shapefile format to Atlas*GIS and additional GIS editing to correct for post–census year changes in administrative geography, extracts of the Census Bureau's sophisticated and carefully compiled TIGER (Topologically Integrated and Geographically Encoding and Referencing) system files for 1990 and 2000 were used for mapping county-level results of the most recent elections. Digital cartographic data derived indirectly from earlier U.S. census DIME (Dual Independent Map Encoding) files for 1970 and 1980 as modified and distributed by Strategic Mapping Inc. for use with Atlas*GRAPHICS or Atlas*GIS were used as a basis for mapping elections from the 1970s to the late 1980s. GIS editing also was applied to the Atlas*GIS files to accommodate post–census year changes in administrative geography after 1970 and 1980.

Historical United States County Boundary Files is the principal digital data source used for identifying state and county boundaries as they existed prior to 1970. It is an extraordinary but relatively little known series of cartographic data files compiled and digitized by Carville Earle and his research assistants in the Department of Geography and Anthropology at Louisiana State University. The files contain GIS data that encode latitude-longitude positions for line segments that depict the boundaries of counties in those states admitted to the Union at the time of each census from 1790 to 1970. Creation of these files involved the laborious compilation of dispersed archival materials followed by the tedious and time-consuming activity of manually geo-coding from paper source maps using a computer-driven digitizing graphics tablet.

Although indispensable, Earle's files required considerable additional GIS editing to produce revised versions suitable for use in preparing maps for the *Atlas*. The original files were created on a state-by-state basis and distributed in a now-outmoded file format. As a result, the individual files for each state for a given census year had to be digitally translated and then concatenated into a single, larger composite file for the United States as a whole. The creation of a large composite file of the boundaries of all U.S. counties at the time of a particular decennial census usually uncovered numerous edge-matching gaps or overlaps between counties located along misaligned state boundaries. Problems of this sort are quite common in historical geographical research because of discrepancies in the style, projection, scale, and cartographic generalization of archival maps from different sources. Other more subtle base-map inconsistencies may be traceable to the shortcomings of older surveying technologies or to different geographical datum assumptions about the earth's degree of ellipticity. Efforts to correct the edge-matching problems, as well as other problems, involved visual examination of relevant printed maps, on-screen GIS overlay of geospatially correct but modern era TIGER files, and GIS editing to ensure that common borders between adjacent polygons are truly and visually coincident.

Also among the many cartographic sources consulted is William Thorndale and William Dollarhide's *Map Guide to the U.S. Federal Censuses, 1790–1920* (1987), which proved useful for visual cross-checking while editing the census-year county boundary files derived from Earle's files. In Thorndale and Dollarhide's compilation, a helpful and important feature is having the outlines of counties darkly overprinted on lighter base maps that show modern county boundaries. Also helpful were Census Bureau maps published in various decennial volumes and a February 1996 microcomputer summary compilation of population census data that includes a table showing the first census year by which a county had been formed. Uncertainties involving state, territorial, or county boundaries in the United States' early years were sometimes resolved by examining Francis Paul Prucha's *Atlas of American Indian Affairs* (1990) for information on the times and geographical configurations of Native American land cessions, because a formal transfer of lands from Native Americans to European Americans was usually a necessary precondition to white settlement and governmental organization.

Identifying changes in boundary configurations between census years posed a difficult problem. Tabular data sources used to ascertain county voting histories usually were sufficient to determine the time of appearance of a new county in relation to the quadrennial presidential election cycle, although spelling and other variations in county names sometimes presented difficulties. In many instances, the identity and boundary configuration for a county organized between census years could be inferred from the known geographical arrangement that had prevailed at the time of the subsequent decennial census. Counties, however, were sometimes organized and then unorganized, reorganized, or merged with other counties more than once between census years, with the consequence that the subsequent census year configurations were not always secure foundations for mapping elections in non-census years. Appendix materials in Burnham's *Presidential Ballots* were helpful for tracing county boundary changes during the mid-to-late nineteenth century. Appendix materials in Dubin's *United States Presidential Elections* also were helpful for tracing county-boundary changes during the late eighteenth to early nineteenth centuries for states that chose electors from districts. Paullin and Wright's *Atlas of the Historical Geography of the United States* and Hewes and Gannett's *Scribner's Statistical Atlas of the United States* also proved helpful.

Adrian B. Ettlinger's AniMap Plus is the cartographic data source that proved most valuable in tracing inter-censual boundary changes. This computer-based atlas contains more than 2,000 maps that show county and other boundary changes from colonial times to the present for each state and for the United States as a whole. Designed for graphical display on fairly low-resolution computer screens, the maps were compiled through extensive archival research and represent an unrivaled integrated compilation of otherwise very fragmented and elusive visual cartographic materials on U.S. geographical history. As with printed map source materials, the maps from AniMap were used as aids in on-screen digital GIS editing of cartographic base files derived or revised from TIGER, AtlasGRAPHICS, and Atlas*GIS files and Historical United States County Boundary Files.

CARTOGRAPHIC MAPPING PROCEDURES

Once the necessary foundation materials had been assembled involving votes cast and location, maps were produced in a two-stage procedure. In the first stage, Atlas*GIS was used to create a set of draft maps displaying the party identity of the presidential candidate who led in popular votes in each county, the proportion of popular votes received in each county by those candidates who received at least 2 percent of all popular votes cast nationally, and the presidential slate or slates that won electoral votes in each state. An additional draft map also was created for those few elections decided in the U.S. House of Representatives because of the failure of any candidate to receive an electoral college majority.

The advantages of digital map compilation using GIS technology were considerable at this stage, because apparent map errors trapped through visual examination of initial draft maps could be linked computationally to underlying data values and to geographical coordinates and topology and, if necessary, corrected using GIS database management and editing techniques. In addition, the use of GIS technology made it possible to systematically address map design refinements, such as the choice of the Albers conical equal-area projection for all maps and the choice of a standardized set of revealing choropleth class-breaks statistically and conceptually suitable for representation of presidential election results over an extended series

of election outcomes. GIS technology is of unrivaled utility in taking numerical values (such as voting percentages) linked to digital geographical coordinates and transforming them into temporary map displays viewable on computer screens. It suffers, however, from many shortcomings when the aim is to produce aesthetically attractive as well as informative maps for presentation in print.

The second stage of the map production process involved using Adobe Illustrator, a vector-based illustration software package, to transform map files exported from Atlas*GIS into aesthetically refined maps suitable for printing and viewing by a wide audience. Unlike GIS technology, illustration software, such as Adobe Illustrator, offers almost unlimited flexibility in establishing the appearance, scale, and positioning of graphic elements on maps. In short, whatever can be done with pen and ink, manual color rendering, and graphic arts photography can also be accomplished using this software. The matter of color selection is the map design issue that most warrants elaboration, although a number of other map design features—such as selection of font style and size, choice of line style and line weight, the scale of principal county-level maps versus inset state-level maps, positioning of graphic elements, and so on—were dealt with at this stage.

Considerable thought, visual experimentation, trial and error, and discussion led to the color schemes ultimately adopted. The main concerns regarding color selection involved conceptual issues of ideological similarities and differences among parties and candidates contesting the presidency at different times, perceptual aspects of human cognition in relation to map reading tasks, and constraints presented by color map reproduction technology. An added layer of complexity in color selection involved choosing color hues and intensities to symbolize qualitative as well as quantitative information. The main type of qualitative information pertained to political party affiliations, and the main type of quantitative information concerned statistical variations in levels of popular and electoral votes.

In the end, it was decided to give somewhat higher priority to the practical considerations of map clarity, legibility, and reproducibility as printed documents than to the political nuances of ideological similarities or differences among parties and candidates. Although real and important distinctions of ideological orientations or of programmatic objectives have not been entirely overlooked in the map symbolization scheme, some strange bedfellows do appear under the same party colors as a result of efforts to minimize the risks of otherwise creating maps that graphically communicate election information in confusing or unclear ways. So, for example, the use of the same red hue to represent Federalists, National Republicans, Whigs, and modern Republicans and the same blue hue to represent Anti-Federalists, Jeffersonian Republicans, Jacksonians, and modern Democrats should not be interpreted as implying that these are merely temporally variant names of otherwise ideologically identical parties. Eighteenth-century Federalists are certainly not the same as twenty-first-century Republicans, nor are early nineteenth-century Jeffersonian Republicans the same as late twentieth-century Democrats. Cartographic experiments revealed the risk of producing unreadable or unprintable maps too great if somewhat different shades of blues and reds were used to more acutely depict different historically contingent party coalitions.

Another map design consideration involved ensuring the availability of sufficient intensity variations of each hue depicting a party (in order to represent different levels of popular electoral support) and that each hue intensity is visually distinguishable from all others. These visual differences had, of course, to be retainable when reproduced using available printing technology. The color hues and intensities were chosen with the assistance of the computer program ColorBrewer (Brewer, Hatchard and Harrower, 2003) to make the *Atlas* maps as visually clear and legible as possible while conveying essential information about election history and election geography. The program generates color series maximally differentiable from one another and experimentally optimized for map reproduction through offset printing using CYMK (cyan, yellow, magenta, black) inks.

The chosen hues and hue intensities generally have the following interpretations:

Major parties under the long-running two-party system
- Shades of red: Federalists, Whigs, and modern Republicans
- Shades of blue: Anti-Federalists, Jeffersonian Republicans, and Democrats

Relevant minor parties
- Shades of green: the leading third-party or splinter candidate
- Shades of orange: the second-leading third-party or splinter candidate
- Shades of purple: the third-leading third-party or splinter candidate

Other elements
- Light yellow: No Returns, represents unorganized sub-areas within states or counties for which popular ballot data are nonexistent or missing
- Medium brown: Appointed Electors, represents states in which presidential electors are appointed rather than elected
- Light brown: Not Voting, represents state-level areas that were organized but not formally voting (for example, the Confederacy and Reconstruction states)
- Medium grey: Pre-Statehood, represents pre-statehood territories (for example, the Old Northwest Territories, the Louisiana Purchase) or areas of residents ineligible to vote (pre-1964 Washington, D.C.)
- Light grey: Foreign, represents foreign areas (for example, Canada, Spanish Florida)

Special circumstances occasionally prompted departures from the established color conventions. For example, four opposing presidential candidates all ran under the same party label in 1824, making it impossible to use only blue to represent Jeffersonian Republican Party affiliation. There also were other elections in which more than one strong candidate competed for electoral votes in one or more states under the same party label, such as the contests of 1860, 1912, or 1948. The maps sometimes simplify the details of more complex elections out of practical necessity. For these and other reasons, comprehensive understanding requires that readers direct their attention to the maps as well as to the individual election vignettes.

---

1. In 1961 the Thirteenth Amendment to the Constitution gave the District of Columbia electoral voting rights. The District's three votes raised the electoral college total to 538, with a majority of 270 votes needed to be elected president.

2. Florida in 1868 and Colorado in 1876 represent two additional isolated instances of legislature-selected presidential electors.

3. An isolated instance of district-selected electors occurred in Michigan in 1892.

4. Listing of the electoral slate on the ballot generally died out in the early twentieth century. It was last used in Vermont in 1980.

5. Until the 1960 election, Maine held presidential voting in September rather than in November.

6. Philip S. Klein, *Pennsylvania Politics, 1817–1832: A Game without Rules* (Philadelphia: University of Pennsylvania, 1940), 251.

7. James S. Chase, *Emergence of the Presidential Nominating Convention, 1789–1832* (Urbana: University of Illinois Press, 1973), 244.

8. Ibid., 306.

9. Frederick Jackson Turner, *The United States, 1830–1850* (Gloucester, Mass.: Pete Smith, 1958), 409.

1788–1789

PRESIDENTIAL ELECTION

CANDIDATE	POPULAR VOTE PERCENTAGE	ELECTORAL COLLEGE VOTE PERCENTAGE AND (VOTE)*
George Washington (Virginia)	93.3	94.5 (69)
Vice Presidential Selection: John Adams (Massachusetts)		

Map 1

The election of 1788–1789 was the first presidential election held under the terms of the newly ratified U.S. Constitution. In less than thirteen years after the Declaration of Independence of July 4, 1776, the former British colonists had won the Revolutionary War, established the Continental Congress, and instituted a constitutional federal government. Among the new Constitution's provisions were the creation of a strong federal office of the presidency and a rather complex indirect system of electors for selecting among candidates for that office. Ratification of the Constitution by New Hampshire, the required ninth state, on June 21, 1788, set in motion the constitutional process of elections for Congress and the president. The Constitution enumerated the number of presidential electors allocated to each state until a formal census could be held. The term *electoral college,* used to identify the collective body of electors from each state, does not appear in the Constitution but became common in the early nineteenth century.

The United States held its first presidential election in late 1788 and early 1789, and on February 4, 1789, presidential electors met in their respective states to cast the first electoral votes. The states then forwarded the results to the new Congress. On March 4, 1789, the first session of the First Congress (1789–1791) met in New York City but did not have a quorum. The House of Representatives and Senate eventually convened, opened, and confirmed the presidential electoral vote on April 6, 1789.

The leadership of Gen. George Washington of Virginia had been pivotal in the victory over Great Britain, and Washington had played a decisive leadership role as president at the Constitutional Convention in Philadelphia. As expected, Washington received 69 electoral votes, or one vote from every elector participating. John Adams

of Massachusetts, who came in second, became vice president in accordance with the stipulations in the Constitution. On April 30, 1789, in New York City, Washington was inaugurated as the first U.S. president, at which point the United States of America had an established and functioning government.

As required by the Constitution, each state determined the method for choosing its presidential electors. They used three general methods: election by state legislature, a statewide winner-take-all system based on the popular vote of qualified white male citizens statewide, and election based on the popular vote by district (see Table 1). As the popular and electoral college maps illustrate, among the original thirteen states, North Carolina and Rhode Island did not participate in the first election, as they had not yet ratified the Constitution. New York also did not participate, because its legislators could not decide on a final list of electors. In the remaining ten states, Connecticut, Georgia, New Jersey, and South Carolina chose electors in their legislatures. Massachusetts and New Hampshire chose electors by a combination of popular vote and final selection by their legislatures. Delaware and Virginia chose electors by popular vote by district, while Maryland and Pennsylvania chose electors by popular vote in a winner-take-all poll. The latter system would become the system of choice by the 1820s and remain so into the twenty-first century.

In most states with popular voting, eligible voters were presented a ballot with a list, or ticket, of electors' names. The ballot could be considered competitive only in winner-take-all Maryland and Pennsylvania, where voters had a choice between two slates of electors of particular political sentiments—either the so-called Federalist list, which supported the ratification of the Constitution and a strong central government, or the Anti-Federalist list, which generally had not supported

Two electors from Maryland and two from Virginia did not vote.

the ratification of the Constitution and favored decentralized government. Because Maryland and Pennsylvania were the only two states with a somewhat competitive choice, their voting records are the most complete for the first election. The Federalist list won every county in every state and is depicted on the popular vote map as a Washington majority. As evident from the candidate map, only in a few counties did the Washington ticket win less than 65 percent of the vote.

The election of Washington was a forgone conclusion, with national leaders having settled on him almost unanimously during the 1788 ratification process. As the hero of the revolution, Washington entered the first presidential election as the only plausible choice. He ran unopposed with nationwide support. Indeed, Washington was the unanimous victor in the electoral college. Although the first presidential election was devoid of political parties and a competitive election, political differences did exist.

REFERENCE: Jensen, Merrill, and Robert A. Becker, eds. *The Documentary History of the First Federal Elections, 1788–1790.* 4 vols. Madison: University of Wisconsin Press, 1976–1984.

1792

PRESIDENTIAL ELECTION

~

Candidates	Popular Vote Percentage	Electoral College Vote Percentage and (Vote)*
George Washington (Virginia)	88.9	97.8 (132)
Vice Presidential Selection: John Adams (Massachusetts)		
Anti-Federalist scattering	11.1	0 (0)

Map 2

During the 1780s, political sentiment was generally divided between the Federalists and Anti-Federalists. The Federalists favored ratification of the proposed Constitution and establishment of a strong central government to replace the weak Continental Congress system. The Anti-Federalists opposed ratification, believing that the Constitution placed too much power in the hands of the federal government and too little in those of the states. Although most states ratified the Constitution by comfortable margins, a geography of political sentiment for and against it clearly existed. Support for the Constitution was strongest in most parts of New England, cities, and coastal commercial areas of the Mid-Atlantic and the South. Anti-Federalist sentiment was strongest in non-coastal upcountry areas and rural counties.

Political parties did not exist during George Washington's first presidential term (1789–1793). Within the cabinet, however, differences in philosophy of governance began to split the administration. Alexander Hamilton, secretary of the Treasury and a former Revolutionary War aide to Washington, held great sway with the president. Hamilton had a "nationalist" conception of the United States, viewing it as an economic whole rather than a group of independent constituent states. Hamilton and other nationalists believed that promotion of the economic interests of the commercial elite, bankers, and those involved in manufacturing and trade would enhance the strength of the nation. One of Hamilton's more important initiatives was the establishment of a national bank, which favored the commercial interests of the Northeast and those involved in exporting and importing. Hamilton desired a strong central government administered by an educated elite, while

Secretary of State Thomas Jefferson led those with a philosophy of limited government and the strong belief that the government should also support and defend the small farmer and planter. For example, Jefferson questioned whether the Constitution allowed the establishment of a national bank and whether central government power could become too pervasive.

In Congress, one bloc of senators and representatives generally supported the Hamiltonian view of government, and another bloc supported more limited government. Many who supported the administration and Hamilton's governing concept came from many of the areas of Federalist support during the ratification period, that is, New England and other coastal commercial areas of the Mid-Atlantic and some areas of the South. The anti-administration bloc for more limited government tended to hail from rural areas, the South, and inland areas.

The one thing that Jefferson and Hamilton did agree on in 1792 was that Washington should run for a second term. Washington reluctantly agreed to do so. The nation again united behind Washington in spite of political or regional differences. Two new states, Kentucky and Vermont, had by then joined the original thirteen. Connecticut, Delaware, Georgia, New Jersey, New York, North Carolina, Rhode Island, South Carolina, and Vermont—nine of the fifteen states participating in the vote—did not have popular elections, choosing instead to select electors in their state legislatures. Virginia and Kentucky (once part of Virginia) both had a popular vote and selected electors by district. Massachusetts had a popular vote with the legislature having the final say on electors. Maryland, New Hampshire, and Pennsylvania employed a winner-take-all system of popular voting. Only in

Two Maryland electors and one Vermont elector did not vote.

Pennsylvania was there a semblance of a competitive race. There, two slates of electors appeared on the ballot, with the Washington-pledged slate winning every county but two in which returns are available. As the 1792 electoral college map illustrates, Washington again received one vote from every participating elector, making a clean sweep.

In 1790 a census of the population determined for the first time the number of presidential electors allocated to each state. The Constitution instructs that a census be conducted every ten years and that seats in the House of Representatives be reapportioned based on the results. In turn, the number of seats allotted a state determines the number of its presidential electors—one elector for every seat (in addition to two electors based on Senate representation). Since the first census, in 1790, the House has been reapportioned as required every ten years with the exception of 1920.

Members of the pro-administration bloc as well as the anti-administration bloc supported Washington's reelection. Perhaps the most interesting geographic aspect of the 1792 election was the vote for vice president. During this period, prior to the ratification of the Twelfth Amendment, each elector voted for two candidates. The winner became president, and the runner-up became vice president. The pro-administration bloc supported vice president Adams for reelection as well, but many supporters of Jefferson's limited government philosophy backed New York governor George Clinton for vice president. The final electoral vote count was Washington 132, Adams 77, Clinton 50, Jefferson 4, and Aaron Burr 1. Clinton's electoral votes came from his native New York and the three southern states of Virginia, North Carolina, and Georgia; Jefferson's electoral votes came from Kentucky; and Burr's single electoral vote came from South Carolina.

The first four years of the United States gave birth to several precedents involving the presidency, Congress, and the judiciary. Numerous foreign and domestic policy issues confronted the new nation and would play roles in the next and several succeeding elections. Although political parties did not formally exist, voting blocs in Congress were recognized, and newspapers, books, and citizens of the constituent states debated philosophies of governance.

REFERENCE: Rose, Lisle A. *Prologue to Democracy: The Federalists in the South, 1789–1800.* Lexington: University of Kentucky Press, 1968.

PRESIDENTIAL ELECTION

Candidates	Popular Vote Percentage	Electoral College Vote Percentage and (Vote)
Federalist		
John Adams (Massachusetts)	52.2	51.4 (71)
Vice Presidential Nominee: Thomas Pinckney (South Carolina)		
Republican		
Thomas Jefferson (Virginia)	47.8	49.3 (68)
Vice Presidential Nominee: Aaron Burr (New York)		

Map 3

During the second administration of George Washington (1793–1797), the Federalists and the Republicans emerged as distinct political parties. Some historians consider the Republicans to have formed as early as the summer of 1791, when Thomas Jefferson and James Madison traveled together in the north to rally politicians opposed to the policies of Alexander Hamilton. Nevertheless, by the Fourth Congress (1795–1797), voting blocs were beginning to associate with self-identified labels, and an early form of loose party competition ensued.

These first parties are not to be confused with the organized formal political parties with national presidential nominating conventions and well-thought-out campaigns that developed in the 1830s and 1840 and are somewhat similar to parties today. For the most part, the followers of George Washington, John Adams, Alexander Hamilton, and the pro-administration congressional bloc coalesced as the Federalist Party in Congress and the states. The followers of Thomas Jefferson, James Madison, and the anti-administration congressional voting bloc formed the Republican Party (which is not the same as the modern-day Republican Party, which was founded in 1854).

The domestic issues separating the two new parties resembled the positions of the previous congressional blocs. The Federalists favored a strong national government to support emerging industries, trade, and manufacturing and commerce in general. They tended to be traditional churchgoers and wealthier, older, and better educated than the Republicans. The Republicans favored a strict constructionist interpretation of federal involvement in the economy and supported expanding voting rights to all white males. Small farmers and planters tended to support them.

Foreign policy became part of a presidential campaign for the first time in 1796. The French Revolution and consequent violence had disturbed the more traditional and conservative Federalists. On the other hand, Jefferson and many Republicans were sympathetic to the overthrow of the monarchy and the establishment of a more democratic government. The Republicans viewed the Jay Treaty of 1795, signed by the Washington administration to clarify relations with Britain, as pro-British, while the Federalists labeled the Republicans pro-French.

With two clear-cut political groups established, Washington's announcement that he would refuse to serve a third term set the stage for the first competitive U.S. presidential election. Federalist leaders almost unanimously supported Vice President John Adams of Massachusetts. With many elite, conservative, and commercially oriented Federalists living in the South, the party attempted to geographically "balance the ticket" in the vice presidential race by selecting as their preferred candidate Thomas Pinckney, a Revolutionary War hero, former governor of South Carolina, and former U.S. minister to Britain and Spain. The Republicans chose as their presidential candidate Thomas Jefferson, who would prove to be one of the most charismatic and intelligent leaders in U.S. history. Jefferson had resigned from the second Washington cabinet in 1793 to divorce himself from constant political clashes. Because Jefferson came from Virginia, the Republicans selected Sen. Aaron Burr of New York as their preferred vice presidential candidate in an attempt to attract votes from all sections of the country.

The 1796 election was close. Half of the sixteen states—Connecticut, Delaware, New Jersey, New York, Rhode Island, South Carolina, Vermont and the newly admitted state of Tennessee—chose presidential electors in their state legislatures. Kentucky, Maryland, North Carolina, and Virginia held popular votes, selecting electors by district. Massachusetts and New Hampshire also had a popular vote, but allowed the legislature the final say in electors. Georgia and Pennsylvania had a winner-take-all system of popular voting.

Somewhat complete county-level election data exist only for Maryland, Georgia, and Pennsylvania, where two slates of pledged electors appeared on the ballot. In Pennsylvania, Adams carried the more developed southeastern region, except for Philadelphia, where Jefferson was popular. Carrying Philadelphia city and county by a wide margin allowed the Republicans to win the state with a slim 50.3 percent of the vote. In Georgia, Jefferson won all but two counties and carried the state with more than 70 percent of the vote. In Maryland, Adams won the plantation-based commercial agriculture counties in the southern Chesapeake Bay, but there is no other clear geographical pattern to the vote in that state. The Federalists won a majority of the district-elected electors.

In the final electoral count, Adams won 71-68. A change in any state vote, or for that matter, a change in any two elector district votes, would have given the election to Jefferson. The electoral vote in this first contested election was sharply divided between north and south. Adams won all five states in his home region of New England. (Maine was part of Massachusetts until separation and statehood in 1820.) Adams also won the Mid-Atlantic coastal commercial states of Delaware, New Jersey, and New York. Jefferson won all the states adjacent to and south of his home state of Virginia, in addition to, as mentioned above, barely carrying Pennsylvania.

Under the original system of elections established by the Constitution, Republican Jefferson, who received the second highest number of electoral votes, became vice president to the Federalist Adams. Though personally friendly at first, Adams and Jefferson became political adversaries and after four years were unfriendly to say the least. In the emerging competitive electoral process, the Federalists and Republicans would pit these same two leaders against each other in 1800.

REFERENCES: Dauer, Manning J. *The Adams Federalists.* Baltimore, Md.: Johns Hopkins Press, 1953.

Hoadley, John F. *Origins of American Political Parties, 1789–1803.* Lexington: University Press of Kentucky, 1986.

1800

PRESIDENTIAL ELECTION

Candidates	Popular Vote Percentage	Electoral College Vote Percentage and (Vote)
Republican		
Thomas Jefferson (Virginia)	61.3	52.9 (73)
Vice Presidential Nominee: Aaron Burr (New York)		
Federalist		
John Adams (Massachusetts)	38.7	47.1 (65)
Vice Presidential Nominee: Charles Cotesworth Pinckney (South Carolina)		

Map 4

John Adams had been elected president in 1796 by a narrow margin. During his administration, Federalist domestic economic policy had flourished. Foreign policy issues began to grow in importance as the 1800 election approached, with a major conflict looming with France. The French, like many Americans who sided with the Republican Party, continued to regard the Jay Treaty as too pro-British. The French government seemingly allowed, and even encouraged, privateers to capture and take U.S. ships and cargo, a policy that had led to engagements between French and U.S. naval forces. A real war seemed likely. In an effort to defuse tensions, the Adams government dispatched ministers to France, where they were offered bribes. The resulting XYZ Affair exacerbated anti-French feelings in the United States, even among some Republicans. Adams's peace initiatives managed to avoid war with France, though oddly the peace angered Alexander Hamilton and other conservative Federalists. Opponents of the peace broke with the administration and formed a dissident faction, the so-called High Federalists, going into the 1800 election.

On the domestic front, several laws passed by the Federalist-controlled Congress worried true believers in an unfettered democracy. The Alien and Sedition Acts of 1798, which were clearly anti-immigration (and in reality anti-French), allowed the imprisonment of foreigners in times of war. The Sedition Act made it a crime to voice or commit a "conspiracy or revolt" against the government, obviously an effort to stifle opposition to Adams's Federalist administration. A number of Republican newspaper editors were arrested and tried, and some were convicted of sedition. In Virginia and Kentucky, Republican-friendly state legislatures even proposed that states had the right to judge the constitutionality of federal laws that infringe on the Bill of Rights. The Alien and Sedition Acts were clear examples of the philosophies of the two parties—Jeffersonian democracy of limited decentralized government and power, states rights, and freedom of the common man versus the elite Federalist concept of strong central government from above. The 1800 election tested these ideas.

With the growing role of political parties becoming more accepted and recognized, and with Congress serving as the meeting place for politicians from all over the nation, representatives and senators became central in the selection of presidential candidates. Congressional Republicans and congressional Federalists met separately in unofficial caucuses to discuss and nominate candidates. For the 1800 election, the Federalists decided to back President Adams, though with some opposition from the High Federalists. They chose South Carolinian Charles Cotesworth Pinckney, brother of Vice President Thomas Pinckney, for the second slot. The

Republicans again chose Thomas Jefferson as the presidential nominee and New York's Aaron Burr as their vice presidential candidate.

The 1800 election was an extremely close affair in which a change in one state would have altered the outcome. This election featured the highest proportion of states without a popular vote for electors. The same sixteen states that had participated in the 1796 election did so again, but in 1800 eleven opted for their legislatures to choose electors. From this election forward, however, popular voting for president gained ground, especially in the 1820s; by 1832 only South Carolina would continue to select electors by legislature. During the early 1800s, the parties that controlled the state legislature of course determined the state's presidential electors. Having the New Yorker Burr on the ticket in 1800 may in fact have helped determine the composition of the New York legislature, which was elected just before the presidential election. The new state legislature was majority Republican, whereas the previous one had been Federalist controlled. Adams had carried New York in 1796, but the newly elected legislature supported Jefferson in 1800. New York was the only state that switched support from 1796 to 1800, which handed the election to Jefferson.

Five states had popular voting for president in 1800: Kentucky, Maryland, and North Carolina selected electors by district, while Virginia and Rhode Island selected theirs on a winner-take-all basis. Good county election returns are available for all but Kentucky. In Maryland, the districts split, five for Adams and five for Jefferson. Adams received his strongest support in the counties of the southern Chesapeake Bay and those with plantations along the lower Potomac River valley. In North Carolina, Adams won four districts, and Jefferson took eight. As the popular vote map shows, Adams had pockets of support on the central coast and in the upper Cape Fear River valley counties centered on the town of Fayetteville and Cumberland County. Some historians consider this subregion one of the longest and strongest Federalist areas outside of New England. Jefferson's Virginia supported its native son with 77.3 percent of the vote; Adams only carried nine scattered counties and one town. In Rhode Island, Adams carried three of five counties and the state with 52.2 percent of the vote. The geography of the national vote as seen on the electoral college map is similar to that of 1796: Adams carried the New England states, coastal New Jersey, and Delaware and had pockets of support in the southern states, including in Maryland and North Carolina. Jefferson dominated in the South and carried Pennsylvania and this time New York.

The 1800 electoral vote was one of the most historic. In the previous three elections, political leaders had taken measures that ensured that the presidential and vice presidential candidates did not receive the same number of votes. In 1800, however, Jefferson won the presidential election with 73 votes to Adams's 65, but Republican vice presidential candidate Burr also received 73 votes, making the vote for the presidency a tie. In case of a tie, the Constitution directs that the election be decided by the House of Representatives. The lame duck Sixth Congress (1789–1801) had a clear Federalist majority. In the House election system, each state got one vote, determined by the majority vote of its delegation. In the case of a tie in the delegation, the state casts a blank ballot. On February 6, 1801, the House of Representatives met to vote for president with nine of sixteen votes needed to win. For thirty-five ballots the results stood at Jefferson 8 and Burr 6, with 2 blank. On February 17, 1801, on the thirty-sixth ballot, the House elected Jefferson after Federalist representatives in Vermont and Maryland broke the deadlock by switching their vote. The Twelfth Amendment, ratified in 1804, calls for separate balloting for president and vice president to avoid a repeat of the situation that evolved in 1800.

The 1800 election was one of the first peaceful transfers of governmental power from one political party to another. In addition, the triumph of broad-based Jeffersonian democracy over elitist Federalist philosophy became permanent. The Federalists declined rapidly, and the Republicans rose as the dominant political party, until they became so large that they split into factions in the 1820s.

REFERENCES: Ferling, John E. *Adams vs. Jefferson: The Tumultuous Election of 1800*. New York: Oxford University Press, 2004.

Risjord, Norman K. *Chesapeake Politics, 1781–1800*. New York: Columbia University Press, 1965.

Weisberger, Bernard A. *America Afire: Jefferson, Adams, and the Revolutionary Election of 1800*. New York: HarperCollins, 2000.

1804

PRESIDENTIAL ELECTION

CANDIDATES	POPULAR VOTE PERCENTAGE	ELECTORAL COLLEGE VOTE PERCENTAGE AND (VOTE)
Republican		
Thomas Jefferson (Virginia)	71.8	92.0 (162)
Vice Presidential Nominee: George Clinton (New York)		
Federalist		
Charles Cotesworth Pinckney (South Carolina)	28.2	8.0 (14)
Vice Presidential Nominee: Rufus King (New York)		

Map 5

In an attempt at conciliation, President Thomas Jefferson famously said in his March 1801 inaugural speech, "We are all Republicans; we are all Federalists." In the next four years, Jefferson brought Republican limited government to the United States, while at the same time retaining many Federalist economic policies, and even occasionally adopting the Federalists' more expansive interpretation of the Constitution.

The acquisition of the Louisiana Territory from France in 1803 perhaps represents Jefferson's biggest deviation from Republican philosophy. The Louisiana Purchase nearly doubled the size of the United States and made it one of the largest nations in the world, but did the Constitution allow such an action? A strict constructionist, Jefferson nonetheless moved forward with the deal, which easily passed in the Republican-controlled Congress. Of interest, New England Federalists opposed the purchase not because of any constitutional qualms, but because they feared that it might cause a geopolitical imbalance, with the new western territory emerging and gaining power at the expense of their own region. After the purchase had been secured, Jefferson, in an imaginative move, sent explorers Meriwether Lewis and William Clark to survey the Missouri River and sent Zebulon Montgomery Pike to find the source of the Mississippi River.

The first Jefferson administration (1801–1805) had been a time of peace and prosperity. The Federalists were poorly organized, associated with an elitist governing philosophy, and buffeted by the wave of Jeffersonian democracy and the increasing franchise of white males. The popular Jefferson oversaw a moderate administration and lived in an unpretentious style in keeping with Republican philosophy. In February 1804, Republican members of Congress held the first official, organized presidential caucus, nominating Jefferson for president and George Clinton of New York for vice president. The Republicans replaced Vice President Aaron Burr because of his acceptance of Federalist presidential votes in the 1801 House presidential election and his running for the New York governorship in 1804 against a Republican candidate. The disorganized Federalists failed to hold a caucus, but eventually their leaders asked South Carolinian Charles Cotesworth Pinckney, the 1800 vice presidential candidate, to stand for president. Former New York senator Rufus King was chosen as the vice presidential candidate. Again, both parties had one northerner and one southerner on their tickets.

In 1804 the trend began in the move away from legislatures selecting presidential electors and toward selection by popular vote. In only six states did legislatures elect electors in 1804, down from eleven in 1800. Kentucky, Maryland, North Carolina, and Tennessee had popular election by districts. Massachusetts, New Hampshire, New Jersey, the newly admitted state of Ohio, Pennsylvania, Rhode Island, and Virginia had winner-take-all popular votes. Only Maryland,

Massachusetts, and Pennsylvania held actual contests of two opposing electoral slates, yielding a somewhat complete set of county voting data. As the 1804 popular vote map shows, in Maryland the Federalists won some southern Chesapeake Bay counties and gained two of the eleven district-elected electors. In Pennsylvania, Pinckney won only one county. In North Carolina, a few counties again went Federalist in the upper Cape Fear River valley. The staunchly Federalist Massachusetts went shockingly for Jefferson, who won a total of 53.3 percent of the state ballot.

The 1804 poll was the first election after enactment of the Twelfth Amendment, which separated the contests for president and vice president. Unlike the 1796 and 1800 elections, the one held in 1804 was not close. Pinckney won the electoral votes of just Connecticut and Delaware, along with the aforementioned two votes from Maryland. Jefferson won with 162 electoral votes (92 percent) to Charles Cotesworth Pinckney's 14 votes (8 percent). Jefferson's victory was of overwhelming proportion in all regions and sections. The 1804 election heralded the ascension of the Jeffersonian Republican Party to political dominance.

REFERENCE: Goodman, Paul, ed. *The Federalists vs. the Jeffersonian Republicans.* New York: Holt, Rinehart and Winston, 1967.

1808

PRESIDENTIAL ELECTION

CANDIDATES	POPULAR VOTE PERCENTAGE	ELECTORAL COLLEGE VOTE PERCENTAGE AND (VOTE)*
Republican		
James Madison (Virginia)	64.5	69.3 (122)
Vice Presidential Nominee: George Clinton (New York)		3.4 (6)
Federalist		
Charles Cotesworth Pinckney (South Carolina)	33.2	26.7 (47)
Vice Presidential Nominee: Rufus King (New York)		
Independent Republican		
James Monroe (Virginia)	2.3	0 (0)

Map 6

The second term of President Thomas Jefferson (1805–1809) lacked the same degree of peace and prosperity as his first. War between the British and French in 1803 caused havoc in international trade, in which the United States had become increasingly involved. The United States wanted to maintain its neutrality and ocean trade with both powers. The two nations, however, attempted to prevent the United States from trading with the other. Their warships stopped U.S. merchant ships to search them for forbidden cargo and also to impress American sailors suspected of being deserters from their side. After three Americans were killed and others impressed from the merchant ship *Chesapeake* in June 1807, the Jefferson administration decided against war, but asked Congress to enact an embargo of trade with both powers. Though the Embargo Act of December 1807 was intended to force the British and French to cease their harassment at sea, it instead primarily punished American exporters, farmers, planters, and merchants. The embargo hit New England particularly hard.

In 1808 Jefferson followed George Washington's precedent and declined a third presidential term. Jefferson handpicked Secretary of State James Madison, from his home state of Virginia, as his party's nominee. Although not totally without dissent,

the Republican congressional caucus reaffirmed various state caucuses in selecting Madison. Vice President George Clinton of New York remained on the ticket for regional balance and to help win his key home state. Public anger over the economic losses caused by the embargo had breathed new life into the faltering Federalist Party, whose leaders and state gatherings once again nominated the 1804 team of Charles Cotesworth Pinckney from South Carolina for president and former New York senator Rufus King for vice president.

The 1808 campaign focused on the embargo and the inability to protect U.S. trade and the economy. Voting in most states took place in November 1808, and presidential electors voted on December 7. Congress announced the electoral college results in February 1809, with Madison receiving 122 votes to Pinckney's 47. Jefferson's strength of personality and the power of the Republicans in the South helped carry Madison to a comfortable victory. The Federalist vote was concentrated as usual in New England. Pinckney carried four of the five New England states, but only one other state, strongly Federalist Delaware. Madison carried his home state of Virginia and all states west and south of Virginia. In New York, an anti-Madison faction of the Republican Party cast six of the state's thirteen electoral

One Kentucky elector did not vote.

votes for president for fellow New Yorker Clinton. Regardless, Clinton still received the most votes for vice president and was reelected to that office. He became the first vice president to serve under two presidents.

In 1808 seven of the seventeen states had legislature-chosen presidential electors. As in the previous election, Kentucky, Maryland, North Carolina, and Tennessee held popular elections by district. New Hampshire, New Jersey, Ohio, Pennsylvania, Rhode Island, and Virginia had winner-take-all popular votes. As the popular vote map illustrates, the Federalists showed their strength in the southern Chesapeake Bay counties in Maryland and won two of the eleven Maryland districts. The Federalists also again did well in the upper Cape Fear River valley and coastal North Carolina and won three of the fourteen North Carolina districts. In Pennsylvania, Madison carried every county and won the state with more than three-fourths of the popular vote. Madison received more than three-fourths of the vote in his home state, where his chief opposition was not the Federalist candidate, but fellow Republican James Monroe. A Monroe-pledged slate carried nine Virginia counties and received more than 17 percent of the popular vote. Pinckney carried seven of thirteen counties in New Jersey, but lost the state, taking only slightly more than 44 percent of the total vote. Pinckney managed to carry Rhode Island and New Hampshire with 54 percent and 52 percent, respectively.

The 1808 election further demonstrated the weakness of the Federalists and the dominance of the Republicans, even in a time of national crises and economic downturn. The actions of Britain and France outraged most Americans, who accepted some action by the government. Nevertheless, New Englanders saw the embargo as more anti-British than anti-French and believed that it hurt their region much more than the Mid-Atlantic states or the South. Some Federalists, including Massachusetts senator John Quincy Adams, son of the venerable Federalist president, resisted their party. Adams's generally independent voting record and support of the national interest in the *Chesapeake* incident led him out of the party and into the Republican ranks. Harassment of U.S. merchant vessels on the high seas continued into President Madison's first term (1809–1813) and led to the War of 1812.

REFERENCE: Munroe, John A. *Federalist Delaware, 1775–1815*. New Brunswick, N.J.: Rutgers University Press, 1954.

1812

PRESIDENTIAL ELECTION

CANDIDATES	POPULAR VOTE PERCENTAGE	ELECTORAL COLLEGE VOTE PERCENTAGE AND (VOTE)*
Republican		
James Madison (Virginia)	50.7	58.7 (128)
Vice Presidential Nominee: Elbridge Gerry (Massachusetts)		
Independent Republican–Federalist		
De Witt Clinton (New York)	47.1	40.8 (89)
Vice Presidential Nominee: Jared Ingersoll (Pennsylvania)		
Independent Federalist		
Rufus King (New York)	2.2	0 (0)

Map 7

As an emerging North Atlantic trading nation, the United States unavoidably became involved in the Napoleonic Wars of early nineteenth-century Europe. In 1803 the British-French declaration of war had led to interference in U.S. overseas shipping and commerce and passage of the Embargo Act of 1807. After the 1808 election, continued impressments, seizures, and general harassment of U.S. shipping by the British as well as the French brought calls for action not from New Englanders, whose ships were the most likely to be stopped, but from southerners and westerners.

Trouble with Native Americans on the western frontier fed into U.S. troubles on the high seas. In the Northwest Territories, Chief Tecumseh of the Shawnee had built an Indian confederacy to resist white expansion, some argued with help from British Canada. Conflict between the Indian alliance and settlers came to a climax in November 1811, when Indiana territorial governor William Henry Harrison defeated an Indian force at Tippecanoe Creek. Supposed British involvement in the frontier Indian Wars further exacerbated anti-British feeling in Congress and the nation.

In 1812 events on the high seas intensified. President James Madison called for a renewed embargo but reluctantly deferred to the Twelfth Congress (1811–1813),

which had a vast Republican majority and wanted tougher action. Among the new congressional members was a group of young so-called War Hawks, who pressed for a declaration of war with Great Britain. Prominent among them were Speaker of the House Henry Clay of Kentucky and John C. Calhoun of South Carolina. The War Hawks were not only anti-British, but also pro-expansionist, eyeing Spanish Florida (ally of the British) and British Canada. In June 1812, Congress declared war on Great Britain. Federalists and representatives from New England and commercial areas of the Mid-Atlantic states voted against the war. New Englanders—generally pro-British—also opposed expansion, fearing further diminution of their region's power. Republicans and representatives from the South and West generally voted for the war.

In the month before the declaration of war, the Republican congressional caucus renominated Madison for president. The Republicans then chose Massachusetts Republican governor Elbridge Gerry for vice president. Many state legislatures also caucused and endorsed the Madison nomination, as did most Republican newspapers. Commercial New York, however, had been injured by the various embargos and talk of war. The vast majority of the Republican legislative

One Ohio elector did not vote.

caucus nominated Republican New York City mayor De Witt Clinton, son of former Republican vice president George Clinton, for president. Clinton accepted, ambitiously thinking that he could unite New England and Mid-Atlantic antiwar Republicans and Federalists and win the election. Federalist leaders met in New York City in September 1812, and the weakened party decided to endorse Clinton as the lesser of two Republican evils, rather than select a separate Federalist candidate. They chose Philadelphia lawyer and jurist Jared Ingersoll as their vice presidential nominee. Given the nature of Clinton's affiliations and endorsements, he is here listed as an Independent Republican–Federalist for the 1812 election.

The war with Britain started badly in the summer and fall of 1812. The British and their Indian allies captured Detroit and Fort Dearborn (Chicago) in August. Republican and Federalist opponents of the conflict began calling it "Mr. Madison's War." Nevertheless, Madison won reelection, with the general populace supporting the president in wartime, though support was sharply divided geographically. As the electoral college map indicates, Clinton carried all the coastal New England states, his home state of New York, and the coastal, commercial Mid-Atlantic states of Delaware and New Jersey. Madison carried his home state of Virginia and again every state south and west of Virginia, receiving 128 electoral votes (58.7 percent). He also won Pennsylvania with 62.6 percent of the vote, enough to secure its critical twenty-five electoral votes and Republican victory.

As the popular vote map indicates, nine of the eighteen states, including newly admitted Louisiana, chose presidential electors in their legislatures. No county-level election returns are available for the two western states of Ohio and Tennessee. Clinton did well in New England, carrying almost all counties with popular elections. In Maryland, one of the four states in which electors were chosen by district, Clinton did well in the southern Chesapeake Bay counties, where Federalists had always been popular, and in plantation counties along the lower Potomac River valley. Maryland was the only state to split its electoral vote, with 6 for Madison and 5 for Clinton. In Virginia, the state Federalist Party voted not to support Clinton and instead put forth a slate pledged to Federalist Rufus King. As the popular vote map indicates, the Federalist slate won the Eastern Shore counties and a line of counties in western Virginia. In the end, Madison carried the state with nearly 73 percent of the vote.

After the declaration of war, many New England merchants continued to trade illegally with Great Britain. The War of 1812 dragged on much longer than most Americans thought it would. The election of 1812 proved again not only the strength of the dominant Republican Party, but also that the nation was extremely divided geographically in party affiliation and domestic and foreign policy. Actions by northeastern Federalists during the war would doom their party into becoming a minor regional party before its demise.

REFERENCE: Broussard, James H. *The Southern Federalists, 1800–1816*. Baton Rouge: Louisiana State University Press, 1978.

1816

PRESIDENTIAL ELECTION

CANDIDATES	POPULAR VOTE PERCENTAGE	ELECTORAL COLLEGE VOTE PERCENTAGE AND (VOTE)*
Republican		
James Monroe (Virginia)	67.4	82.8 (183)
Vice Presidential Nominee: Daniel Tompkins (New York)		
Federalist		
Rufus King (New York) and others	15.8	15.4 (34)
Vice Presidential Nominee: None		
John E. Howard (Maryland) received the most votes		
Independent Republicans	16.8	0 (0)
Scattering and unpledged electors		

Map 8

The War of 1812 dominated the second administration of James Madison. In 1813 U.S. forces captured and burned the capital of Upper Canada, York (Toronto), and Commodore Oliver Perry defeated the British in a naval engagement on Lake Erie. The following year, British forces captured and burned Washington, D.C., in August. Republicans, especially the congressional War Hawks, vigorously supported the war, as did most of the South and West. Nearly all Federalists and most of New England and the Mid-Atlantic coastal towns, particularly those involved in commerce and trade with England, vigorously opposed it.

In December 1814 and January 1815, three fateful events occurred that would influence U.S. politics and presidential elections. First, New England Federalists held a convention in Hartford, Connecticut, in December and January, at which they drafted a number of proposals for protecting New England's interests. A minority of delegates argued that secession would be in order if the central government failed to address their interests. Second, after the convention, news reached the East that Gen. Andrew Jackson had defeated the British in January in the Battle

of New Orleans. Jackson's accomplishment represented an overwhelming victory for the United States that not only thrust Jackson into prominence as a national hero, but also gave the Americans the last great victory of an inconclusive war. Third, news spread to the United States that the Treaty of Ghent had been signed in December in Belgium ending the war. (Word of the signing had not reached the United States before the Battle of New Orleans.) The treaty was as inconclusive as the war itself, but many Americans interpreted the Battle of New Orleans and other victories—holding their own against the greatest empire in the world—as a national triumph.

A number of political winners emerged from the War of 1812: Republicans, westerners, southerners, the Madison administration and Virginians in general, the War Hawks, and in the long term Gens. Andrew Jackson and William Henry Harrison. Among the political losers, besides the western Indians who had sided with the British, stood the Federalists and Hartford Convention participants, who appeared to be pro-British appeasers and regionally self-centered in a time of national crises and war.

One Delaware and three Maryland electors did not vote.

With the ascent of the War Hawks, a new generation of Republicans emerged in Congress and the nation. These "New" Republicans were more willing than the "Old" Republicans to embrace westward expansion, protective markets, and even internal improvements, in essence co-opting many Federalist programs. In 1816 Madison and Congress even re-chartered the National Bank to expire in 1836, an obvious step toward continued expanded federal power. By the time of the 1816 presidential election, two things had become certain: Secretary of State James Monroe of Virginia was the Republican front-runner, and the Federalists were fatally weakened. In March 1816, the Republican congressional caucus confirmed Monroe's nomination, though in a surprisingly close caucus vote. Monroe beat out the more personable and dynamic William H. Crawford of Georgia by only a 65 to 54 margin. In addition, some in the caucus objected to the undemocratic nature of the caucus system in selecting candidates for the highest office in the land. The caucus selected a northerner, Gov. Daniel Tompkins of New York, as the vice presidential candidate. The Federalists did not hold a caucus, and New England leaders agreed that any winning presidential electors among them should cast their vote for the previous vice presidential candidate, Rufus King of New York. The Federalist vice presidential vote was left to each state. In the end, John E. Howard, a former Federalist senator from Maryland, received the most Federalist vice presidential votes.

The 1816 campaign was perhaps as uneventful as the unopposed elections of George Washington. As the popular vote map illustrates, nine states selected their presidential electors by legislature, including newly admitted Indiana. Ten states had popular elections for president. County returns are unavailable for North Carolina, Ohio, and Tennessee. Kentucky, Maryland, and Tennessee held elections by district, while all others chose electors on a winner-take-all basis. The Federalists prevailed in a few counties in southern Maryland and some in New Hampshire. In Maryland, the Federalists won three of the eleven districts, but at the time of the electoral college vote, these three cast no ballot. In addition, one of the four Federalist ballots in Delaware was not cast. In New Hampshire, the Federalists won nearly 47 percent of the vote, but lost the state under the winner-take-all system. In Pennsylvania, two lists of electors appeared on the ballot, with one pledged to Monroe and the other "unpledged," indicating dissident Republicans (supported by Federalists) who opposed the caucus nomination system. The irregular, or dissident, unpledged slate won ten Pennsylvania counties and Philadelphia and is designated Independent Republicans on the 1816 leading candidates map.

The final results show Rufus King receiving 34 electoral votes, from the Federalist-dominated legislatures of Massachusetts, Connecticut, and Delaware. James Monroe carried the rest of the nation, winning 183 electoral votes. In the Fifteenth Congress (1817–1819), the Federalists represented less than 30 percent of the House and Senate combined. After a brief Federalist revival prior to and at the beginning of the War of 1812, one large, umbrella-like Republican Party dominated the nation.

REFERENCE: Higginbotham, Sanford W. *The Keystone in the Democratic Arch: Pennsylvania Politics, 1800–1816.* Harrisburg: Pennsylvania Historical and Museum Commission, 1952.

1820

PRESIDENTIAL ELECTION

~

CANDIDATES	POPULAR VOTE PERCENTAGE	ELECTORAL COLLEGE VOTE PERCENTAGE AND (VOTE)*
Republican		
James Monroe (Virginia)	80.6	98.3 (231)
Vice Presidential Nominee: Daniel D. Tompkins (New York)		
Federalists and others (Independent Republicans and scattering)	19.4	0.4 (1)

Map 9

The landslide presidential election of James Monroe in 1816 heralded the beginning of the so-called Era of Good Feeling, a time in which the United States was essentially a one-party nation, with the Republican Party dominating presidential, congressional, and most state elections. Federalists comprised less than 10 percent of the Senate, and in the House they represented only a few districts. Harkening back to the era of George Washington, many considered political parties to be divisive, and a one-party state a worthy goal. The first Monroe administration was not, however, without controversy.

In 1819 Missouri applied for admission to the Union. Southerners, many of them with slaves, had initially settled the territory. These settlers first inhabited the lowlands along the Mississippi River valley and up the Missouri River valley where tobacco could be grown. More than one-sixth of Missouri's population consisted of slaves when it applied to enter the Union. The state constitution called for its admittance as a slave state, but northern congressmen voiced concern over the expansion of slavery into a territory that far north. Congress therefore passed two amendments to the Missouri statehood bill to control and regulate slavery there and to eventually eliminate the institution in the state. This interference infuriated southern congressmen. The argument over the moral, ethical, and legal status of slavery brought out by Missouri statehood would plague U.S. politics to the point of civil war.

The Missouri antislavery amendments passed the House of Representatives in part because of northern gains in population relative to the South's. The Senate,

however, remained evenly divided between slave states, which permitted slavery, and free states, which had banned slavery through state constitutions. Between 1815 and the 1820 election, Indiana (free) and Mississippi (slave) and Illinois (free) and Alabama (slave) were admitted to the Union, thus preserving the slave-free balance in the Senate. The admission of Missouri would not only destroy that balance, but also geographically expand slavery into the north. Congress delayed Missouri's admission until 1820, when both sides agreed to compromise legislation admitting Missouri as a slave state but otherwise "forever" banning slavery north of Missouri's southern-most boundary, 36° 30' north latitude, which became known as the Missouri Compromise Line. Also as part of the compromise, the Maine portion of Massachusetts was admitted as a separate and free state, thus preserving the slave-free balance in the Senate. The Missouri Compromise passed because enough northern representatives went along with the settlement in a desire to stop the expansion of slavery north and to generally prevent sectional strife. The election of 1820 lacked political party conflict, but not sectional conflict and struggle.

The Republicans called their congressional nominating caucus in April 1820, but it was sparsely attended. Sensing displeasure in Congress and the nation over this method of presidential selection, the caucus never put forth an official recommendation. Regardless, President James Monroe and Vice President Daniel D. Tompkins emerged as consensus candidates. With the Federalist Party all but dead, even the Panic of 1819 failed to arouse opposition. The lack of opposition resulted

One elector each from Tennessee, Mississippi, and Pennsylvania did note vote.

in virtually no campaigning and, not surprisingly, voter apathy and low turnout. Monroe's victory in the electoral college was almost unanimous. One faithless Republican New Hampshire elector voted for John Quincy Adams, allegedly so that George Washington would remain the only unanimously elected president. Three other electors did not vote. This represented the zenith of the one-party state in U.S. politics.

Twenty-four states participated in the 1820 election. Nine states' legislatures still appointed presidential electors. Of the fifteen states with popular voting, Illinois, Kentucky, Maine, Maryland, Massachusetts, and Tennessee voted by district. In Illinois, Monroe won all the districts, but in three counties an alternative list won the majority of the vote. In Maryland, the Republicans carried all counties for the first time. In Massachusetts, the Monroe slate carried only two of the fourteen counties, but nevertheless, the Federalist-oriented electors voted unanimously for him. In Pennsylvania, an opposition antislavery ticket supporting De Witt Clinton appeared on the ballot and received votes, but failed to carry a county. The two Washington elections and the election of 1820 are the only uncontested U.S. presidential elections.

In the late 1810s and early 1820s, the Republican Party grew so much that it literally encompassed all political ideologies and leanings across the country. Given the party's broad political spectrum and popularity in different localities—each with geographical self-interests—it seemed inevitable that political, economic, and regional factions would arise. Throughout Monroe's second term, various candidates with strong personalities and representing a variety of political philosophies and regions emerged to contest the position of Republican standard-bearer in 1824.

Reference: Cunningham, Noble E. *The Presidency of James Monroe.* Lawrence: University Press of Kansas, 1996.

1824

PRESIDENTIAL ELECTION

~

Candidates	Popular Vote Percentage	Electoral College Vote Percentage and (Vote)
Republican		
Andrew Jackson (Tennessee)	41.3	37.9 (99)
John Quincy Adams (Massachusetts)	30.9	32.2 (84)
Henry Clay (Kentucky)	13.0	14.2 (37)
William Crawford (Georgia)	11.2	15.7 (41)
Republican Vice Presidential Nominee: John C. Calhoun (South Carolina)		

In the 1820 presidential election, President James Monroe had run unopposed. In the 1824 election, four major candidates ran for the highest office in one of the most hotly contested presidential elections. Although the United States was still a one-party, Republican-dominated nation, a new generation of political leaders had begun to emerge. The older generation of national leaders, including Washington, Adams, Jefferson, Madison, and Monroe, had been involved in crafting the Declaration of Independence, leading the American Revolution, and in drafting and ratifying the Constitution. The successor generation of Republican leaders had all come of political age after the establishment of the constitutional system. The era of the founding presidents had come to a close.

 Map 10

The political philosophies within the Republican Party in 1824 covered a wide range. At one end, the "Old" Republicans believed in a Jeffersonian interpretation of limited powers for the federal government, while at the other end the "New" Republicans felt that federal power should be constitutionally extended, especially in areas aiding national economic and commercial growth. During Monroe's second term, five natural leaders emerged to contest the 1824 race: William H. Crawford of Georgia, John C. Calhoun of South Carolina, Henry Clay of Kentucky, John Quincy Adams of Massachusetts, and Andrew Jackson of Tennessee. Almost every region and section of the nation thus was represented. All five candidates corresponded with state and local leaders and traveled to state legislatures, local party meetings, and conventions to pick up nominations and endorsements as early as 1822, but primarily in 1823 and 1824. Crawford was extremely well liked in the party and had almost beat Monroe in the 1816 Republican presidential caucus. As secretary of the Treasury under Monroe, Crawford represented much of the Old Republican philosophy. Crawford unfortunately suffered a paralyzing stroke in September 1823. His health improved during 1824, but he never fully recovered. Calhoun, the youngest candidate, withdrew his name from consideration, sensing strong Jackson support during his travels in 1824. All factions immediately began to court Calhoun for the vice presidency, and he eventually became the consensus candidate for the post.

Clay had been Speaker of the House since 1811. A young War Hawk along with Calhoun, Clay had cultivated congressional friendships and acquired a national stature. He was perhaps the chief proponent of the New Republican philosophy of expanded federal government. Clay's American System program for U.S. economic growth and development became one of the central issues of debate from the mid-1820s through the mid-1850s. The American System consisted fundamentally of three pillars: a protective tariff to foster American industry; a national bank to promote a strong currency and stable financial system; and federally sponsored internal improvement and development of harbors, canals, river navigation, road networks, and railroads, which would unite the nation in a modern integrated economy.

Adams, the son of former president John Adams, also supported the American System. New England and adjacent areas of the northeast formed the core of emerging industry and finance, and merchants there were eager to take advantage of the expanding markets of the West. Adams, who served as President Monroe's secretary of state from 1817 to 1825, had broken with the Federalist Party of his father over British impressments and the War of 1812 and had earned strong New Republican credentials.

Jackson, the political outsider, was an American hero best known for his exploits in the Indian Wars and the Battle of New Orleans during the War of 1812. Although he served for short periods as a representative and a senator from Tennessee, his political philosophy was the least known among all the candidates. Jackson ran a campaign based on his cult status and being a westerner, a common man of the people, and a defender of the small farmer and expansion of the franchise to all white males.

In February 1824, Crawford won the Republican caucus despite his poor health. The caucus, however, was sparsely attended and had been under fire for some time as an undemocratic and elitist method of selecting the president. Supporters of Clay, Adams, and Jackson had all campaigned actively. The caucus's support of Crawford played directly into Jackson's hands, allowing him to emphasize broadening the franchise to encourage greater popular voting for president. By 1824 Crawford's health and the caucus issue had greatly diminished the support he had initially received, though he retained some popularity in the South. Adams, though strong in New England, was much less popular in the West and the South. Clay's popularity lay in the West. Only Jackson's popularity extended to all regions, with the possible exception of New England.

By the time of the election, only six states retained the somewhat archaic method of choosing electors in the state legislature. Eighteen of the twenty-four states now selected electors directly, through popular election. Illinois, Kentucky, Maine, Maryland, Missouri, and Tennessee used the district method, with the others adopting a winner-take-all system. The expanded popular franchise, combined with better record keeping, made the 1824 election a breakthrough campaign in the ability to map and analyze county-level voting patterns in presidential elections. Although the president is elected indirectly through the electoral college, rather than a nationwide popular vote, consideration of the size and geography of the popular vote is important to understanding the electoral process.

In 1824 no candidate received a majority of the popular vote. Jackson came closest, with 41.3 percent, followed by Adams, Clay, and Crawford. Furthermore, no candidate won an electoral vote majority: Jackson received 99 electoral votes, followed by Adams with 84, Crawford with 41, and Clay with 37. The 1824 electoral college map shows strong home state and regional support among the candidates.

Adams carried all of New England and did well in neighboring New York. Clay carried his home state of Kentucky and neighboring Ohio and Missouri. Crawford carried his home state of Georgia and won a majority of the voters in Virginia, where his candidacy was favored by Virginians Madison and Monroe. Jackson won his home state of Tennessee and showed great strength throughout the South and West. Maryland was the only state voting by district to split the vote, with Crawford winning one district, Adams three, and Jackson seven. The split vote in Delaware, Louisiana, and New York, which had legislatively appointed electors, resulted from faithless electors with factional loyalties in this complex, multicandidate election. Meanwhile, Calhoun, the consensus vice presidential candidate, took that office.

For the second time in the United States' short history, the presidential election went to the House of Representatives for adjudication. The Twelfth Amendment stipulates that only the three leading presidential candidates are eligible for House consideration when no majority exists. This eliminated Clay and incited a rush to court his supporters.

The run-up to the House vote in February 1825 produced intense politicking and public debate. Crawford's health denied him serious consideration, while Jackson's supporters claimed that their man had received the most popular and electoral votes and therefore deserved the presidency. Washington "insiders" questioned Jackson's inexperience and feared his impetuous nature and unknown stances on political and economic policies. Some old-line Federalists considered him a "commoner" or an uneducated rural westerner. Clay, out of the race, threw his support to Adams, whom he and his supporters viewed as the only viable option with respect to government experience and support for the American System.

In accordance with the Constitution, the vote in the House is by state, with each delegation casting one vote as determined by the majority of that delegation. The winning candidate needed a majority, that is, thirteen of the twenty-four states. Adams won on the first ballot with a vote of thirteen. Seven states went for Jackson and four for Crawford. Comparison of the maps depicting the House and electoral votes reveals the switches in votes by the states. Crawford took Georgia and Virginia in both votes and picked up North Carolina and Delaware in the House. Jackson lost Illinois and Louisiana to Adams in the House, and the split vote in Maryland also went to Adams. The critical votes that determined the House election, however, came from Kentucky, Missouri, and Ohio, the three states Clay won in the electoral college. In the House vote, they all switched to Adams, giving him the presidency.

The 1824 popular vote map allows for detailed analysis of this multicandidate ballot. Adams carried every county in New England. He also captured votes in the southern Chesapeake Bay counties with old Federalist ties, some western Virginia counties supporting internal improvements, and areas in Ohio with Yankee settlements. Crawford swept most counties in Virginia. Clay carried almost all of this home state of Kentucky and did well in neighboring Indiana, Ohio, and Missouri, where many migrants from Kentucky had settled. Jackson carried almost every county in Alabama, Mississippi, and Tennessee and did well in North Carolina. Jackson showed surprising strength in two northern states, New Jersey and Pennsylvania, carrying the latter with a percentage—76.1—second only to that of his home state of Tennessee. This geographic anomaly deserves additional discussion.

The Mid-Atlantic was the only region without a favorite son in the election, and Jackson was especially popular among rural, western, and Scotch-Irish Pennsylvanians. In a campaign somewhat devoid of substantive issues, the personality and hero status of Jackson proved appealing. Because of this overwhelming grassroots support for Jackson, the other candidates chose not to spend much time and money in the Keystone State. Jackson's victory in neighboring New Jersey was nowhere near as large as his showing in Pennsylvania, but he carried nine of the thirteen counties and the state with 51.8 percent of the vote over his nearest competitor, Adams.

Eight days after being voted president, Adams nominated Clay to be secretary of state. The Jacksonians howled with indignation, alleging the appointment a "corrupt bargain" in exchange for the Clay states of Kentucky, Missouri, and Ohio. Jacksonians' ire over the outcome in the House and the Clay nomination split the ruling Republican Party into two warring factions. One camp, headed by Adams and Clay, favored the American System of protective tariffs, federal aid for internal improvements, a national bank, and a generally nationalist approach to U.S. economic development and promotion of industrial, commercial, and financial interests. The other group, headed by Jackson and like-minded Old Republicans, such as Martin Van Buren of New York, favored a more limited federal government, had doubts about the constitutional basis for a national bank and internal improvements, and favored the interests of the small farmer and planter. These two competing visions carried forward from the mid-1820s through the mid-1850s, when a much more sectional party system emerged.

REFERENCES: Ershkowitz, Herbert. "The Election of 1824 in New Jersey." *Proceedings of the New Jersey Historical Society* 84 (April 1966): 113–132.

Klein, Philip S. *Pennsylvania Politics, 1817–1832.* Philadelphia: University of Pennsylvania, 1940.

1828

PRESIDENTIAL ELECTION

~

Candidates	Popular Vote Percentage	Electoral College Vote Percentage and (Vote)
Andrew Jackson (Tennessee)	56.0	68.2 (178)
Vice Presidential Nominee: John C. Calhoun (South Carolina)		
John Quincy Adams (Massachusetts)	43.6	31.8 (83)
Vice Presidential Nominee: Richard Rush (Pennsylvania)		

The 1828 presidential election represents a transition election between the caucus nominations of the past and national conventions of established political parties that would become the standard. During the administration of President John Quincy Adams (1825–1829), U.S. politics, including congressional affiliations, was generally divided between the followers of Adams and those of Andrew Jackson. Most of Adams's followers eventually called themselves the National Republicans. (After the dissolution of the National Republicans following the 1832 election, many of its former members would participate in organizing the Whig Party.) The Jacksonians evolved into the Democrat-Republicans. (By the mid-1830s they would become the Democratic Party.)

The turmoil of the 1824 election had hardly dissipated when the Tennessee legislature nominated Jackson for president a few months after Adams's inauguration. Vice President John C. Calhoun, who broke with Adams over alleged regional bias, switched factions to become Jackson's running mate for 1828, creating a particularly strong southern and western flavor to the ticket. Since Jackson and Calhoun both came from slave states, southerners in general were much more trusting of Jackson and Calhoun than of the New Englander Adams. Adams eventually accepted Richard Rush of Pennsylvania as his running mate in 1828, giving his ticket a decidedly northeastern flavor.

The issues in the campaign were clear-cut. The incumbent Adams favored a protective tariff, a national bank, and federal appropriations for internal improvements. Jackson, being more evasive on the issues, based his campaign on the "cor-

Map 11

rupt bargain" of 1824–1825, his war hero status, and being the so-called champion of the common man and rural farmers in comparison to Adams, the former Federalist and New Englander. Jackson's strategy perhaps worked, especially as the white male franchise continued to expand. More than three times as many voters cast popular ballots in the 1828 election than had done so in the 1824 election. Both political camps launched a number of unsavory personal attacks.

The Tariff of 1828 was perhaps the primary and most immediate issue of the campaign. Though complex in its regional effects, it was called the Tariff of Abominations by southerners, who generally considered any tariff to be detrimental to their agricultural region and beneficial to the more manufacturing-oriented Northeast. In addition, the tariff raised the possibility of foreign governments retaliating with tariffs on southern cotton, potentially making this commodity much more expensive on the world market. High tariffs made goods more expensive for western farmers, so Jackson men in Congress maneuvered for provisions to the tariff bill favoring several western products, including hemp and flax. In 1824 Kentucky, Missouri, and Ohio had gone to Adams, and many historians believe that the machinations on behalf of the western states helped move these three states into Jackson's column in 1828.

In the popular presidential ballot, Jackson received 56 percent of the vote to Adams's 43.6 percent. It was the second time that a sitting president had been ousted, Adams's father, John Adams, having been the first, in 1800. With expansion of the white male franchise becoming the norm, only South Carolina and Delaware lacked popular voting in 1828, still choosing presidential electors in their state legislatures. The electoral college result proved to be more decisive than the popular vote count, with 178 votes (68.2 percent) for Jackson and 83 votes (31.8 percent) for Adams.

The geographical component of the 1828 electoral college result is a stark one, as vividly illustrated on the electoral college map. Adams won New England, Delaware, and New Jersey, while Jackson carried the entire South and the trans-Appalachian West. An examination of balloting in individual states on the popular vote map illustrates in most states a clear, if not overwhelming, preference for one candidate or the other. For example, Adams received more than 70 percent of the vote in Connecticut, Massachusetts, Rhode Island, and Vermont, while Jackson won more than 80 percent in Alabama, Georgia, Mississippi, and Tennessee. Only in Ohio, where Jackson took 51.6 percent of the vote, was the contest close.

Analysis of the popular vote map provides exceptional insight into country-wide trends. Adams swept virtually all of the New England counties and most of New Jersey. Adams lost the majority of district-selected presidential electors in a close New York race, in spite of carrying numerous counties in northeastern and western New York. In western New York, a cluster of counties originally settled by New Englanders and known as the Burned-Over District, for its "fires of evangelical enthusiasm," had developed its own brand of political, cultural, and religious heritage with Federalist roots and New England religious and social leanings. Over the next several elections, this subregion would emerge as a distinctive area of voting and political party support. Its political heritage and Yankee origins were unmistakable. A cluster of counties in northeastern New York also had been settled by New Englanders.

Martin Van Buren, an ardent Jacksonian and head of the powerful Albany Regency political organization, appeared on the ballot in New York and was elected governor. The Tammany Society helped Van Buren and Jackson secure votes in New York City. In fact, in New York County (Manhattan), Jackson beat Adams 15,435 to 9,638, taking the three presidential electors for that congressional district. From the mid-1820s through the mid-1830s, New York City elected three pro-Jackson representatives to the House of Representatives every two years.

The Western Reserve (or New Connecticut) area of northeastern Ohio was another distinctive subregion voting for Adams. This area was given to Connecticut as part of the general arrangement during the ceding of trans-Appalachian land by the original states in the 1780s. Much of the Western Reserve was sold to settlers from Connecticut and to other New Englanders. These settlers, like those in western New York, brought with them their northeastern political heritage. Two other pockets of strong Adams support in Ohio also related to original settlement. The Ohio Company, incorporated in Massachusetts in the 1780s, established Marietta, Ohio,

and sold land—a band of counties along the Ohio River in the southeastern portion in an area called the Ohio Company Purchase—mainly to New Englanders. The other pocket was the Virginia Military Tract, a cluster of counties in west-central Ohio between the Sciota and Miami Rivers. Populated mostly by Kentuckians and Virginians, many of these settlers were Methodists and other southerners with anti-slavery sentiments who desired to settle in free Ohio. They shared the American System economic views of Kentuckian Henry Clay and became staunch Whig supporters in the 1830s and beyond. These three areas of Ohio that went to Adams were surrounded by pro-Jackson areas that became Democratic in the 1830s and beyond. Migrants from the upper South and Pennsylvania settled these lands. The three Ohio subregions remained distinctive in their voting patterns through the Whig era and into the twentieth century. These areas experienced influxes of additional settlers, but as is the case with other subregions in early U.S. history, the initial settlement hearth theory and the establishment of political culture are important to understanding their voting patterns.

Jackson carried the vast majority of the counties in the South. In Kentucky in 1824, Clay had won a large victory over Jackson, but Adams's secretary of state did not come close to helping his political ally carry the state in 1828. In other southern regions, however, several developed commercial locales or districts supporting internal improvements stand out as pro-Adams. The commercial and plantation areas of the Chesapeake Bay counties of Maryland supported Adams, as they had supported Federalist candidates in previous elections. These counties gave the majority of Maryland's district-chosen electors to Adams in a close election. Southern Louisiana, site of the commercially important city and port of New Orleans and in general home to wealthy French- and Spanish-Catholic sugar plantation owners, was another area of the South favoring Adams. In contrast, northern Louisiana and the "Florida parishes" of northeastern Louisiana, areas mainly settled by southern Anglo-Americans, supported Jackson. The north-south, Anglo-Cajun divide of Louisiana remains a distinct feature in U.S. cultural geography to this day.

In general, the election of 1828 is a classic in U.S. political geography. At the time, each candidate symbolized his state and region, and each supported the economic and political interests of his region to solidify his base. In the end, each region voted for its favorite son and economic and social interests. Of note, Andrew Jackson was the first president not to hail from either Virginia or Massachusetts. His election signaled the growing political power of the trans-Appalachian West in Congress and the electoral college. Ascent from humble roots and efforts to spread the franchise to all white males are two of the trademarks of Jacksonian democracy.

REFERENCE: Cayton, Andrew R. L. *The Frontier Republic: Ideology and Politics in the Ohio Country, 1780–1825*. Kent, Ohio: Kent State University Press, 1986.

1832

PRESIDENTIAL ELECTION

~

Candidates	Popular Vote Percentage	Electoral College Vote Percentage and (Vote)*
Democrat Republican		
Andrew Jackson (Tennessee)	54.2	76.0 (219)
Vice Presidential Nominee: Martin Van Buren (New York)		
National Republican		
Henry Clay (Kentucky)	37.4	17.0 (49)
Vice Presidential Nominee: John Sergeant (Pennsylvania)		
Anti-Masonic		
William Wirt (Maryland)	7.8	2.4 (7)
Vice Presidential Nominee: Anis Ellmaker (Pennsylvania)		

Map 12

fter the 1828 election, national political alignments revolved around President Andrew Jackson, whose actions during his first term (1829–1833) became a lightning rod for criticism or for loyal support. The prevailing identifiers of political affiliation were either as a Jackson man or simply anti-Jackson. Jackson's followers called themselves Republicans or "Democratic" Republicans, to assert lineage from Thomas Jefferson and the Jeffersonian Republicans. (By the mid-to-late 1830s, the Democratic Republicans would become known simply as the Democrats.) The disparate anti-Jackson group attempted to develop a "National" Republican Party, also attempting by name to claim direct descent from the Jeffersonian Republicans.

The 1832 presidential election was extraordinary in U.S. political history because it occasioned the first national nominating conventions. These gatherings heralded the recognition of the role and final acceptance of political parties in the political system and the beginning of the formalization of national party structures and democratic presidential nomination procedures. The Anti-Masonic Party, a new small grouping, held the first national convention in September 1831 in

Baltimore, Maryland. With two other larger parties forming at this time, the Anti-Masonic Party can be considered the nation's first "third party." The party originated in the Burned-Over District of western New York, an area of religious and reformist fervor. As the party's name implies, the party began as an anti-Freemason movement with the goal of ridding "secret society" members from public life. The party, owing to the New England roots of most of its founders, was also a moralist Christian movement, antislavery, and anti-alcohol. Zealously anti-Jackson, the Anti-Masonics adopted many of the economic policies of John Quincy Adams, Henry Clay, and the National Republicans. They, however, viewed the slave owning, drinking, Mason Clay as morally corrupt. The Anti-Masonics chose William Wirt of Maryland as their presidential candidate and Anis Ellmaker of Pennsylvania as their vice presidential pick.

Anti-Jackson individuals of many political backgrounds met in December 1831 in Baltimore as the National Republican convention. They nominated Henry Clay of Kentucky, the clear voice of opposition to Jackson in Congress and long-time experienced national figure. To balance the ticket and to favor banking and

Two Maryland electors did not vote.

commercial interests in the important swing state of Pennsylvania, Philadelphia lawyer John Sergeant received the vice presidential nomination. In May 1832, the Jacksonians also met in Baltimore to confirm many state legislatures' nomination of Jackson to a second term and to nominate a vice presidential candidate. They needed a new vice presidential candidate because Vice President John C. Calhoun of South Carolina had become antagonistic toward Jackson over personal and tariff-related issues. They selected devoted Jackson supporter and former secretary of state Martin Van Buren of New York.

Of the main campaign issues in 1832, perhaps the national bank was most symbolic of Jackson and his philosophy of limited government and states' rights. Anti-Jackson politicians in Congress had introduced the issue of an early re-chartering, which Jackson vetoed, calling the bank hostile to states' rights, unconstitutional, and monopolistic. In addition, he accused the institution of being "aristocratic," supporting the activities of rich merchants, and an affront to the common man, whom Jackson, of course, defended. The National Republicans viewed a national bank as sound fiscal and currency policy that would allow the country to grow and develop economically and as especially important to areas involved in commercial farming, manufacturing, and trading. The National Republicans also favored a nationalist program involving a protective tariff and federal support of internal improvements and opposition to Jackson's alleged abuse of presidential power. They cited as an example of Jackson's autocratic rule his choosing to ignore Supreme Court rulings on Indian removal and Indian policy, especially with respect to the expulsion of the Cherokee nation from the East Coast to present-day Oklahoma.

Rural noncommercial small farmers, laborers, and mechanics related to Jackson during this period of good economic times, which produced a comfortable victory for him in 1832. He won 54.2 percent of the popular vote to Clay's 37.4 percent and Wirt's 7.8 percent. The electoral vote count overwhelmingly favored Jackson, who received 219 votes, with 49 for Clay and 7 for Wirt. All states except South Carolina held popular elections. In South Carolina, antitariff nullification fervor had reached such proportions that the legislature turned its back on all three national candidates. Opposition to Jackson resulted not only from his having supported the onerous Tariff of 1832, but also from his penning a strenuous warning to supporters of nullification. The South Carolina legislature gave the state's 11 electoral votes (4 percent of the national total) to Virginia governor John Floyd, a leader of the States' Rights bloc in the Virginia legislature and a nullification sympathizer. The electoral college map depicts Jackson's sweeping victory, with Clay carrying only his home state of Kentucky, part of Maryland, Delaware, and southern New England.

The popular vote map also illustrates the overwhelming nature of the Jackson victory, which is even more striking when compared to the map for the 1828 elec-

tion. Jackson carried almost every county in the South. For example, in Alabama, Georgia, and Mississippi, Jackson slates received essentially 100 percent of the vote. Clay and the business-friendly National Republicans received support from only three areas of the South: the area including the commercially important city and port of New Orleans and the area of French- and Spanish-Catholic wealthy sugar plantation owners in southern Louisiana; the commercial and plantation areas of the Chesapeake Bay counties of Maryland (which had supported Adams in 1828 and previously Federalist candidates); and Kentucky (though not every county).

In the North, Clay did not do as well as the New Englander Adams had in the previous election. For example, Jackson carried most of the counties in Maine and New Hampshire. This represented a historic change in New England politics. New Hampshire had given their neighbor Adams 93 percent of the vote in 1824 and 54 percent in 1828, but in 1832 the Democrats won the state with some 55 percent of the popular vote (and would dominate it for the next twenty years). Jacksonian support came from the poorer hill towns and farming regions in the state. An extremely strong state Democratic Party organized in the 1830s and stigmatized the National Republicans, and later Whigs, as wealthy Federalists and aristocratic Congregationalists. In addition, economic change would sweep the state with total National Republican and Whig acceptance, but Democratic questioning and caution with respect to the financial effects on farmers and small towns.

Elsewhere in the North, Clay had pockets of support in areas of historic New England settlement: northeastern New York, the western New York Burned-Over District, and the Western Reserve area of northeastern Ohio. In 1832 western New York, Pennsylvania, and many parts of New England were emerging areas of strong Anti-Masonic support. The National Republicans and Anti-Masonics cooperated in New York and Pennsylvania, but not in Vermont. In New York, the Anti-Masonic candidate did not appear on the ballot, so majorities in the western counties voted for Clay. The candidate map for Wirt clearly shows the other two areas of Anti-Masonic support. In Vermont, Wirt won a plurality of 40.5 percent although both major parties appeared on the ballot. In Pennsylvania, the Anti-Masonic and anti-Jackson forces supported Wirt in a "Union" ticket, with Clay not appearing on the ballot. On the map, therefore, several counties show an Anti-Masonic majority, including Erie County on Lake Erie, which was predominantly settled by Yankees and was a geographical link between western New York and the Western Reserve. In the commercially important city of Philadelphia, home of the National Bank, the Union ticket won with 5,476 votes for Wirt to 3,267 for Jackson. The vote in rural Philadelphia County was generally split.

The election of 1832 witnessed the reelection of a popular president in good economic times. It is part of the democratizing period of U.S. political development that saw presidential nominating conventions of state delegates triumph over the elite congressional caucus system, the white male vote expanding, and voters of all states, except one, directly selecting presidential electors. After Jackson, political parties, not individuals, would dominate the electoral landscape. The era of formal national organized political parties had arrived, and the era of larger-than-life individuals, such as Washington, Jefferson, and Jackson, commanding the political process ended.

REFERENCES: Cole, Donald B. *Jacksonian Democracy in New Hampshire, 1800–1851.* Cambridge, Mass.: Harvard University Press, 1970.

Connolly, Michael J. *Capitalism, Politics and Railroads in Jacksonian New England.* Columbia: University of Missouri Press, 2003.

1836
PRESIDENTIAL ELECTION

CANDIDATES	POPULAR VOTE PERCENTAGE	ELECTORAL COLLEGE VOTE PERCENTAGE AND (VOTE)
Democrat		
Martin Van Buren (New York)	50.8	57.8 (170)
Vice Presidential Nominee: Richard M. Johnson (Kentucky)		
Whig		
William Henry Harrison (Ohio)	36.6	24.8 (73)
Hugh White (Tennessee)	9.7	8.8 (26)
Daniel Webster (Massachusetts)	2.7	4.8 (14)
Vice Presidential Nominee: Francis P. Granger (New York)		

After the 1832 election, the loosely formed National Republican coalition disintegrated. As President Andrew Jackson began his second term (1833–1837), political alignment in Congress and the nation continued to center around being a Jackson supporter or anti-Jackson. The anti-Jackson faction in Congress, which included Henry Clay and Daniel Webster, decided to form a new coalition party. By 1834 the term *Whig* was increasingly used to identify this anti-Jackson grouping. The name derived from the British antiroyalist party, and it seemed fitting for Jackson's opponents given their contention that he had become an autocratic ruler. As Jackson's second term came to an end, Jacksonians tended to refer to their party as Democratic Republican or Democrat.

Jackson selected long-time loyalist and vice president Martin Van Buren to succeed him, a selection greeted with some resistance and controversy, especially among southern Democrats. In fact, the Democratic Republican convention was held early, before others could organize against him, in May 1835, to ensure Van Buren's nomination. To balance the ticket geographically, the party selected Richard M. Johnson of Kentucky as its vice presidential candidate.

The Whigs were also experiencing some turmoil. Unable to agree on an acceptable candidate, they attempted an unprecedented geo-electoral strategy: They

Map 13

selected two candidates to run in the two disparate sections—in the South, Hugh White of Tennessee, and in the North, William Henry Harrison of Ohio. In Massachusetts, a list of electors pledged to favorite son Daniel Webster represented the Whigs on the ballot. Knowing White and Harrison incapable of obtaining a majority of presidential electors, the Whigs hoped to throw the election into the House of Representatives.

The election issues resembled those in previous campaigns. Most Whigs, coming from National Republican ranks, supported the general thrust of Henry Clay's American System. They favored a national bank, a protective tariff, and federally sponsored internal improvements. Some southerners also joined the coalition as a reaction against Jackson and Van Buren on the nullification issue. On the opposite end of the political spectrum, most northern Anti-Masonics also joined the Whig coalition. The Democrats, on the other hand, defended a limited federal government, states' rights, and protection of the people over the powerful. Most poor white noncommercial farmers and many recent immigrants felt the Democrats more welcoming and sympathetic to their condition. As each party formed, intraparty regional differences emerged. Western and southern Democrats favored vigorous land acquisition and westward expansion. Northern Whigs, generally middle-class, displayed a strong religious and moral reform element. Slavery as an underlining issue generally divided the northern and southern wings of each party, especially the Whigs.

In the 1836 national ballot, the electorate chose Van Buren as their eighth president, giving him 50.8 percent of the vote. In the electoral college, Van Buren received 170 of the 294 votes (57.8 percent), 22 more than the 148 needed for victory. The regional Whig candidates ran surprisingly well, and the election was close in a number of states. In Pennsylvania, which had 30 electoral votes, Van Buren won 91,466 votes (51.2 percent) to Harrison's 87,235 (48.8 percent). A switch of a few thousand popular votes in Pennsylvania would have thrown the presidential election into the House of Representatives, as the Whigs had hoped. In the end, however, strong state Democratic Party organizations saved Van Buren, as he carried the frontier West, most of the Northeast, and a sufficient number of states in the South. Again, South Carolina was the only state not to select electors by popular vote. As in 1832, the South Carolina legislature turned its back on all the national candidates and gave its 11 electoral votes to pro-nullification senator Willie P. Mangum, a Jacksonian turned Whig from North Carolina.

The 1836 popular vote map pattern symbolizes the Whig-Democrat era (1836–1856) of presidential elections. In Congress, the geography of roll-call voting patterns on slavery and other issues of the day, such as the tariff and internal improvements, revealed extreme regional divisions. Across the nation, however, a rough sectional balance prevailed in congressional parties and presidential elections. In other words, sectional issues existed, but not sectional parties. This does not mean that the popular vote maps are an example of randomness. In each election during this period, distinct regions and subregions of strong and weak popular support for one party or another are discernible and often had decisive consequences for the electoral vote of a state and sometimes the nation.

The Whig's favorite-son strategy is illustrated on the 1836 popular vote map. Harrison carried his home state of Ohio, receiving strong support in the Western Reserve region. He also carried numerous counties in the neighboring states of Indiana and Kentucky. In addition, he took the old Federalist-Adams-National Republican areas of Delaware, Maryland, and New Jersey. The previously strong Anti-Masonic fervor of Vermont helped carry this state for the Whigs. Southern

Whig candidate White won his home state of Tennessee and neighboring Georgia. An interesting pattern developed in the Deep South from central Georgia through Alabama and into the Mississippi River valley counties of Arkansas, Louisiana, and Mississippi. In this band of fertile soil, plantation agriculture spread westward from the Carolinas to the extensive plantation area along the Mississippi River. Because of the plantations, this area had a very high concentration of slaves. This so-called black belt—characterized by high-density African American counties—is still evident in twenty-first century census maps. In this region, plantation owners and others connected to the commercial agricultural economy favored the economic policies of the Whigs and voted as such. Plantation society was not, however, pervasive in the counties of northern Georgia and northern Alabama. In this area of Appalachia and poorer soil, many impoverished rural white farmers admired Andrew Jackson and tended to vote Democrat.

Van Buren carried most of his home state of New York, except for the western Burned-Over District. He also carried Pennsylvania, where his margin in the northern tier of counties was sufficient for him to outpoll Harrison statewide. Van Buren also had a better-than-average Democratic showing in New England. In 1832 New Hampshire and Maine had gone to Jackson, as a strong Jackson party had formed in these states. Dislike of the southerner Clay was strong enough to hand Van Buren razor-thin victories in Connecticut and Rhode Island, but over the next forty years, these two former Federalist-Adams-National Republican states would vote solidly Whig and then Republican in virtually every election.

Jackson and his supporters viewed the 1836 election as a referendum on his presidency. Farmers in frontier Arkansas, Illinois, and Missouri also thought as much and voted for his hand-picked successor Van Buren. A few months after Van Buren's inauguration, the Panic of 1837 hit. The Whigs blamed Van Buren, the Democrats, and their banking and other policies for the worst economic depression in U.S. history to that time. The Whigs would exploit this opportunity to take their party from virtual nonexistence to the White House in a few short years.

REFERENCE: Holt, Michael F. *The Rise and Fall of the American Whig Party: Jacksonian Politics and the Onset of the Civil War.* New York: Oxford University Press, 1999.

1840

PRESIDENTIAL ELECTION

CANDIDATES	POPULAR VOTE PERCENTAGE	ELECTORAL COLLEGE VOTE PERCENTAGE AND (VOTE)
Whig		
William Henry Harrison (Ohio)	52.9	79.6 (234)
Vice Presidential Nominee: John Tyler (Virginia)		
Democrat		
Martin Van Buren (New York)	46.8	20.4 (60)
Vice Presidential Nominee: None		

Within a month of the inauguration of President Martin Van Buren in March, the country suffered the Panic of 1837, its worst economic depression to that time. The panic and the resulting economic downturn dominated politics the next four years. The Democrats remained loyal to Van Buren and renominated him at their May 1840 convention. The personal life of Vice President Richard M. Johnson caused much discontent, so the Democrats did not present an official vice presidential nominee, leaving this selection up to each state. The Democrats also officially changed the name of their convention and party from Democratic Republican to Democratic. That year, the Democrats presented the first party platform, clearly stating their positions, which included limited government and a strict interpretation of the Constitution, no federal constitutional power to conduct internal improvement programs or create a national bank, and states' rights, especially with respect to slavery. The drafting of a platform has been a major component of presidential nominating conventions ever since. The Whig convention, held late in 1839, nominated its 1836 northern candidate, William Henry Harrison of Ohio. To balance the ticket geographically and ideologically, the Whigs chose former Jackson supporter and states' rights advocate John Tyler from Virginia.

The state of the economy dominated the campaign. The opposition of the Democrats and Van Buren to the now-defunct national bank, and his introduction of the independent treasury concept, helped fuel the idea of a Democratic-inspired

Map 14

panic. The 1840 election featured the first modern, organized, and media- and personality-oriented campaign. The Democrats had formed numerous state party structures and operated newspapers in every region, including in New England. The Whigs mimicked the Democrats' organization and even exceeded it in tactics. Their primary strategy was to criticize and demonize Van Buren, particularly in portraying him as an aristocrat living a lavish lifestyle in the White House while the country suffered economically. On the other hand, the Whigs spun William Henry Harrison—a man of wealth who resided in a comfortable mansion on the banks of the Ohio—into a common man who lived in a log cabin and drank hard cider. They also portrayed him as the Indian War hero at Tippecanoe. The rollicking nature of the campaign appealed to the rural white male masses, who were eligible to vote in record numbers.

The slogan "Tippecanoe and Tyler too" is emblematic of the clever nature of the campaign. With Harrison, a northern, pro–American System nationalist, teamed with southern former Jacksonian states' rightist Tyler, one northern Whig said of the ticket, "There is a rhyme, but no reason." Such was the state of the era's two major political parties—rough coalitions of sometimes disparate factions ignoring slavery as long as possible to maintain a southern electoral base.

The results of the 1840 election surprised no one. Harrison received 52.9 percent of the vote to 46.8 percent for Van Buren. The electoral college vote reveals the decisive nature of the election, with Harrison receiving 234 votes (79.6 percent) to Van Buren's 60 (20.4 percent). As the electoral map indicates, Van Buren carried only seven states—three on the frontier, three in the South, and one in the North. South Carolina, the only state not to have a popular vote for presidential electors, was among these. Concerned that a pro-tariff Whig might gain the presidency, South Carolinian John C. Calhoun rejoined the Democratic Party in 1840 and influenced the legislature to support Van Buren. The Democratic platform's strong states' rights position on the slavery issue swayed some southerners to return to the party after Jackson's departure.

Van Buren failed to carry his home state of New York, receiving 212,733 votes to Harrison's 226,001. The vote was close in Pennsylvania, where 144,018 votes were cast for Harrison (50.1 percent) and 143,675 (49.9 percent) for Van Buren, the difference being a Harrison majority of 2,881 in the city of Philadelphia. The 1840 popular vote map displays a pattern similar to that of 1836, though with a much more extensive area of victory for the Whigs. The New England states, with the exception of New Hampshire, rejoined the Whig fold. Western and northeastern New York helped keep Van Buren's native state out of his column. Harrison won his home state of Ohio, and Kentucky clearly displayed its Whig heritage, giving him 64.2 percent of the popular vote, the largest margin of victory in any state. Harrison also made a strong showing in the old Federalist-Adams-National Republican areas of Chesapeake Maryland, Delaware, New Jersey, and the coastal areas of Virginia and North Carolina. The Whig-oriented black belt portions of Georgia and Alabama, which emerged in 1836, are also clearly evident. Even more visible is the pro-Whig commercial plantation region straddling the Mississippi River from New Orleans to the "bootheel" of Missouri.

The campaign of 1840 represented a triumph of Whig coalition building and clever campaigning during an extremely bad economic period. Economic hard times usually seal the electoral fate of incumbent candidates and parties, and this held true in 1840. The popular vote map illustrates that even in a time of nonsectional parties, readily identifiable political subregions of Whig and Democratic support still existed. The Whigs' victory would be short-lived. Harrison was inaugurated on March 4, 1841, but he died on April 4, 1841, having developed pneumonia after presenting his lengthy inaugural address in cold, rainy weather. John Tyler became the first vice president to ascend to the highest office on the occasion of the death of the president. Harrison's death was a major blow to the Whigs, as Tyler's views as a states' rights southerner differed greatly from those of Whigs on the tariff and other nationalist commercial interests.

REFERENCE: Silbey, Joel H. *Martin Van Buren and the Emergence of American Popular Politics.* Lanham, Md.: Rowman and Littlefield, 2002.

1844

PRESIDENTIAL ELECTION

CANDIDATES	POPULAR VOTE PERCENTAGE	ELECTORAL COLLEGE VOTE PERCENTAGE AND (VOTE)
Democrat		
James K. Polk (Tennessee)	49.5	61.8 (170)
Vice Presidential Nominee: George Dallas (Pennsylvania)		
Whig		
Henry Clay (Kentucky)	48.1	38.2 (105)
Vice Presidential Nominee: Theodore Frelinghuysen (New Jersey)		
Liberty		
James Birney (New York)	2.3	0 (0)
Vice Presidential Nominee: Thomas Morris (Ohio)		

Map 15

The Whigs had selected John Tyler as the running mate of William Henry Harrison to balance their ticket in 1840, although Tyler did not ascribe to their general constitutional and economic philosophies. Upon Harrison's death in April 1841, Tyler assumed the presidency. After several years of conflict between Tyler and congressional Whigs, the party literally expelled Tyler. With the incumbent president politically ostracized, the Whigs as well as the Democrats looked to different candidates for the 1844 election. Whig founder and congressional and national leader Henry Clay again accepted the presidential nomination, twenty years after his first attempt. The Whigs chose northerner Theodore Frelinghuysen of New Jersey as their vice presidential nominee.

The Democrats were ready to renominate an old party leader, former president Martin Van Buren, with the blessing of party founder Andrew Jackson. In the period leading up to the convention, however, western territorial expansion, especially the annexation of Texas, emerged as an issue. Southerners generally favored Texas joining the Union as a slave state, while northerners generally opposed it. Van Buren's announcement of his opposition to the annexation doomed his nomina-

tion, as it led to an almost total withdrawal of support from the southern wing of the party. Much indecision and turmoil ensued at the May 1844 Democratic convention. After eight ballots, the Democrats nominated James K. Polk, a dark horse compromise candidate from Tennessee. Although Polk had been governor, representative, and Speaker of the House, he was a relative political unknown who lacked the national name recognition and reputation of Clay. The Democrats chose long-time party loyalist and Pennsylvania lawyer George Dallas for its vice presidential nominee.

Polk, an aggressive expansionist and pro-annexationist, embodied the philosophy of Manifest Destiny, which was popular at the time. The Democratic Party platform aggressively made clear the party's stance as pro-Texas annexation and pro-westward expansion. The Democrats cleverly added Oregon to its expansion rhetoric to extend the policy beyond the addition of slave-owning Texas, proposing a national policy of expansion along the northern tier as well. This appeased and even appealed to some northerners. Clay, on the other hand, issued a weak statement opposing the annexation of Texas. During the campaign Clay tried to make the tariff and other American System issues the primary divide. The Democrats' strong advocacy of the expansion issue, however, made that the primary focus of the campaign. Recognizing this, Clay issued another weak statement, this time announcing the possibility of his supporting annexation, hoping to please southern voters. The tactic failed to satisfy northerners or southerners, but did manage to shift the campaign's momentum toward the Democrats and the unfamiliar Polk.

Clay and Polk both owned slaves. While the Democrats openly accepted slavery, the Whigs tried their best to ignore it. Some people in the North, however, would not let the issue be muted. In 1840 a one-issue antislavery third party, the Liberty Party, had formed, but had received little support. Better organized in 1844, the party nominated noted abolitionist James G. Birney of New York for president and Thomas Morris of Ohio for vice president. The party gained ballot access in twelve northern states and ran a vigorous campaign attacking the moral, religious, and ethical tenants of the institution of slavery. A constituency of northern, religious, middle-class Whigs sympathized with the Liberty Party. Dismayed by the Texas issue, this small but critical portion of the northern Whig vote turned to Birney.

The 1844 presidential election was extremely close. Polk won 49.5 percent of the popular vote to Clay's 48.1 percent. Virtually all of the remaining 2.4 percent went to the Liberty Party. In the electoral college, however, Polk handily won 170 votes to Clay's 105. The vote was razor thin in six states. In fact, in the case of the biggest prize of all, New York's 36 electoral votes, Polk won with only a plurality, 237,588 votes (48.9 percent) to 232,482 votes (47.9 percent) for Clay. The difference of 15,812 (3.3 percent) votes went to the Liberty Party. Many historians believe that if the Liberty Party had not been on the ballot, Clay would have won New York, and the switch of these thirty-six votes would have given Clay his long-sought-after presidency. In the end, Clay only carried most of the old Federalist-Adams-National Republican states of New England and the coastal North. Clay also won his home state of Kentucky and even Polk's neighboring home state of Tennessee. Polk carried all the western frontier states of Jacksonian voters, the Deep South, newly Democratic Maine and New Hampshire, and most important, New York and Pennsylvania, the evenly divided Mid-Atlantic swing states of the era.

The pattern of the 1844 popular vote map resembles the general pattern of the Whig-Democrat-era maps of previous elections. In contrast, however, to the Whig areas expanding and the Democratic areas subsiding in the 1840 map, in 1844 the Democratic areas expanded, and the Whig areas contracted. The Democrats and Whigs had pockets of support in all regions of the country. Whig Party strongholds in 1844 consisted of four New England states, western New York, Ohio (including the Western Reserve region), Chesapeake Maryland, Delaware, New Jersey, Kentucky, and plantation areas along the black belt across the Deep South and the lower Mississippi River valley and southern Louisiana. In the North, the map shows numerous counties with a Whig plurality for the first time rather than a Whig majority. In virtually all these counties, the Liberty Party ran so strong that it reduced the Whig vote to less than 50 percent. Although Birney received only 2.3 percent of the vote nationally, he garnered significant support in many parts of New England and areas of Yankee migration, such as western New York, northeastern Ohio, southern Michigan, and northern Illinois.

In the South, Clay carried only his native Kentucky, North Carolina, and Tennessee. The popular vote map shows two sections of North Carolina clearly expressing Whig sympathies. Coastal North Carolina was a commercial area with old Federalist ties. In western North Carolina, the mountainous portion of the state, the population felt that the internal improvements the Whigs proposed would help tie them into the national economy. Tennessee also went for Clay in 1844 and was, in general, where the Whigs were competitive during this era. Flat and fertile southwestern Tennessee in the Mississippi valley, home to plantations and commercial farming, supported the Whigs. Eastern Appalachian Tennessee was also a Whig stronghold in support of internal improvements. Tennessee, like many other states, also had areas of Democrat or Whig support motivated by local issues, local leaders, newspapers, a history of domestic migration and internal settlement, immigration, or the strength of organized parties. In general, individual counties can confound subregional and regional patterns by quirks of local individuals, circumstances, and history.

In 1844 the candidate elected president received less than a majority of the popular vote, the second time this had occurred. Nevertheless, Polk and the Democrats took the victory as a mandate for Manifest Destiny. The process had begun, however, even before Polk took office, with lame duck president Tyler pushing Texas statehood and Congress approving it. As president, Polk continued the process, acquiring the Oregon Territory from Britain and starting a war with Mexico in 1846.

REFERENCE: Howe, Daniel Walker. *The Political Culture of the American Whigs.* Chicago: University of Chicago Press, 1979.

1848

PRESIDENTIAL ELECTION

Candidates	Popular Vote Percentage	Electoral College Vote Percentage and (Vote)
Whig		
Zachary Taylor (Louisiana)	47.3	56.2 (163)
Vice Presidential Nominee: Millard Fillmore (New York)		
Democrat		
Lewis Cass (Michigan)	42.5	43.8 (127)
Vice Presidential Nominee: William O. Butler (Kentucky)		
Free Soil		
Martin Van Buren (New York)	10.1	0 (0)
Vice Presidential Nominee: Charles Francis Adams (Massachusetts)		

Map 16

In the four years of the Polk administration (1845–1849), the United States realized Manifest Destiny, extending its control of territory to the Pacific Coast. Negotiations for the Oregon Territory and the successful Mexican-American War extended the United States almost to its present-day continental boundaries. Polk, severely ailing, did not run for a second term and died four months after leaving office. Both major parties had to find acceptable candidates in an era of growing sectional differences.

In the months leading up to the 1848 election, the major focus of politics turned again to slavery, particularly its fate in the newly acquired territories. The issue of slavery divided both parties. Views on it varied and included total abolition, keeping it legal only in the South but banning it in the newly acquired territories, and allowing it in the new territories only along the southern tier. The Democratic Party had historically supported states' rights and the constitutional underpinning allowing for slavery in the South. In the 1840s, however, the New York Democratic Party split into two factions: the liberal antislavery Barnburners and the more traditional Hunkers. Both were allowed representation at the Democratic national convention, but both walked out. The Whigs were similarly divided between Conscience Whigs, who opposed slavery, and Cotton Whigs, who did not oppose slavery (and were primarily from the South).

With these sectional rifts as backdrop, the Democrats met in May in Baltimore and nominated Sen. Lewis Cass of Michigan for the presidency. Cass adopted a compromise position with respect to slavery's expansion in an attempt to defuse the issue and regional tensions. His doctrine of "popular sovereignty" left it to the voters of each new territory and new state to decide whether their constitutions should allow slavery within their borders. As was the custom in this era, a geographically balanced ticket was required, so the Democrats selected as their vice presidential nominee Gen. William O. Butler, a War of 1812 and Mexican-American War veteran from Kentucky.

The Whigs met in June in Philadelphia to select a candidate. The precedent of nominating a war hero to the highest office dated back to Washington and included Jackson and Harrison and even the Democratic vice presidential nominee that year. The Whigs turned to Gen. Zachary Taylor, hero of the Mexican-American War from Louisiana. To balance the ticket, Millard Fillmore, a former representative and New York state comptroller, received the vice presidential nomination. Taylor's nomination took the military strategy to the extreme, in that he was a career military man with no civilian administrative or political experience, had never voted, and had never voiced a public opinion on the great issues of the day. One thing, however, was certain about Taylor—he held large plantations in Louisiana and Mississippi and owned more than a hundred slaves. His nomination disappointed many Conscience Whigs.

In the summer of 1848, unhappiness over the major-party nominations by some northern Whigs, Democrats, and Liberty Party members led to the creation of the Free Soil Party. Meeting in Buffalo, New York, in August, the Free Soilers nominated former president Martin Van Buren, a Democrat and a Barnburner, for president. They selected for the vice presidency a fellow northerner from Massachusetts, Conscience Whig Charles Francis Adams, the son of former president John Quincy Adams. As opposed to the more abolitionist Liberty Party, the Free Soilers believed that the existence of slavery in the South had constitutional protections. They stated accordingly, "We therefore propose no interference by Congress with slavery within the limits of any state." Although antislavery, the Free Soilers' main platform in 1848 was the prevention of slavery's expansion to new U.S. territories. Their other platform positions weighed in on such issues as the tariff and internal improvements. They also promoted homesteading, the granting of frontier surveyed public lands to settlers. The Free Soil Party was thus more than a one-issue party, advocating other concerns important to northerners. The party's campaign theme of "Free soil, Free speech, Free labor, and Free men" reflected their total platform and foreshadowed the future of northern politics.

A new federal law directed that the states for the first time hold presidential and congressional elections on one date, the first Tuesday in November, so on November 7, 1848, most citizens voted in unison. Only South Carolina chose its electors via state legislature. Despite the impact of the Free Soil Party, the campaign ended as the nonconfrontational Whigs had hoped. Taylor won a plurality victory with 47.3 percent of the vote to Cass's 42.5 percent. The newly formed Free Soil Party won a remarkable 10.1 percent of the vote. It appeared on the ballot in every free state and even received a few votes in the slave states of Delaware and Maryland. Van Buren outpolled Cass in Massachusetts, New York, and Vermont, although these states delivered popular pluralities to Taylor. In the electoral college, Taylor received 163 votes (56.2 percent) to Cass's 127 votes (43.8 percent). The sectional distribution of electoral votes was balanced, emblematic of the general balance of congressional and presidential parties during the Whig-Democrat era. As the electoral college maps shows, Taylor carried the historically Whig states in the North (including Massachusetts), historically Whig border states (including Delaware, Kentucky, and Maryland), and historically Whig states in the South (including Louisiana and Tennessee). The Democrat Cass carried his entire home region of northwestern states and frontier states with Jacksonian voters. Cass also carried newly Democratic states in the North (Maine and New Hampshire) along with normally southern Democratic states (South Carolina and Virginia). In addition, Cass did well in the newly admitted frontier states of Iowa and Texas, the latter grateful for Democratic support for annexation.

The popular vote map shows areas of similar Whig and Democratic strength as seen in preceding elections. Taylor carried his home state with the help of plantation areas in southern Louisiana and the Mississippi River valley. Whig patterns in Kentucky, North Carolina, and Tennessee were remarkably stable. The map clearly shows the Whig wins in many instances in the North to be plurality victories because of the Free Soil vote. Taylor carried the swing state of Pennsylvania because of strong support in the more developed counties along transportation and communication lines in the southern portion of the state. The northern tier of Pennsylvania counties, home to poorer, noncommercial farmers, primarily voted for Cass.

The Free Soil candidate map illustrates noteworthy patterns foreshadowing the future. Almost all counties registering 10 percent or more votes for it are located in the "Deep North," the extreme northern states or the northern portion of the northern states. For example, in Ohio, the strongest support for the Free Soilers came from the northeastern Western Reserve area. In Illinois, the Free Soilers received strong support in northern counties, but scant backing in the southern ones. Southern Illinois, southern Indiana, and much of southern Ohio experienced significant migration from slaveholding border states. Much of the population with southern roots in southern Illinois and southern Indiana admired Andrew Jackson, held sympathetic or neutral views on slavery, and tended to vote Democratic. In addition, commercial wheat farming in southern and southeastern Illinois lagged because of physical geography features involving soil, topography, and other factors. Furthermore, the southern portion of Illinois, Indiana, and Ohio had commercial links, via the Ohio and Mississippi Rivers, to the Democratic South. The more northerly counties of Illinois, on the other hand, were quickly developing commercial agricultural economies and tended to be settled by northerners, many with New England roots.

The presidential election of 1848 highlighted the ongoing tenuous alliance of the nation's sections within the two major parties. These alliances once again illustrate severe strains over regional issues, in this instance, the expansion of slavery into newly acquired territories. Many historians believe that the nonsectional Whig and Democratic parties actually held the United States together in the antebellum period. The Whigs and the Democrats would in a few years again try to preserve the Union with the Compromise of 1850.

REFERENCE: Rayback, Joseph G. *Free Soil: The Election of 1848*. Lexington: University Press of Kentucky, 1970.

Turner, Frederick Jackson. *The United States, 1830–1850*. Gloucester, Mass.: Peter Smith, 1958.

1852
PRESIDENTIAL ELECTION

CANDIDATES	POPULAR VOTE PERCENTAGE	ELECTORAL COLLEGE VOTE PERCENTAGE AND (VOTE)
Democrat		
Franklin Pierce (New Hampshire)	50.8	85.8 (254)
Vice Presidential Nominee: William Rufus de Vane King (Alabama)		
Whig		
Winfield Scott (Virginia)	43.9	14.2 (42)
Vice Presidential Nominee: William Graham (North Carolina)		
Free Soil		
John P. Hale (New Hampshire)	4.9	0 (0)
Vice Presidential Nominee: George Washington Julian (Indiana)		

The 1848 election of southern general Zachary Taylor put a political unknown in the White House. Much to the shock and dismay of southern politicians and slave owners, Taylor began to unravel the delicate sectional political balance in Congress and the nation. After the 1849 gold rush, Taylor recommended the immediate admission of California as a state, although its state constitution would likely ban slavery and give the free states a majority in the Senate. The California question and slavery in general threatened the very existence of the Union.

In early 1850, Henry Clay, and later Sen. Stephen A. Douglas of Illinois, fashioned a series of compromise legislation—the Compromise of 1850—to defuse "forever" the sectional question of slavery. The most important pieces of the compromise called for admitting California as a free state, admitting New Mexico and Utah under popular sovereignty (allowing those states' voters to determine the status of slavery within their borders), ending the slave trade in the District of Columbia, and enacting a stringent fugitive slave law. Taylor opposed parts of the compromise, but he died unexpectedly in July 1850. Millard Fillmore, who succeed-

Map 17

ed Taylor, supported the compromise laws and signed each one as it passed Congress.

Many northerners rejected the Fugitive Slave Act, which required the arrest and return to the South of runaway slaves, considering it particularly onerous among the compromise laws. Despite the hopes of the majorities in the North and the South, the act and slavery in general became central to the 1852 presidential campaign with the publication that year of *Uncle Tom's Cabin,* Harriet Beecher Stowe's classic antislavery novel. The Whigs and Democrats both tried to sidestep the slavery issue by fully endorsing the compromise in their party platforms.

The Democratic convention met in July in Baltimore to select a presidential candidate from four possible choices: Lewis Cass, James Buchanan, William L. Marcy, and Stephen A. Douglas. None of these frontrunners, however, could assemble a winning coalition. After forty-nine ballots, they nominated a compromise candidate, New Hampshire's Franklin Pierce, who had the near unanimous support of the New England delegations. A former member of the House and the Senate, Pierce was known to be friendly, even sympathetic, to southern concerns. To balance the ticket, the Democrats selected William Rufus de Vane King of Alabama for vice president.

The Whigs met in July in Baltimore as well and also required a large number of ballots to choose a candidate. The Compromise of 1850 divided the Whigs more than it did the Democrats, with mostly northern Conscience Whigs opposed to it and the mostly southern Cotton Whigs favoring it. Many Cotton Whigs liked President Fillmore for his support of the compromise. After more than fifty ballots, however, Fillmore's supporters still could not rally a winning coalition. The party therefore turned to a compromise candidate, Gen. Winfield Scott, a Virginian of Mexican-American War fame. Secretary of the Navy William Graham of North Carolina received the vice presidential nomination.

A gathering of Free Soilers, antislavery Democrats, Conscience Whigs, and old Liberty Party members convened in Pittsburgh in August 1852 for the Free Soil Democratic Convention. The good feelings surrounding the Compromise of 1850 and the return of the Barnburner Democrats to the Democratic Party, including 1848 Free Soil nominee Martin Van Buren, had generally weakened the Free Soilers' position among the electorate. The Free Soil Democrats nominated Free Soil senator John P. Hale of New Hampshire and George Washington Julian of Indiana for president and vice president, respectively. The party thus carried on the mantle of the Free Soil tradition with a slight name change to the Free Soil Democratic Party. The votes for John P. Hale are designated in the 1852 election maps as Free Soil. The party platform went further than the previous Free Soil platform in condemning slavery, including the Compromise of 1850, which it viewed as proslavery.

In the election, Pierce won a slight majority, with 50.8 percent of the popular vote. Scott took 43.9 percent of the popular vote, and Hale earned 4.9 percent, less than half of the more than 10 percent that the Free Soilers received in 1848. As the electoral college map shows, Pierce's victory was overwhelming. He carried every state but four. His 254 votes (85.8 percent) to Scott's 42 (14.2 percent) ranks among the biggest sweeps in competitive U.S. electoral history. Scott squeaked by with nar-

row victories in the traditional Whig states of Kentucky, Tennessee, and Vermont and a plurality in Massachusetts. The Whig Party appeared to be broken locally as well as nationally.

The 1852 popular vote map illustrates the sweeping nature of the Democratic victory, especially in the Deep South and frontier West. Whig pockets, though reduced in size, remain evident in the traditional areas of Kentucky, southwestern and eastern Tennessee, and Vermont, the string of plantation counties along the lower Mississippi River valley, southern Louisiana, the Western Reserve region of northeastern Ohio, Chesapeake Maryland, and western and coastal North Carolina. The flight of southern Whigs to the Democratic Party is illustrated by the decline in the number of southern counties carried by the Whigs in 1852 compared to in previous elections.

The Free Soil Democratic vote of John P. Hale is telling geographically. Free Soil support remained strong in New England, northeastern Ohio, southern Michigan, northern Illinois, and southern Wisconsin. The geographic patterns of the vote for the Free Soilers of 1848 and the Free Soil Democrats of 1852 represent precursors of the even stronger sectional cleavages to come in the next presidential election.

The 1852 passing of Whig founders Henry Clay of Kentucky and Daniel Webster of Massachusetts and the division of the Whigs between antislavery Conscience and proslavery Cotton factions doomed the coalition that initially began as an anti–Andrew Jackson pro-nationalist movement in the 1830s. The election of 1852 marked the beginning of the end of the Whig-Democrat era, a significant and identifiable party system with an identifiable geography of large pockets, or subregions, of strong party support in all regions. The next two elections set in motion a new era in U.S. electoral geography featuring regional, or sectional, parties.

REFERENCE: Blue, Frederick J. *The Free Soilers: The Party Politics, 1848–1854*. Urbana: University of Illinois Press, 1973.

INTRODUCTION AND INDEX TO THE MAPS

The *Historical Atlas of U.S. Presidential Elections, 1788–2004* is the only reference work to map the first fifty-five presidential elections by counties. Two sets of maps allow for analysis of voting patterns on several different levels.

Maps indicating the popular vote results in each election appear at the top of right-hand pages and depict the winning candidate and party in each county, allowing for longitudinal analysis of electoral patterns for every county, state, region, and section of the United States from 1788 through 2004. These maps cover the major-party candidates and third-party candidates receiving at least 2 percent of the vote. These popular vote maps use two different color intensities for each candidate to differentiate plurality and majority levels of support for the county winner. These color variations also allow independent analysis of party vote patterns. The identification of plurality winners is particularly useful for examining three-way races or contests involving even more candidates. Maps in the lower right-hand corner indicate how each state voted in the electoral college. In the lower left-hand corner, two pie charts depict popular vote and electoral college vote percentages. Visual comparisons can be easily made between popular votes received and the electoral college margin. The unique set of maps on left-hand pages depicts the level of support for the individual candidates in every county of the country. The popular vote for each candidate is divided into five levels of support from which county, state, and regional strengths can be discerned. The county boundaries on all maps are as they existed at the time of each election.

1788–1789 Presidential Election: Popular Support for Leading Candidate

Washington

Percentage of
Popular Vote

Under 1

1 to 34

35 to 49

50 to 64

65 or more

Foreign

Pre-Statehood

No Returns

Appointed Electors

Did Not Participate

Map
1

1788-1789 Presidential Election: Popular and Electoral Votes

Map 1

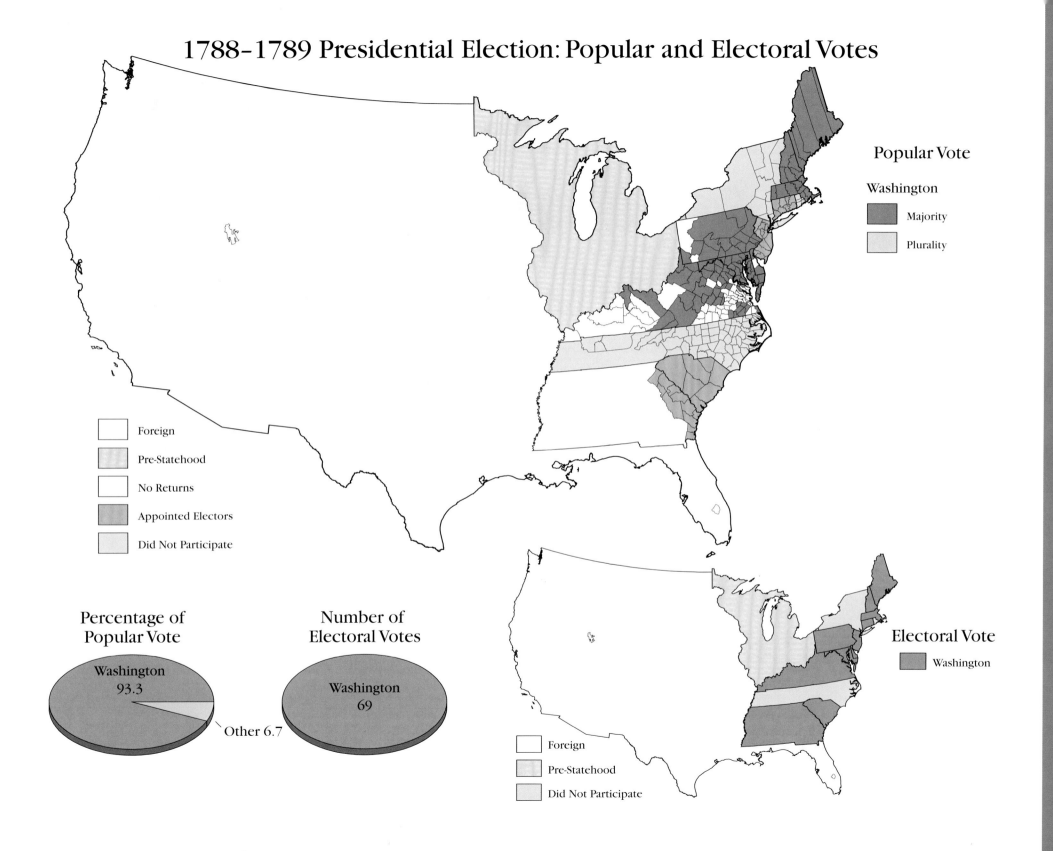

Popular Vote

Washington

- Majority
- Plurality

Foreign

Pre-Statehood

No Returns

Appointed Electors

Did Not Participate

Percentage of Popular Vote

Washington 93.3

Other 6.7

Number of Electoral Votes

Washington 69

Electoral Vote

Washington

Foreign

Pre-Statehood

Did Not Participate

Map
2

1792 Presidential Election: Popular Support for Leading Candidate

Washington

Percentage of
Popular Vote

Under 1

1 to 34

35 to 49

50 to 64

65 or more

Foreign

Pre-Statehood

No Returns

Appointed Electors

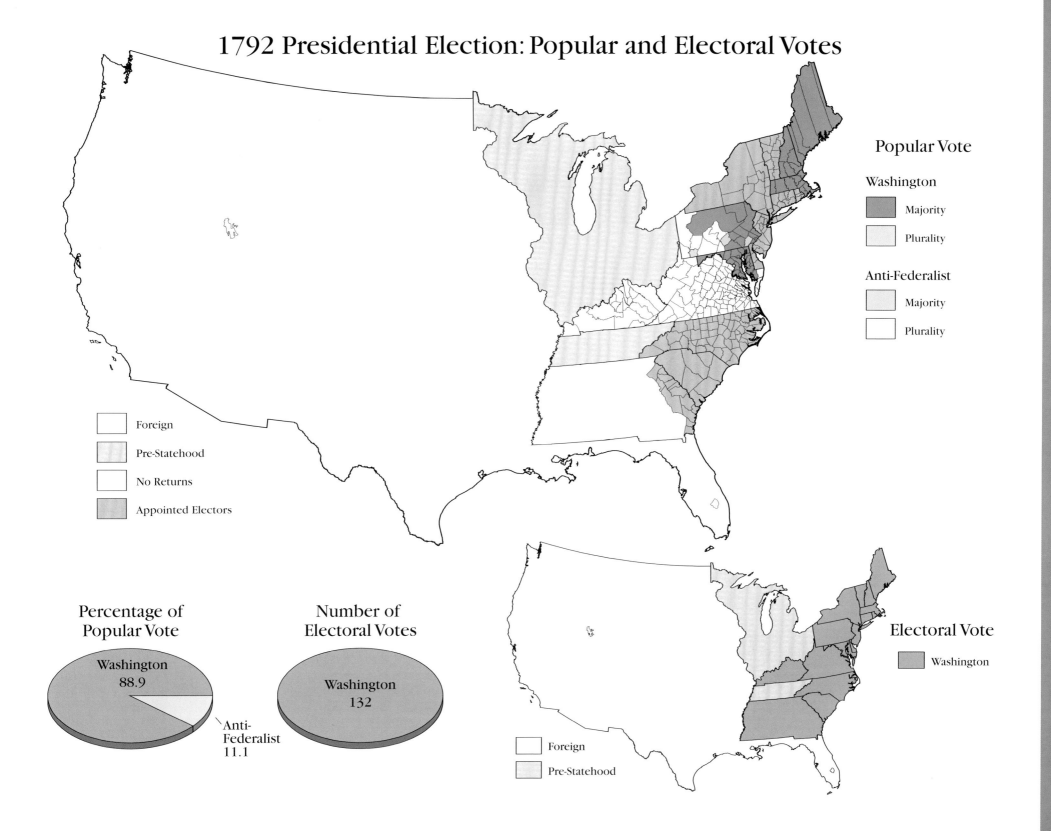

1792 Presidential Election: Popular and Electoral Votes

Map 2

Popular Vote

Washington
- Majority
- Plurality

Anti-Federalist
- Majority
- Plurality

- Foreign
- Pre-Statehood
- No Returns
- Appointed Electors

Percentage of Popular Vote

Washington 88.9

Anti-Federalist 11.1

Number of Electoral Votes

Washington 132

Electoral Vote

- Washington

- Foreign
- Pre-Statehood

Map
3

1796 Presidential Election: Popular Support for Leading Candidates

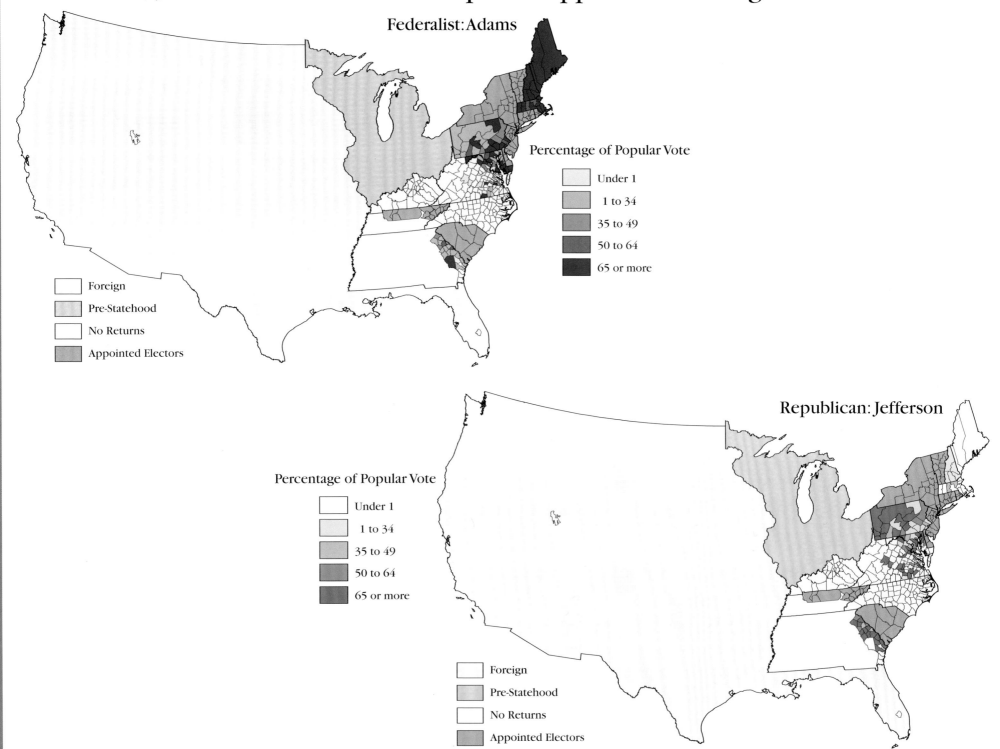

Federalist: Adams

Percentage of Popular Vote

- Under 1
- 1 to 34
- 35 to 49
- 50 to 64
- 65 or more

- Foreign
- Pre-Statehood
- No Returns
- Appointed Electors

Republican: Jefferson

Percentage of Popular Vote

- Under 1
- 1 to 34
- 35 to 49
- 50 to 64
- 65 or more

- Foreign
- Pre-Statehood
- No Returns
- Appointed Electors

1796 Presidential Election: Popular and Electoral Votes

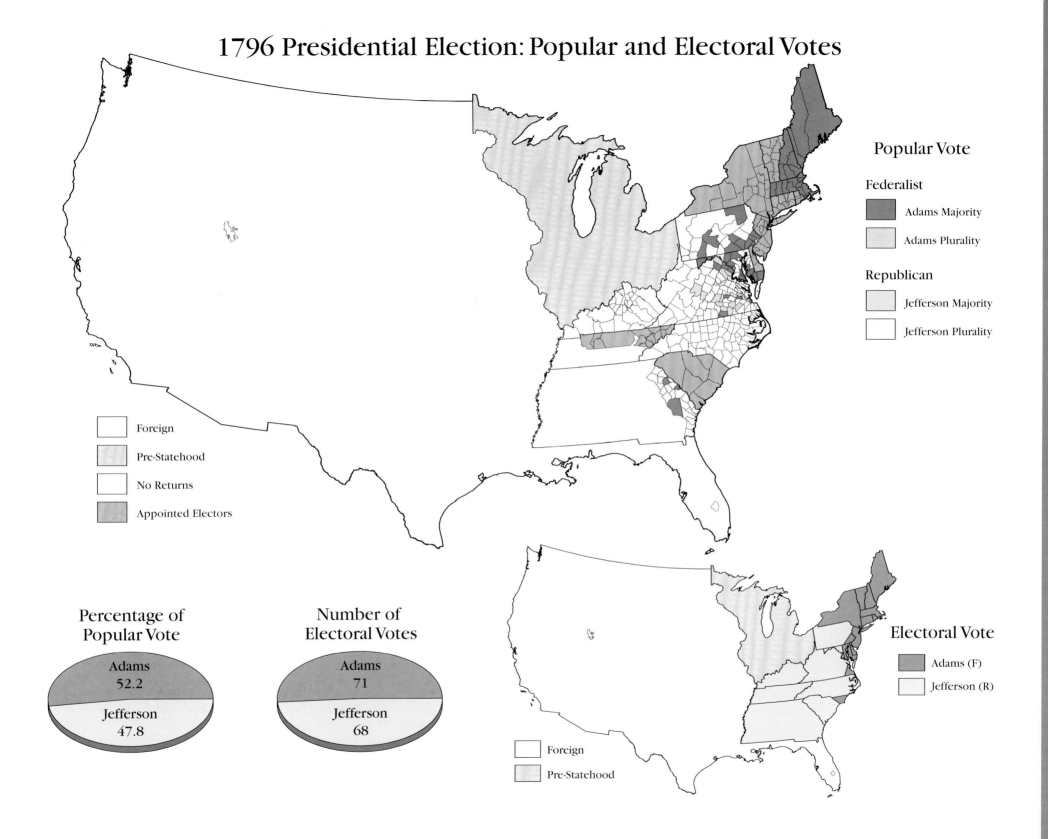

Map 3

Popular Vote

Federalist
- Adams Majority
- Adams Plurality

Republican
- Jefferson Majority
- Jefferson Plurality

- Foreign
- Pre-Statehood
- No Returns
- Appointed Electors

Percentage of Popular Vote
Adams 52.2
Jefferson 47.8

Number of Electoral Votes
Adams 71
Jefferson 68

Electoral Vote
- Adams (F)
- Jefferson (R)

- Foreign
- Pre-Statehood

Map 4

1800 Presidential Election: Popular Support for Leading Candidates

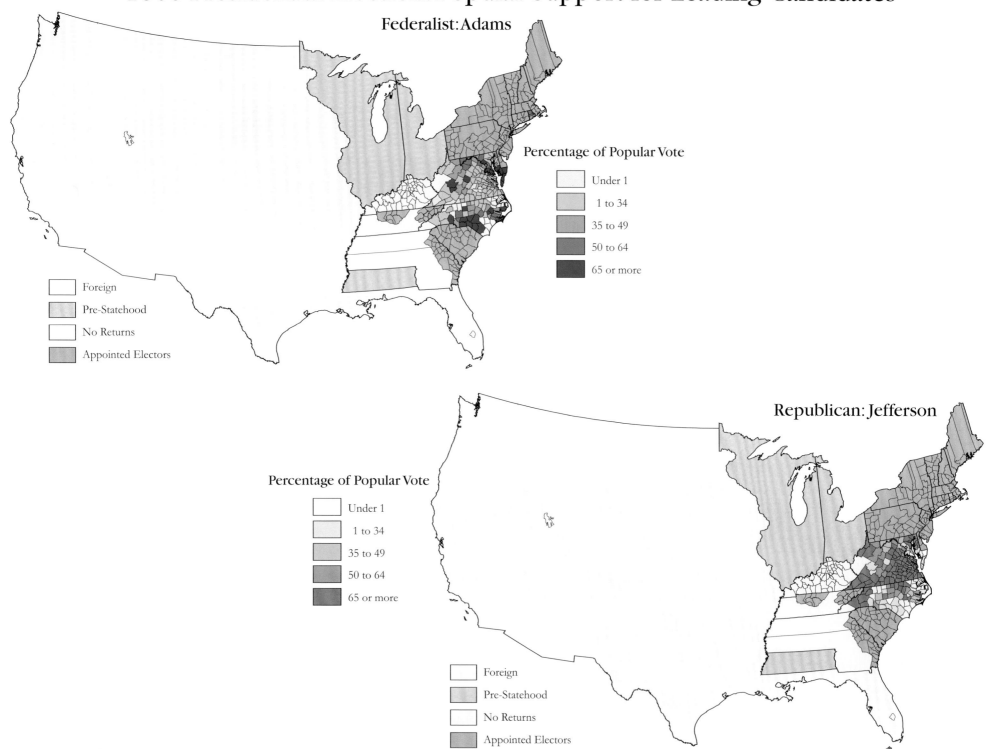

Federalist: Adams

Percentage of Popular Vote

- Under 1
- 1 to 34
- 35 to 49
- 50 to 64
- 65 or more

- Foreign
- Pre-Statehood
- No Returns
- Appointed Electors

Republican: Jefferson

Percentage of Popular Vote

- Under 1
- 1 to 34
- 35 to 49
- 50 to 64
- 65 or more

- Foreign
- Pre-Statehood
- No Returns
- Appointed Electors

1800 Presidential Election: Popular and Electoral Votes

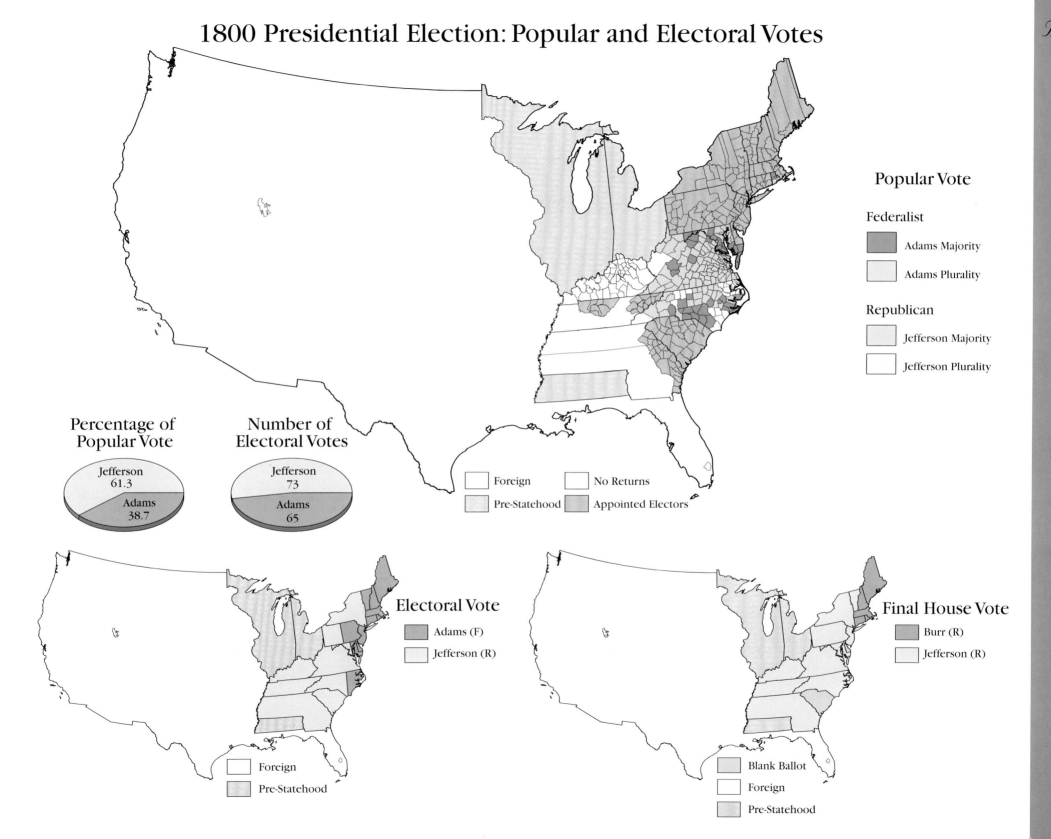

Map
4

Popular Vote

Federalist

- Adams Majority
- Adams Plurality

Republican

- Jefferson Majority
- Jefferson Plurality

- Foreign
- No Returns
- Pre-Statehood
- Appointed Electors

Percentage of Popular Vote

- Jefferson 61.3
- Adams 38.7

Number of Electoral Votes

- Jefferson 73
- Adams 65

Electoral Vote

- Adams (F)
- Jefferson (R)

- Foreign
- Pre-Statehood

Final House Vote

- Burr (R)
- Jefferson (R)

- Blank Ballot
- Foreign
- Pre-Statehood

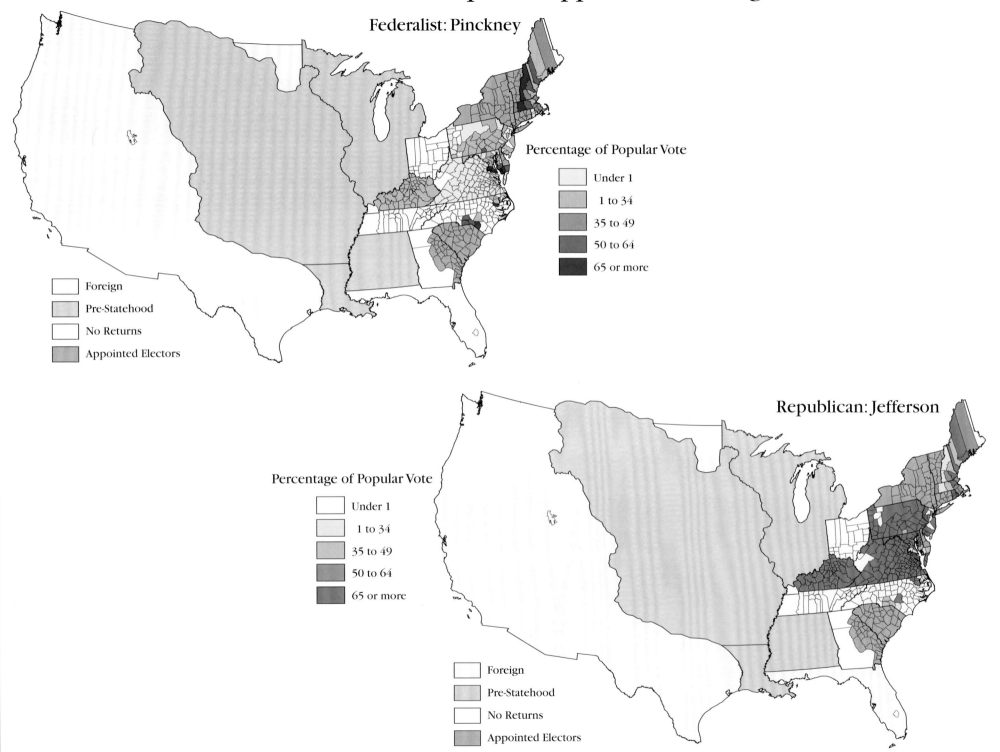

Map
5

1804 Presidential Election: Popular Support for Leading Candidates

Federalist: Pinckney

Percentage of Popular Vote

- Under 1
- 1 to 34
- 35 to 49
- 50 to 64
- 65 or more

- Foreign
- Pre-Statehood
- No Returns
- Appointed Electors

Republican: Jefferson

Percentage of Popular Vote

- Under 1
- 1 to 34
- 35 to 49
- 50 to 64
- 65 or more

- Foreign
- Pre-Statehood
- No Returns
- Appointed Electors

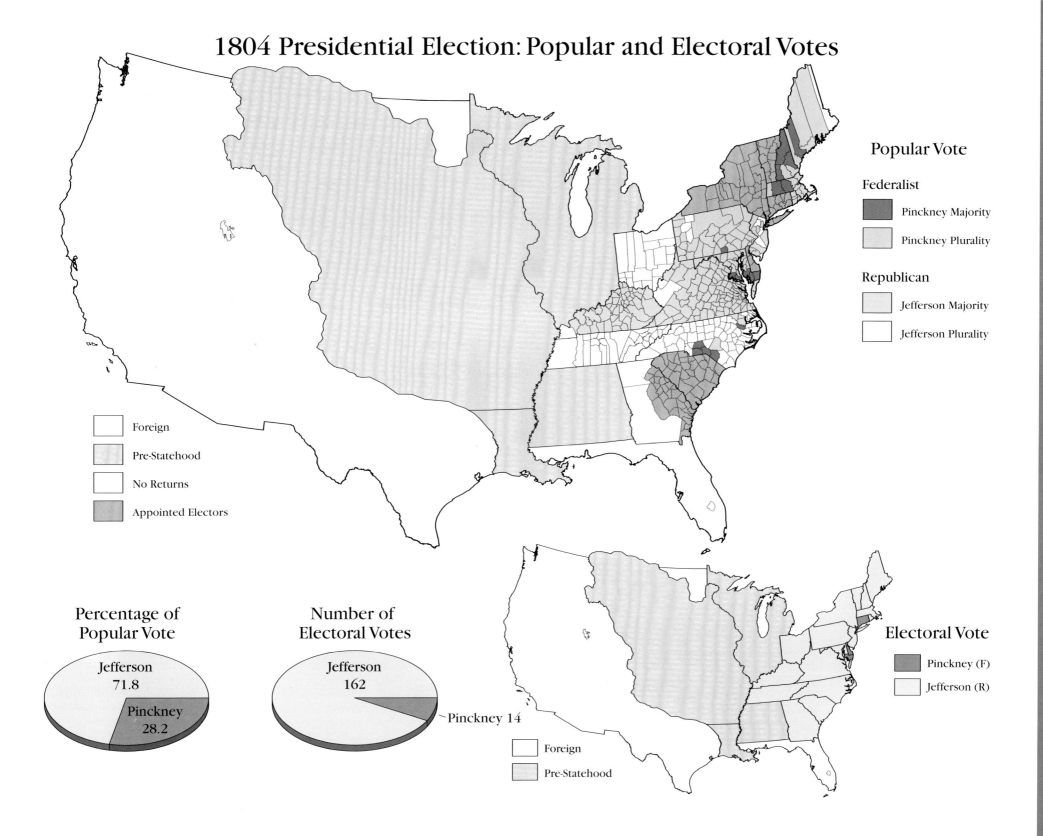

1804 Presidential Election: Popular and Electoral Votes

Map
5

Popular Vote

Federalist

- Pinckney Majority
- Pinckney Plurality

Republican

- Jefferson Majority
- Jefferson Plurality

- Foreign
- Pre-Statehood
- No Returns
- Appointed Electors

Percentage of Popular Vote

Jefferson
71.8

Pinckney
28.2

Number of Electoral Votes

Jefferson
162

Pinckney 14

Electoral Vote

- Pinckney (F)
- Jefferson (R)

- Foreign
- Pre-Statehood

Map
6

1808 Presidential Election: Popular Support for Leading Candidates

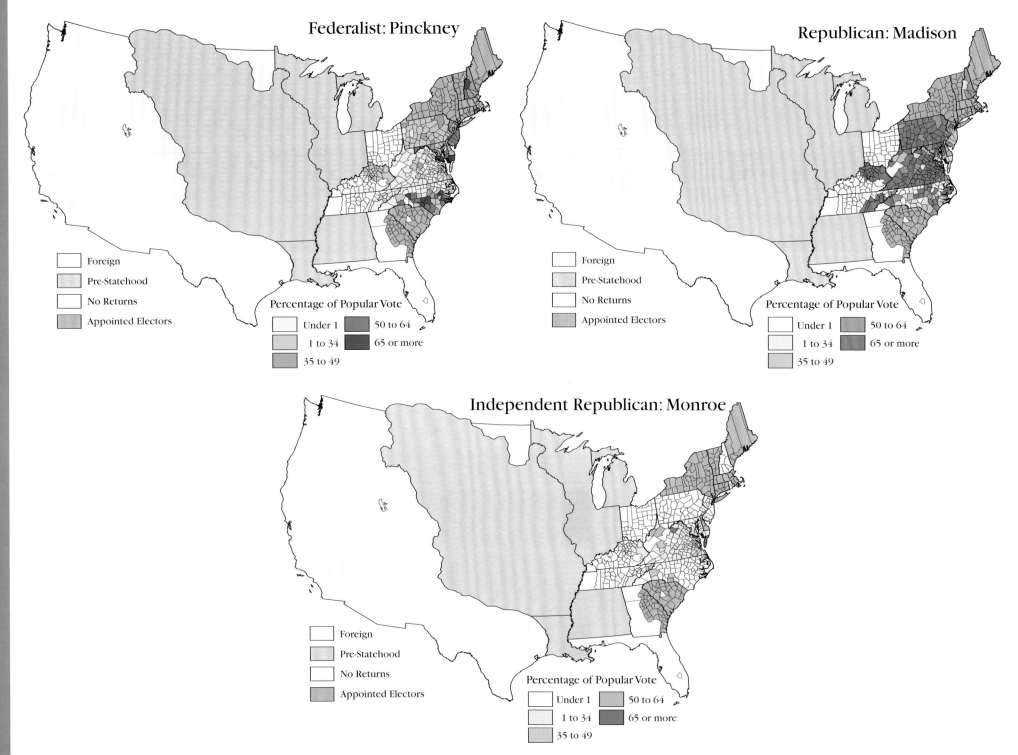

Federalist: Pinckney

Foreign
Pre-Statehood
No Returns
Appointed Electors

Percentage of Popular Vote
Under 1
1 to 34
35 to 49
50 to 64
65 or more

Republican: Madison

Foreign
Pre-Statehood
No Returns
Appointed Electors

Percentage of Popular Vote
Under 1
1 to 34
35 to 49
50 to 64
65 or more

Independent Republican: Monroe

Foreign
Pre-Statehood
No Returns
Appointed Electors

Percentage of Popular Vote
Under 1
1 to 34
35 to 49
50 to 64
65 or more

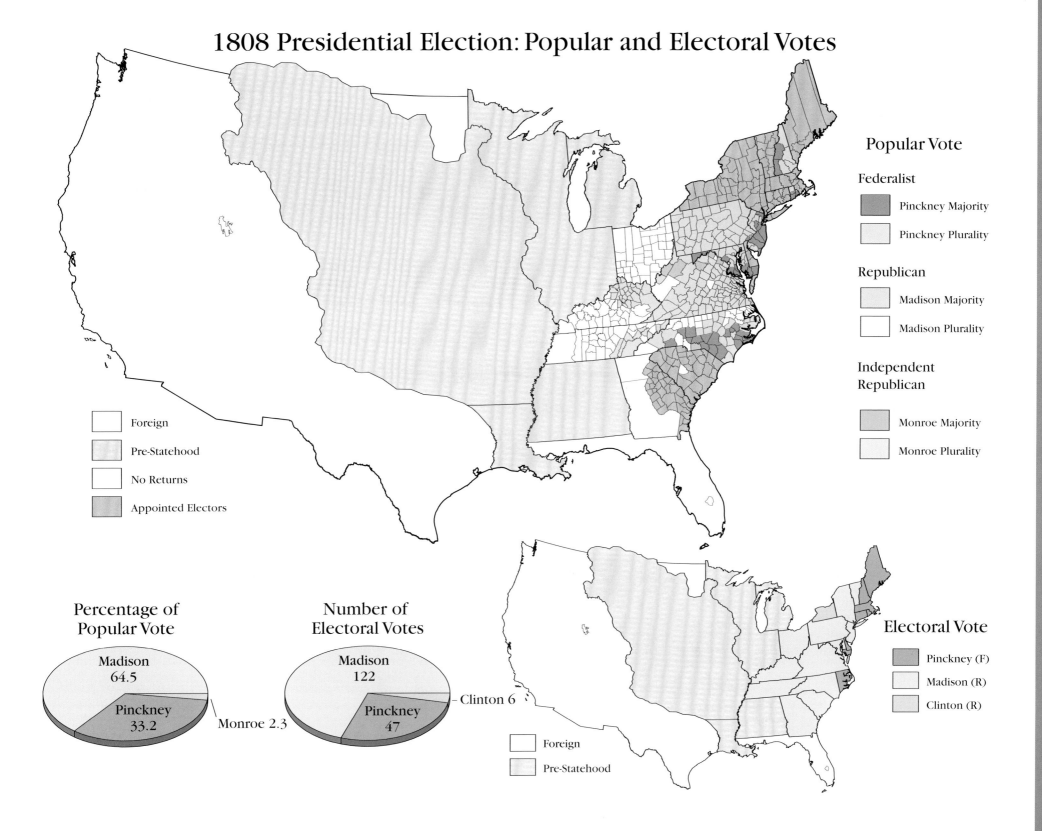

1808 Presidential Election: Popular and Electoral Votes

Map
6

Popular Vote

Federalist

Pinckney Majority

Pinckney Plurality

Republican

Madison Majority

Madison Plurality

Independent Republican

Monroe Majority

Monroe Plurality

Foreign

Pre-Statehood

No Returns

Appointed Electors

Percentage of Popular Vote

Madison
64.5

Pinckney
33.2

Monroe 2.3

Number of Electoral Votes

Madison
122

Pinckney
47

Clinton 6

Electoral Vote

Pinckney (F)

Madison (R)

Clinton (R)

Foreign

Pre-Statehood

Map
7

1812 Presidential Election: Popular Support for Leading Candidates

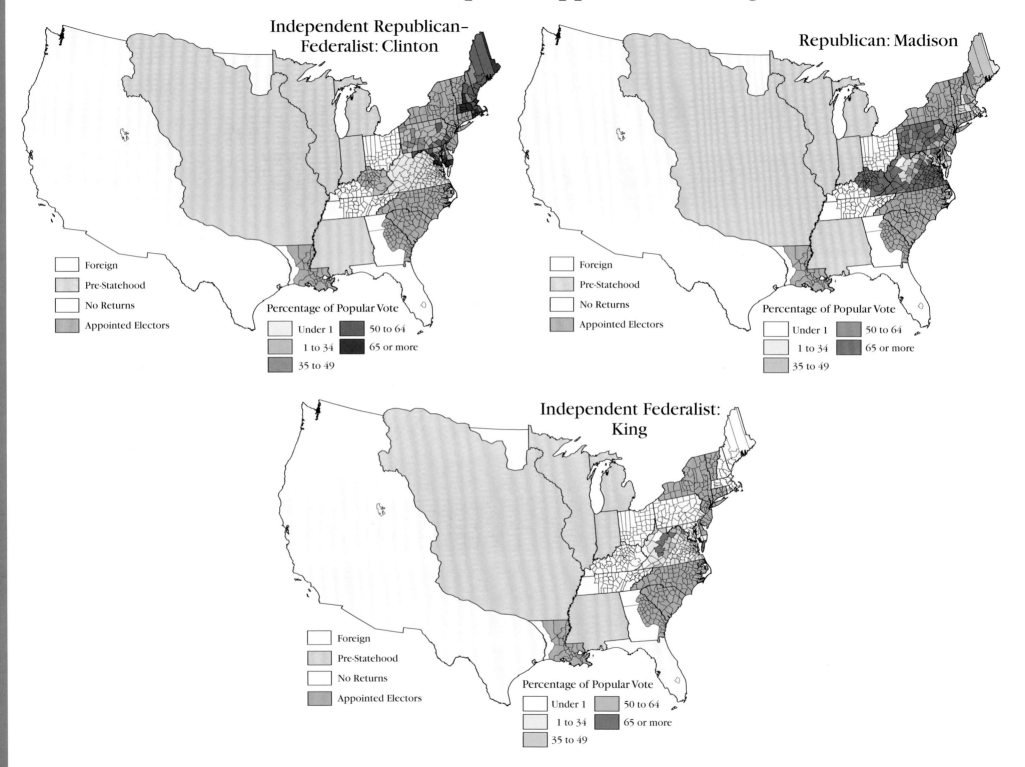

Independent Republican–Federalist: Clinton

Foreign
Pre-Statehood
No Returns
Appointed Electors

Percentage of Popular Vote

Under 1 · 50 to 64
1 to 34 · 65 or more
35 to 49

Republican: Madison

Foreign
Pre-Statehood
No Returns
Appointed Electors

Percentage of Popular Vote

Under 1 · 50 to 64
1 to 34 · 65 or more
35 to 49

Independent Federalist: King

Foreign
Pre-Statehood
No Returns
Appointed Electors

Percentage of Popular Vote

Under 1 · 50 to 64
1 to 34 · 65 or more
35 to 49

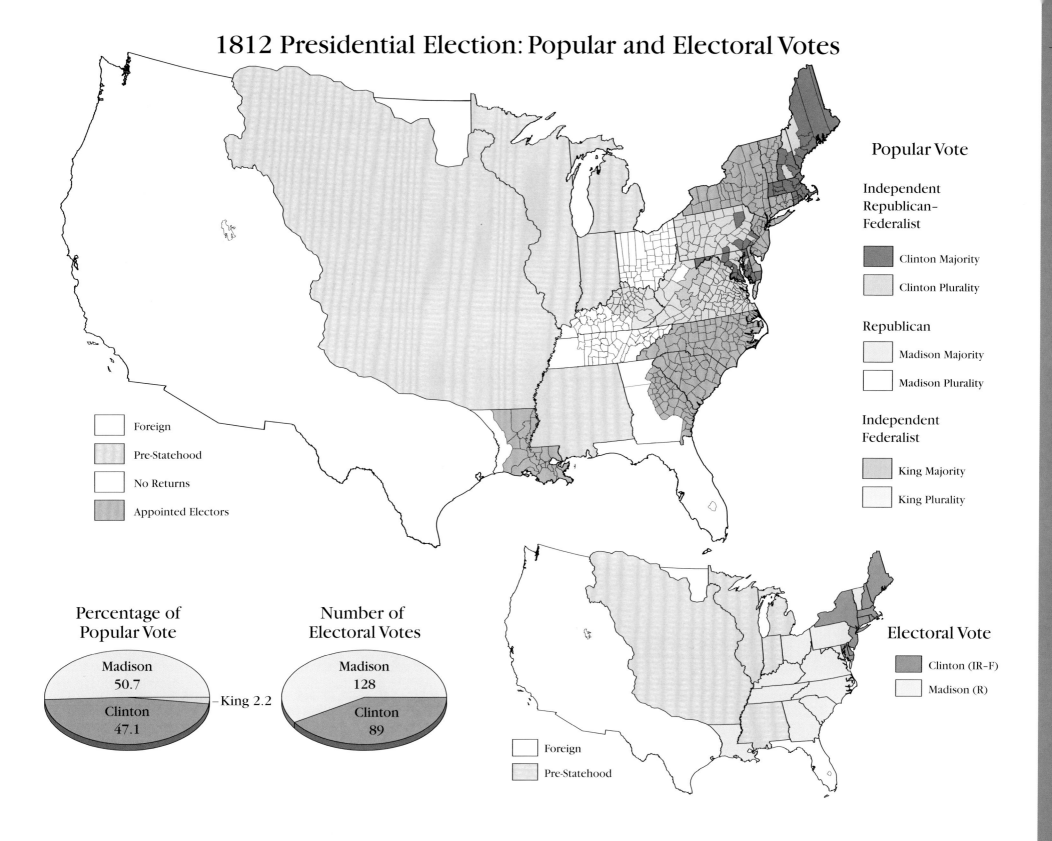

1812 Presidential Election: Popular and Electoral Votes

Map 7

Popular Vote

Independent Republican–Federalist
- Clinton Majority
- Clinton Plurality

Republican
- Madison Majority
- Madison Plurality

Independent Federalist
- King Majority
- King Plurality

- Foreign
- Pre-Statehood
- No Returns
- Appointed Electors

Percentage of Popular Vote
Madison 50.7
Clinton 47.1
— King 2.2

Number of Electoral Votes
Madison 128
Clinton 89

Electoral Vote
- Clinton (IR–F)
- Madison (R)

- Foreign
- Pre-Statehood

1816 Presidential Election: Popular Support for Leading Candidates

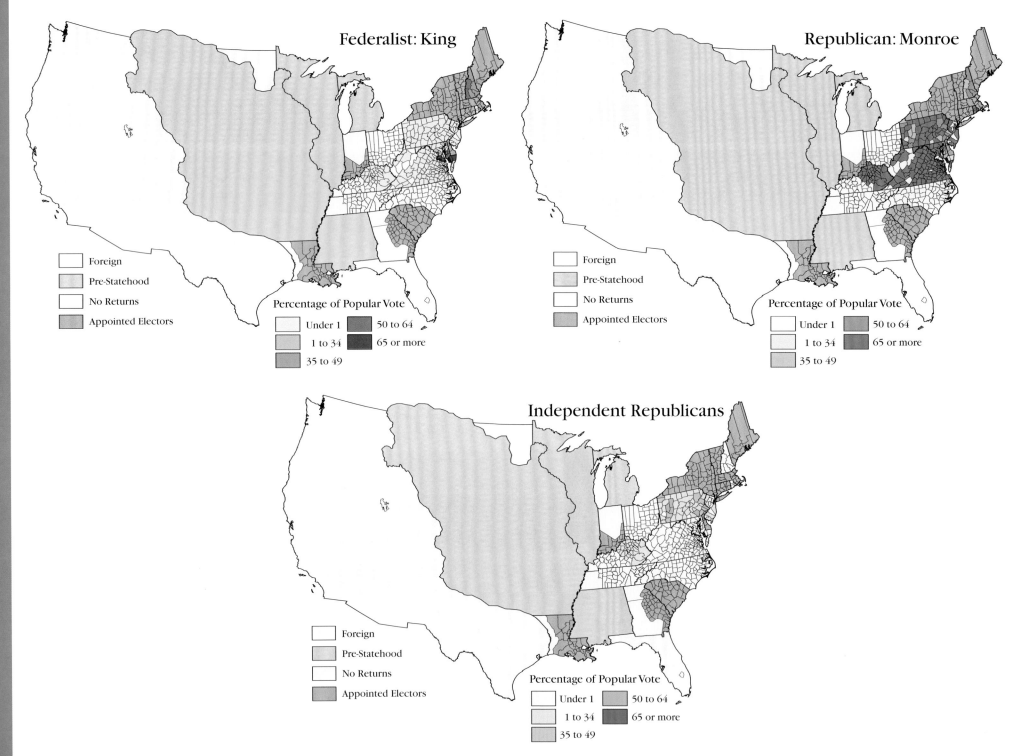

Map 8

Federalist: King

Foreign
Pre-Statehood
No Returns
Appointed Electors

Percentage of Popular Vote
Under 1
1 to 34
35 to 49
50 to 64
65 or more

Republican: Monroe

Foreign
Pre-Statehood
No Returns
Appointed Electors

Percentage of Popular Vote
Under 1
1 to 34
35 to 49
50 to 64
65 or more

Independent Republicans

Foreign
Pre-Statehood
No Returns
Appointed Electors

Percentage of Popular Vote
Under 1
1 to 34
35 to 49
50 to 64
65 or more

1816 Presidential Election: Popular and Electoral Votes

Map
8

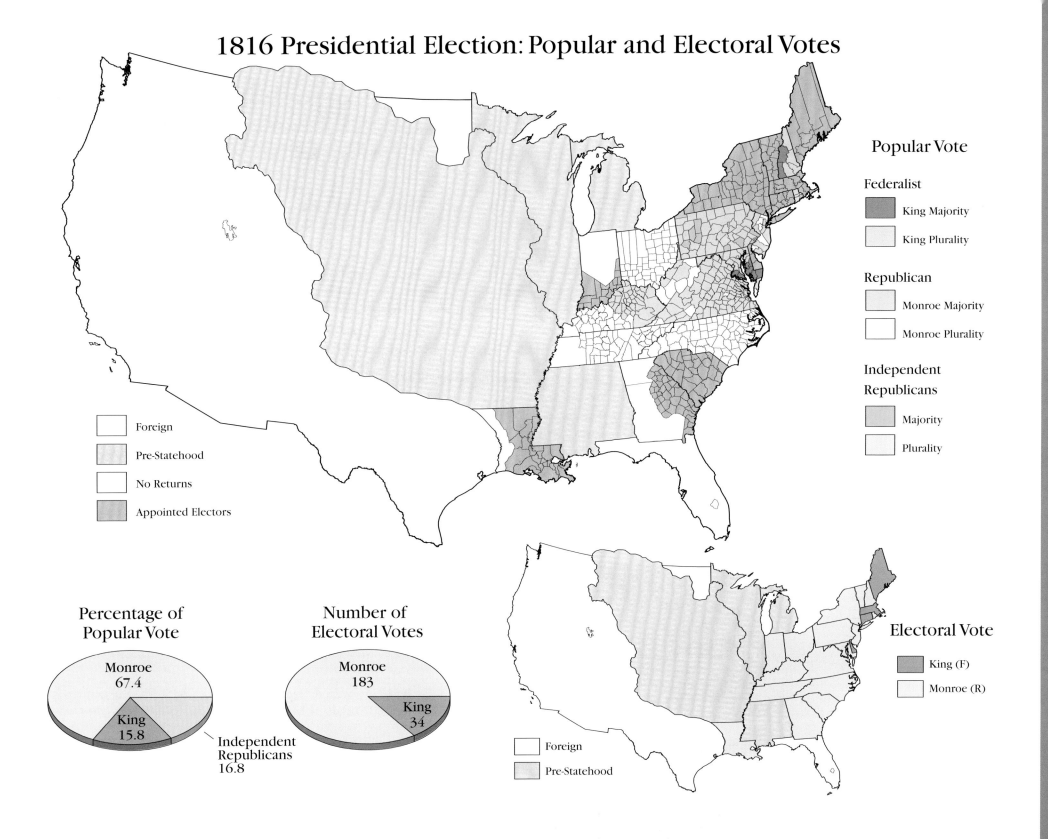

Popular Vote

Federalist

King Majority

King Plurality

Republican

Monroe Majority

Monroe Plurality

Independent
Republicans

Majority

Plurality

Foreign

Pre-Statehood

No Returns

Appointed Electors

Percentage of
Popular Vote

Monroe
67.4

King
15.8

Independent
Republicans
16.8

Number of
Electoral Votes

Monroe
183

King
34

Electoral Vote

King (F)

Monroe (R)

Foreign

Pre-Statehood

Map
9

1820 Presidential Election: Popular Support for Leading Candidates

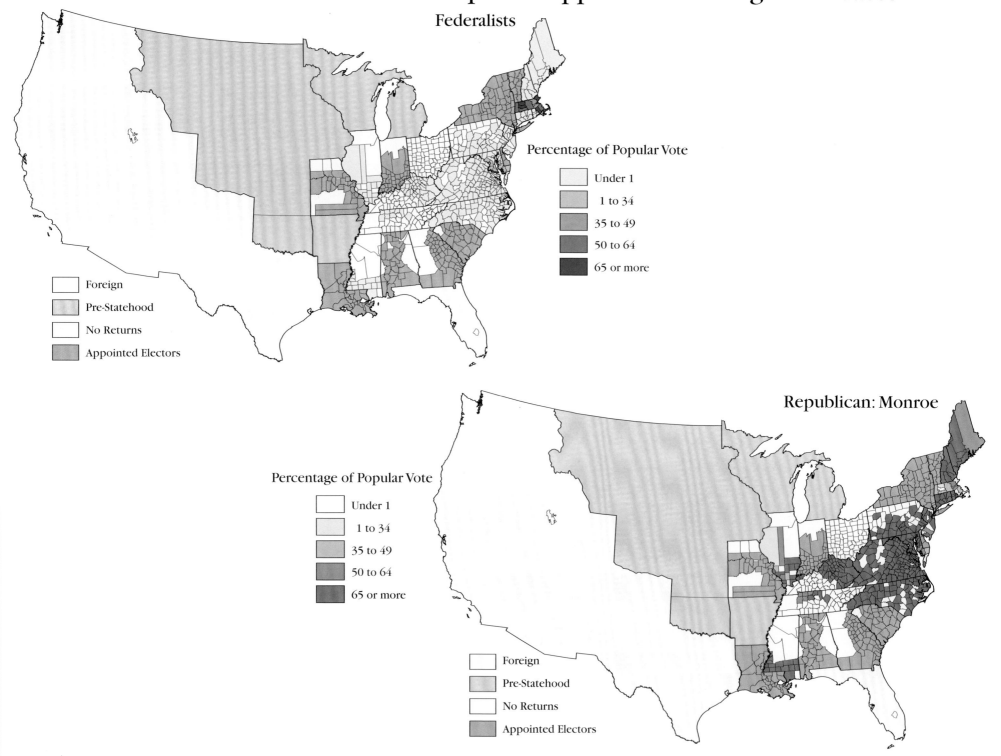

Federalists

Percentage of Popular Vote

Under 1
1 to 34
35 to 49
50 to 64
65 or more

Foreign
Pre-Statehood
No Returns
Appointed Electors

Republican: Monroe

Percentage of Popular Vote

Under 1
1 to 34
35 to 49
50 to 64
65 or more

Foreign
Pre-Statehood
No Returns
Appointed Electors

1820 Presidential Election: Popular and Electoral Votes

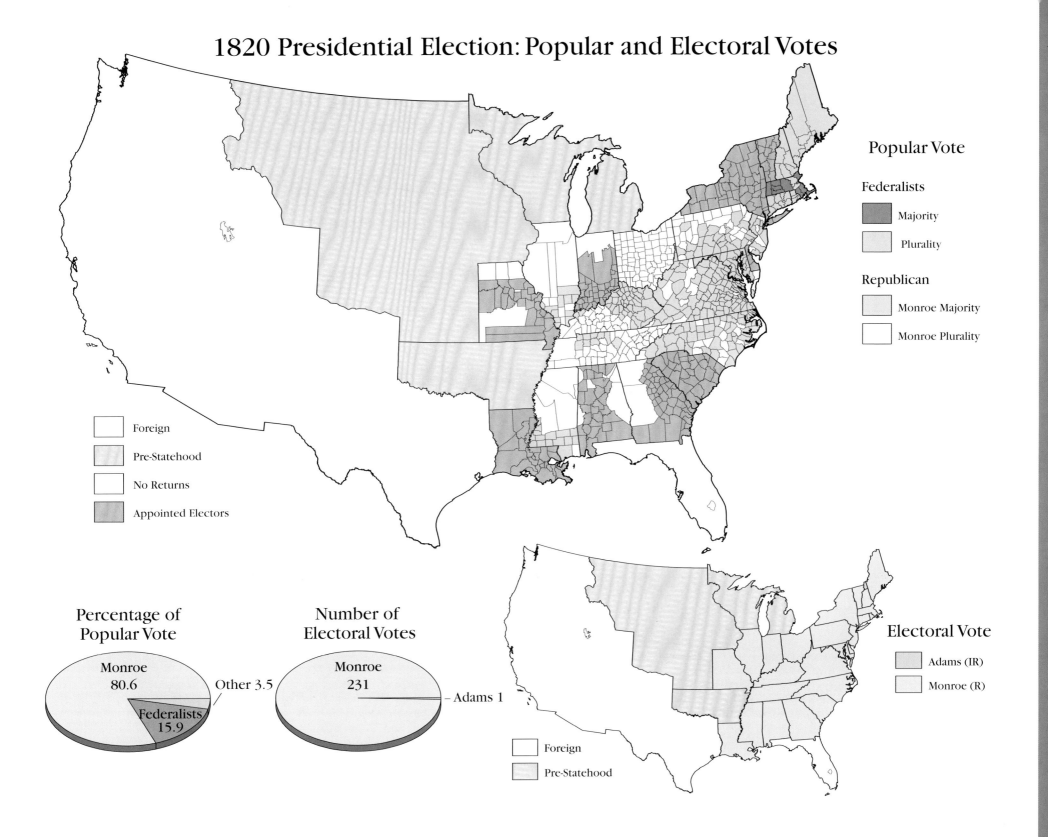

Map 9

Popular Vote

Federalists

- Majority
- Plurality

Republican

- Monroe Majority
- Monroe Plurality

- Foreign
- Pre-Statehood
- No Returns
- Appointed Electors

Percentage of Popular Vote

Monroe 80.6

Other 3.5

Federalists 15.9

Number of Electoral Votes

Monroe 231

– Adams 1

Electoral Vote

- Adams (IR)
- Monroe (R)

- Foreign
- Pre-Statehood

Map
10

1824 Presidential Election: Popular Vote for Leading Candidates

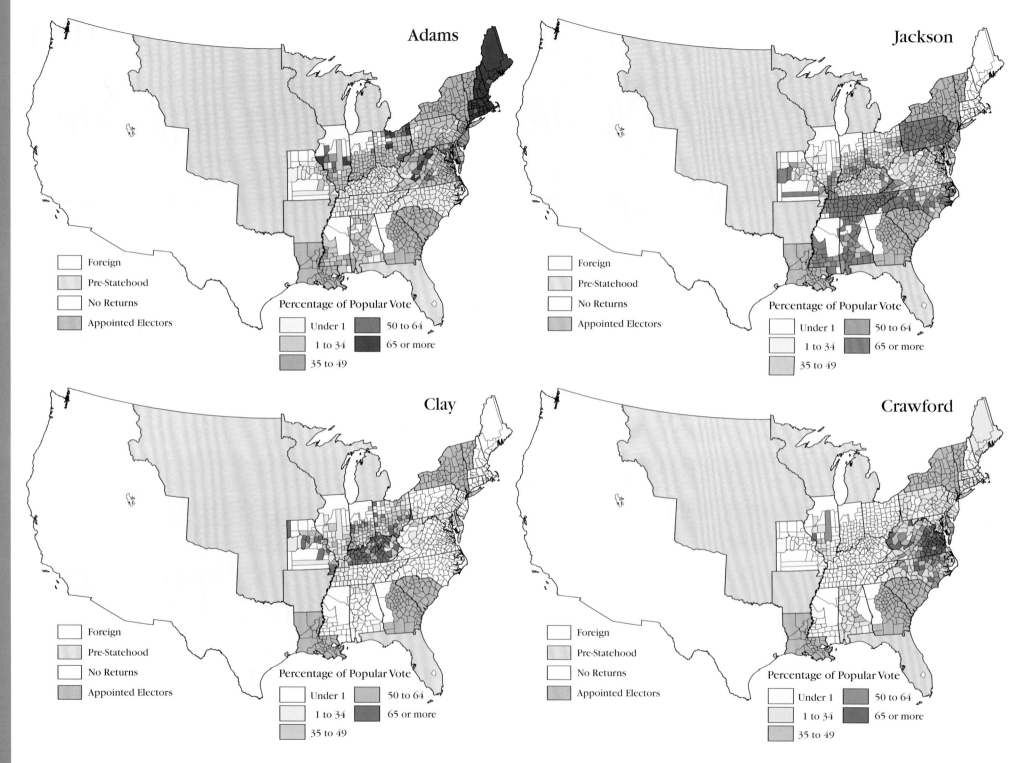

Adams

Jackson

Clay

Crawford

Foreign
Pre-Statehood
No Returns
Appointed Electors

Percentage of Popular Vote

Under 1   50 to 64
1 to 34   65 or more
35 to 49

1824 Presidential Election: Popular and Electoral Votes

Map
10

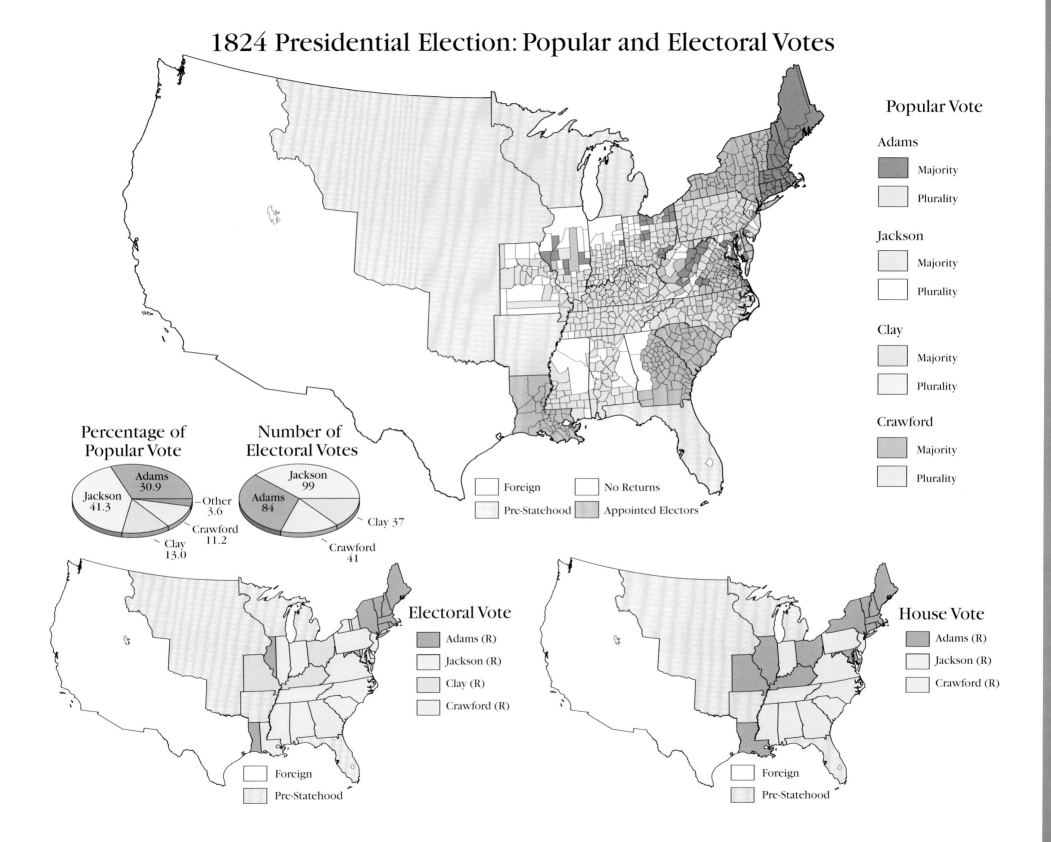

Popular Vote

Adams
- Majority
- Plurality

Jackson
- Majority
- Plurality

Clay
- Majority
- Plurality

Crawford
- Majority
- Plurality

Foreign   No Returns

Pre-Statehood   Appointed Electors

Percentage of Popular Vote

Adams 30.9
Jackson 41.3
Other 3.6
Crawford 11.2
Clay 13.0

Number of Electoral Votes

Jackson 99
Adams 84
Clay 37
Crawford 41

Electoral Vote
- Adams (R)
- Jackson (R)
- Clay (R)
- Crawford (R)

Foreign

Pre-Statehood

House Vote
- Adams (R)
- Jackson (R)
- Crawford (R)

Foreign

Pre-Statehood

Map
11

1828 Presidential Election: Popular Support for Leading Candidates

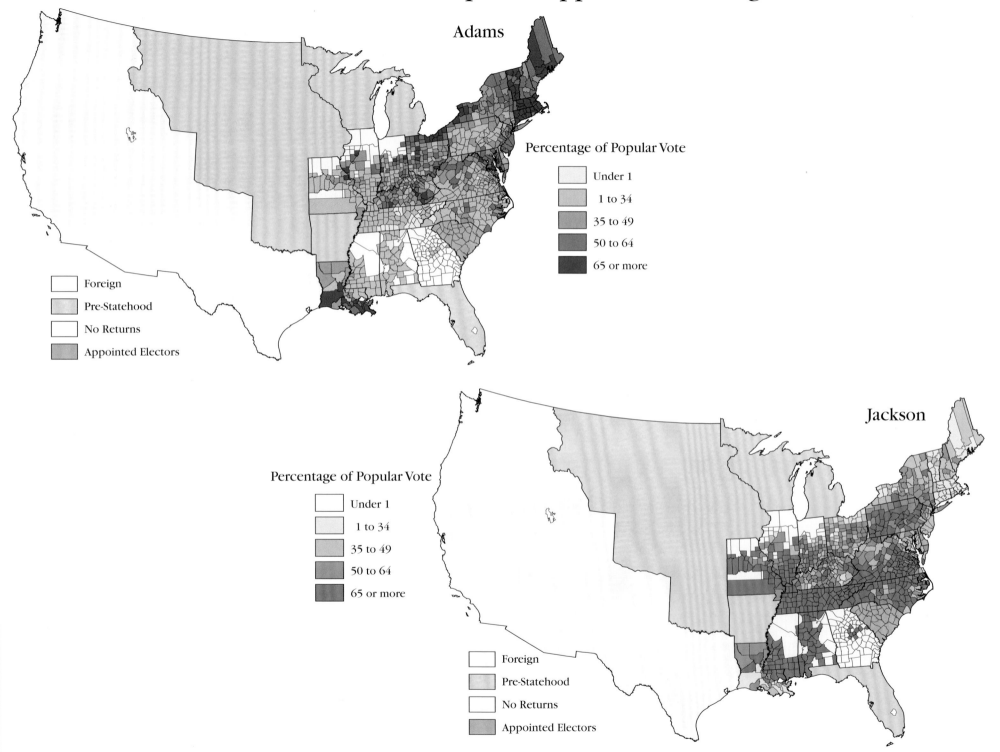

Adams

Percentage of Popular Vote
- Under 1
- 1 to 34
- 35 to 49
- 50 to 64
- 65 or more

- Foreign
- Pre-Statehood
- No Returns
- Appointed Electors

Jackson

Percentage of Popular Vote
- Under 1
- 1 to 34
- 35 to 49
- 50 to 64
- 65 or more

- Foreign
- Pre-Statehood
- No Returns
- Appointed Electors

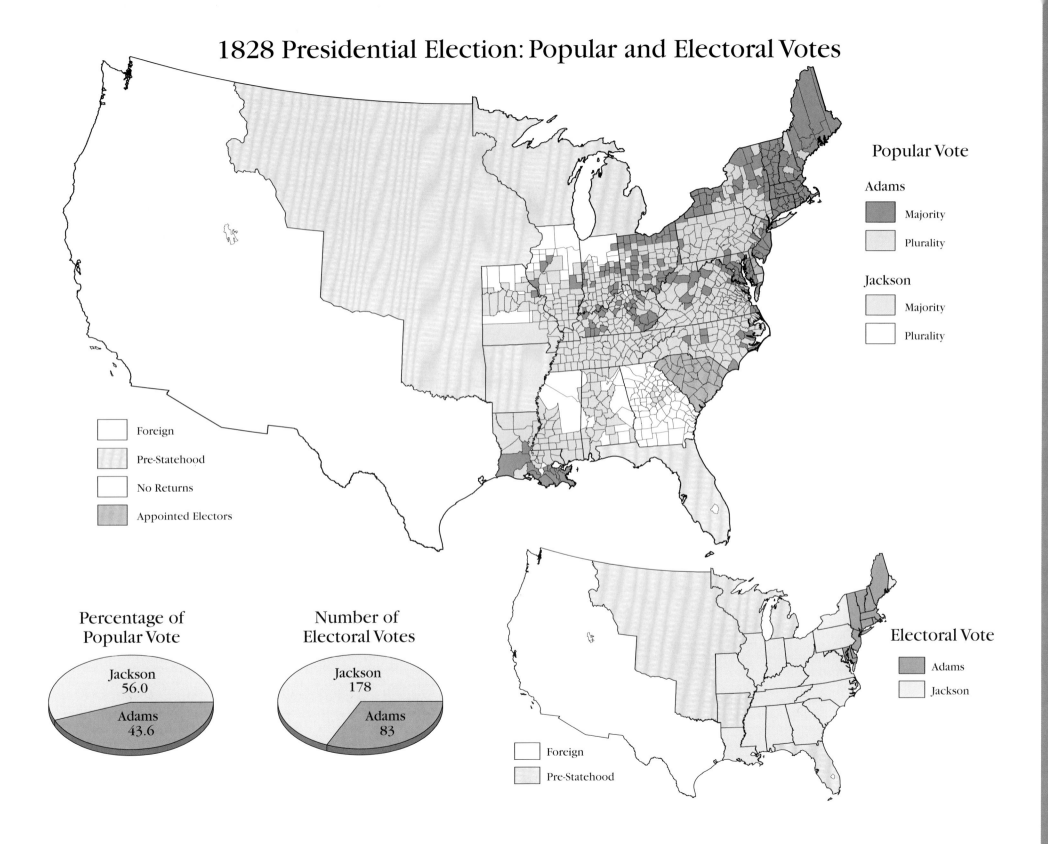

1828 Presidential Election: Popular and Electoral Votes

Map 11

Popular Vote

Adams

Majority

Plurality

Jackson

Majority

Plurality

Foreign

Pre-Statehood

No Returns

Appointed Electors

Percentage of
Popular Vote

Jackson
56.0

Adams
43.6

Number of
Electoral Votes

Jackson
178

Adams
83

Electoral Vote

Adams

Jackson

Foreign

Pre-Statehood

Map 12

1832 Presidential Election: Popular Support for Leading Candidates

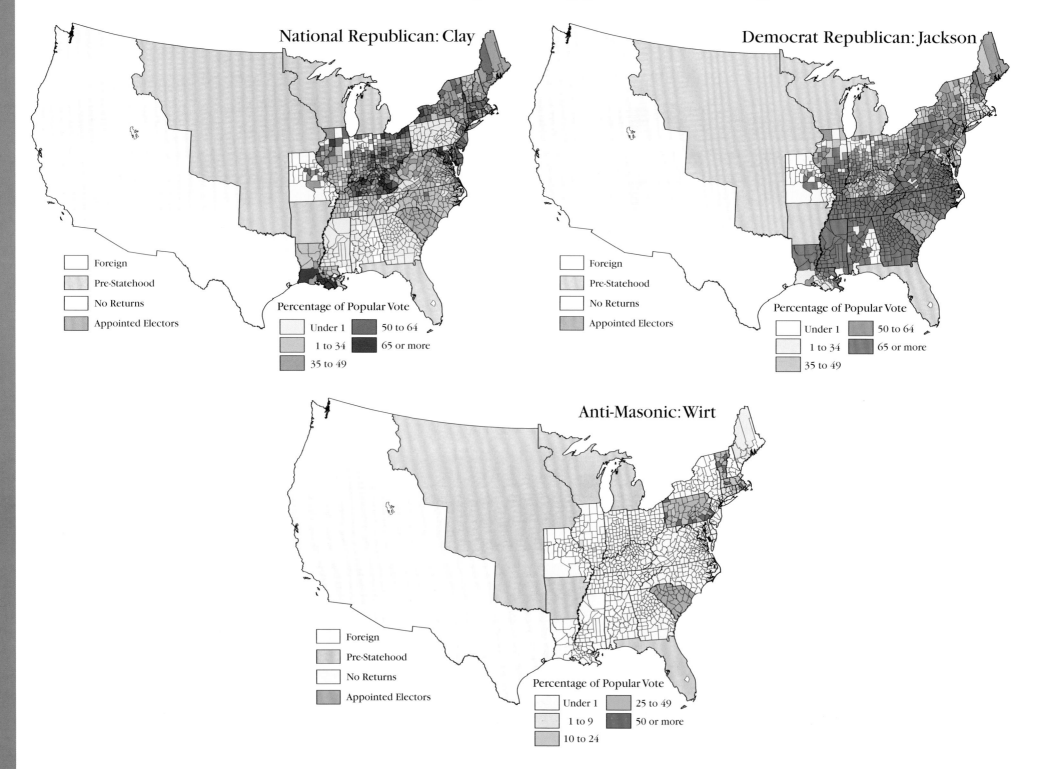

National Republican: Clay

Foreign
Pre-Statehood
No Returns
Appointed Electors

Percentage of Popular Vote

Under 1
1 to 34
35 to 49
50 to 64
65 or more

Democrat Republican: Jackson

Foreign
Pre-Statehood
No Returns
Appointed Electors

Percentage of Popular Vote

Under 1
1 to 34
35 to 49
50 to 64
65 or more

Anti-Masonic: Wirt

Foreign
Pre-Statehood
No Returns
Appointed Electors

Percentage of Popular Vote

Under 1
1 to 9
10 to 24
25 to 49
50 or more

1832 Presidential Election: Popular and Electoral Votes

Map 12

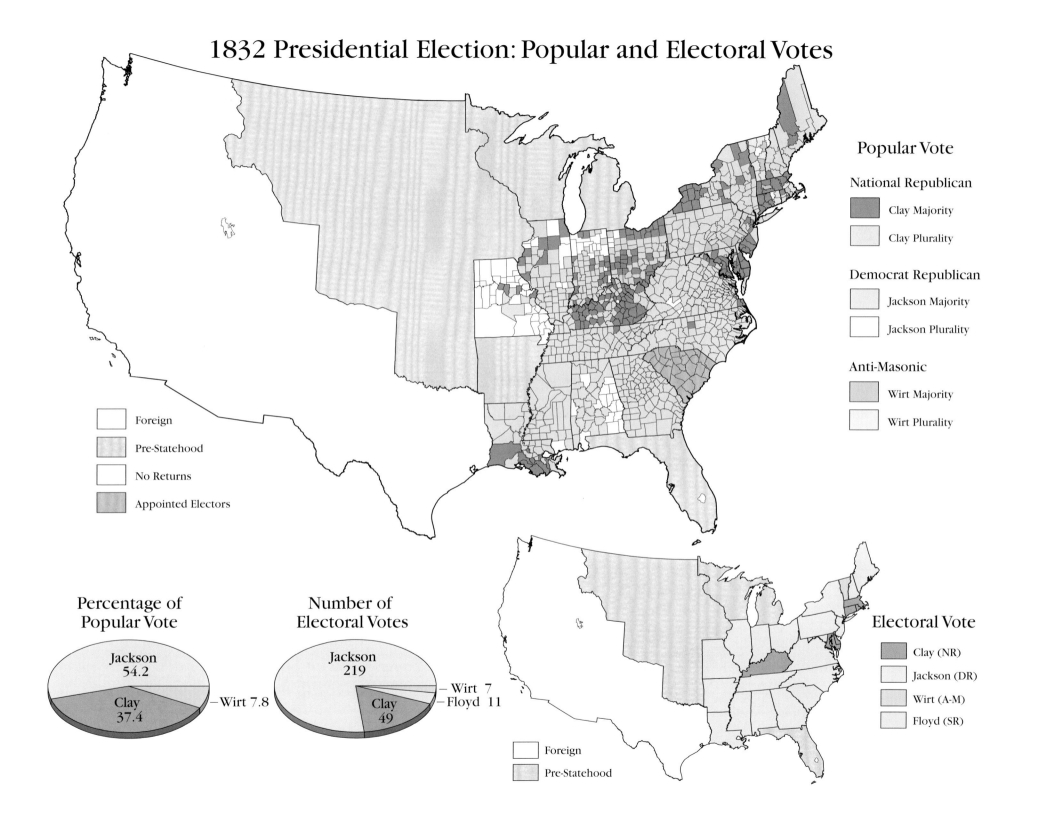

Popular Vote

National Republican
- Clay Majority
- Clay Plurality

Democrat Republican
- Jackson Majority
- Jackson Plurality

Anti-Masonic
- Wirt Majority
- Wirt Plurality

- Foreign
- Pre-Statehood
- No Returns
- Appointed Electors

Percentage of Popular Vote

Jackson 54.2
Clay 37.4
Wirt 7.8

Number of Electoral Votes

Jackson 219
Clay 49
Wirt 7
Floyd 11

Electoral Vote

- Clay (NR)
- Jackson (DR)
- Wirt (A-M)
- Floyd (SR)

- Foreign
- Pre-Statehood

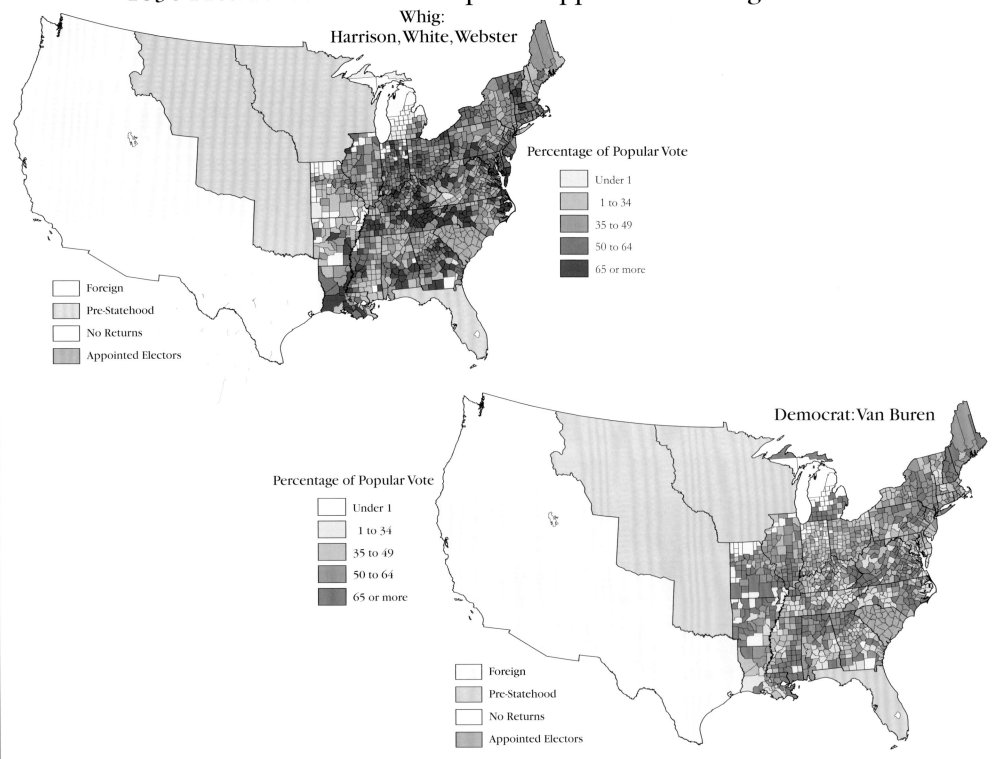

1836 Presidential Election: Popular Support for Leading Candidates

Whig:
Harrison, White, Webster

Percentage of Popular Vote

- Under 1
- 1 to 34
- 35 to 49
- 50 to 64
- 65 or more

- Foreign
- Pre-Statehood
- No Returns
- Appointed Electors

Democrat: Van Buren

Percentage of Popular Vote

- Under 1
- 1 to 34
- 35 to 49
- 50 to 64
- 65 or more

- Foreign
- Pre-Statehood
- No Returns
- Appointed Electors

Map 13

1836 Presidential Election: Popular and Electoral Votes

Map 13

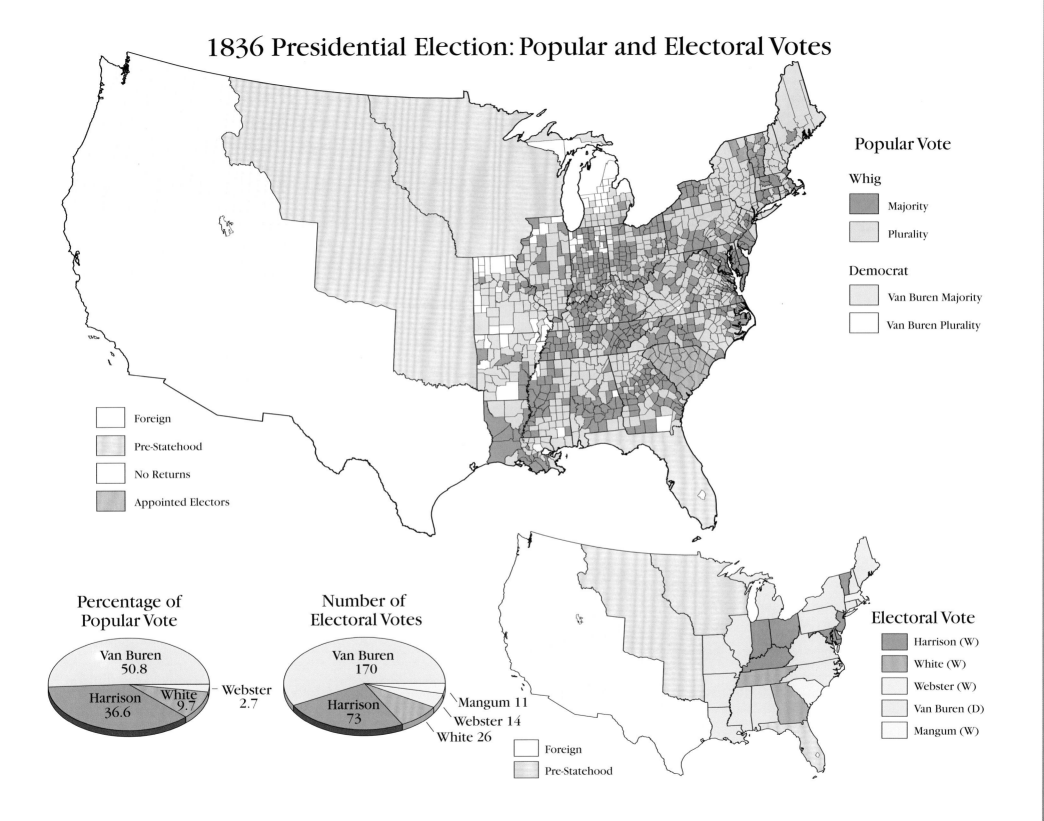

Popular Vote

Whig

Majority

Plurality

Democrat

Van Buren Majority

Van Buren Plurality

Foreign

Pre-Statehood

No Returns

Appointed Electors

Percentage of
Popular Vote

Van Buren
50.8

Harrison
36.6

White
9.7

Webster
2.7

Number of
Electoral Votes

Van Buren
170

Harrison
73

Mangum 11

Webster 14

White 26

Foreign

Pre-Statehood

Electoral Vote

Harrison (W)

White (W)

Webster (W)

Van Buren (D)

Mangum (W)

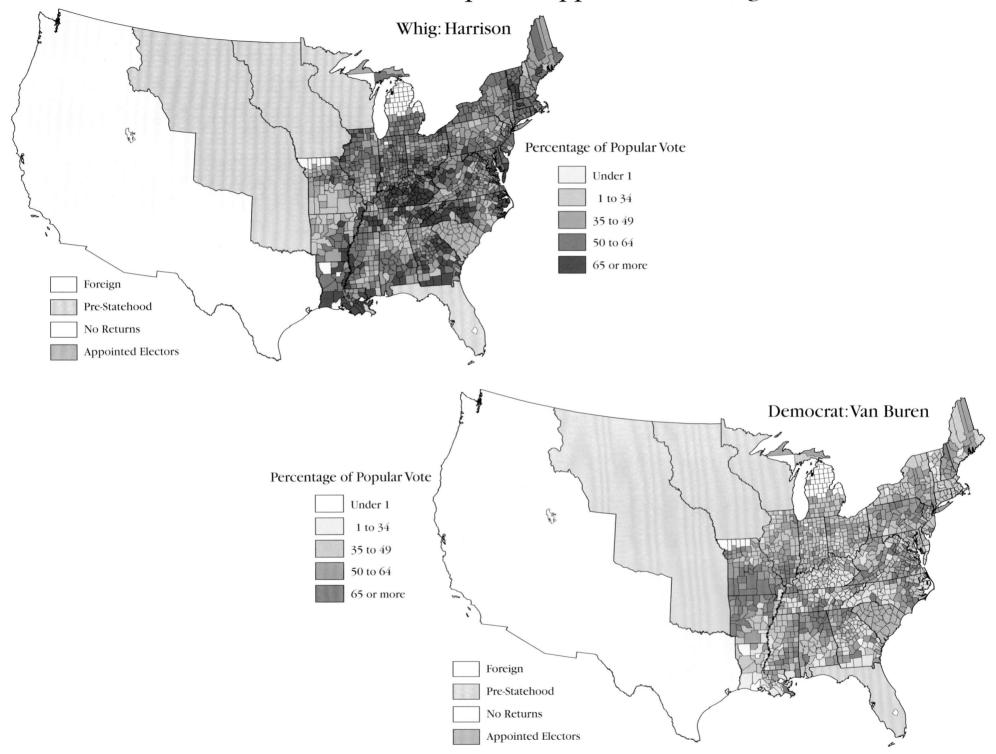

1840 Presidential Election: Popular Support for Leading Candidates

Map
14

Whig: Harrison

Percentage of Popular Vote

- Under 1
- 1 to 34
- 35 to 49
- 50 to 64
- 65 or more

- Foreign
- Pre-Statehood
- No Returns
- Appointed Electors

Democrat: Van Buren

Percentage of Popular Vote

- Under 1
- 1 to 34
- 35 to 49
- 50 to 64
- 65 or more

- Foreign
- Pre-Statehood
- No Returns
- Appointed Electors

1840 Presidential Election: Popular and Electoral Votes

Map 14

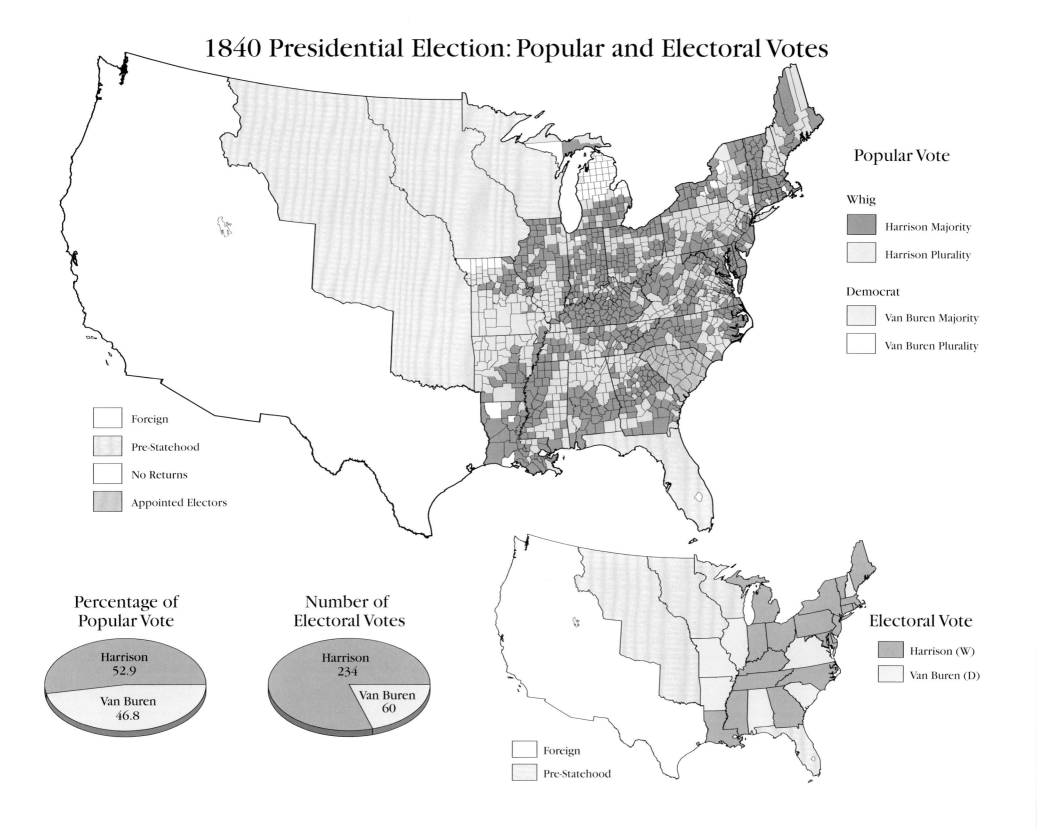

Popular Vote

Whig
- Harrison Majority
- Harrison Plurality

Democrat
- Van Buren Majority
- Van Buren Plurality

- Foreign
- Pre-Statehood
- No Returns
- Appointed Electors

Percentage of Popular Vote

Harrison 52.9

Van Buren 46.8

Number of Electoral Votes

Harrison 234

Van Buren 60

Electoral Vote

- Harrison (W)
- Van Buren (D)

- Foreign
- Pre-Statehood

Map
15

1844 Presidential Election: Popular Support for Leading Candidates

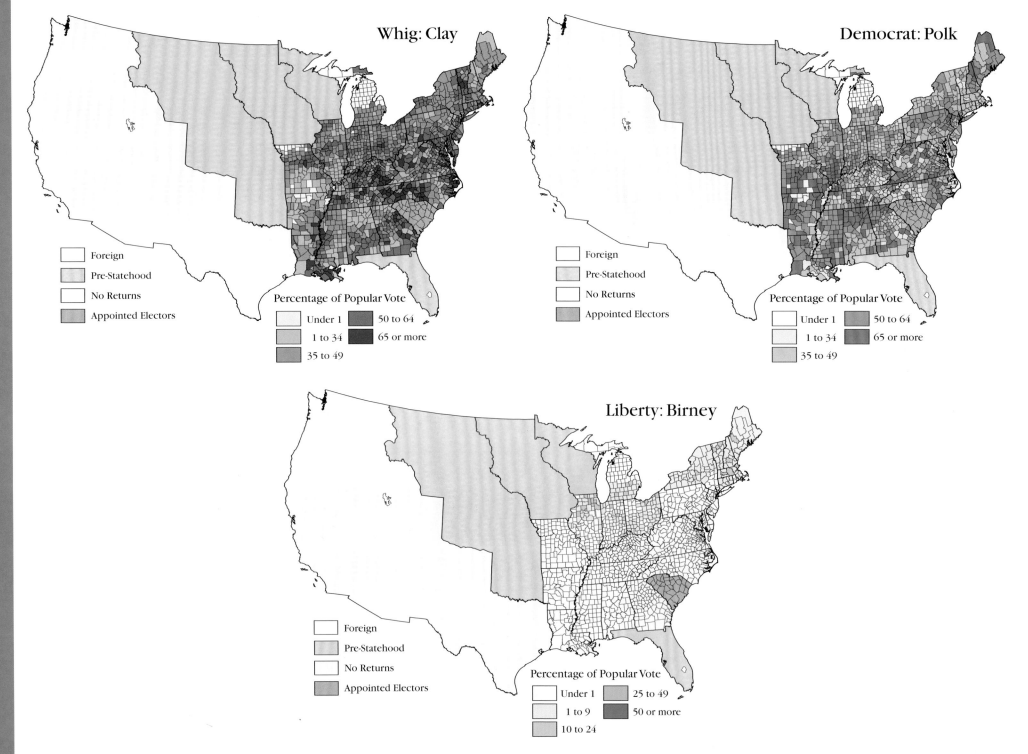

Whig: Clay

Foreign
Pre-Statehood
No Returns
Appointed Electors

Percentage of Popular Vote
Under 1   50 to 64
1 to 34   65 or more
35 to 49

Democrat: Polk

Foreign
Pre-Statehood
No Returns
Appointed Electors

Percentage of Popular Vote
Under 1   50 to 64
1 to 34   65 or more
35 to 49

Liberty: Birney

Foreign
Pre-Statehood
No Returns
Appointed Electors

Percentage of Popular Vote
Under 1   25 to 49
1 to 9   50 or more
10 to 24

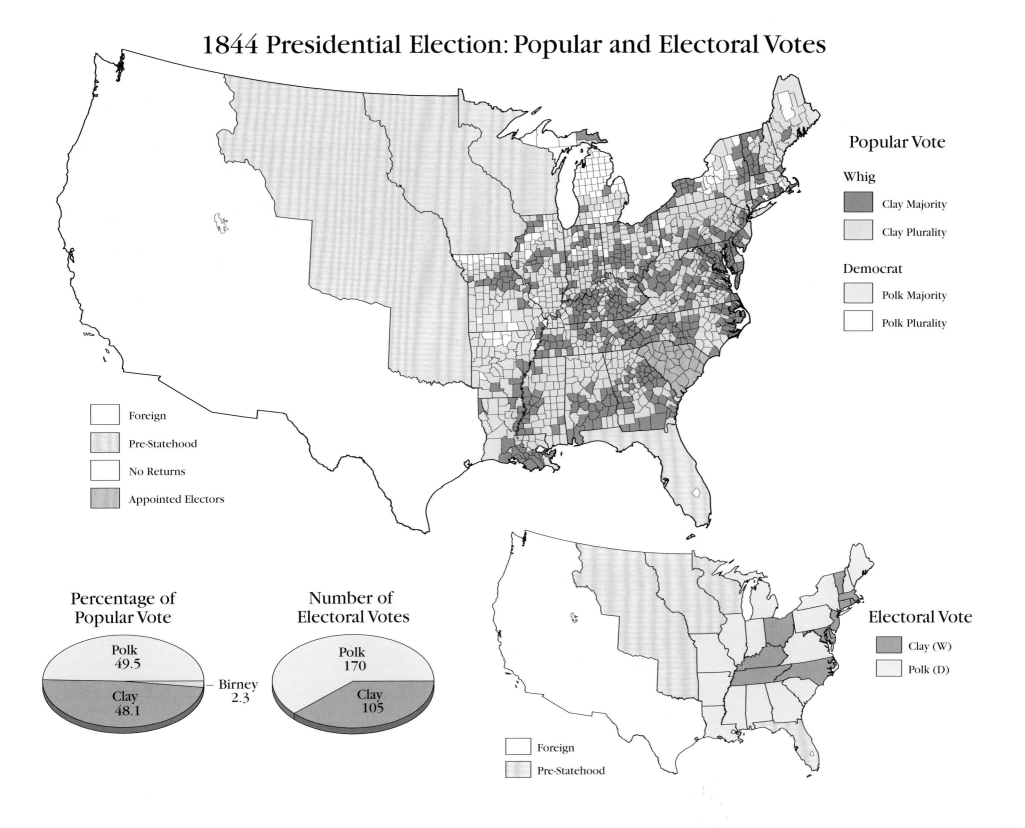

1844 Presidential Election: Popular and Electoral Votes

Map 15

Popular Vote

Whig
- Clay Majority
- Clay Plurality

Democrat
- Polk Majority
- Polk Plurality

- Foreign
- Pre-Statehood
- No Returns
- Appointed Electors

Percentage of Popular Vote
- Polk 49.5
- Clay 48.1
- Birney 2.3

Number of Electoral Votes
- Polk 170
- Clay 105

Electoral Vote
- Clay (W)
- Polk (D)

- Foreign
- Pre-Statehood

Map
16

1848 Presidential Election: Popular Support for Leading Candidates

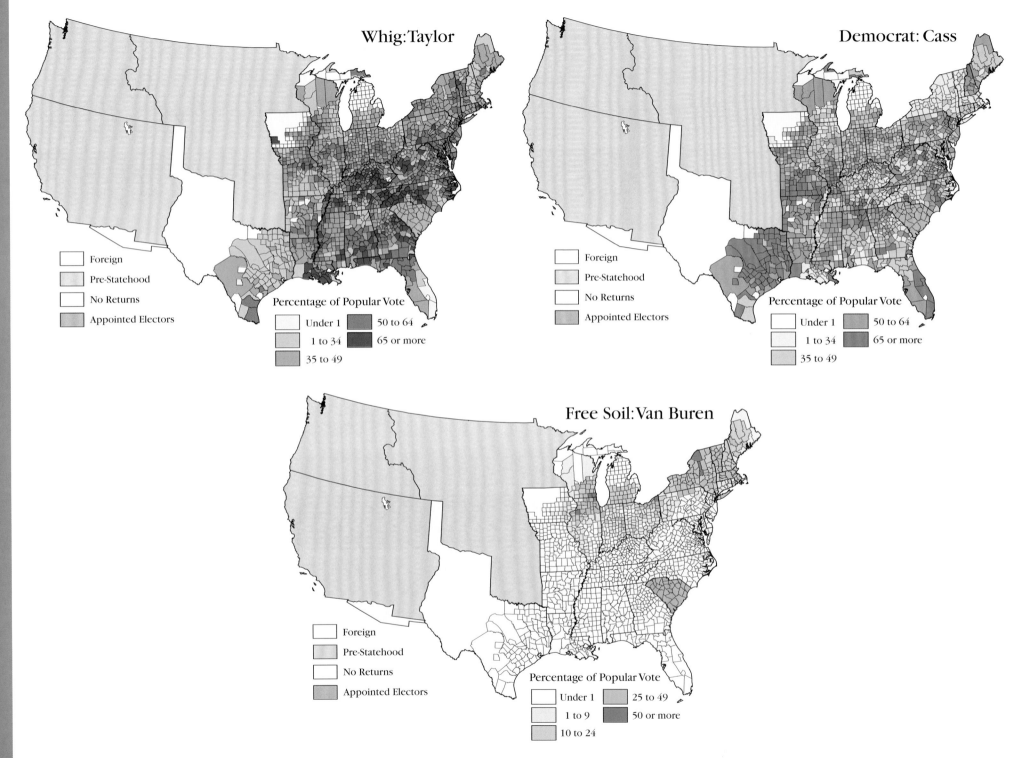

Whig: Taylor

Foreign
Pre-Statehood
No Returns
Appointed Electors

Percentage of Popular Vote
Under 1
1 to 34
35 to 49
50 to 64
65 or more

Democrat: Cass

Foreign
Pre-Statehood
No Returns
Appointed Electors

Percentage of Popular Vote
Under 1
1 to 34
35 to 49
50 to 64
65 or more

Free Soil: Van Buren

Foreign
Pre-Statehood
No Returns
Appointed Electors

Percentage of Popular Vote
Under 1
1 to 9
10 to 24
25 to 49
50 or more

Map 16

1848 Presidential Election: Popular and Electoral Votes

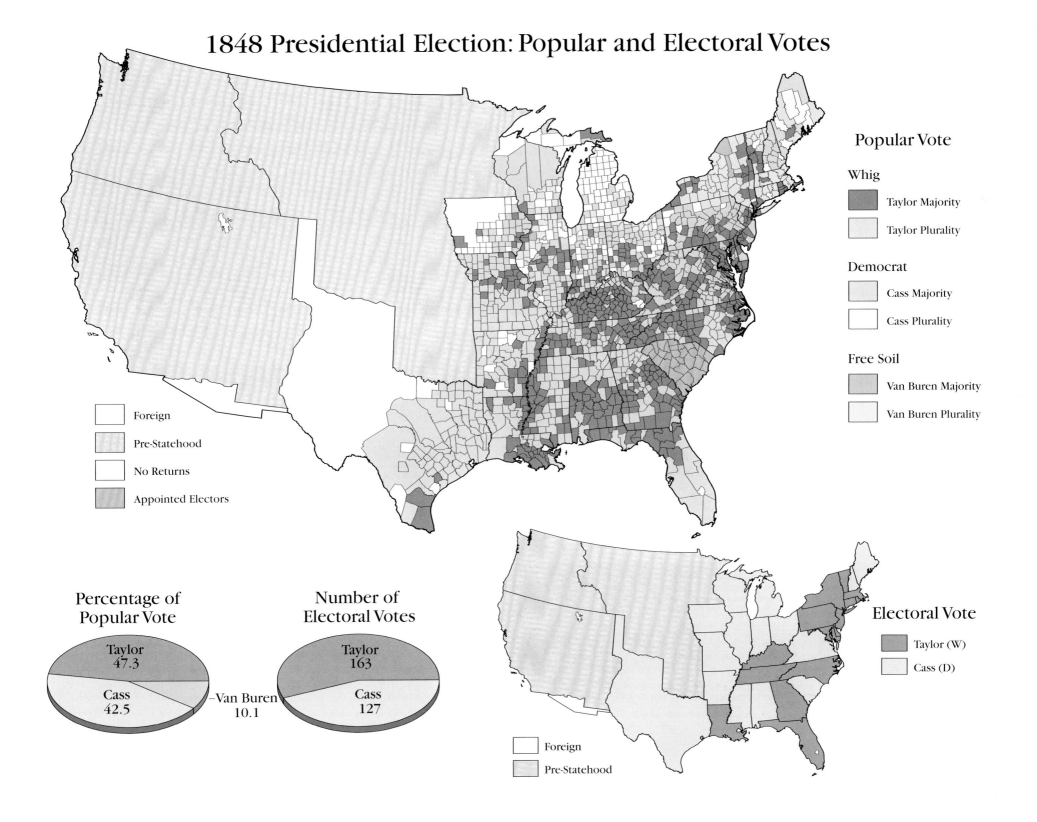

Popular Vote

Whig
- Taylor Majority
- Taylor Plurality

Democrat
- Cass Majority
- Cass Plurality

Free Soil
- Van Buren Majority
- Van Buren Plurality

Foreign

Pre-Statehood

No Returns

Appointed Electors

Percentage of Popular Vote

Taylor 47.3
Cass 42.5
Van Buren 10.1

Number of Electoral Votes

Taylor 163
Cass 127

Electoral Vote
- Taylor (W)
- Cass (D)

Foreign

Pre-Statehood

1852 Presidential Election: Popular Support for Leading Candidates

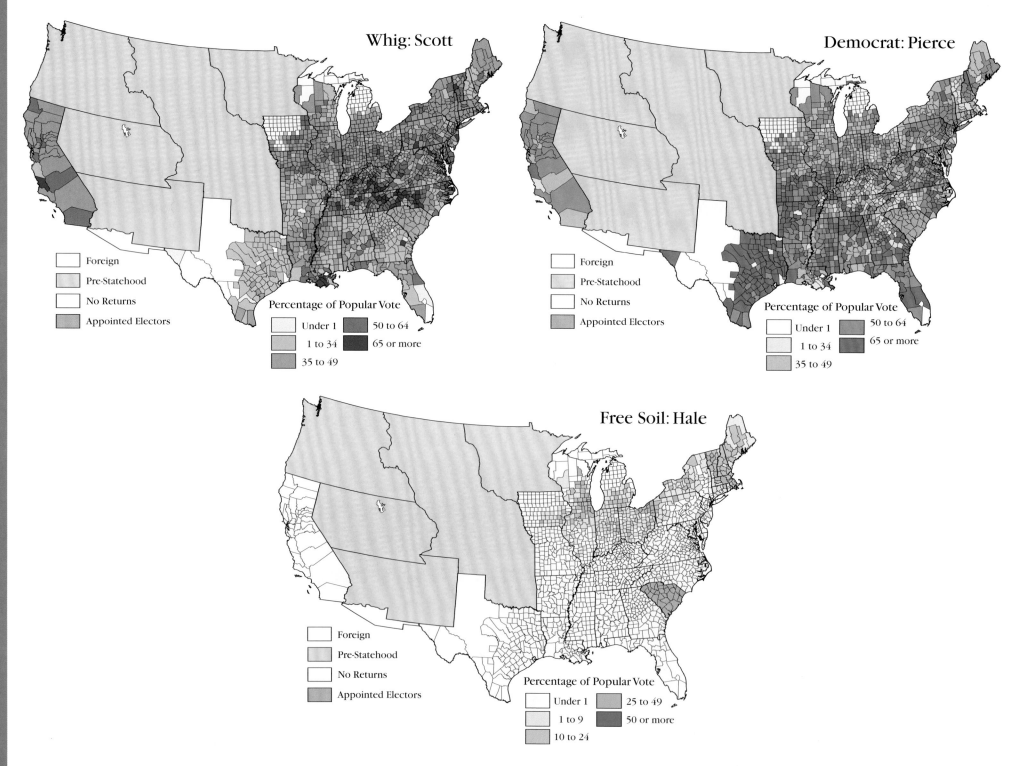

Map
17

Whig: Scott

Foreign
Pre-Statehood
No Returns
Appointed Electors

Percentage of Popular Vote

Under 1 — 50 to 64
1 to 34 — 65 or more
35 to 49

Democrat: Pierce

Foreign
Pre-Statehood
No Returns
Appointed Electors

Percentage of Popular Vote

Under 1 — 50 to 64
1 to 34 — 65 or more
35 to 49

Free Soil: Hale

Foreign
Pre-Statehood
No Returns
Appointed Electors

Percentage of Popular Vote

Under 1 — 25 to 49
1 to 9 — 50 or more
10 to 24

1852 Presidential Election: Popular and Electoral Votes

Map 17

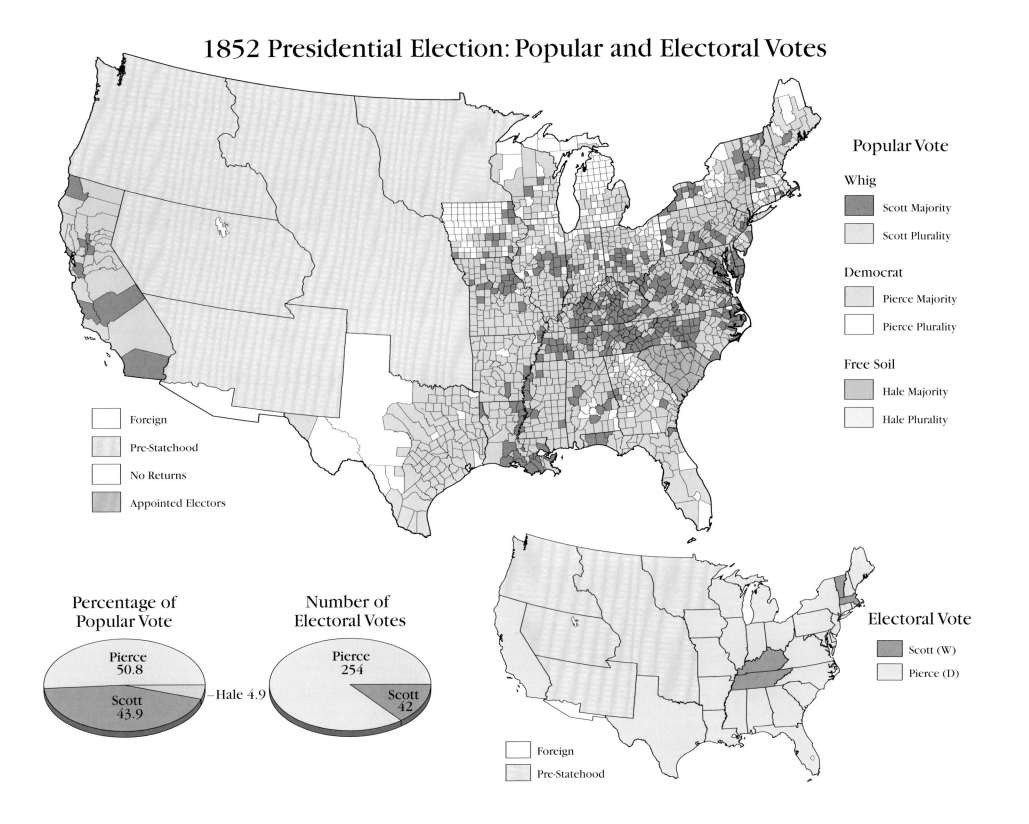

Popular Vote

Whig
- Scott Majority
- Scott Plurality

Democrat
- Pierce Majority
- Pierce Plurality

Free Soil
- Hale Majority
- Hale Plurality

- Foreign
- Pre-Statehood
- No Returns
- Appointed Electors

Percentage of Popular Vote

Pierce 50.8
Scott 43.9
– Hale 4.9

Number of Electoral Votes

Pierce 254
Scott 42

Electoral Vote
- Scott (W)
- Pierce (D)

- Foreign
- Pre-Statehood

Map
18

1856 Presidential Election: Popular Support for Leading Candidates

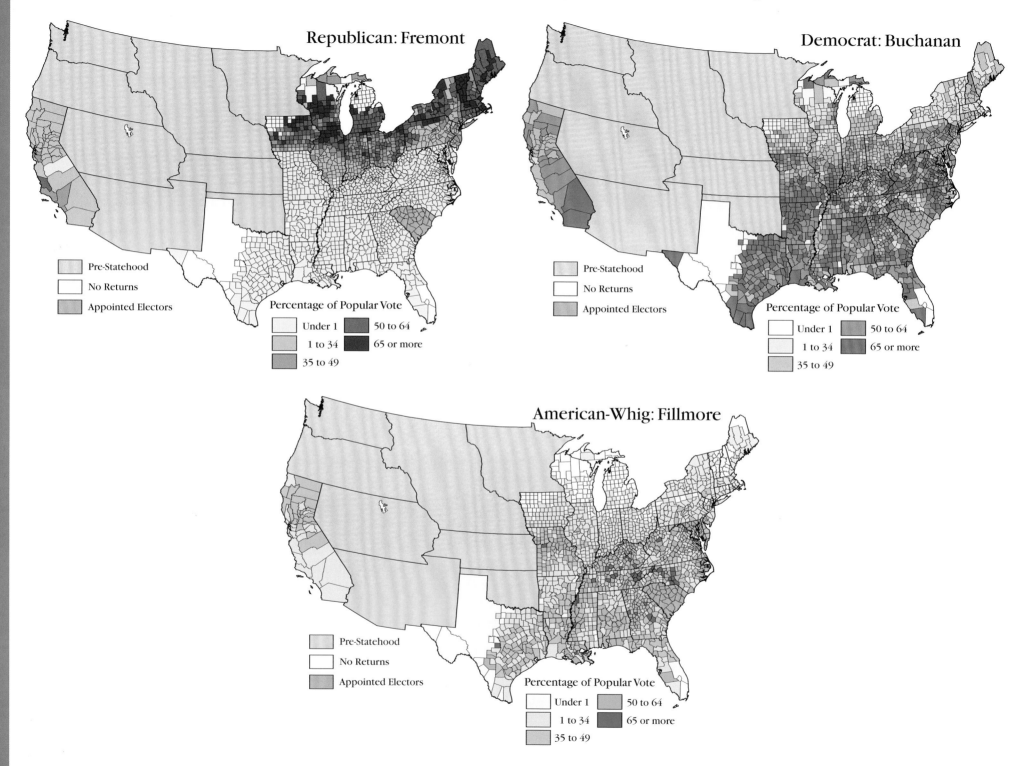

Republican: Fremont

Pre-Statehood
No Returns
Appointed Electors

Percentage of Popular Vote
Under 1
1 to 34
35 to 49
50 to 64
65 or more

Democrat: Buchanan

Pre-Statehood
No Returns
Appointed Electors

Percentage of Popular Vote
Under 1
1 to 34
35 to 49
50 to 64
65 or more

American-Whig: Fillmore

Pre-Statehood
No Returns
Appointed Electors

Percentage of Popular Vote
Under 1
1 to 34
35 to 49
50 to 64
65 or more

1856 Presidential Election: Popular and Electoral Votes

Map 18

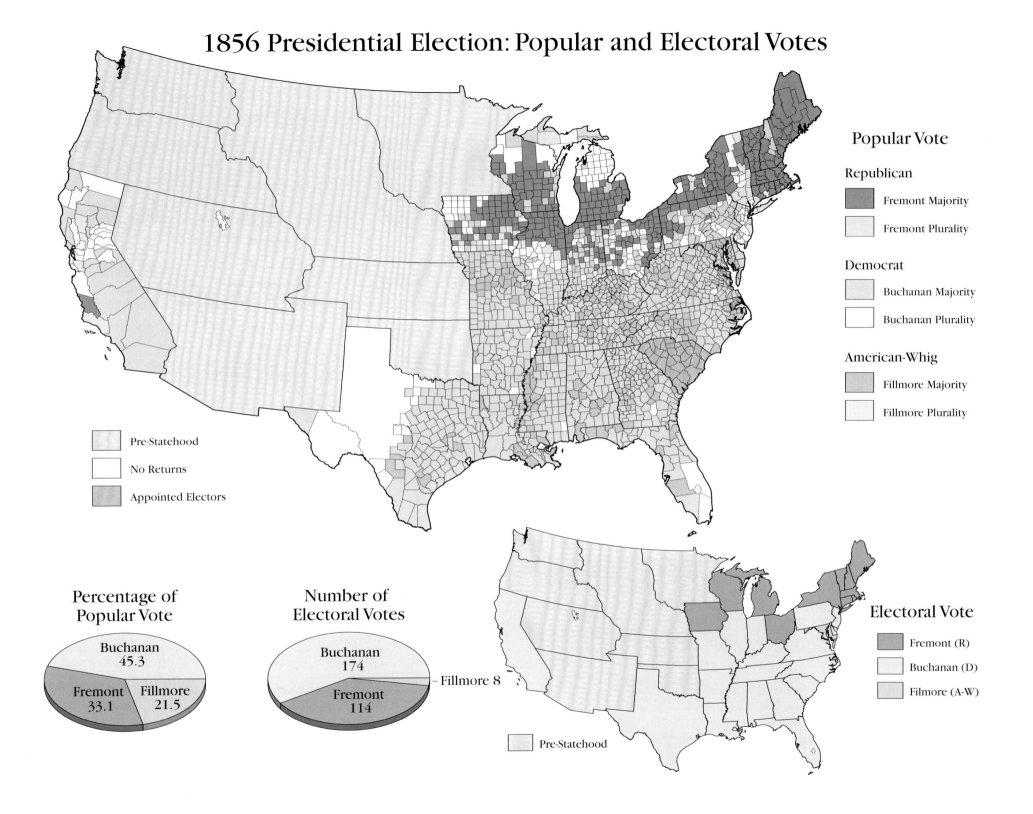

Popular Vote

Republican
- Fremont Majority
- Fremont Plurality

Democrat
- Buchanan Majority
- Buchanan Plurality

American-Whig
- Fillmore Majority
- Fillmore Plurality

- Pre-Statehood
- No Returns
- Appointed Electors

Percentage of Popular Vote

Buchanan 45.3
Fremont 33.1
Fillmore 21.5

Number of Electoral Votes

Buchanan 174
Fremont 114
Fillmore 8

Electoral Vote
- Fremont (R)
- Buchanan (D)
- Filmore (A-W)

- Pre-Statehood

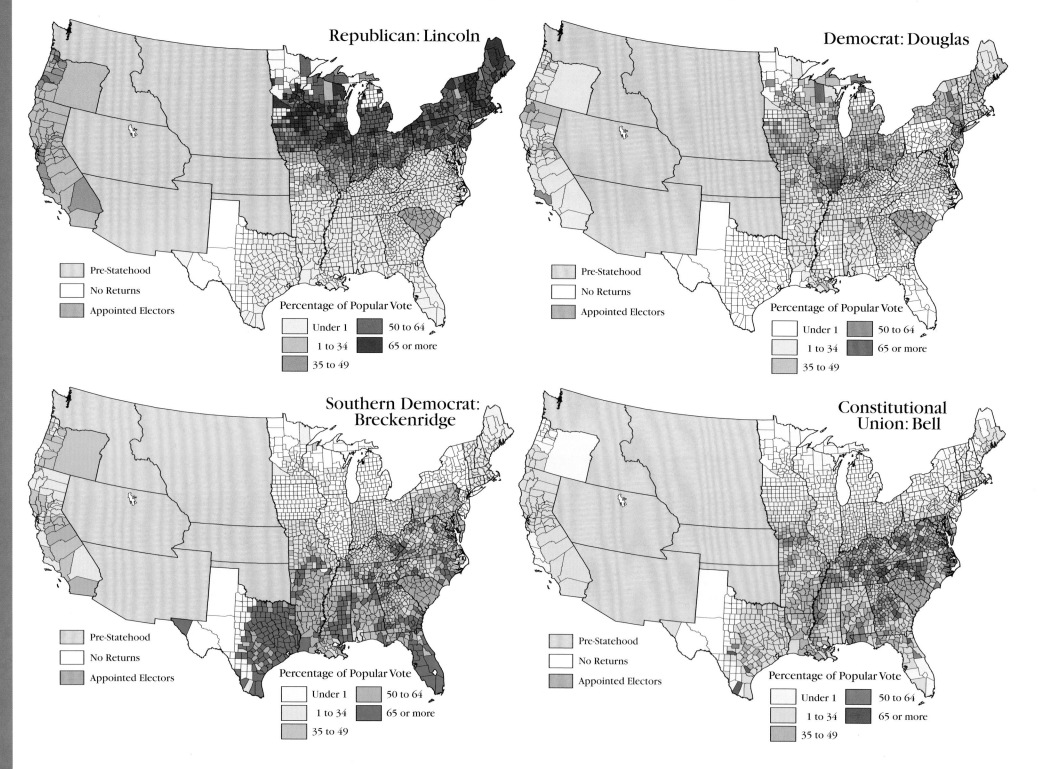

Map
19

1860 Presidential Election: Popular Vote for Leading Candidates

Republican: Lincoln

Pre-Statehood
No Returns
Appointed Electors

Percentage of Popular Vote
Under 1   50 to 64
1 to 34   65 or more
35 to 49

Democrat: Douglas

Pre-Statehood
No Returns
Appointed Electors

Percentage of Popular Vote
Under 1   50 to 64
1 to 34   65 or more
35 to 49

Southern Democrat: Breckenridge

Pre-Statehood
No Returns
Appointed Electors

Percentage of Popular Vote
Under 1   50 to 64
1 to 34   65 or more
35 to 49

Constitutional Union: Bell

Pre-Statehood
No Returns
Appointed Electors

Percentage of Popular Vote
Under 1   50 to 64
1 to 34   65 or more
35 to 49

1860 Presidential Election: Popular and Electoral Votes

Map 19

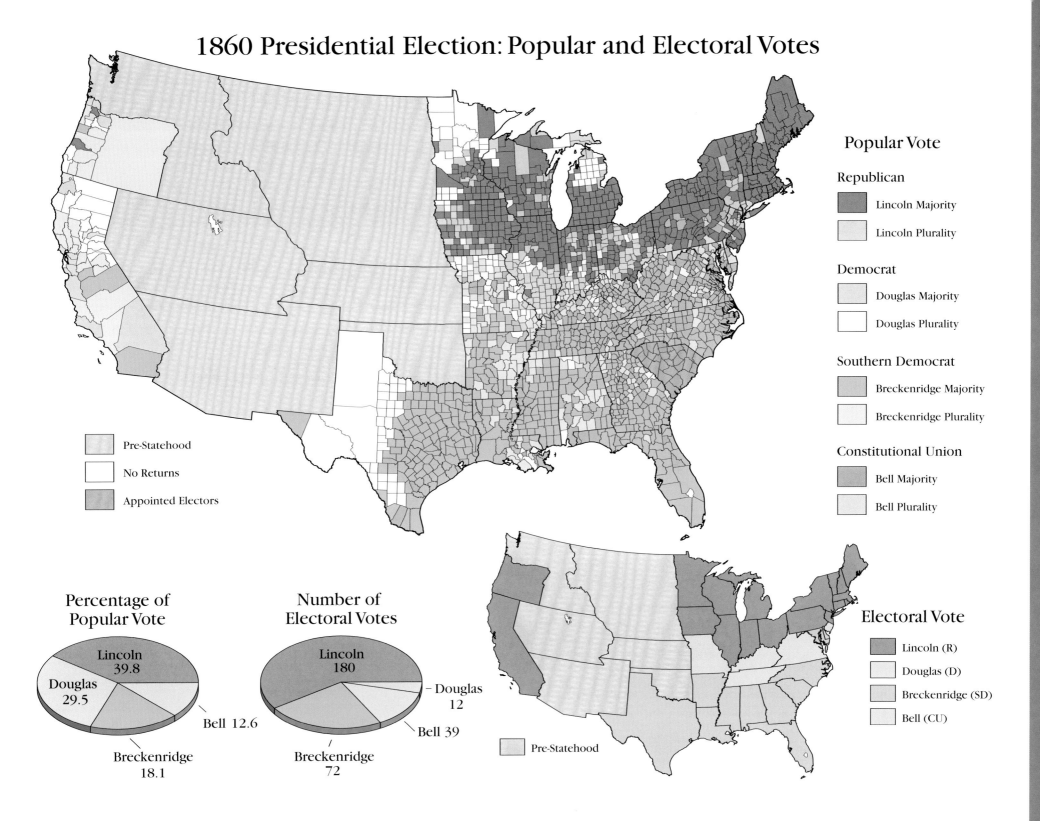

Popular Vote

Republican
- Lincoln Majority
- Lincoln Plurality

Democrat
- Douglas Majority
- Douglas Plurality

Southern Democrat
- Breckenridge Majority
- Breckenridge Plurality

Constitutional Union
- Bell Majority
- Bell Plurality

- Pre-Statehood
- No Returns
- Appointed Electors

Electoral Vote
- Lincoln (R)
- Douglas (D)
- Breckenridge (SD)
- Bell (CU)

- Pre-Statehood

Percentage of Popular Vote

- Lincoln 39.8
- Douglas 29.5
- Bell 12.6
- Breckenridge 18.1

Number of Electoral Votes

- Lincoln 180
- Douglas 12
- Bell 39
- Breckenridge 72

Map 20

1864 Presidential Election: Popular Support for Leading Candidates

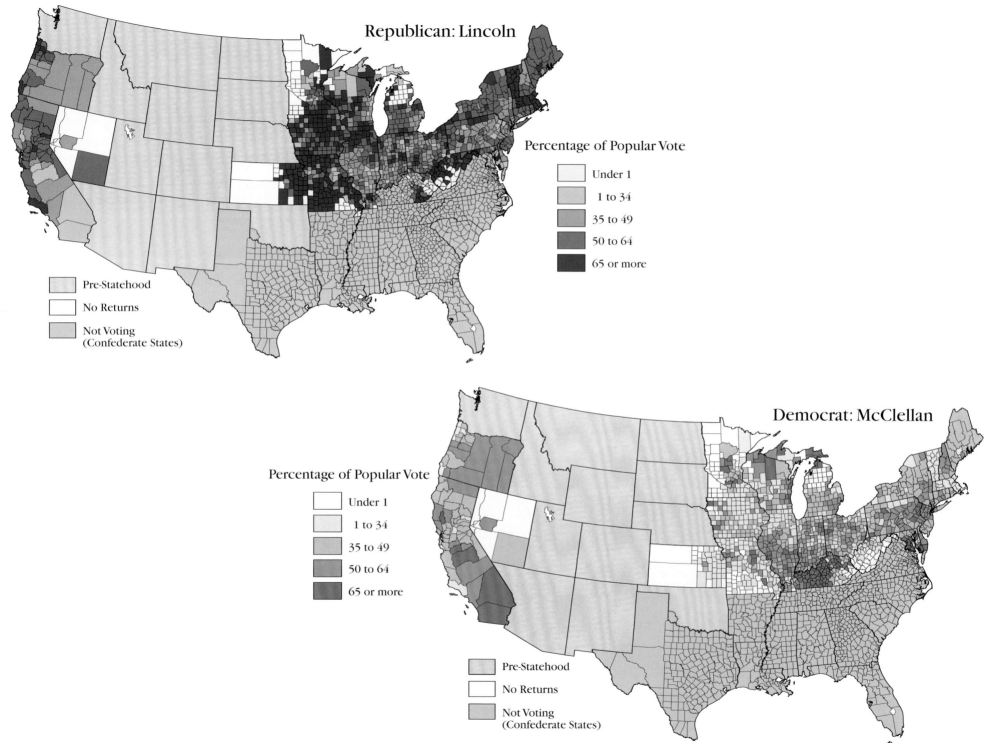

Republican: Lincoln

Percentage of Popular Vote

- Under 1
- 1 to 34
- 35 to 49
- 50 to 64
- 65 or more

- Pre-Statehood
- No Returns
- Not Voting (Confederate States)

Democrat: McClellan

Percentage of Popular Vote

- Under 1
- 1 to 34
- 35 to 49
- 50 to 64
- 65 or more

- Pre-Statehood
- No Returns
- Not Voting (Confederate States)

1864 Presidential Election: Popular and Electoral Votes

Map
20

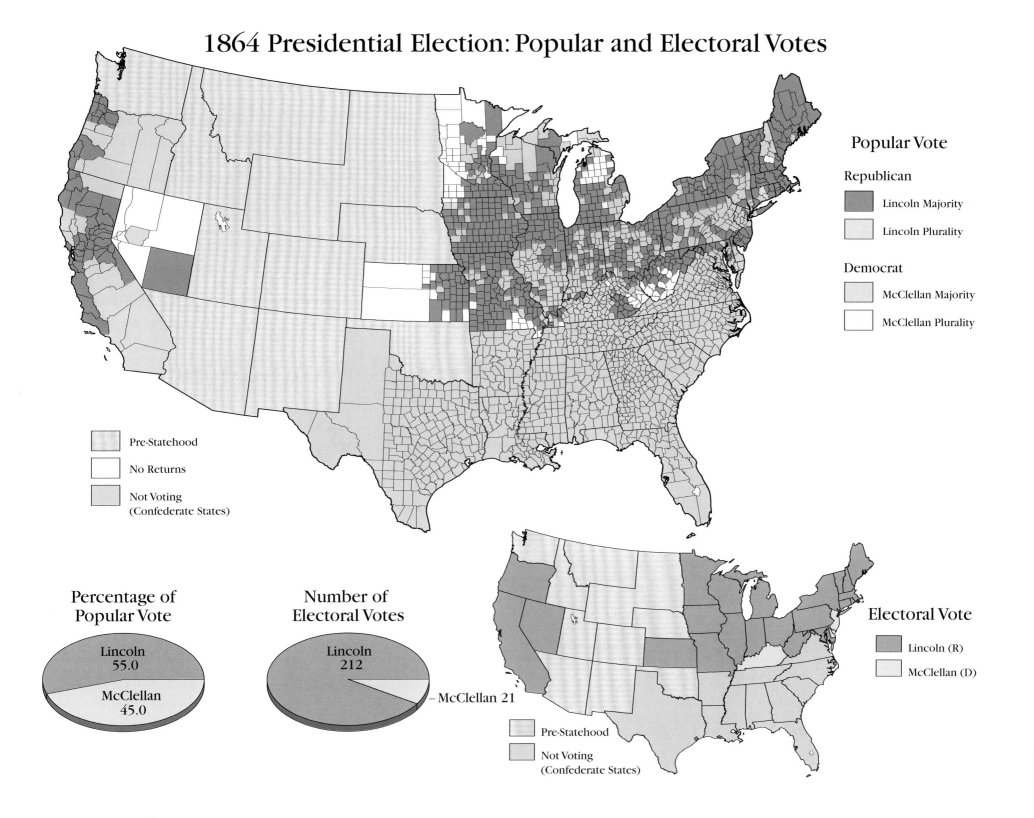

Popular Vote

Republican

- Lincoln Majority
- Lincoln Plurality

Democrat

- McClellan Majority
- McClellan Plurality

Pre-Statehood

No Returns

Not Voting
(Confederate States)

Percentage of Popular Vote

Lincoln 55.0

McClellan 45.0

Number of Electoral Votes

Lincoln 212

– McClellan 21

Electoral Vote

- Lincoln (R)
- McClellan (D)

Pre-Statehood

Not Voting
(Confederate States)

Map
21

1868 Presidential Election: Popular Support for Leading Candidates

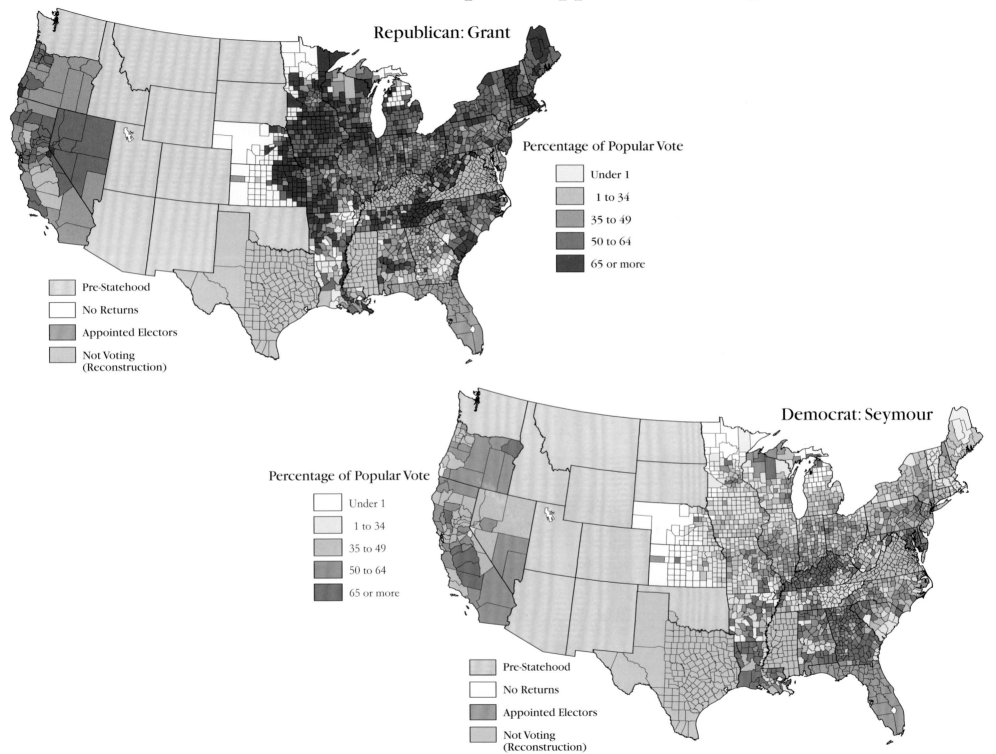

Republican: Grant

Percentage of Popular Vote

- Under 1
- 1 to 34
- 35 to 49
- 50 to 64
- 65 or more

- Pre-Statehood
- No Returns
- Appointed Electors
- Not Voting (Reconstruction)

Democrat: Seymour

Percentage of Popular Vote

- Under 1
- 1 to 34
- 35 to 49
- 50 to 64
- 65 or more

- Pre-Statehood
- No Returns
- Appointed Electors
- Not Voting (Reconstruction)

1868 Presidential Election: Popular and Electoral Votes

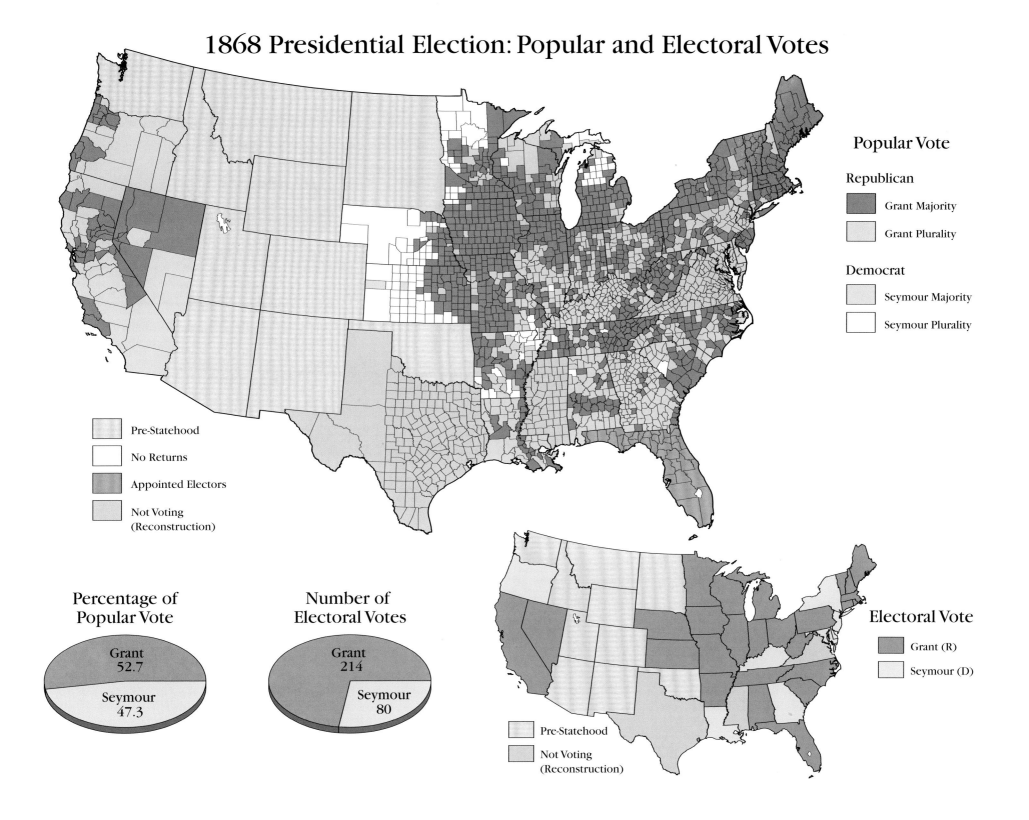

Map
21

Popular Vote

Republican

Grant Majority

Grant Plurality

Democrat

Seymour Majority

Seymour Plurality

Pre-Statehood

No Returns

Appointed Electors

Not Voting
(Reconstruction)

**Percentage of
Popular Vote**

Grant
52.7

Seymour
47.3

**Number of
Electoral Votes**

Grant
214

Seymour
80

Electoral Vote

Grant (R)

Seymour (D)

Pre-Statehood

Not Voting
(Reconstruction)

Map
22

1872 Presidential Election: Popular Support for Leading Candidates

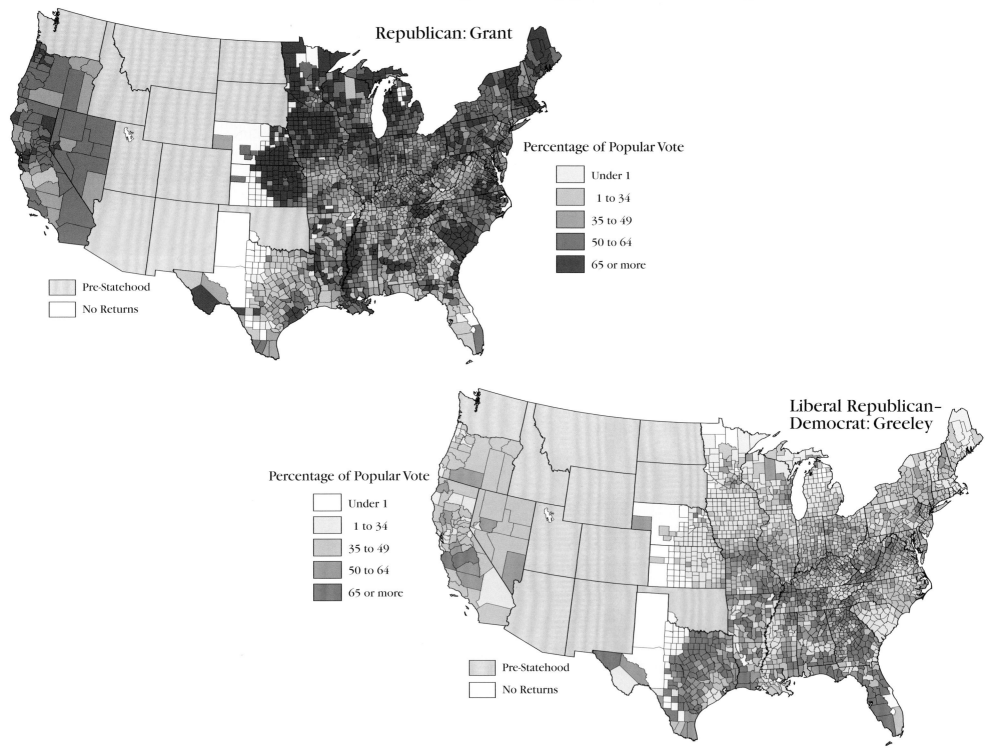

Republican: Grant

Percentage of Popular Vote

Under 1

1 to 34

35 to 49

50 to 64

65 or more

Pre-Statehood

No Returns

Liberal Republican–
Democrat: Greeley

Percentage of Popular Vote

Under 1

1 to 34

35 to 49

50 to 64

65 or more

Pre-Statehood

No Returns

Map
22

1872 Presidential Election: Popular and Electoral Votes

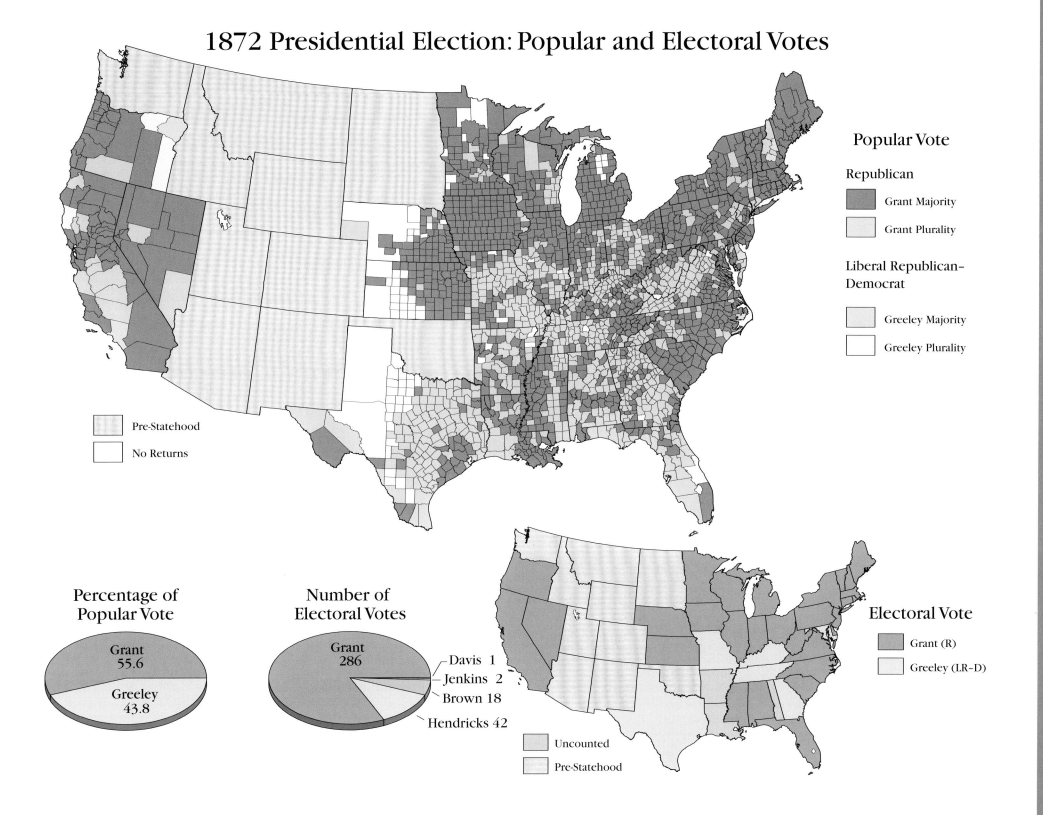

Popular Vote

Republican

- Grant Majority
- Grant Plurality

Liberal Republican–
Democrat

- Greeley Majority
- Greeley Plurality

- Pre-Statehood
- No Returns

**Percentage of
Popular Vote**

- Grant 55.6
- Greeley 43.8

**Number of
Electoral Votes**

- Grant 286
- Davis 1
- Jenkins 2
- Brown 18
- Hendricks 42

Electoral Vote

- Grant (R)
- Greeley (LR–D)

- Uncounted
- Pre-Statehood

1876 Presidential Election: Popular Support for Leading Candidates

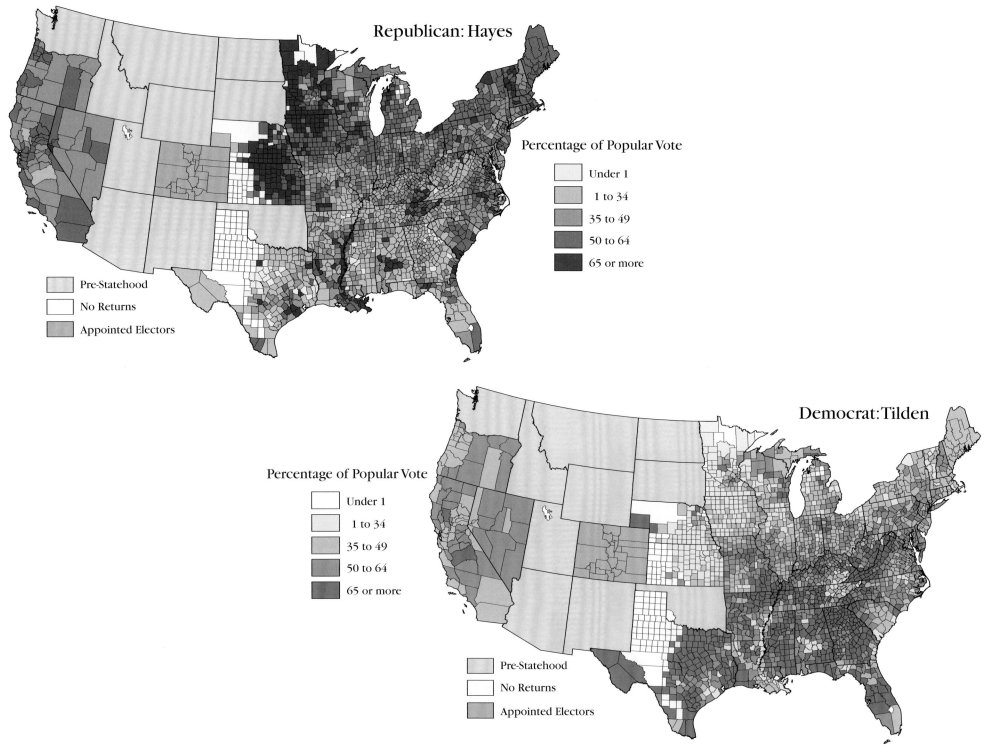

Map 23

Republican: Hayes

Percentage of Popular Vote
- Under 1
- 1 to 34
- 35 to 49
- 50 to 64
- 65 or more

- Pre-Statehood
- No Returns
- Appointed Electors

Democrat: Tilden

Percentage of Popular Vote
- Under 1
- 1 to 34
- 35 to 49
- 50 to 64
- 65 or more

- Pre-Statehood
- No Returns
- Appointed Electors

1876 Presidential Election: Popular and Electoral Votes

Map 23

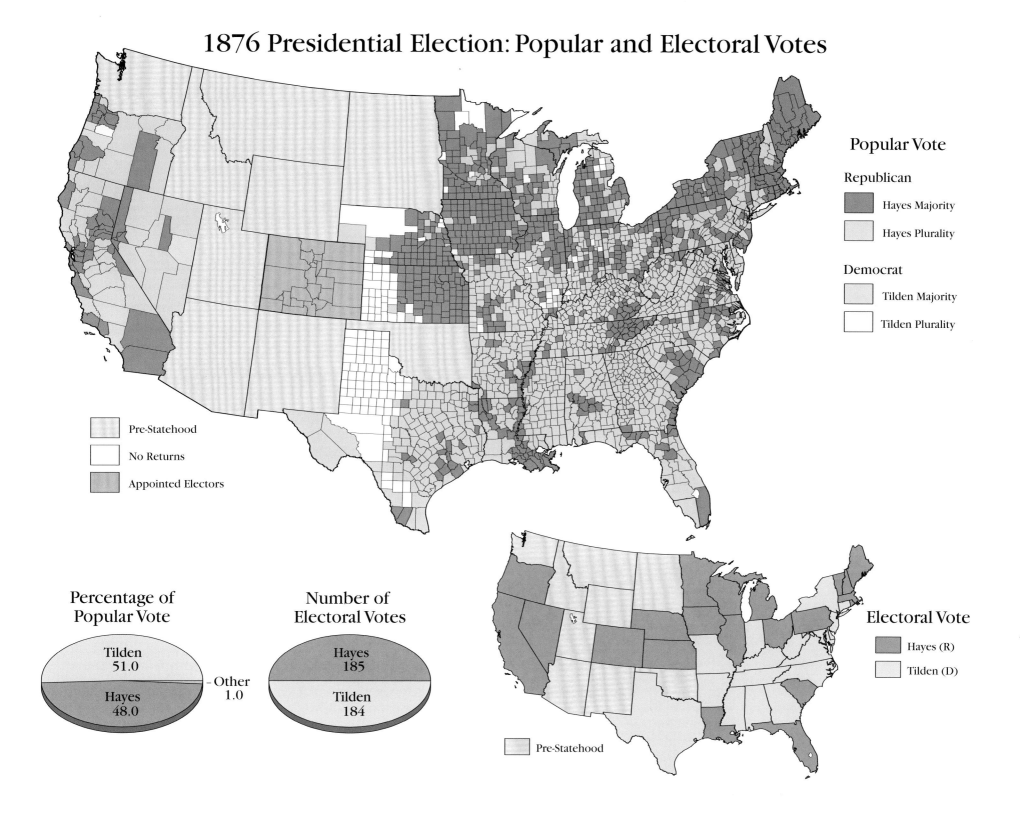

Popular Vote

Republican
- Hayes Majority
- Hayes Plurality

Democrat
- Tilden Majority
- Tilden Plurality

Pre-Statehood
No Returns
Appointed Electors

Percentage of Popular Vote

Tilden 51.0
Hayes 48.0
Other 1.0

Number of Electoral Votes

Hayes 185
Tilden 184

Electoral Vote

- Hayes (R)
- Tilden (D)

Pre-Statehood

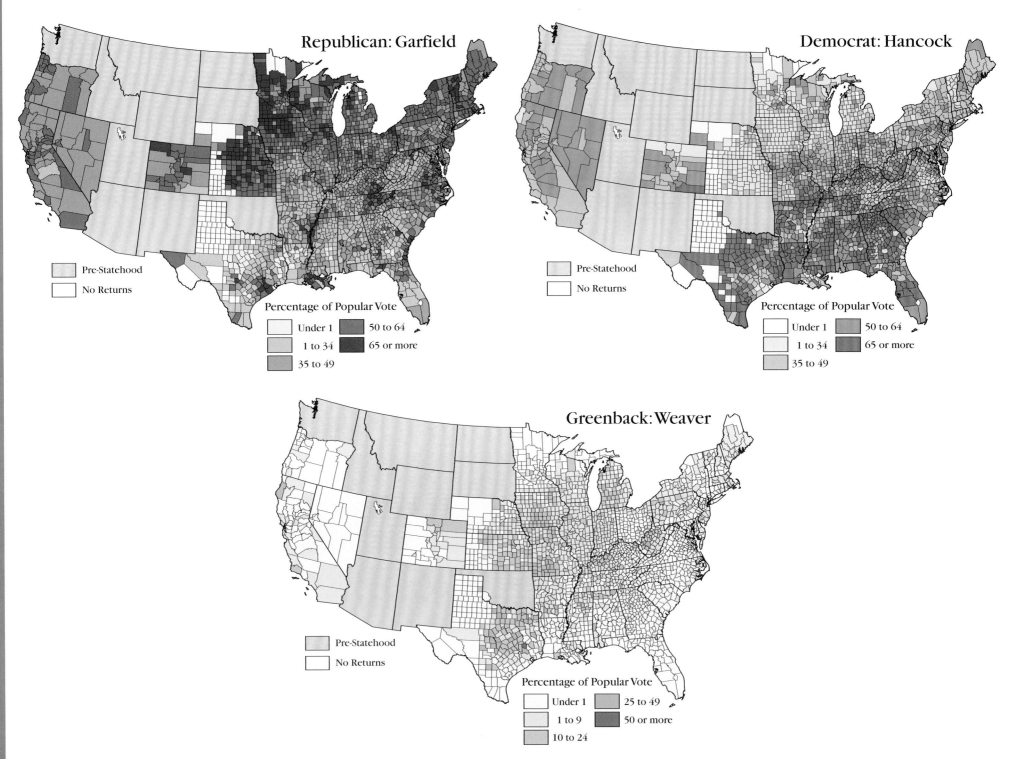

1880 Presidential Election: Popular Support for Leading Candidates

Map 24

Republican: Garfield

Pre-Statehood
No Returns

Percentage of Popular Vote
Under 1
1 to 34
35 to 49
50 to 64
65 or more

Democrat: Hancock

Pre-Statehood
No Returns

Percentage of Popular Vote
Under 1
1 to 34
35 to 49
50 to 64
65 or more

Greenback: Weaver

Pre-Statehood
No Returns

Percentage of Popular Vote
Under 1
1 to 9
10 to 24
25 to 49
50 or more

1880 Presidential Election: Popular and Electoral Votes

Map 24

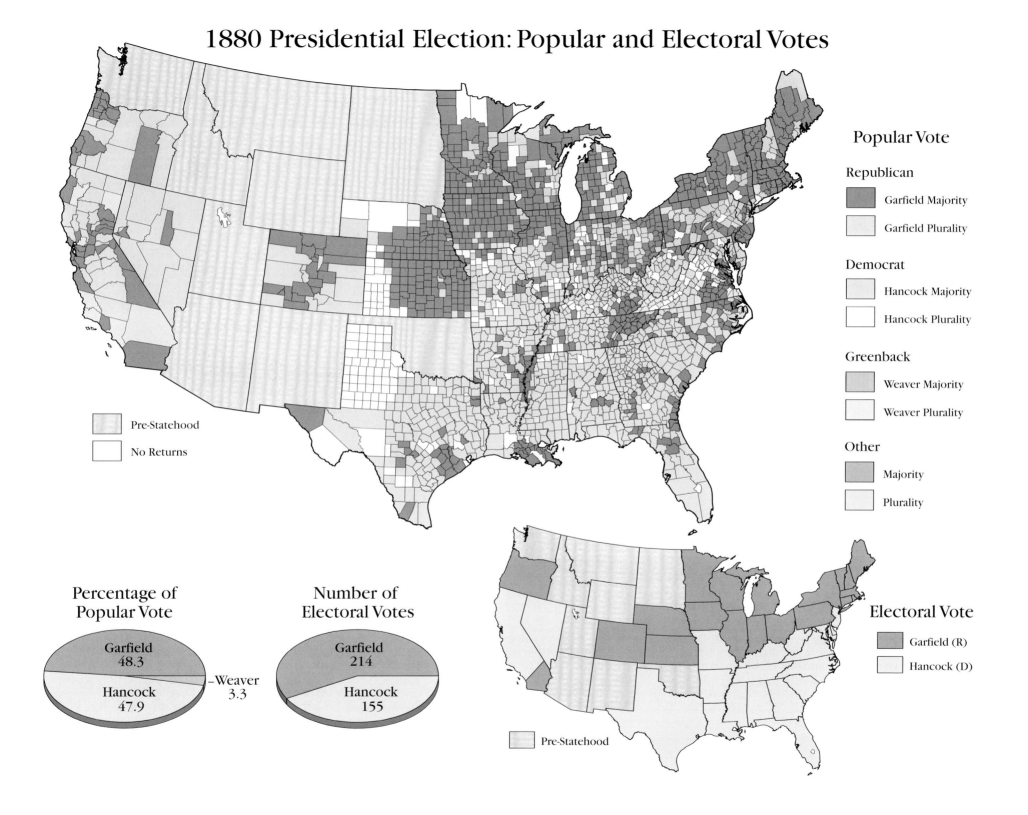

Popular Vote

Republican
- Garfield Majority
- Garfield Plurality

Democrat
- Hancock Majority
- Hancock Plurality

Greenback
- Weaver Majority
- Weaver Plurality

Other
- Majority
- Plurality

- Pre-Statehood
- No Returns

Percentage of Popular Vote

Garfield 48.3
Hancock 47.9
Weaver 3.3

Number of Electoral Votes

Garfield 214
Hancock 155

Electoral Vote
- Garfield (R)
- Hancock (D)

- Pre-Statehood

1884 Presidential Election: Popular Support for Leading Candidates

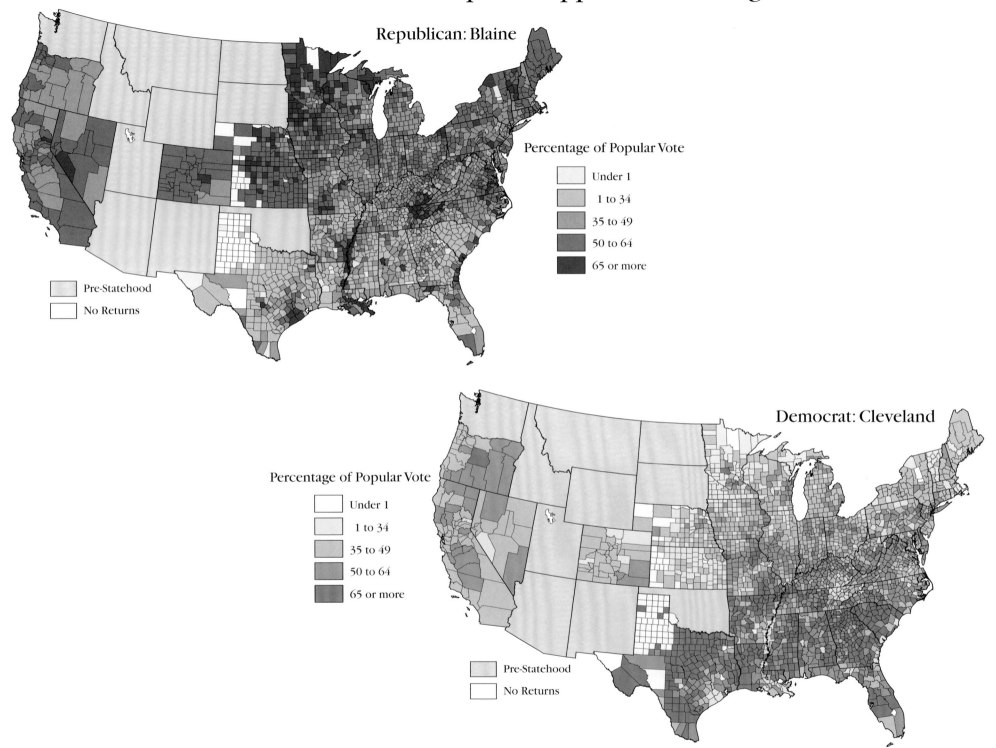

Map 25

Republican: Blaine

Percentage of Popular Vote

- Under 1
- 1 to 34
- 35 to 49
- 50 to 64
- 65 or more

Pre-Statehood

No Returns

Democrat: Cleveland

Percentage of Popular Vote

- Under 1
- 1 to 34
- 35 to 49
- 50 to 64
- 65 or more

Pre-Statehood

No Returns

1884 Presidential Election: Popular and Electoral Votes

Map 25

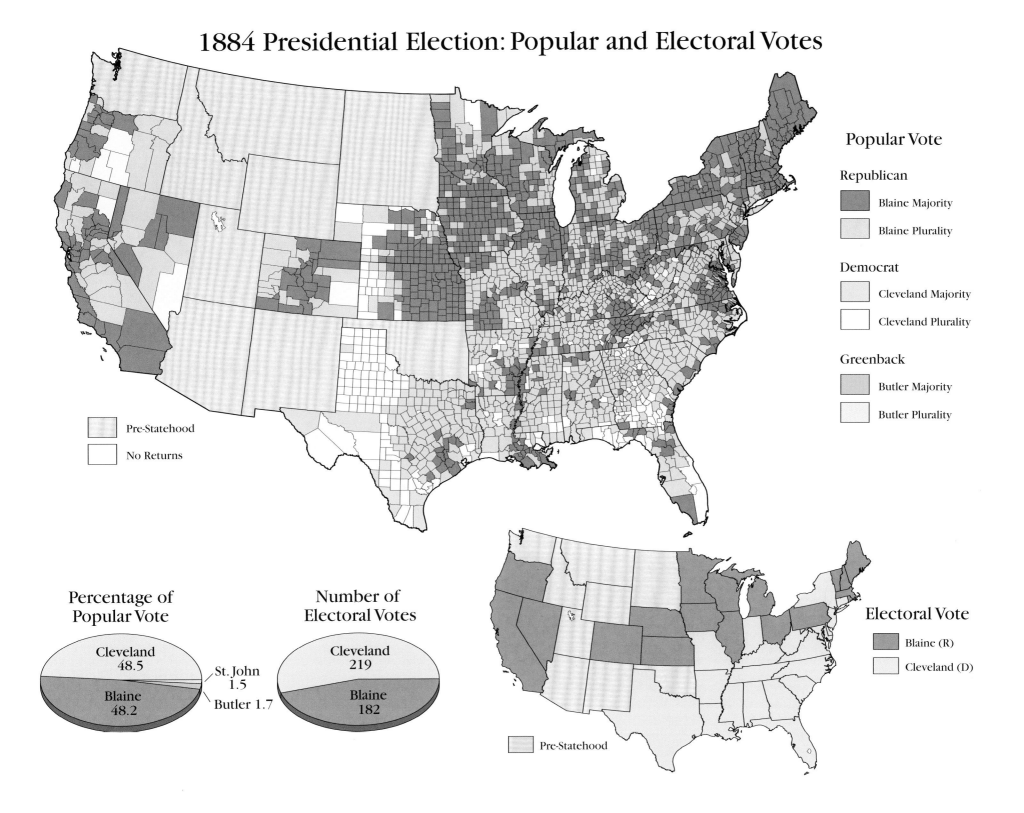

Popular Vote

Republican
- Blaine Majority
- Blaine Plurality

Democrat
- Cleveland Majority
- Cleveland Plurality

Greenback
- Butler Majority
- Butler Plurality

Pre-Statehood

No Returns

Percentage of Popular Vote

Cleveland 48.5
Blaine 48.2
St. John 1.5
Butler 1.7

Number of Electoral Votes

Cleveland 219
Blaine 182

Electoral Vote
- Blaine (R)
- Cleveland (D)

Pre-Statehood

Map
26

1888 Presidential Election: Popular Support for Leading Candidates

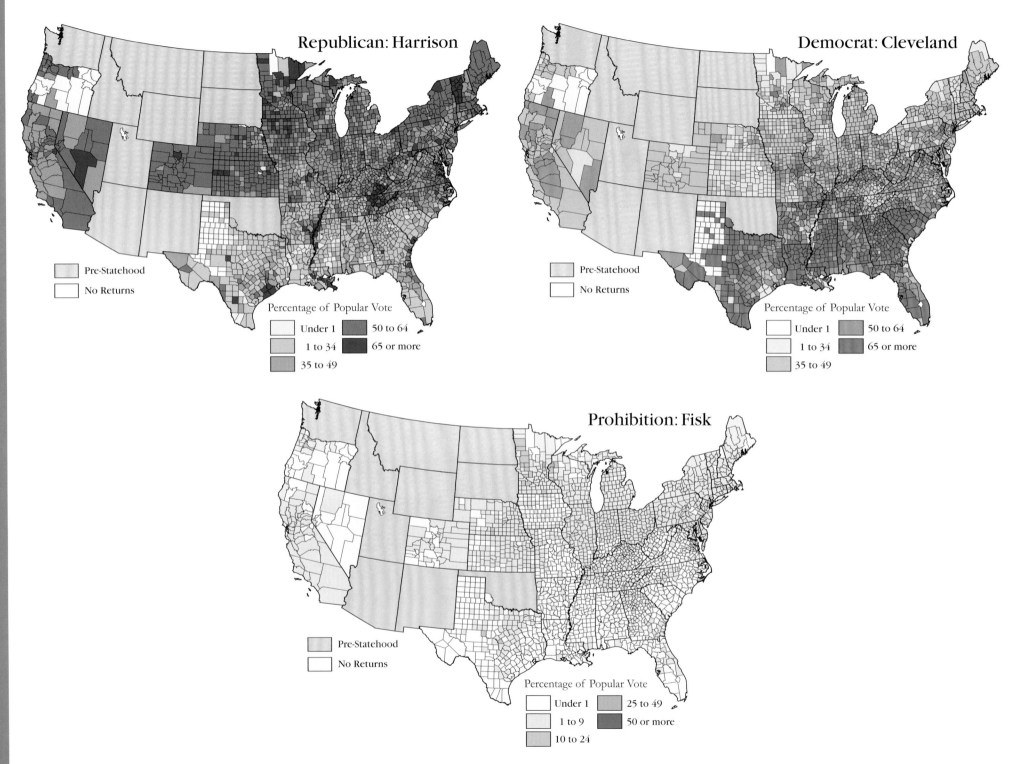

Republican: Harrison

Pre-Statehood

No Returns

Percentage of Popular Vote

Under 1   50 to 64

1 to 34   65 or more

35 to 49

Democrat: Cleveland

Pre-Statehood

No Returns

Percentage of Popular Vote

Under 1   50 to 64

1 to 34   65 or more

35 to 49

Prohibition: Fisk

Pre-Statehood

No Returns

Percentage of Popular Vote

Under 1   25 to 49

1 to 9   50 or more

10 to 24

1888 Presidential Election: Popular and Electoral Votes

Map 26

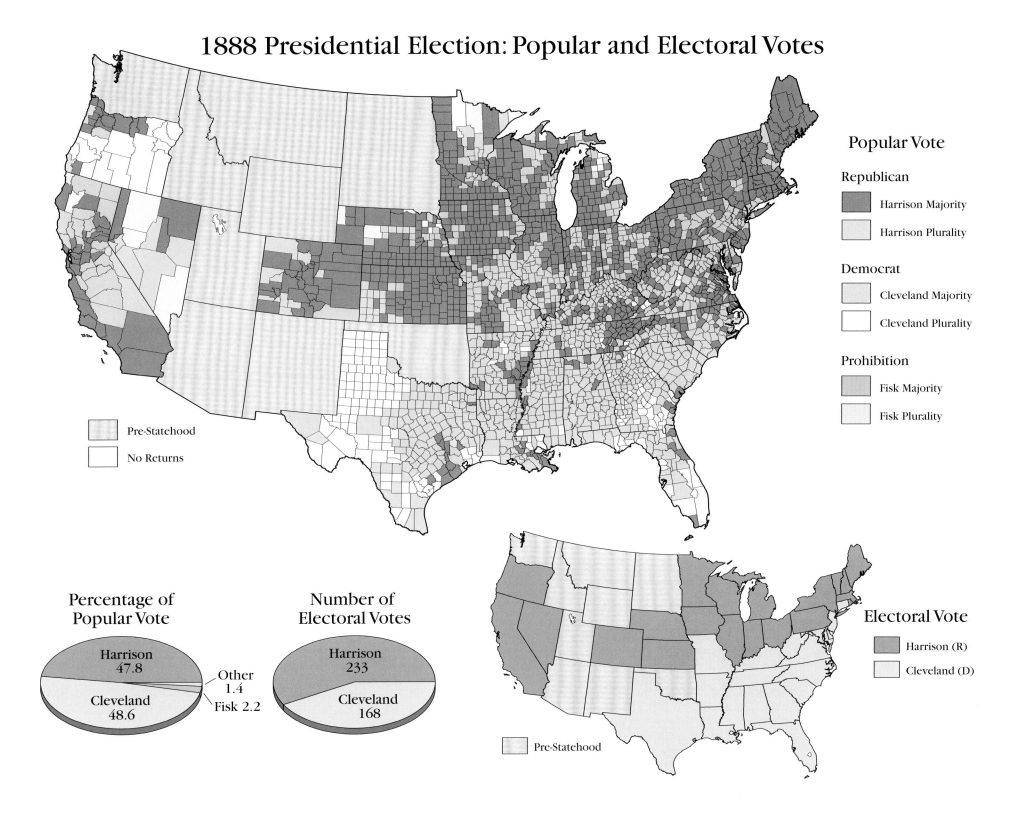

Popular Vote

Republican

- Harrison Majority
- Harrison Plurality

Democrat

- Cleveland Majority
- Cleveland Plurality

Prohibition

- Fisk Majority
- Fisk Plurality

- Pre-Statehood
- No Returns

Percentage of Popular Vote

Harrison 47.8
Cleveland 48.6
Other 1.4
Fisk 2.2

Number of Electoral Votes

Harrison 233
Cleveland 168

Electoral Vote

- Harrison (R)
- Cleveland (D)

- Pre-Statehood

Map
27

1892 Presidential Election: Popular Support for Leading Candidates

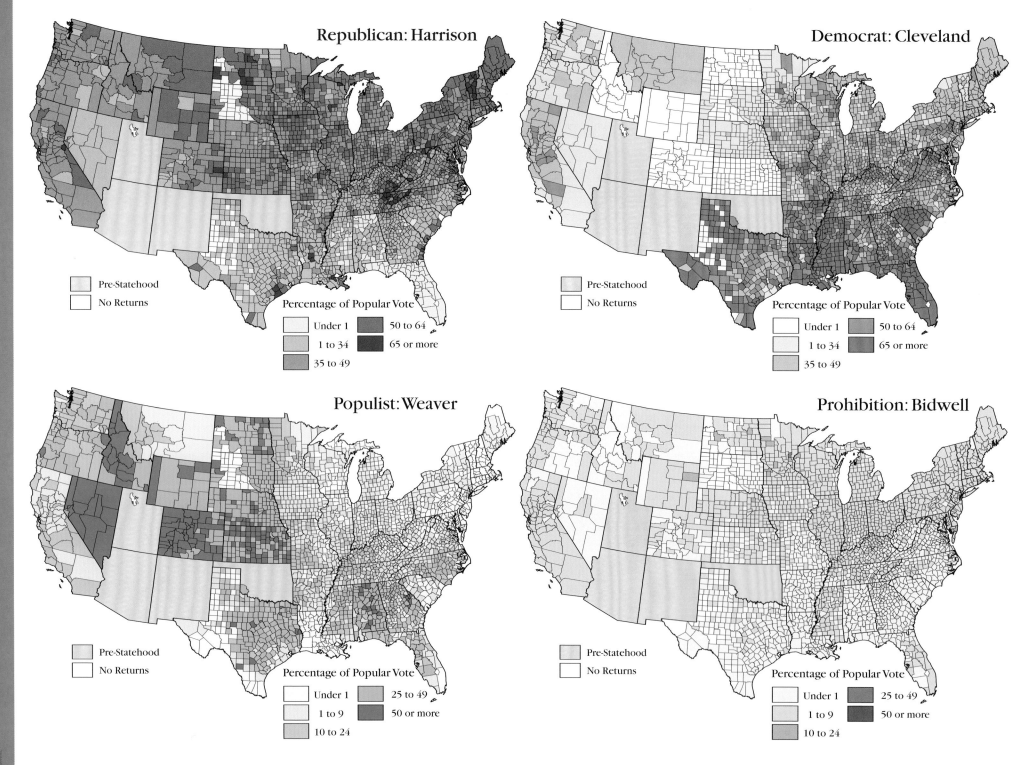

Republican: Harrison

Pre-Statehood
No Returns

Percentage of Popular Vote

Under 1   50 to 64
1 to 34   65 or more
35 to 49

Democrat: Cleveland

Pre-Statehood
No Returns

Percentage of Popular Vote

Under 1   50 to 64
1 to 34   65 or more
35 to 49

Populist: Weaver

Pre-Statehood
No Returns

Percentage of Popular Vote

Under 1   25 to 49
1 to 9   50 or more
10 to 24

Prohibition: Bidwell

Pre-Statehood
No Returns

Percentage of Popular Vote

Under 1   25 to 49
1 to 9   50 or more
10 to 24

1892 Presidential Election: Popular and Electoral Votes

Map 27

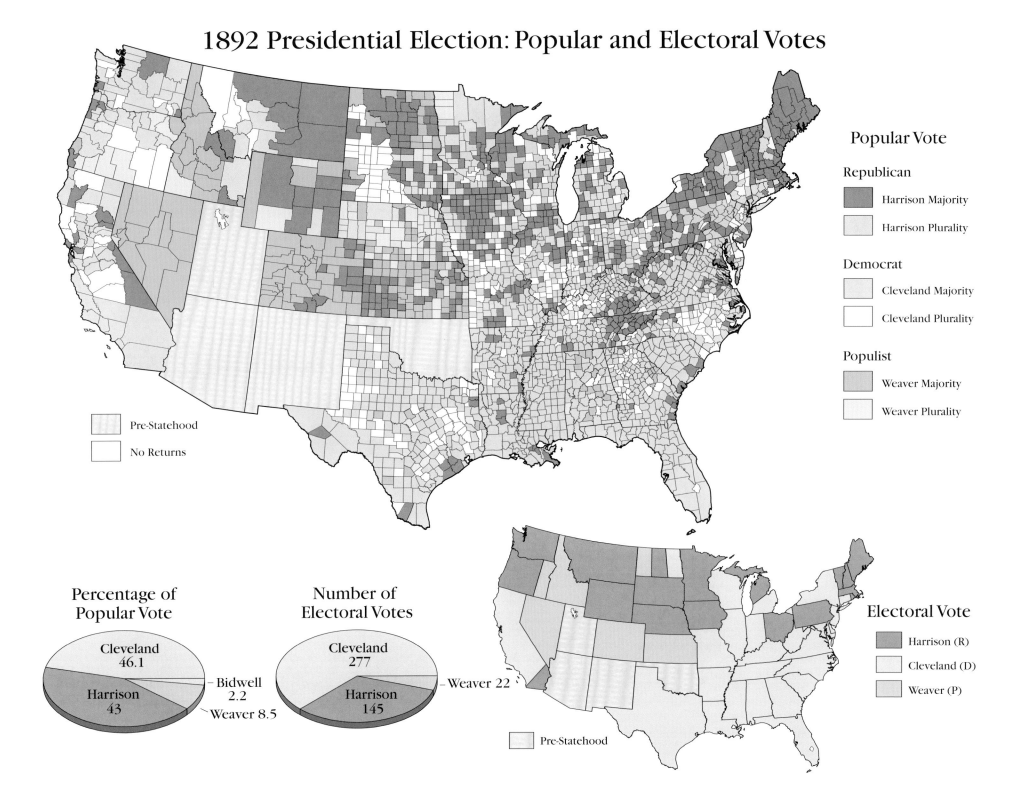

Popular Vote

Republican
- Harrison Majority
- Harrison Plurality

Democrat
- Cleveland Majority
- Cleveland Plurality

Populist
- Weaver Majority
- Weaver Plurality

- Pre-Statehood
- No Returns

Percentage of Popular Vote

- Cleveland 46.1
- Harrison 43
- Bidwell 2.2
- Weaver 8.5

Number of Electoral Votes

- Cleveland 277
- Harrison 145
- Weaver 22

Electoral Vote

- Harrison (R)
- Cleveland (D)
- Weaver (P)

- Pre-Statehood

Map **28**

1896 Presidential Election: Popular Support for Leading Candidates

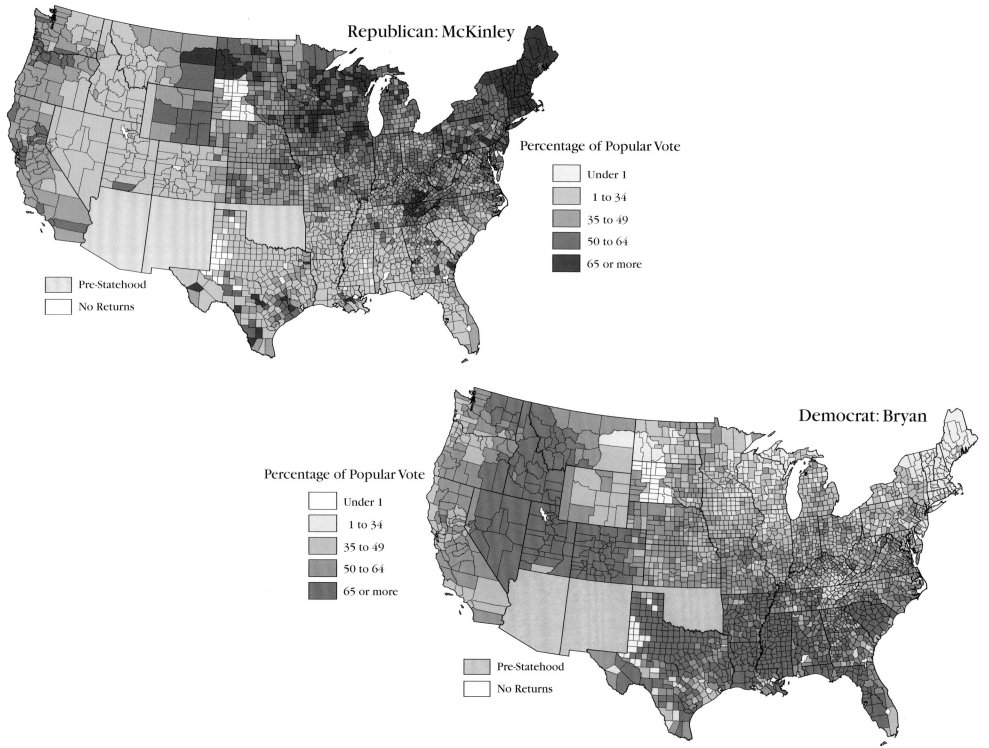

Republican: McKinley

Percentage of Popular Vote

- Under 1
- 1 to 34
- 35 to 49
- 50 to 64
- 65 or more

- Pre-Statehood
- No Returns

Democrat: Bryan

Percentage of Popular Vote

- Under 1
- 1 to 34
- 35 to 49
- 50 to 64
- 65 or more

- Pre-Statehood
- No Returns

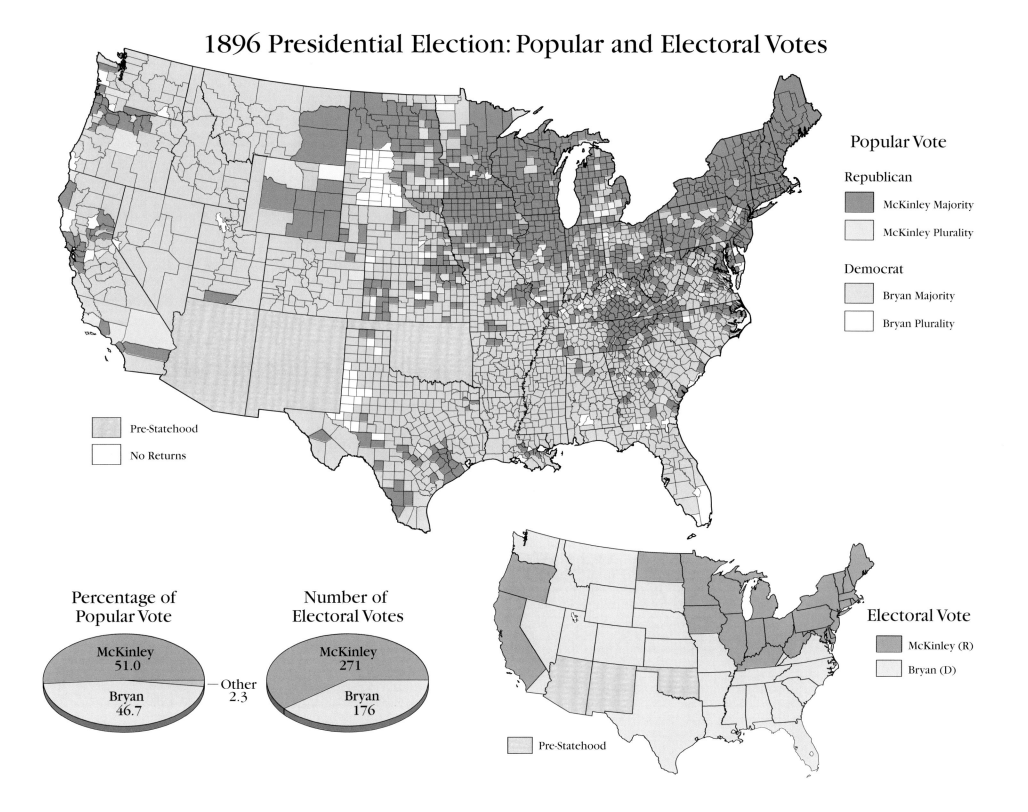

Map
28

1896 Presidential Election: Popular and Electoral Votes

Popular Vote

Republican

McKinley Majority

McKinley Plurality

Democrat

Bryan Majority

Bryan Plurality

Pre-Statehood

No Returns

Percentage of Popular Vote

McKinley 51.0

Bryan 46.7

Other 2.3

Number of Electoral Votes

McKinley 271

Bryan 176

Electoral Vote

McKinley (R)

Bryan (D)

Pre-Statehood

Map
29

1900 Presidential Election: Popular Support for Leading Candidates

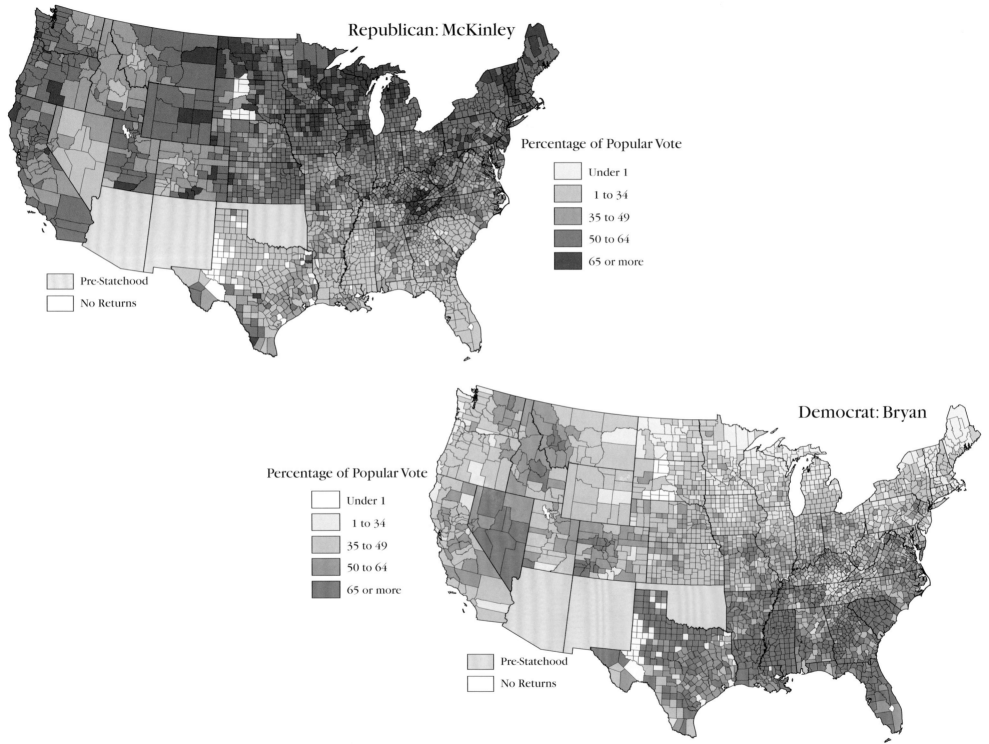

Republican: McKinley

Percentage of Popular Vote

Under 1
1 to 34
35 to 49
50 to 64
65 or more

Pre-Statehood
No Returns

Democrat: Bryan

Percentage of Popular Vote

Under 1
1 to 34
35 to 49
50 to 64
65 or more

Pre-Statehood
No Returns

1900 Presidential Election: Popular and Electoral Votes

Map
29

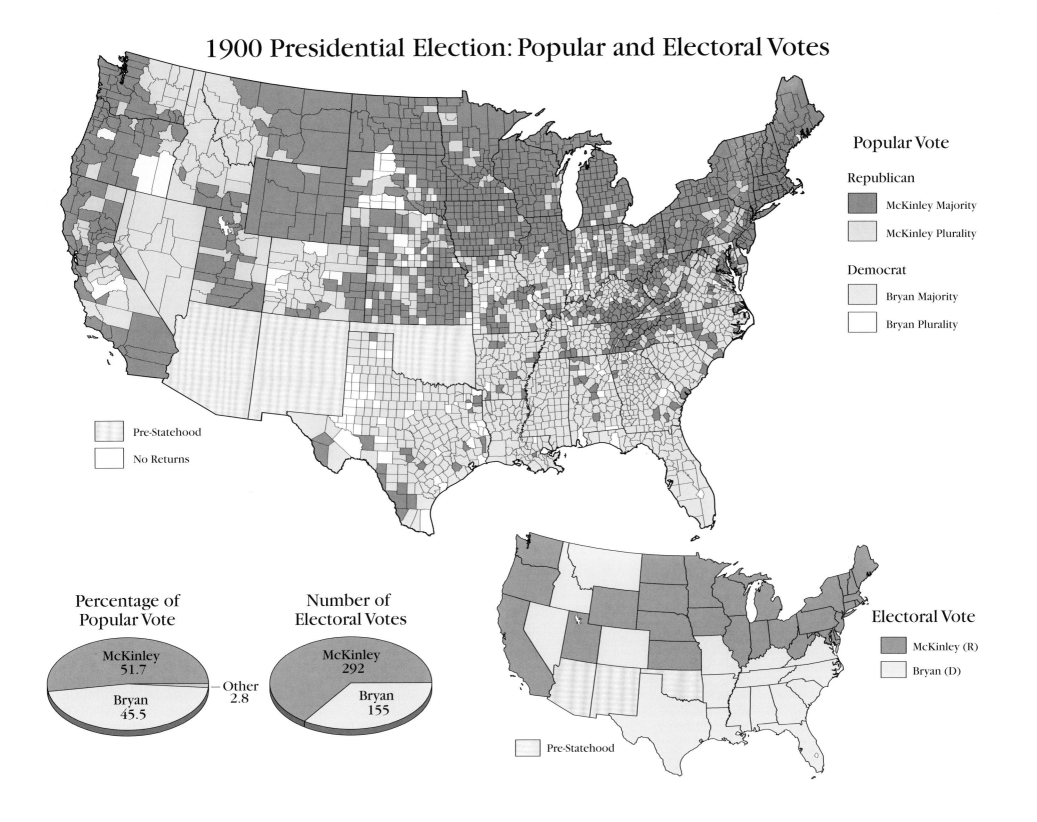

Popular Vote

Republican

- McKinley Majority
- McKinley Plurality

Democrat

- Bryan Majority
- Bryan Plurality

Pre-Statehood

No Returns

Percentage of Popular Vote

- McKinley 51.7
- Bryan 45.5
- Other 2.8

Number of Electoral Votes

- McKinley 292
- Bryan 155

Electoral Vote

- McKinley (R)
- Bryan (D)

Pre-Statehood

Map
30

1904 Presidential Election: Popular Support for Leading Candidates

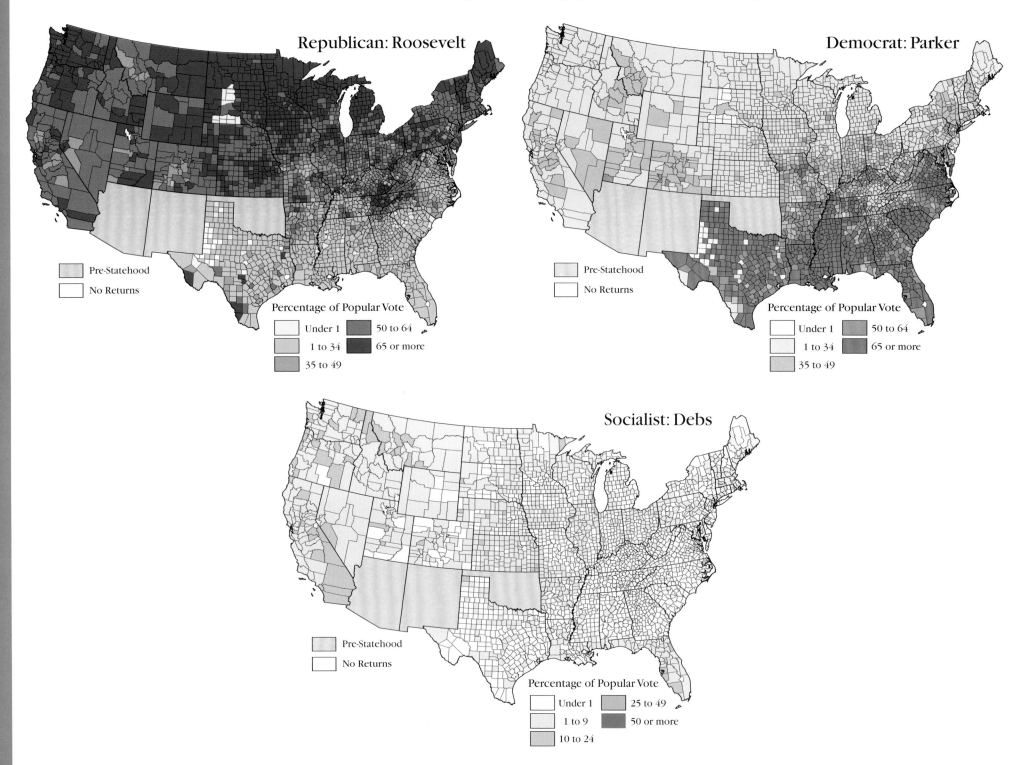

Republican: Roosevelt

Pre-Statehood

No Returns

Percentage of Popular Vote

Under 1 | 50 to 64
1 to 34 | 65 or more
35 to 49

Democrat: Parker

Pre-Statehood

No Returns

Percentage of Popular Vote

Under 1 | 50 to 64
1 to 34 | 65 or more
35 to 49

Socialist: Debs

Pre-Statehood

No Returns

Percentage of Popular Vote

Under 1 | 25 to 49
1 to 9 | 50 or more
10 to 24

1904 Presidential Election: Popular and Electoral Votes

Map 30

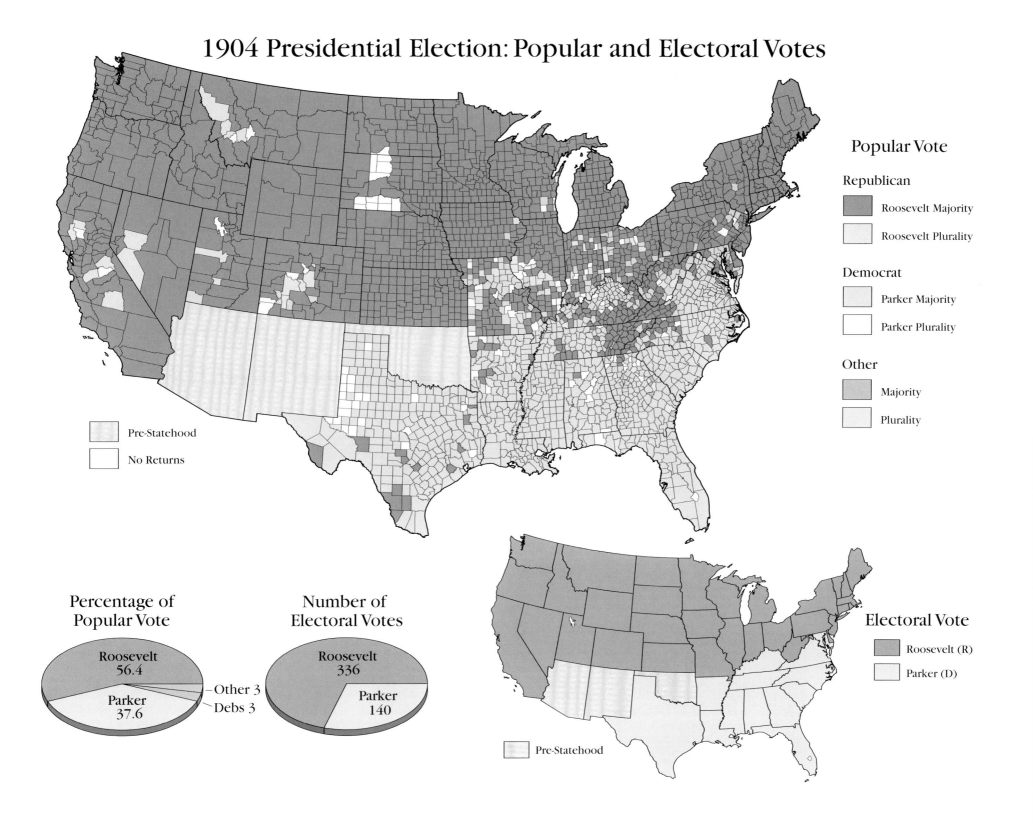

Popular Vote

Republican
- Roosevelt Majority
- Roosevelt Plurality

Democrat
- Parker Majority
- Parker Plurality

Other
- Majority
- Plurality

- Pre-Statehood
- No Returns

Percentage of Popular Vote

Roosevelt 56.4
Parker 37.6
Other 3
Debs 3

Number of Electoral Votes

Roosevelt 336
Parker 140

Electoral Vote
- Roosevelt (R)
- Parker (D)

- Pre-Statehood

Map
31

1908 Presidential Election: Popular Support for Leading Candidates

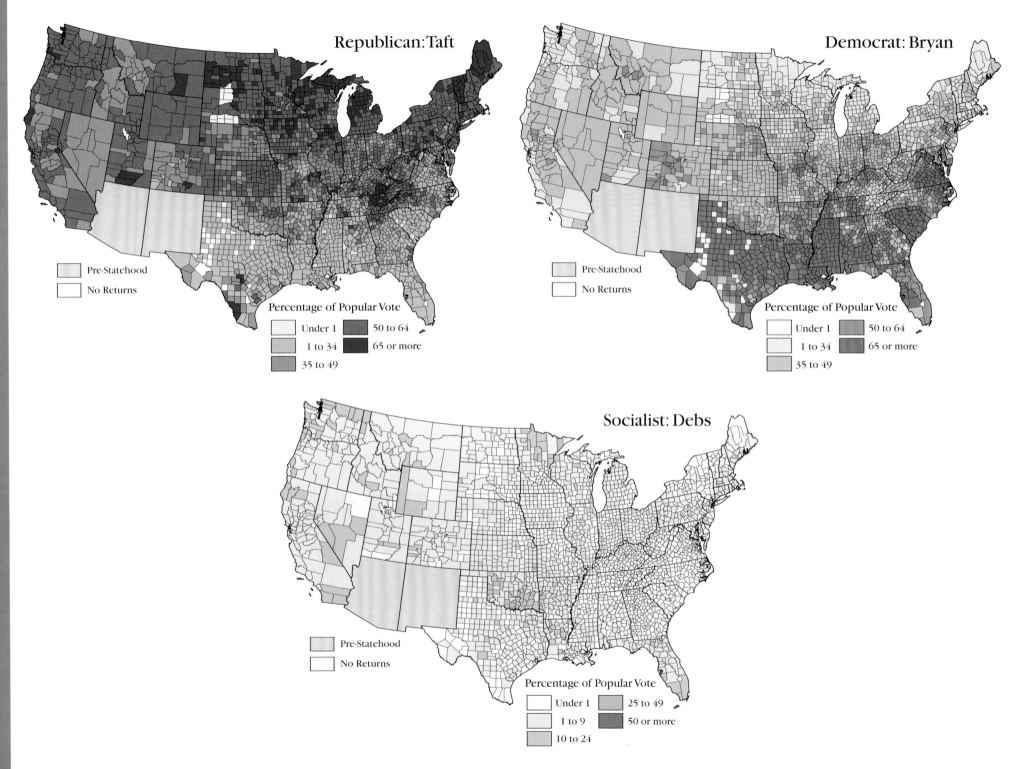

Republican: Taft

Pre-Statehood
No Returns

Percentage of Popular Vote
Under 1   50 to 64
1 to 34   65 or more
35 to 49

Democrat: Bryan

Pre-Statehood
No Returns

Percentage of Popular Vote
Under 1   50 to 64
1 to 34   65 or more
35 to 49

Socialist: Debs

Pre-Statehood
No Returns

Percentage of Popular Vote
Under 1   25 to 49
1 to 9   50 or more
10 to 24

1908 Presidential Election: Popular and Electoral Votes

Map
31

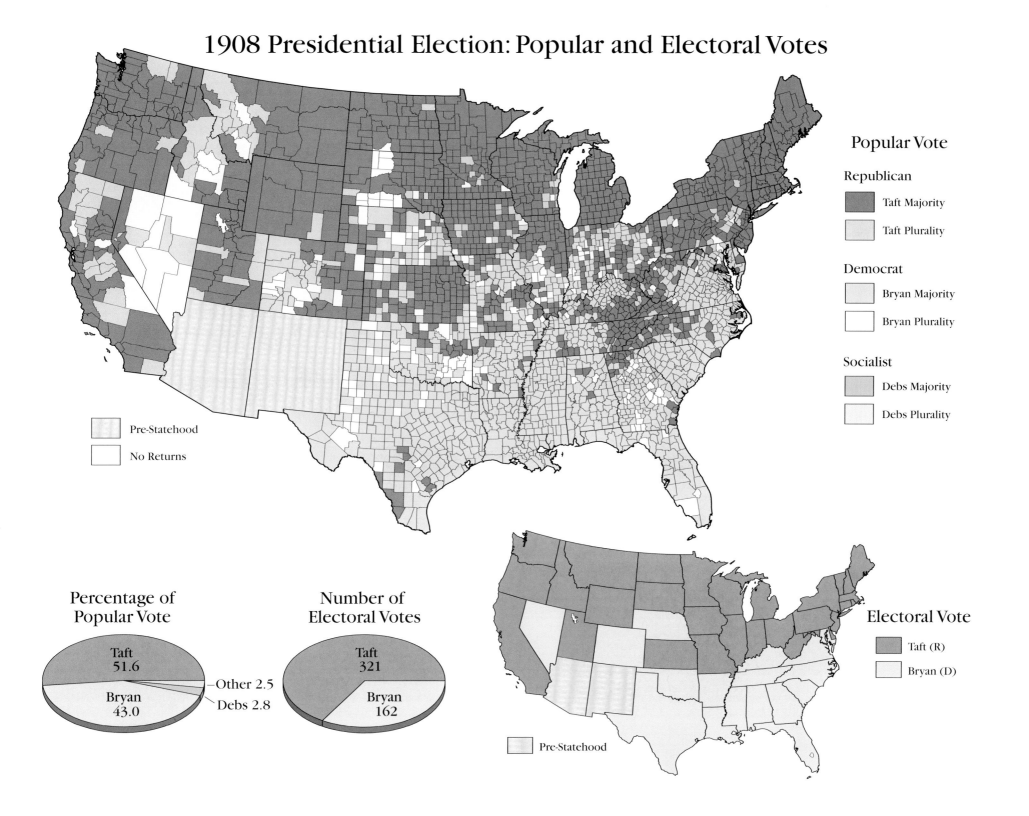

Popular Vote

Republican
- Taft Majority
- Taft Plurality

Democrat
- Bryan Majority
- Bryan Plurality

Socialist
- Debs Majority
- Debs Plurality

Pre-Statehood

No Returns

Percentage of Popular Vote

Taft 51.6
Bryan 43.0
Other 2.5
Debs 2.8

Number of Electoral Votes

Taft 321
Bryan 162

Electoral Vote
- Taft (R)
- Bryan (D)

Pre-Statehood

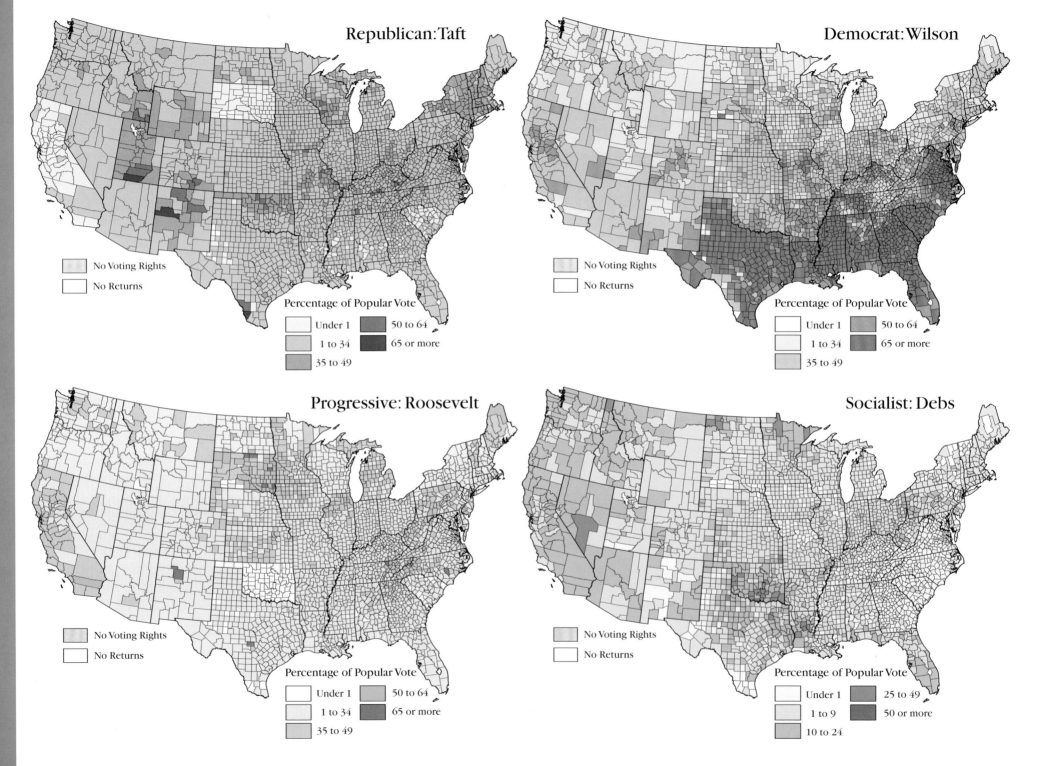

Map
32

1912 Presidential Election: Popular Support for Leading Candidates

Republican: Taft

No Voting Rights

No Returns

Percentage of Popular Vote

Under 1 · 50 to 64
1 to 34 · 65 or more
35 to 49

Democrat: Wilson

No Voting Rights

No Returns

Percentage of Popular Vote

Under 1 · 50 to 64
1 to 34 · 65 or more
35 to 49

Progressive: Roosevelt

No Voting Rights

No Returns

Percentage of Popular Vote

Under 1 · 50 to 64
1 to 34 · 65 or more
35 to 49

Socialist: Debs

No Voting Rights

No Returns

Percentage of Popular Vote

Under 1 · 25 to 49
1 to 9 · 50 or more
10 to 24

1912 Presidential Election: Popular and Electoral Votes

Map 32

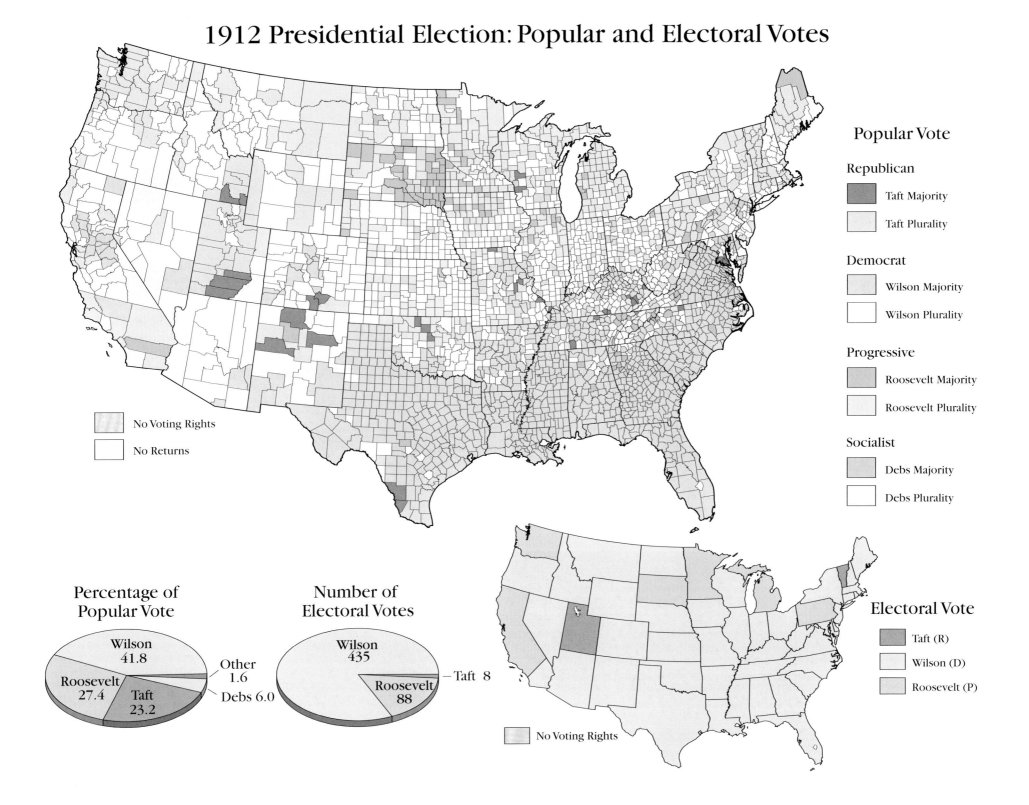

Popular Vote

Republican
- Taft Majority
- Taft Plurality

Democrat
- Wilson Majority
- Wilson Plurality

Progressive
- Roosevelt Majority
- Roosevelt Plurality

Socialist
- Debs Majority
- Debs Plurality

No Voting Rights

No Returns

Percentage of Popular Vote

Wilson 41.8
Roosevelt 27.4
Taft 23.2
Other 1.6
Debs 6.0

Number of Electoral Votes

Wilson 435
Roosevelt 88
Taft 8

Electoral Vote
- Taft (R)
- Wilson (D)
- Roosevelt (P)

No Voting Rights

1916 Presidential Election: Popular Support for Leading Candidates

Map 33

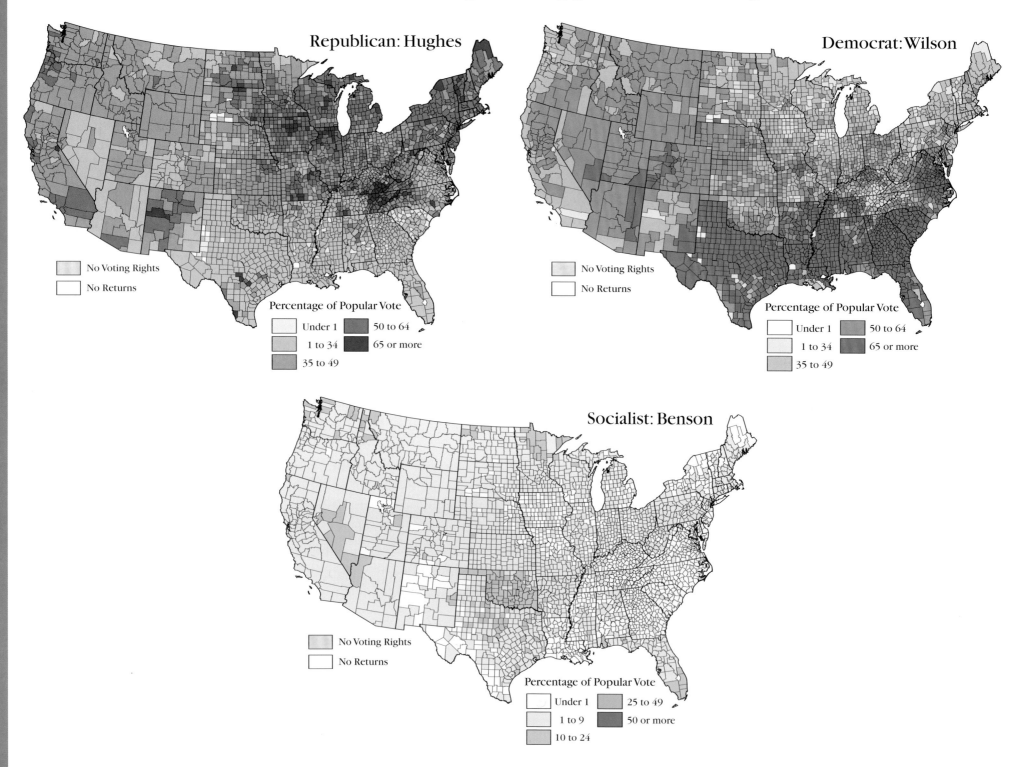

Republican: Hughes

No Voting Rights
No Returns

Percentage of Popular Vote

Under 1
1 to 34
35 to 49
50 to 64
65 or more

Democrat: Wilson

No Voting Rights
No Returns

Percentage of Popular Vote

Under 1
1 to 34
35 to 49
50 to 64
65 or more

Socialist: Benson

No Voting Rights
No Returns

Percentage of Popular Vote

Under 1
1 to 9
10 to 24
25 to 49
50 or more

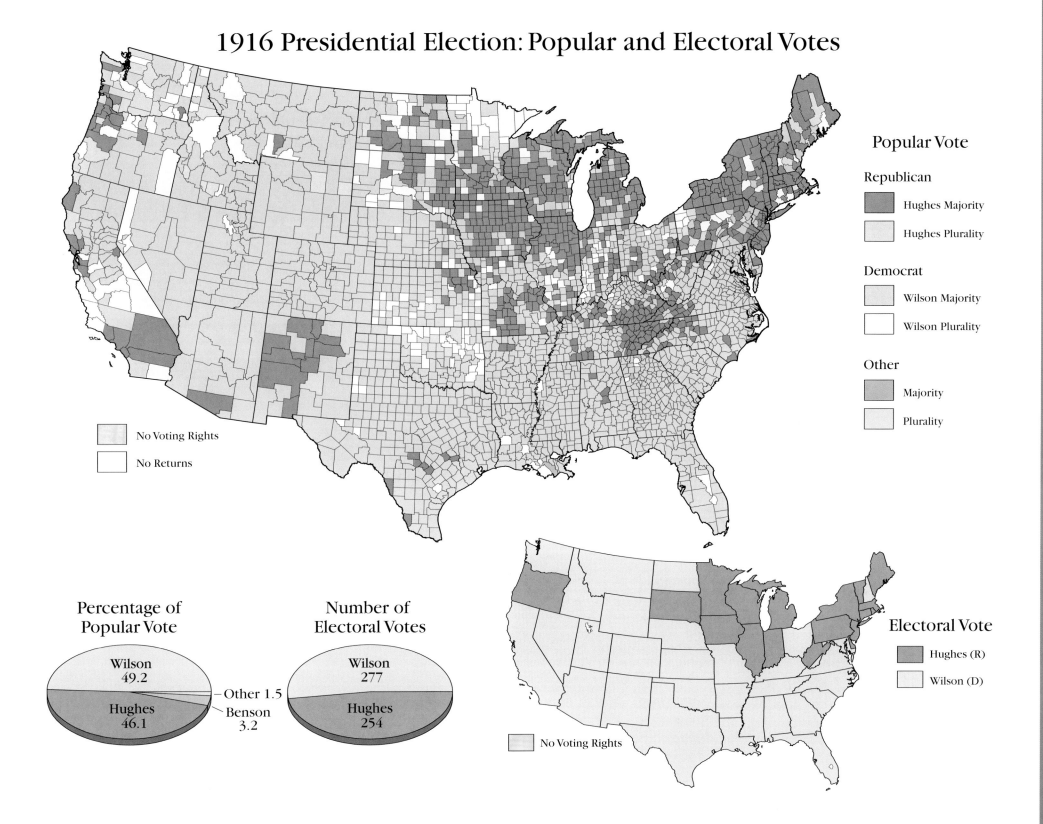

1916 Presidential Election: Popular and Electoral Votes

Map
33

Popular Vote

Republican
- Hughes Majority
- Hughes Plurality

Democrat
- Wilson Majority
- Wilson Plurality

Other
- Majority
- Plurality

No Voting Rights

No Returns

Percentage of Popular Vote

Wilson 49.2

Hughes 46.1

Other 1.5

Benson 3.2

Number of Electoral Votes

Wilson 277

Hughes 254

Electoral Vote
- Hughes (R)
- Wilson (D)

No Voting Rights

Map
34

1920 Presidential Election: Popular Support for Leading Candidates

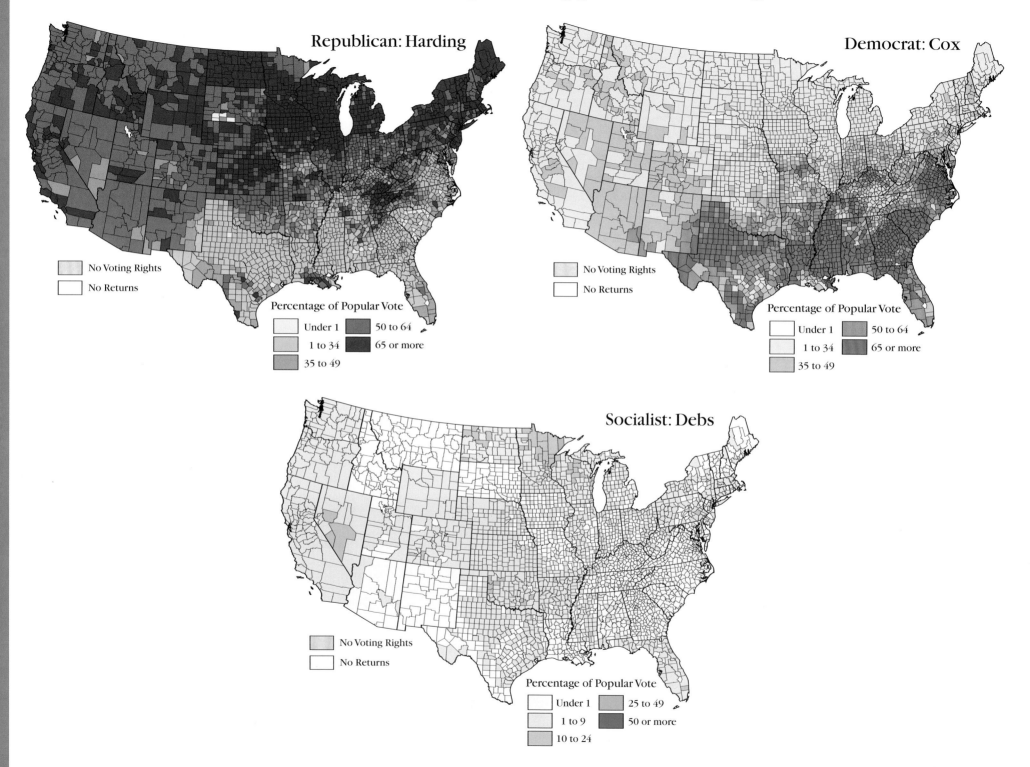

Republican: Harding

No Voting Rights
No Returns

Percentage of Popular Vote

Under 1   50 to 64
1 to 34   65 or more
35 to 49

Democrat: Cox

No Voting Rights
No Returns

Percentage of Popular Vote

Under 1   50 to 64
1 to 34   65 or more
35 to 49

Socialist: Debs

No Voting Rights
No Returns

Percentage of Popular Vote

Under 1   25 to 49
1 to 9   50 or more
10 to 24

1920 Presidential Election: Popular and Electoral Votes

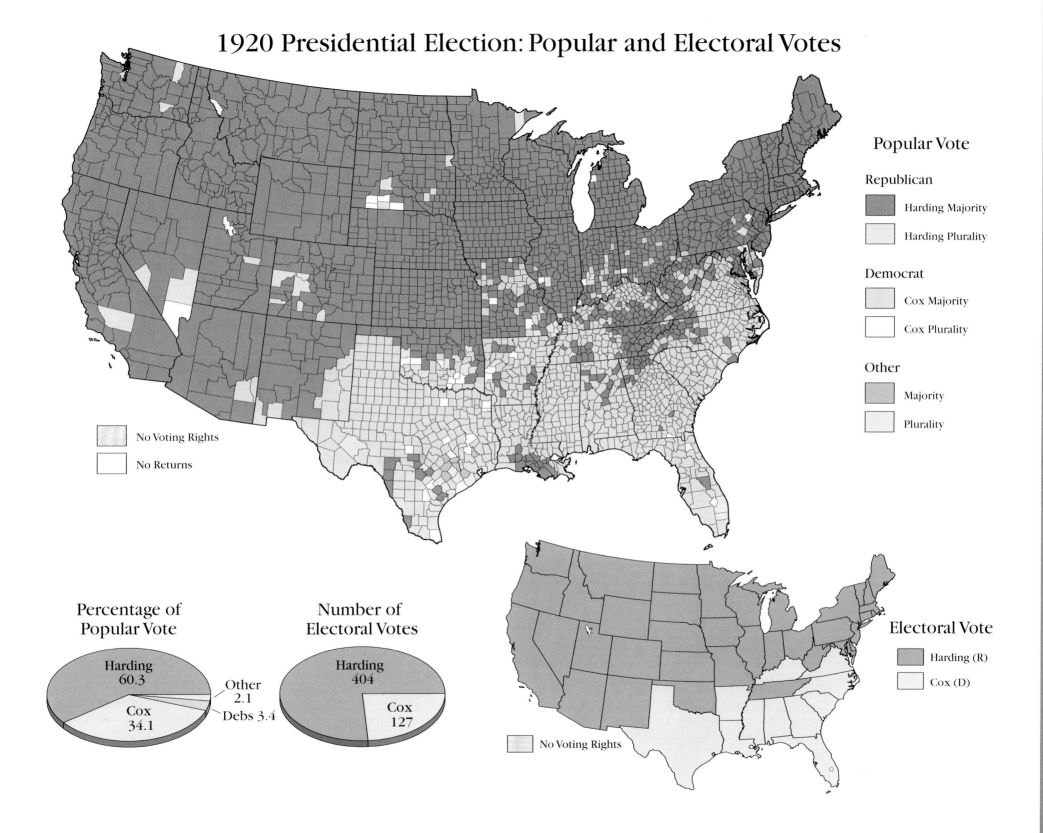

Map 34

Popular Vote

Republican
- Harding Majority
- Harding Plurality

Democrat
- Cox Majority
- Cox Plurality

Other
- Majority
- Plurality

No Voting Rights

No Returns

Percentage of Popular Vote
- Harding 60.3
- Cox 34.1
- Debs 3.4
- Other 2.1

Number of Electoral Votes
- Harding 404
- Cox 127

Electoral Vote
- Harding (R)
- Cox (D)

No Voting Rights

Map
35

1924 Presidential Election: Popular Support for Leading Candidates

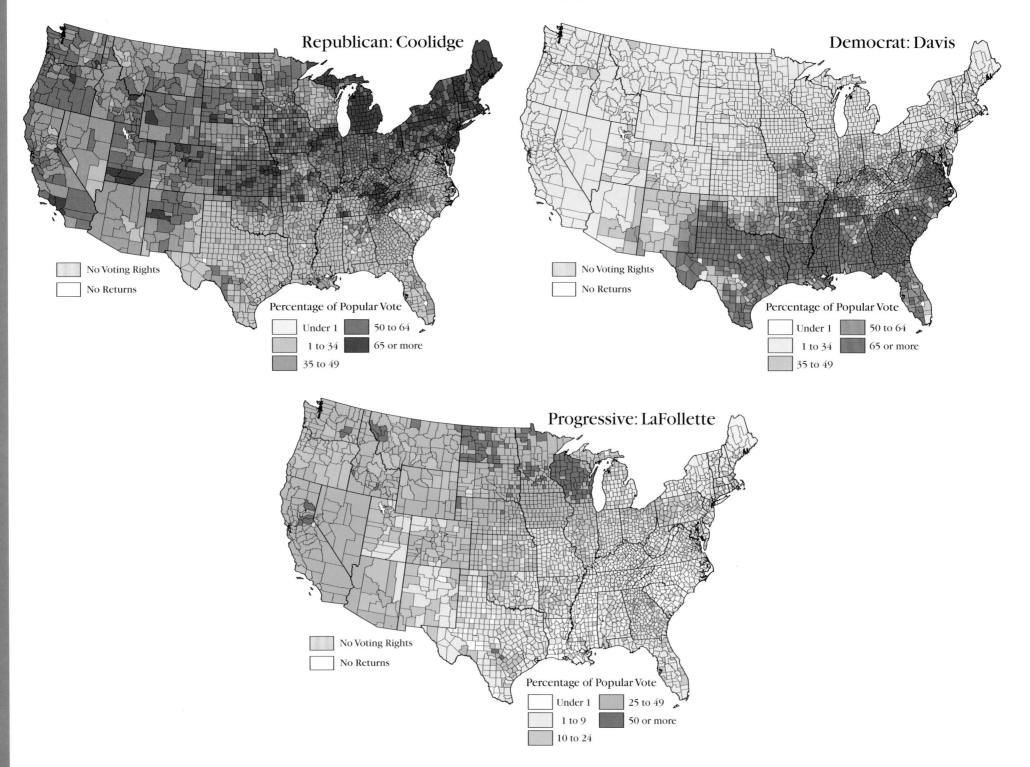

Republican: Coolidge

Democrat: Davis

Progressive: LaFollette

No Voting Rights

No Returns

Percentage of Popular Vote

Under 1 — 50 to 64
1 to 34 — 65 or more
35 to 49

Percentage of Popular Vote

Under 1 — 25 to 49
1 to 9 — 50 or more
10 to 24

1924 Presidential Election: Popular and Electoral Votes

Map
35

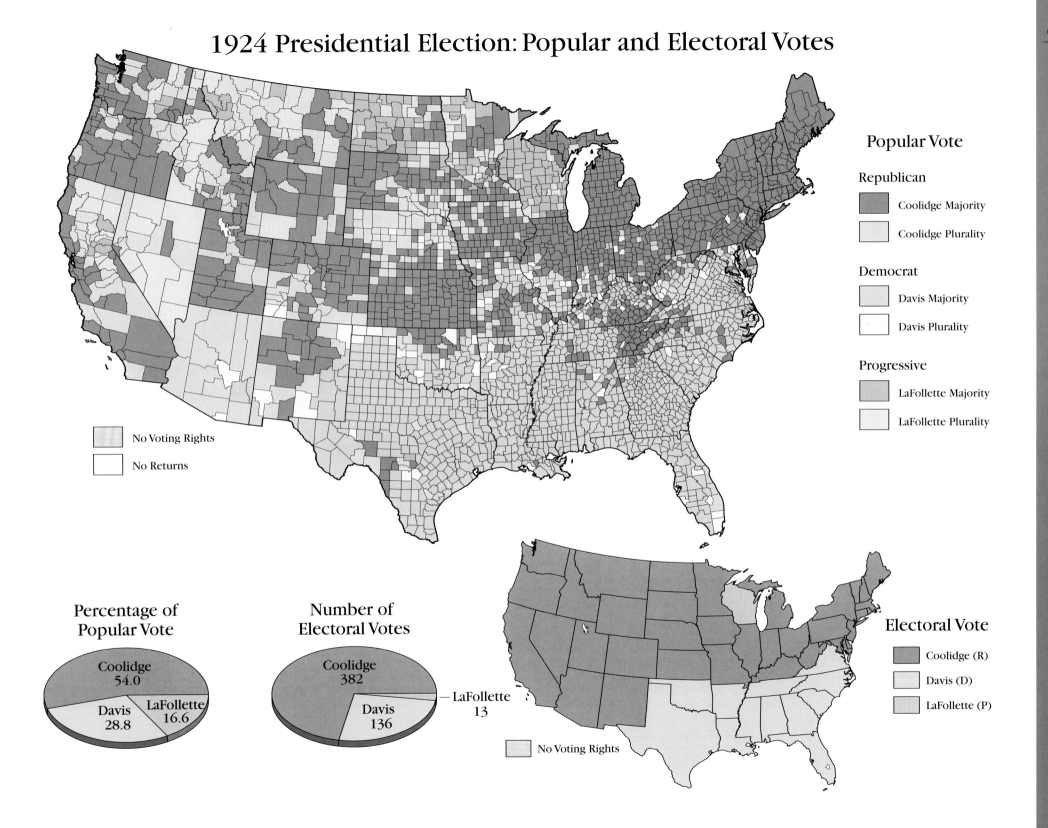

Popular Vote

Republican

Coolidge Majority

Coolidge Plurality

Democrat

Davis Majority

Davis Plurality

Progressive

LaFollette Majority

LaFollette Plurality

No Voting Rights

No Returns

Percentage of Popular Vote

Coolidge 54.0

Davis 28.8

LaFollette 16.6

Number of Electoral Votes

Coolidge 382

Davis 136

— LaFollette 13

Electoral Vote

Coolidge (R)

Davis (D)

LaFollette (P)

No Voting Rights

Map
36

1928 Presidential Election: Popular Support for Leading Candidates

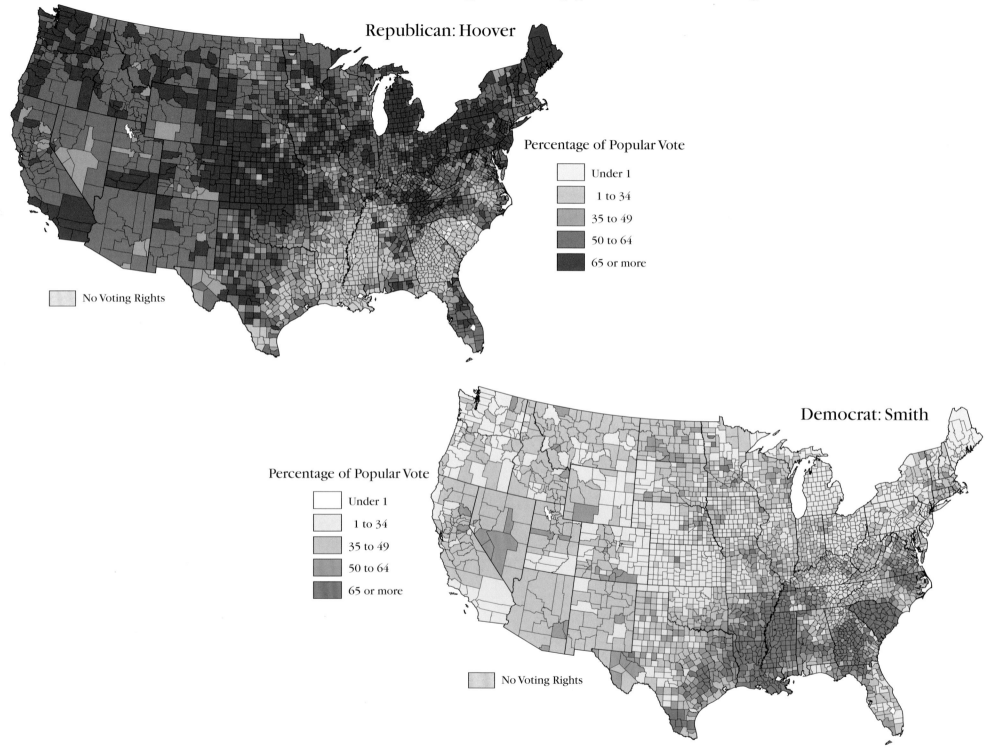

Republican: Hoover

Percentage of Popular Vote

- Under 1
- 1 to 34
- 35 to 49
- 50 to 64
- 65 or more

No Voting Rights

Democrat: Smith

Percentage of Popular Vote

- Under 1
- 1 to 34
- 35 to 49
- 50 to 64
- 65 or more

No Voting Rights

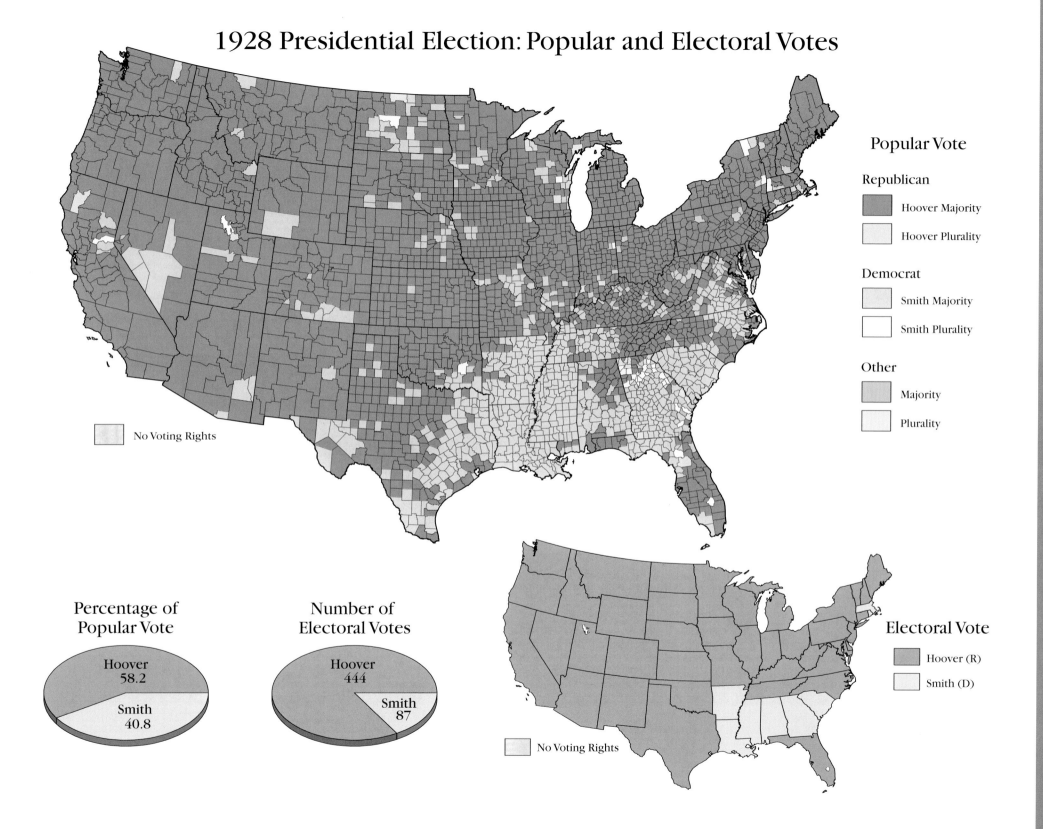

1928 Presidential Election: Popular and Electoral Votes

Map 36

Popular Vote

Republican
Hoover Majority

Hoover Plurality

Democrat
Smith Majority

Smith Plurality

Other
Majority

Plurality

No Voting Rights

Percentage of Popular Vote
Hoover 58.2

Smith 40.8

Number of Electoral Votes
Hoover 444

Smith 87

Electoral Vote
Hoover (R)

Smith (D)

No Voting Rights

1932 Presidential Election: Popular Support for Leading Candidates

Map 37

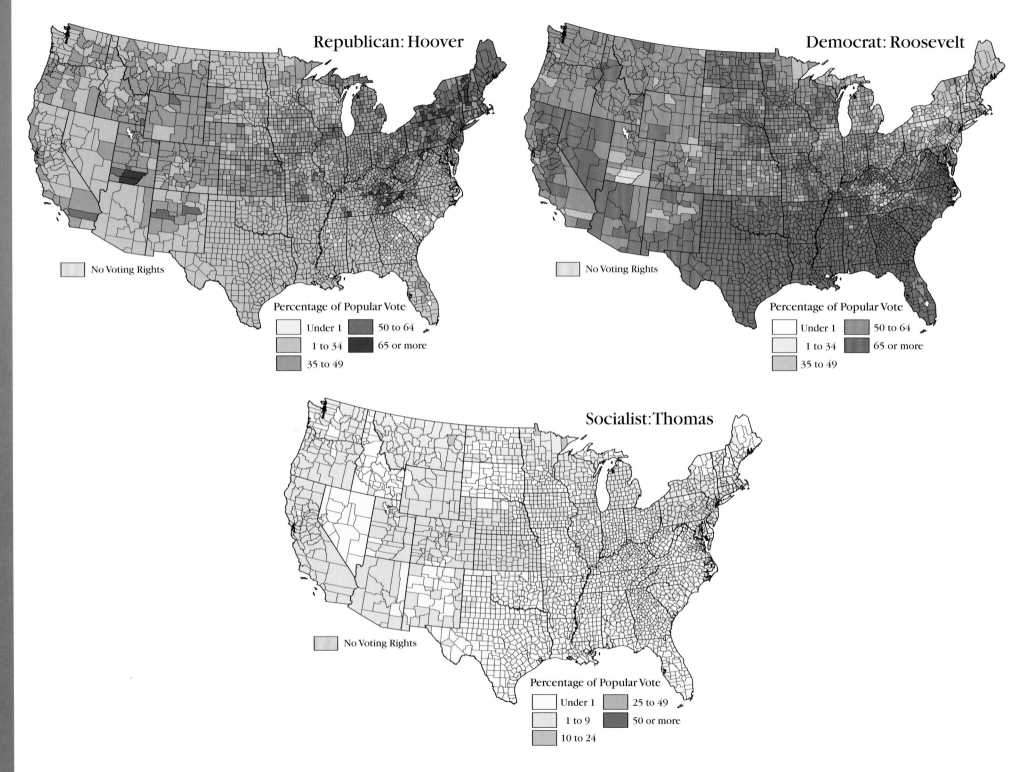

1932 Presidential Election: Popular and Electoral Votes

Map
37

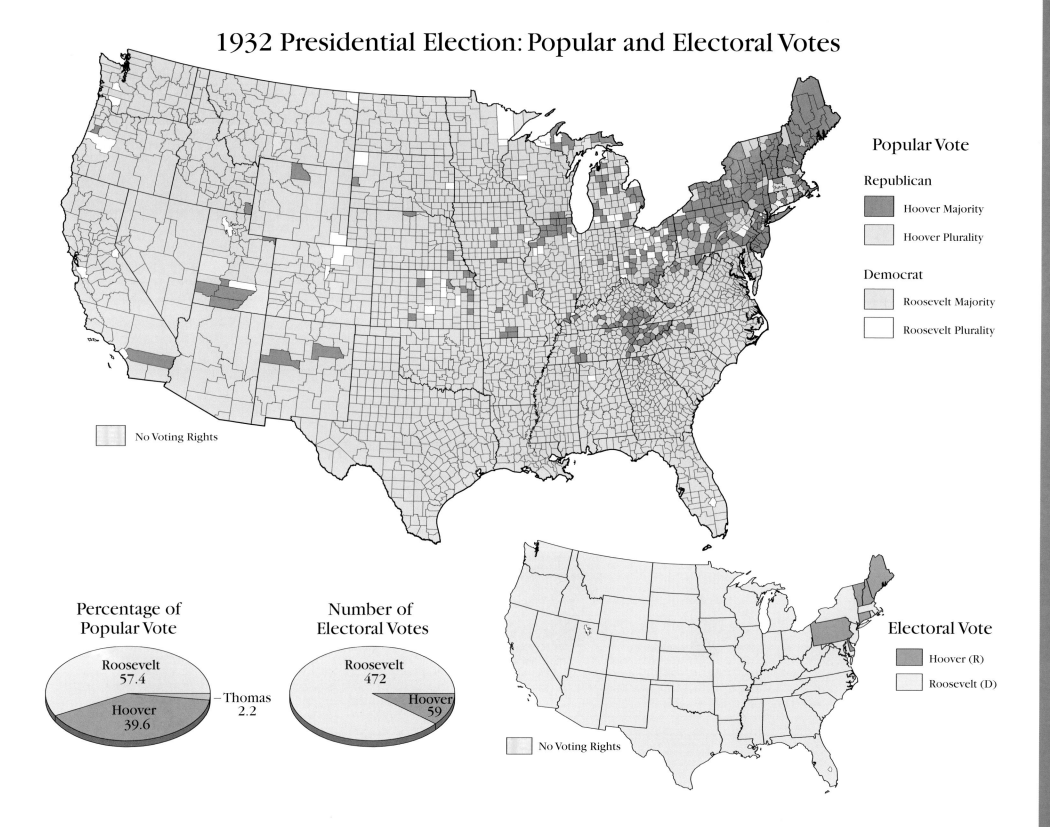

Popular Vote

Republican

Hoover Majority

Hoover Plurality

Democrat

Roosevelt Majority

Roosevelt Plurality

No Voting Rights

Percentage of Popular Vote

Roosevelt 57.4

Hoover 39.6

Thomas 2.2

Number of Electoral Votes

Roosevelt 472

Hoover 59

Electoral Vote

Hoover (R)

Roosevelt (D)

No Voting Rights

Map
38

1936 Presidential Election: Popular Support for Leading Candidates

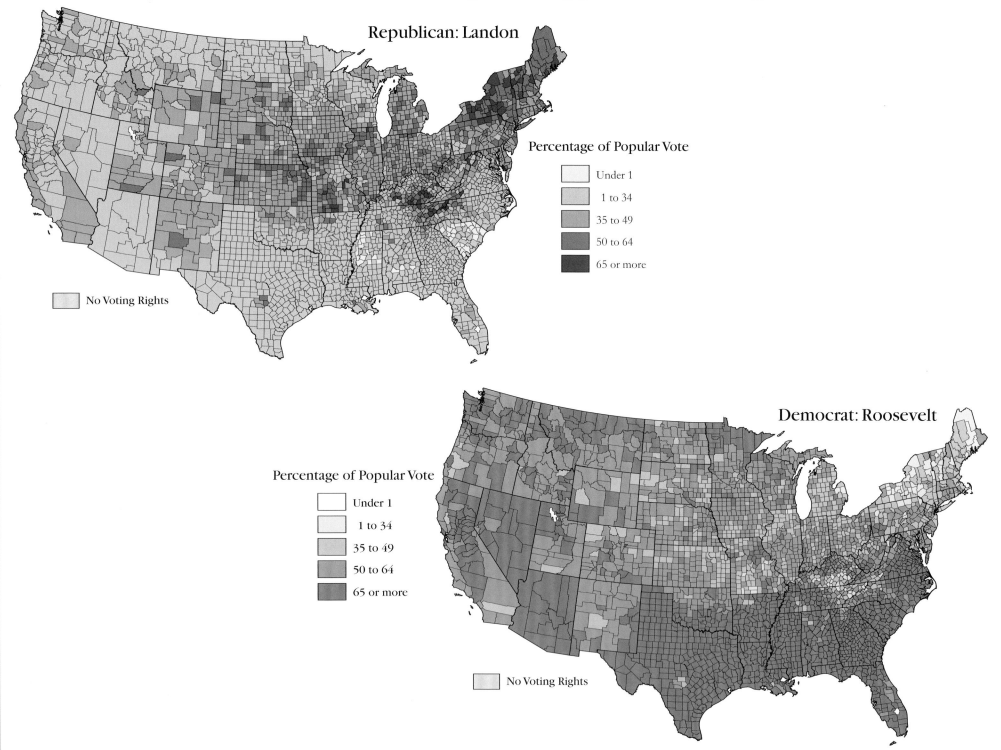

Republican: Landon

Percentage of Popular Vote

- Under 1
- 1 to 34
- 35 to 49
- 50 to 64
- 65 or more

No Voting Rights

Democrat: Roosevelt

Percentage of Popular Vote

- Under 1
- 1 to 34
- 35 to 49
- 50 to 64
- 65 or more

No Voting Rights

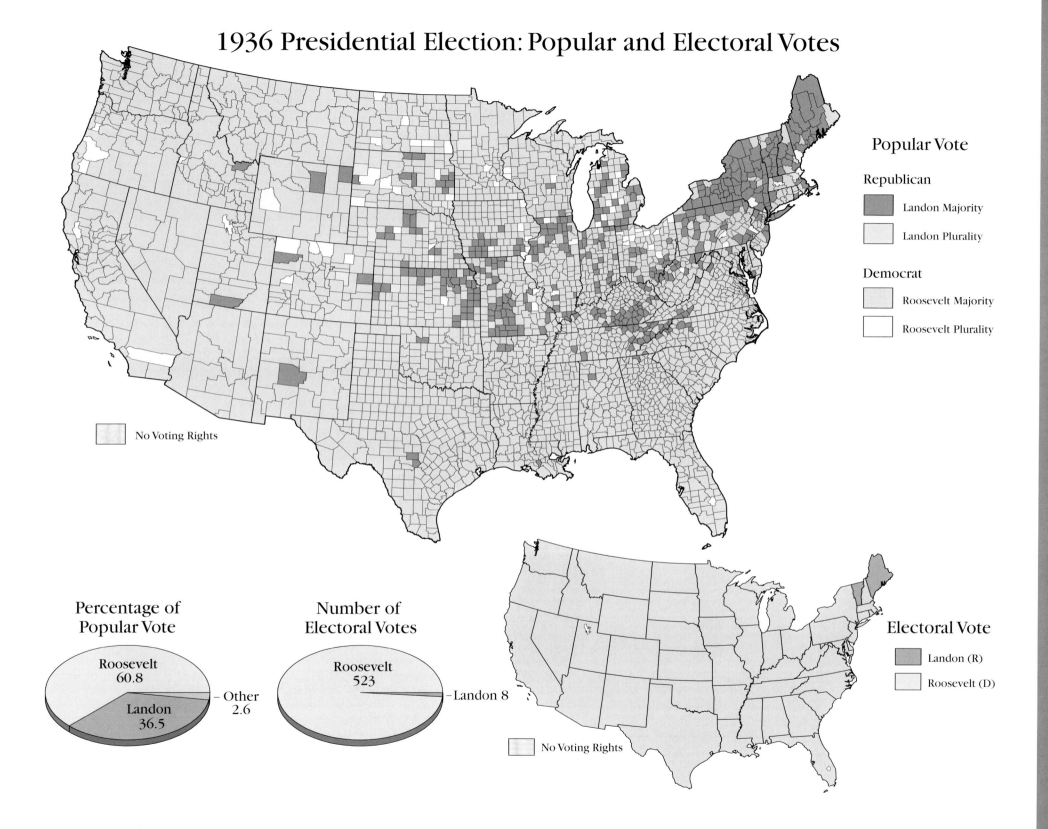

1936 Presidential Election: Popular and Electoral Votes

Map 38

Popular Vote

Republican

Landon Majority

Landon Plurality

Democrat

Roosevelt Majority

Roosevelt Plurality

No Voting Rights

Percentage of Popular Vote

Roosevelt 60.8

Landon 36.5

– Other 2.6

Number of Electoral Votes

Roosevelt 523

– Landon 8

Electoral Vote

Landon (R)

Roosevelt (D)

No Voting Rights

Map
39

1940 Presidential Election: Popular Support for Leading Candidates

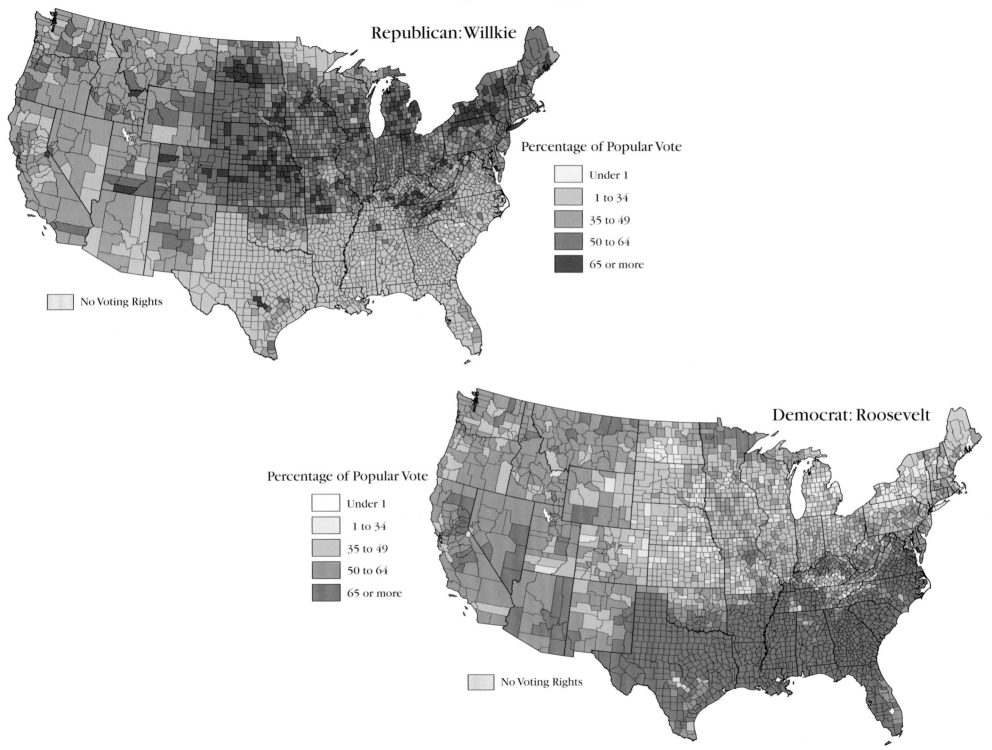

Republican: Willkie

Percentage of Popular Vote

Under 1
1 to 34
35 to 49
50 to 64
65 or more

No Voting Rights

Democrat: Roosevelt

Percentage of Popular Vote

Under 1
1 to 34
35 to 49
50 to 64
65 or more

No Voting Rights

1940 Presidential Election: Popular and Electoral Votes

Map 39

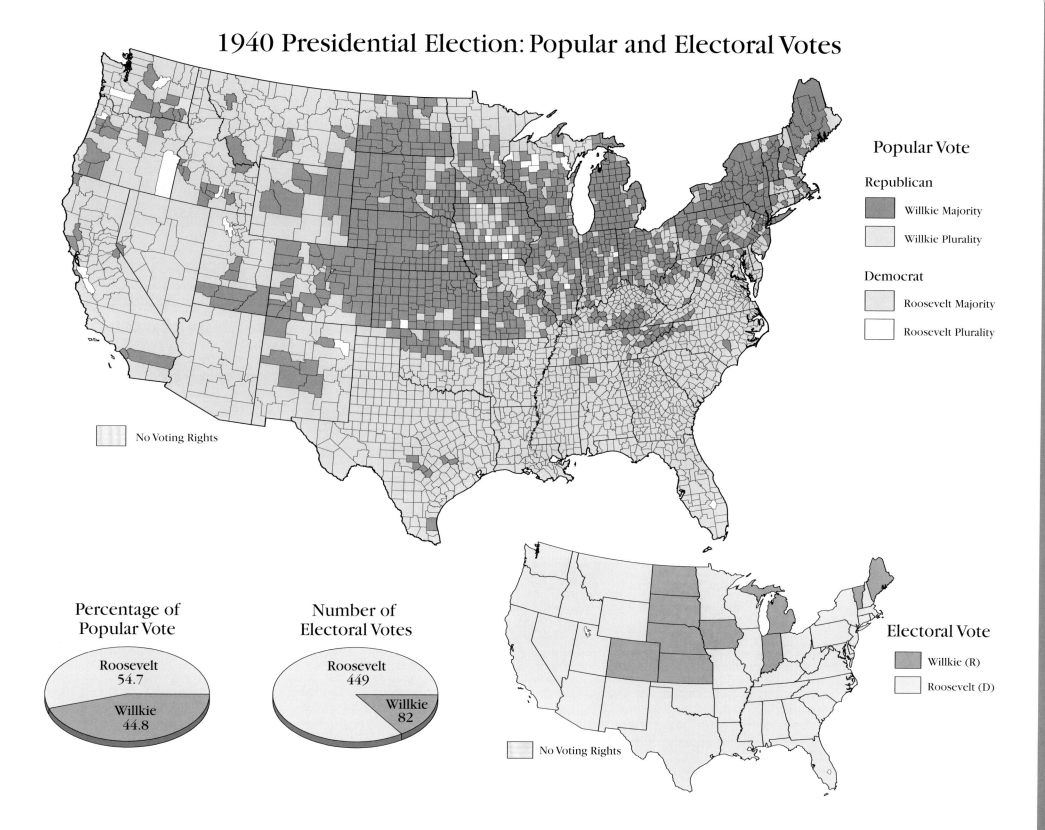

Popular Vote

Republican

Willkie Majority

Willkie Plurality

Democrat

Roosevelt Majority

Roosevelt Plurality

No Voting Rights

Percentage of Popular Vote

Roosevelt 54.7

Willkie 44.8

Number of Electoral Votes

Roosevelt 449

Willkie 82

Electoral Vote

Willkie (R)

Roosevelt (D)

No Voting Rights

Map
40

1944 Presidential Election: Popular Support for Leading Candidates

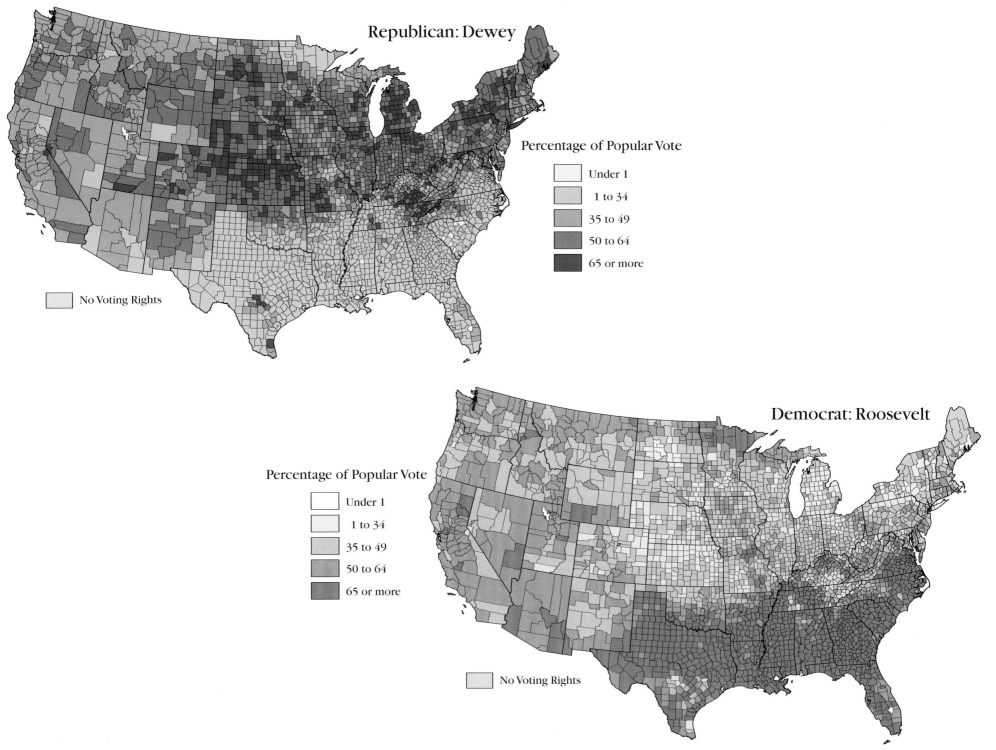

Republican: Dewey

Percentage of Popular Vote

- Under 1
- 1 to 34
- 35 to 49
- 50 to 64
- 65 or more

No Voting Rights

Democrat: Roosevelt

Percentage of Popular Vote

- Under 1
- 1 to 34
- 35 to 49
- 50 to 64
- 65 or more

No Voting Rights

Map
40

1944 Presidential Election: Popular and Electoral Votes

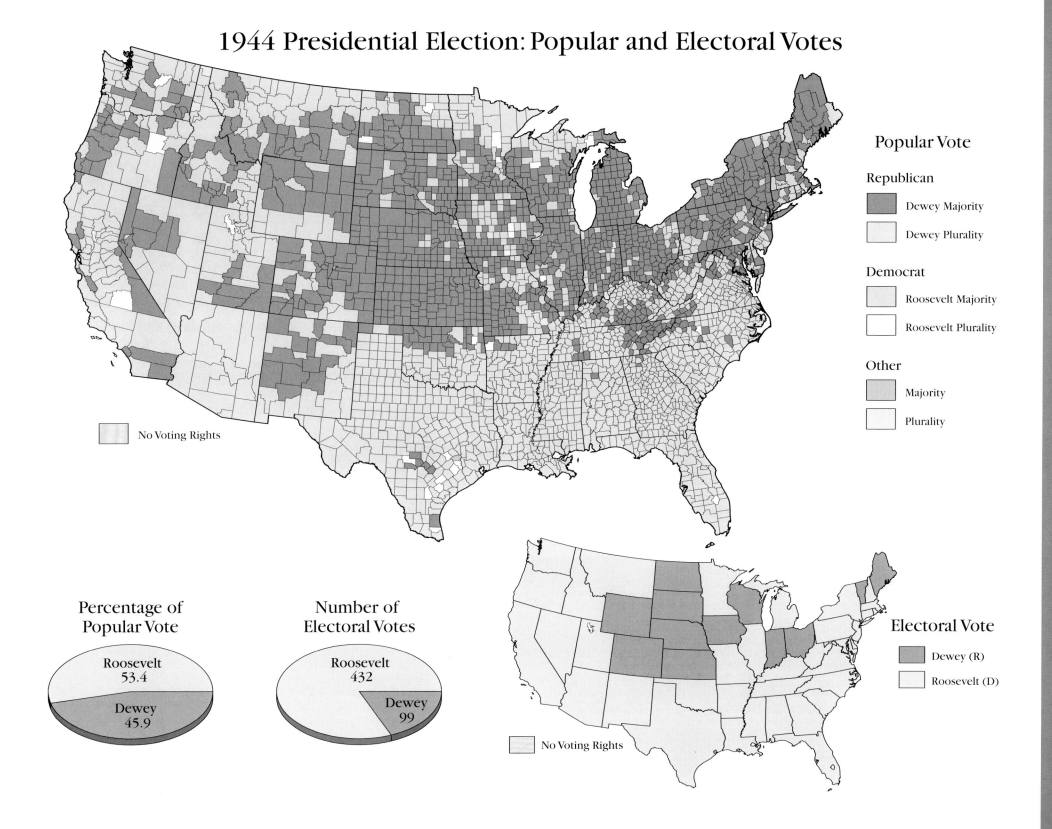

Popular Vote

Republican

Dewey Majority

Dewey Plurality

Democrat

Roosevelt Majority

Roosevelt Plurality

Other

Majority

Plurality

No Voting Rights

Percentage of
Popular Vote

Roosevelt
53.4

Dewey
45.9

Number of
Electoral Votes

Roosevelt
432

Dewey
99

Electoral Vote

Dewey (R)

Roosevelt (D)

No Voting Rights

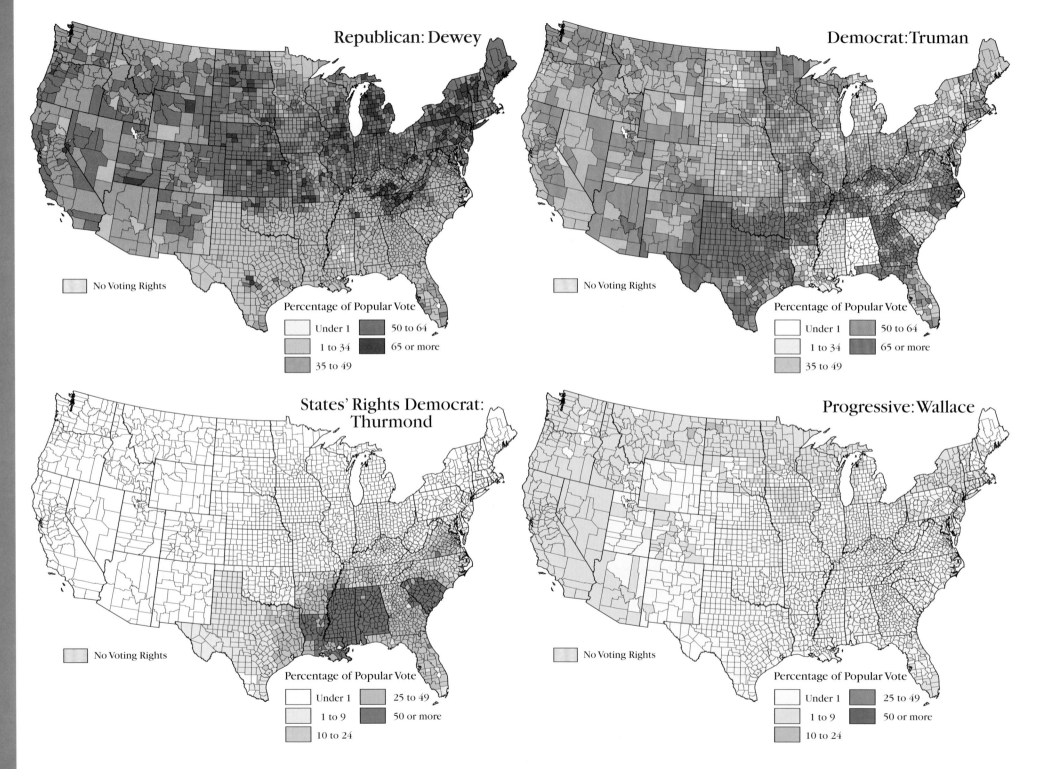

1948 Presidential Election: Popular Support for Leading Candidates

Map 41

Republican: Dewey

No Voting Rights

Percentage of Popular Vote

Under 1   50 to 64
1 to 34   65 or more
35 to 49

Democrat: Truman

No Voting Rights

Percentage of Popular Vote

Under 1   50 to 64
1 to 34   65 or more
35 to 49

States' Rights Democrat: Thurmond

No Voting Rights

Percentage of Popular Vote

Under 1   25 to 49
1 to 9   50 or more
10 to 24

Progressive: Wallace

No Voting Rights

Percentage of Popular Vote

Under 1   25 to 49
1 to 9   50 or more
10 to 24

1948 Presidential Election: Popular and Electoral Votes

Map 41

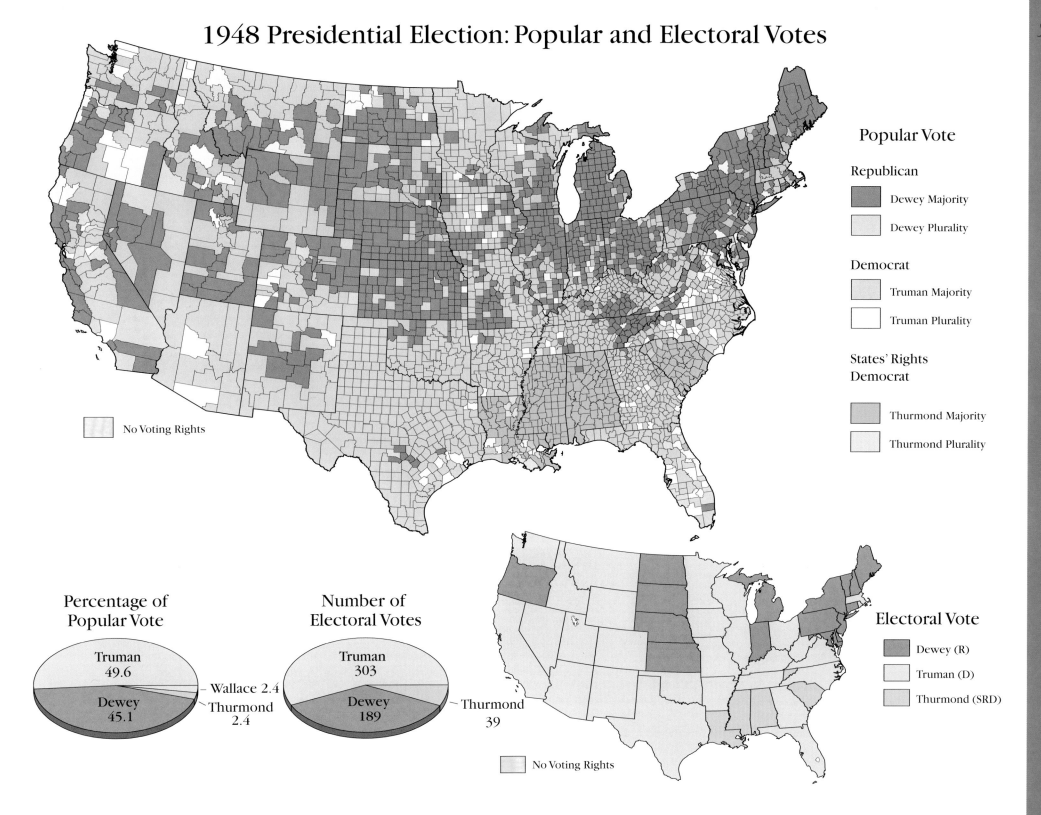

Popular Vote

Republican

Dewey Majority

Dewey Plurality

Democrat

Truman Majority

Truman Plurality

States' Rights Democrat

Thurmond Majority

Thurmond Plurality

No Voting Rights

Percentage of Popular Vote

Truman 49.6

Dewey 45.1

Wallace 2.4

Thurmond 2.4

Number of Electoral Votes

Truman 303

Dewey 189

Thurmond 39

Electoral Vote

Dewey (R)

Truman (D)

Thurmond (SRD)

No Voting Rights

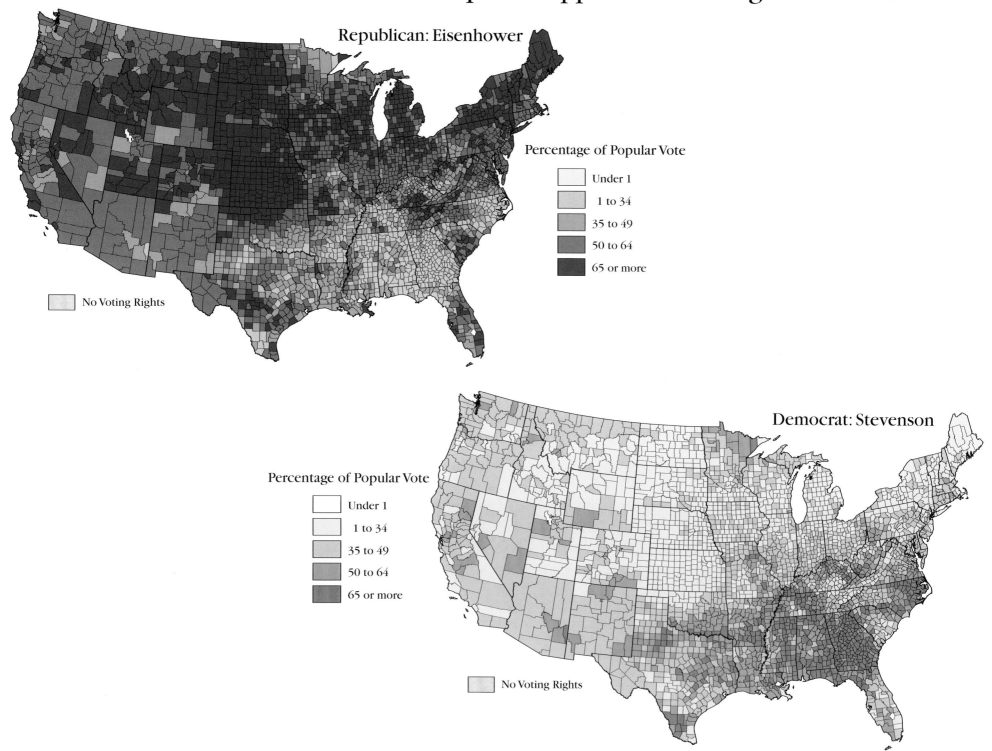

Map
42

1952 Presidential Election: Popular Support for Leading Candidates

Republican: Eisenhower

Percentage of Popular Vote

Under 1
1 to 34
35 to 49
50 to 64
65 or more

No Voting Rights

Democrat: Stevenson

Percentage of Popular Vote

Under 1
1 to 34
35 to 49
50 to 64
65 or more

No Voting Rights

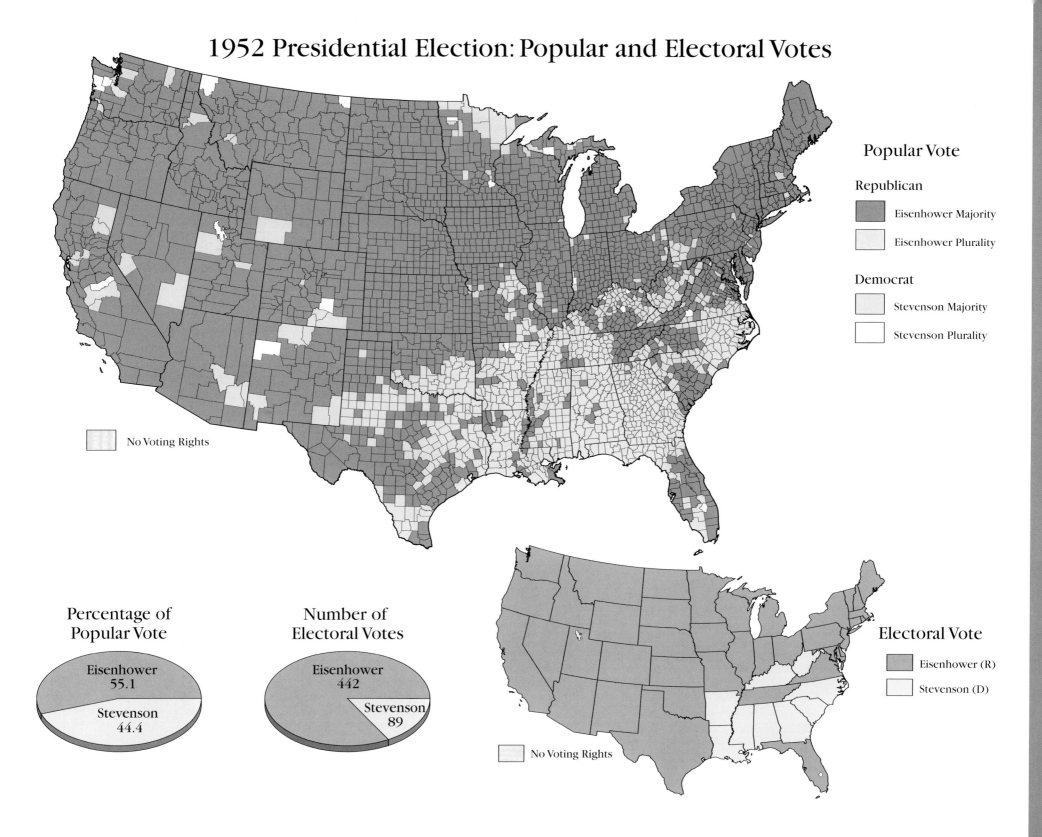

1952 Presidential Election: Popular and Electoral Votes

Map 42

Popular Vote

Republican

Eisenhower Majority

Eisenhower Plurality

Democrat

Stevenson Majority

Stevenson Plurality

No Voting Rights

Percentage of Popular Vote

Eisenhower 55.1

Stevenson 44.4

Number of Electoral Votes

Eisenhower 442

Stevenson 89

Electoral Vote

Eisenhower (R)

Stevenson (D)

No Voting Rights

Map
43

1956 Presidential Election: Popular Support for Leading Candidates

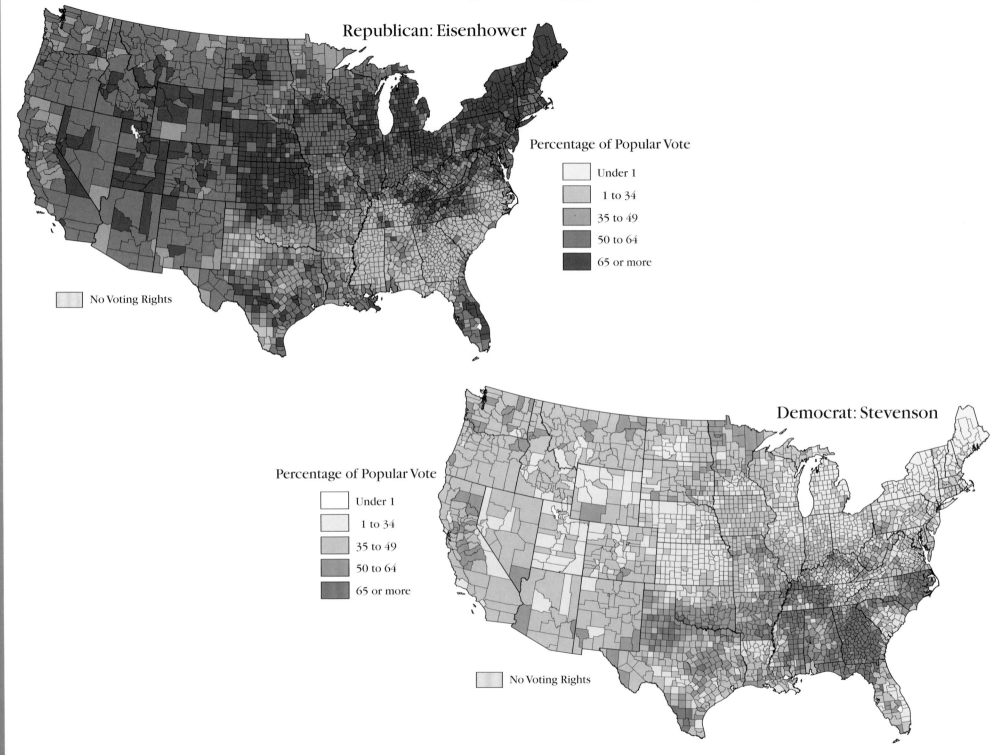

Republican: Eisenhower

Percentage of Popular Vote

Under 1
1 to 34
35 to 49
50 to 64
65 or more

No Voting Rights

Democrat: Stevenson

Percentage of Popular Vote

Under 1
1 to 34
35 to 49
50 to 64
65 or more

No Voting Rights

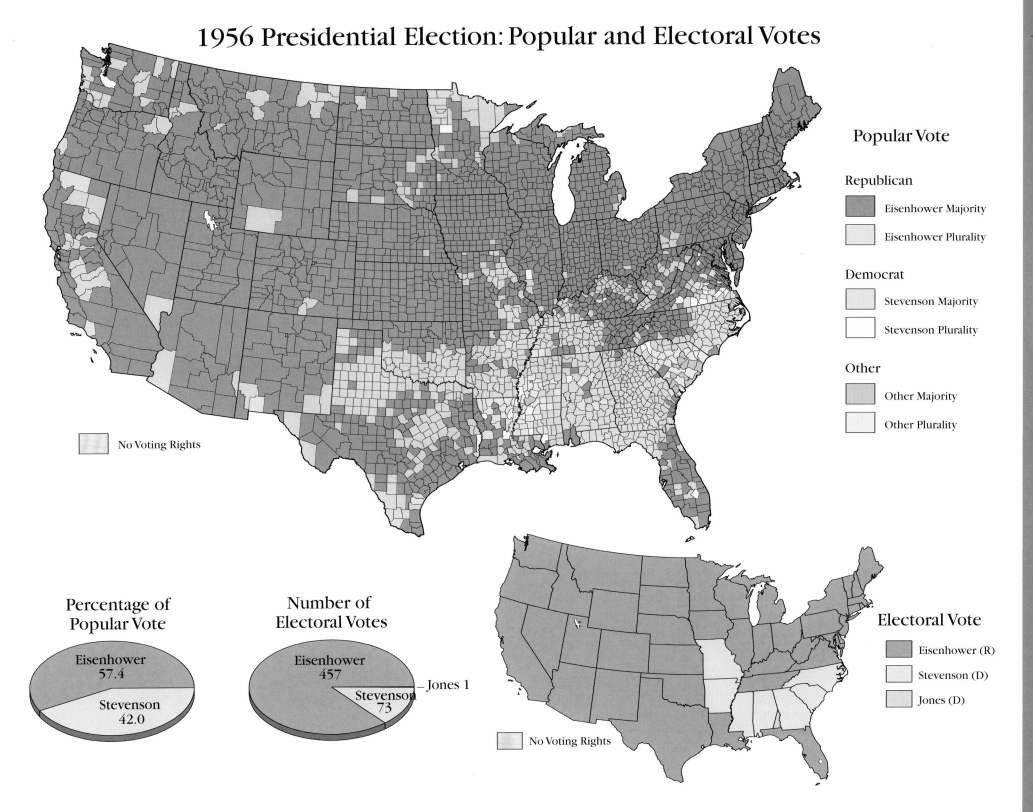

1956 Presidential Election: Popular and Electoral Votes

Map
43

Popular Vote

Republican

Eisenhower Majority

Eisenhower Plurality

Democrat

Stevenson Majority

Stevenson Plurality

Other

Other Majority

Other Plurality

No Voting Rights

Percentage of Popular Vote

Eisenhower
57.4

Stevenson
42.0

Number of Electoral Votes

Eisenhower
457

Jones 1

Stevenson
73

Electoral Vote

Eisenhower (R)

Stevenson (D)

Jones (D)

No Voting Rights

Map 44

1960 Presidential Election: Popular Support for Leading Candidates

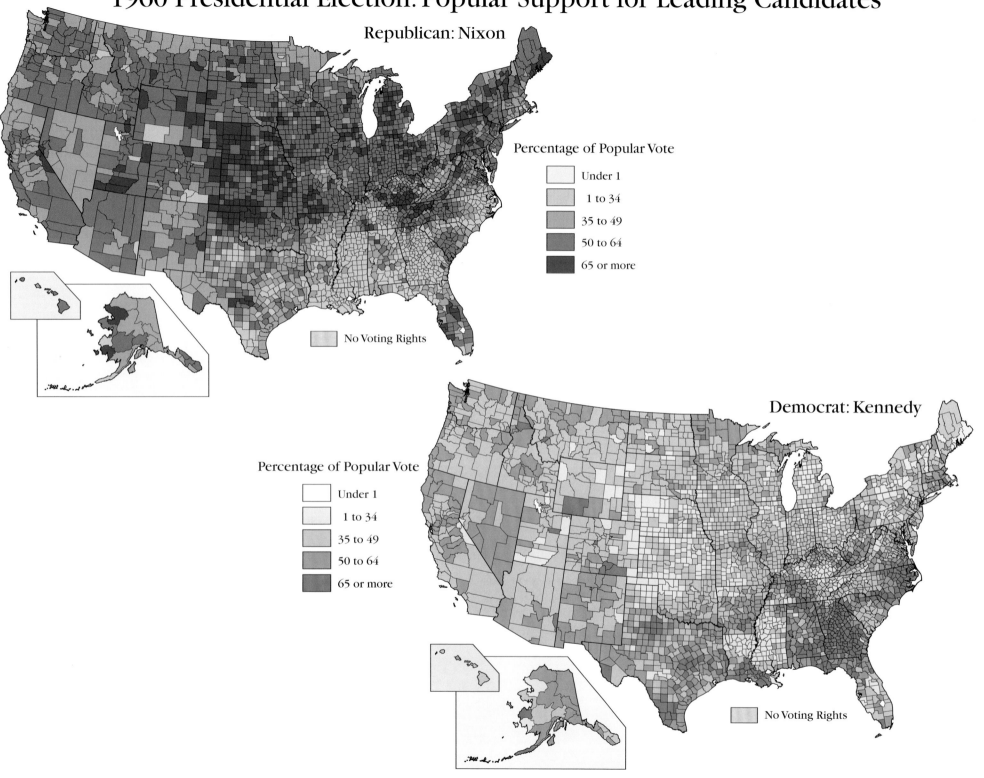

Republican: Nixon

Percentage of Popular Vote

Under 1
1 to 34
35 to 49
50 to 64
65 or more

No Voting Rights

Democrat: Kennedy

Percentage of Popular Vote

Under 1
1 to 34
35 to 49
50 to 64
65 or more

No Voting Rights

1960 Presidential Election: Popular and Electoral Votes

Map 44

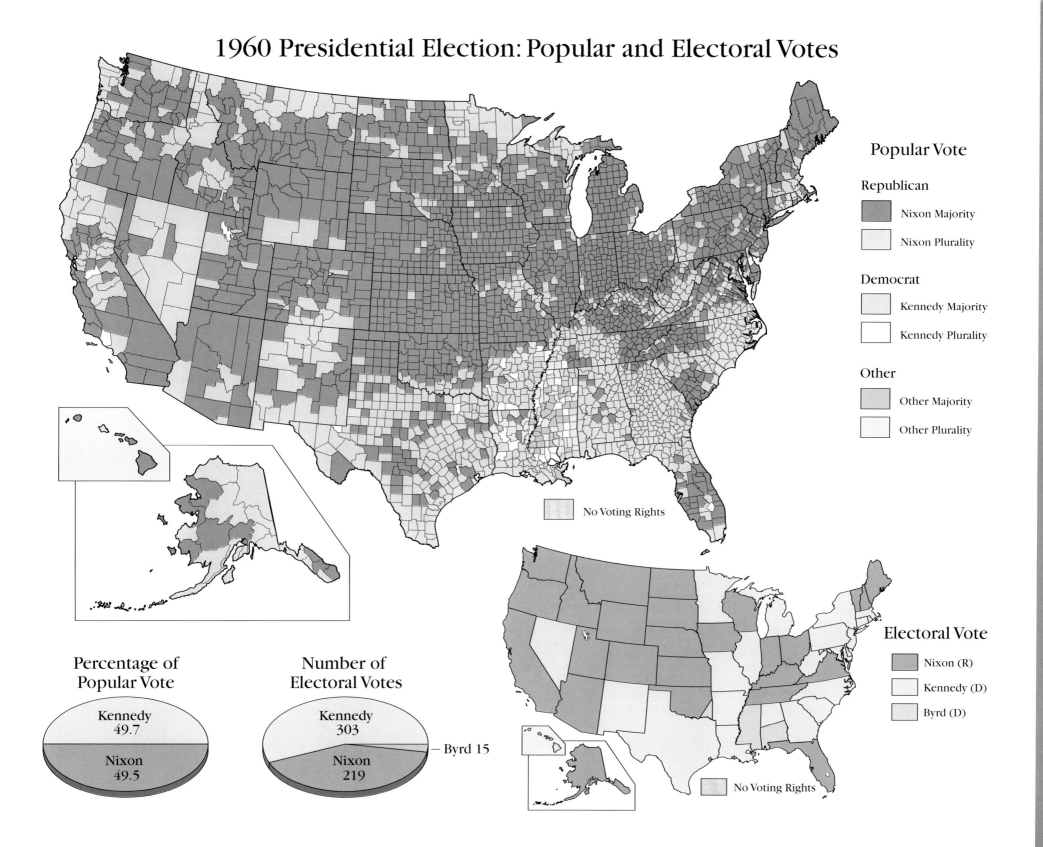

Popular Vote

Republican
- Nixon Majority
- Nixon Plurality

Democrat
- Kennedy Majority
- Kennedy Plurality

Other
- Other Majority
- Other Plurality

No Voting Rights

Percentage of Popular Vote

Kennedy 49.7

Nixon 49.5

Number of Electoral Votes

Kennedy 303

Byrd 15

Nixon 219

Electoral Vote
- Nixon (R)
- Kennedy (D)
- Byrd (D)

No Voting Rights

Map
45

1964 Presidential Election: Popular Support for Leading Candidates

Republican: Goldwater

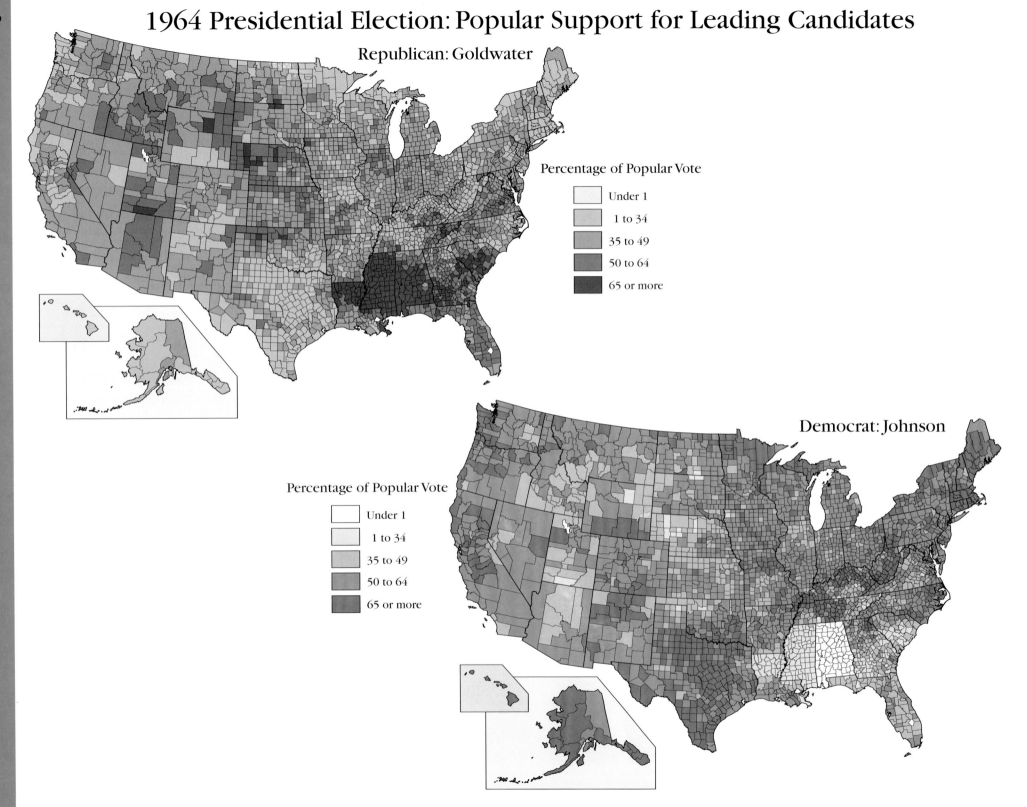

Percentage of Popular Vote

Under 1
1 to 34
35 to 49
50 to 64
65 or more

Percentage of Popular Vote

Under 1
1 to 34
35 to 49
50 to 64
65 or more

Democrat: Johnson

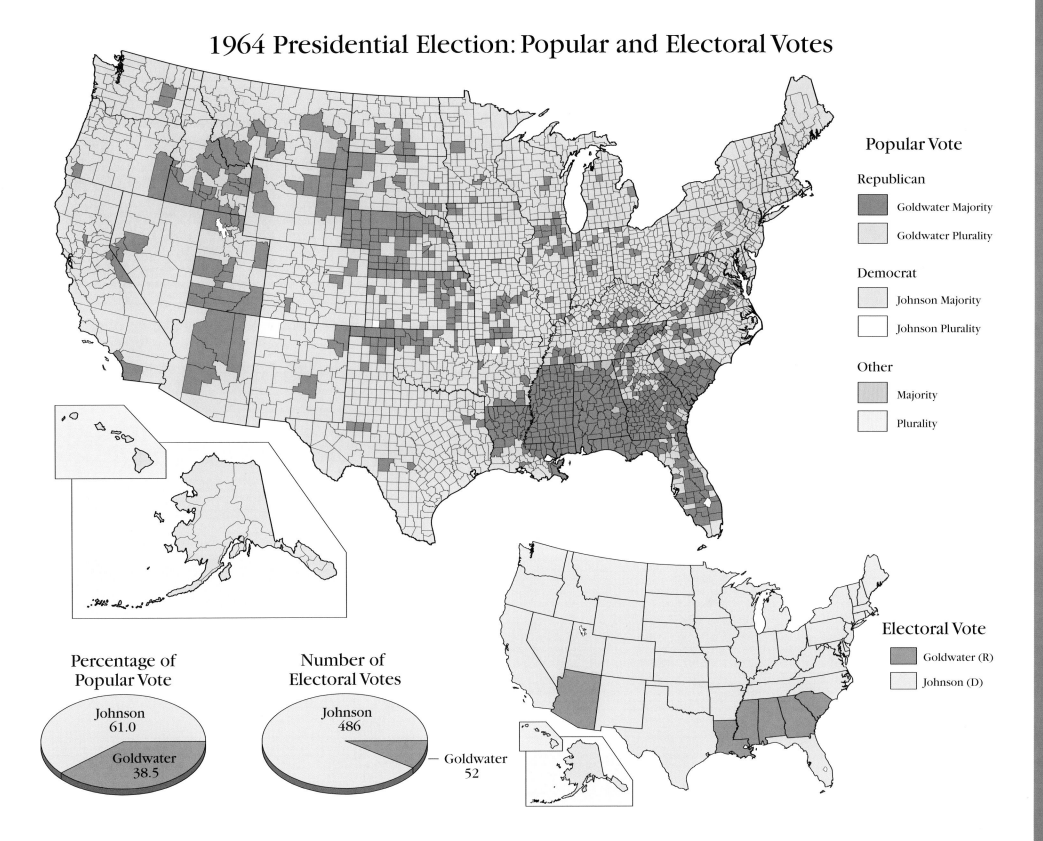

Map
45

1964 Presidential Election: Popular and Electoral Votes

Popular Vote

Republican

Goldwater Majority

Goldwater Plurality

Democrat

Johnson Majority

Johnson Plurality

Other

Majority

Plurality

Electoral Vote

Goldwater (R)

Johnson (D)

Percentage of Popular Vote

Johnson 61.0

Goldwater 38.5

Number of Electoral Votes

Johnson 486

Goldwater 52

1968 Presidential Election: Popular Support for Leading Candidates

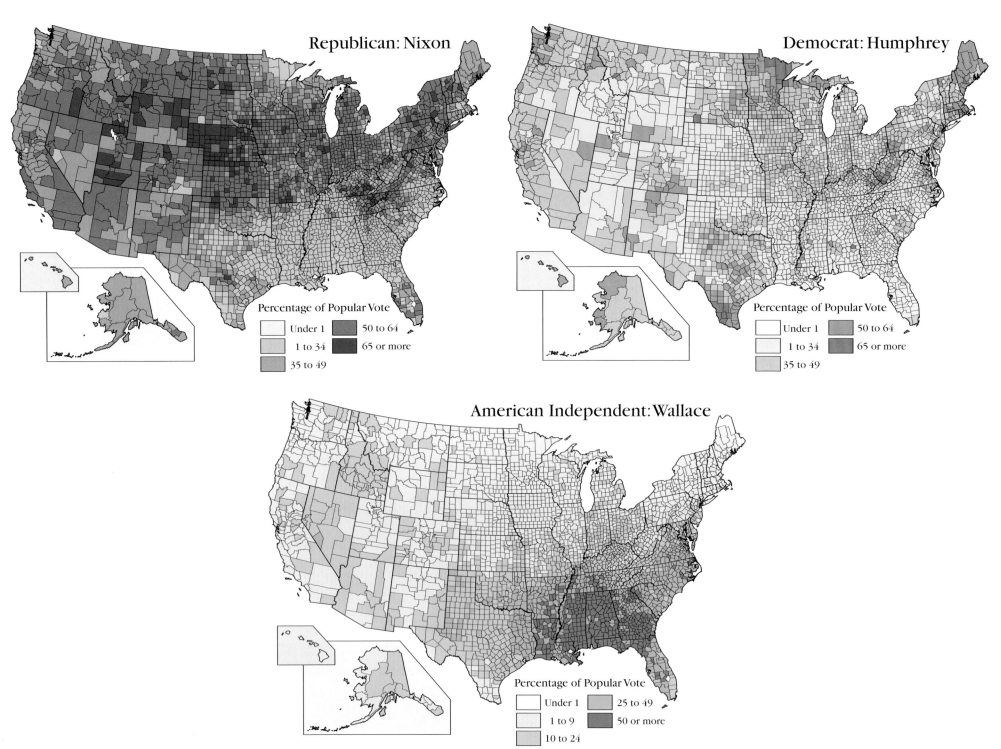

Republican: Nixon

Democrat: Humphrey

Percentage of Popular Vote

Under 1	50 to 64
1 to 34	65 or more
35 to 49	

Percentage of Popular Vote

Under 1	50 to 64
1 to 34	65 or more
35 to 49	

American Independent: Wallace

Percentage of Popular Vote

Under 1	25 to 49
1 to 9	50 or more
10 to 24	

Map
46

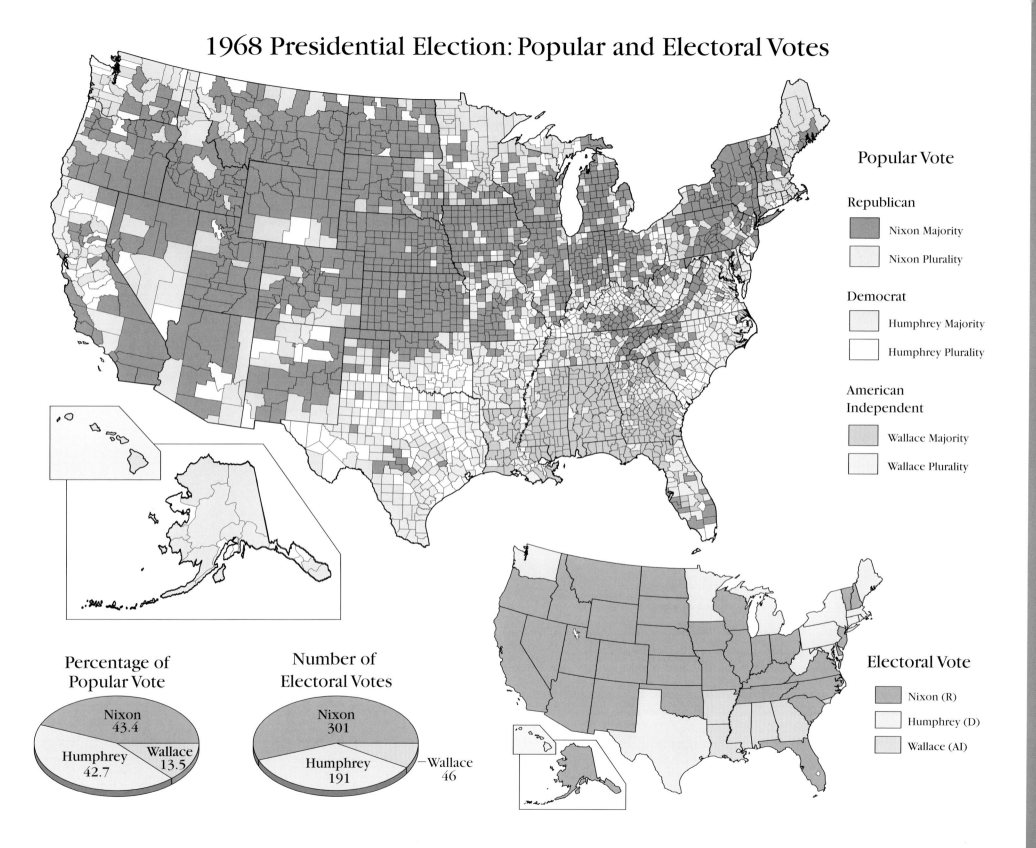

1968 Presidential Election: Popular and Electoral Votes

Map 46

Popular Vote

Republican

Nixon Majority

Nixon Plurality

Democrat

Humphrey Majority

Humphrey Plurality

American Independent

Wallace Majority

Wallace Plurality

Percentage of Popular Vote

Nixon 43.4

Humphrey 42.7

Wallace 13.5

Number of Electoral Votes

Nixon 301

Humphrey 191

Wallace 46

Electoral Vote

Nixon (R)

Humphrey (D)

Wallace (AI)

Map
47

1972 Presidential Election: Popular Support for Leading Candidates

Republican: Nixon

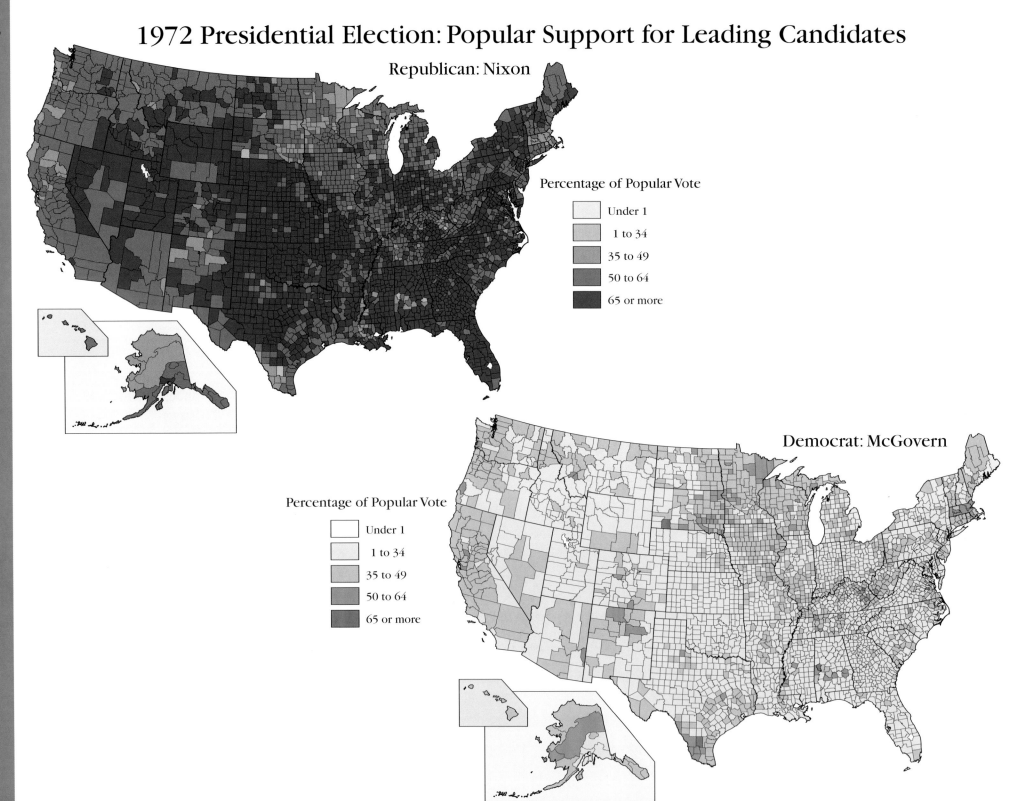

Percentage of Popular Vote

Under 1
1 to 34
35 to 49
50 to 64
65 or more

Democrat: McGovern

Percentage of Popular Vote

Under 1
1 to 34
35 to 49
50 to 64
65 or more

1972 Presidential Election: Popular and Electoral Votes

Map
47

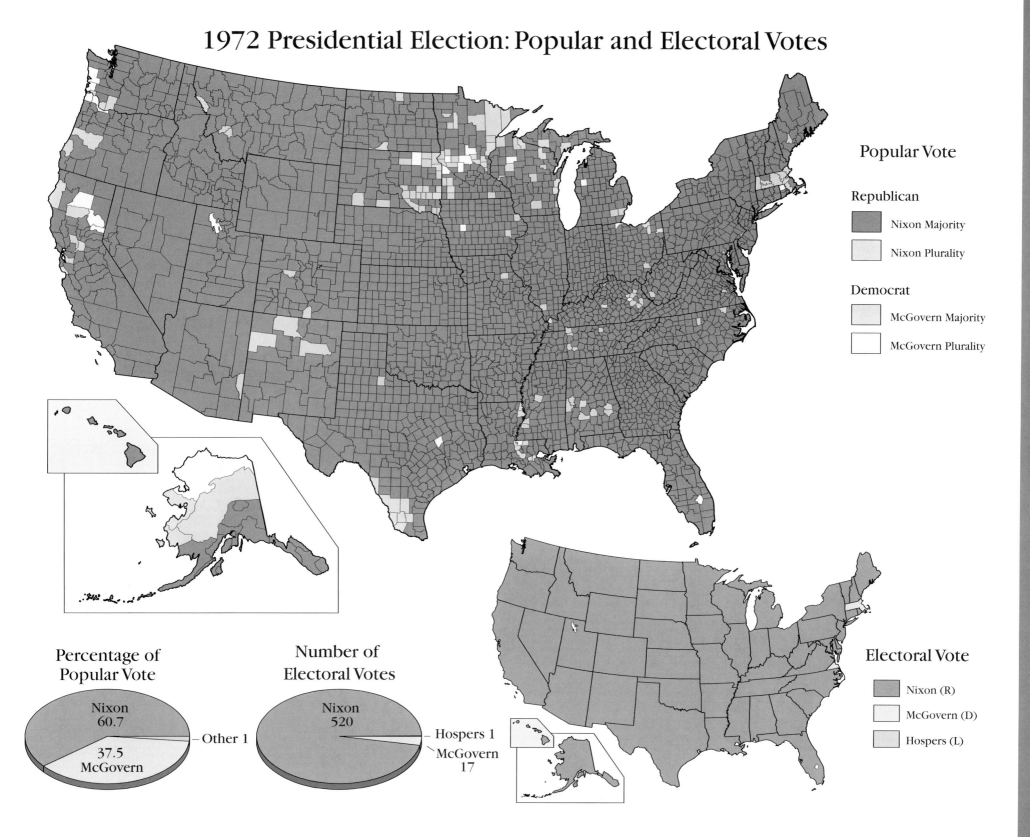

Popular Vote

Republican

Nixon Majority

Nixon Plurality

Democrat

McGovern Majority

McGovern Plurality

Percentage of Popular Vote

Nixon 60.7

37.5 McGovern

— Other 1

Number of Electoral Votes

Nixon 520

— Hospers 1

McGovern 17

Electoral Vote

Nixon (R)

McGovern (D)

Hospers (L)

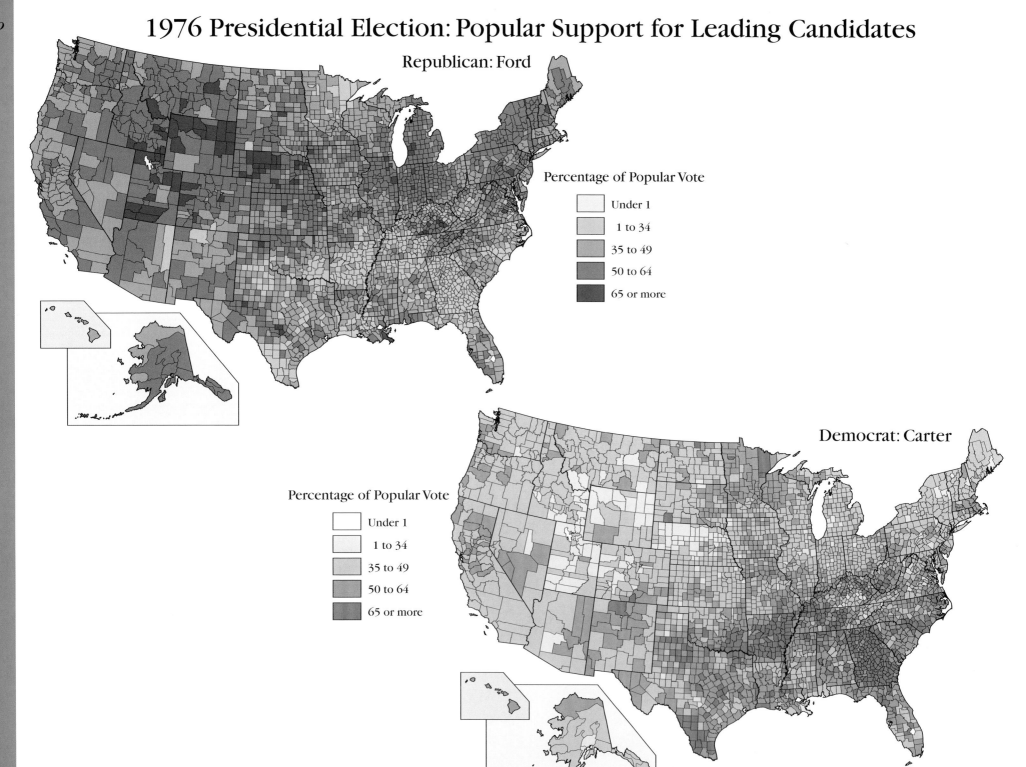

1976 Presidential Election: Popular Support for Leading Candidates

Republican: Ford

Democrat: Carter

Percentage of Popular Vote

- Under 1
- 1 to 34
- 35 to 49
- 50 to 64
- 65 or more

Map 48

1976 Presidential Election: Popular and Electoral Votes

Map
48

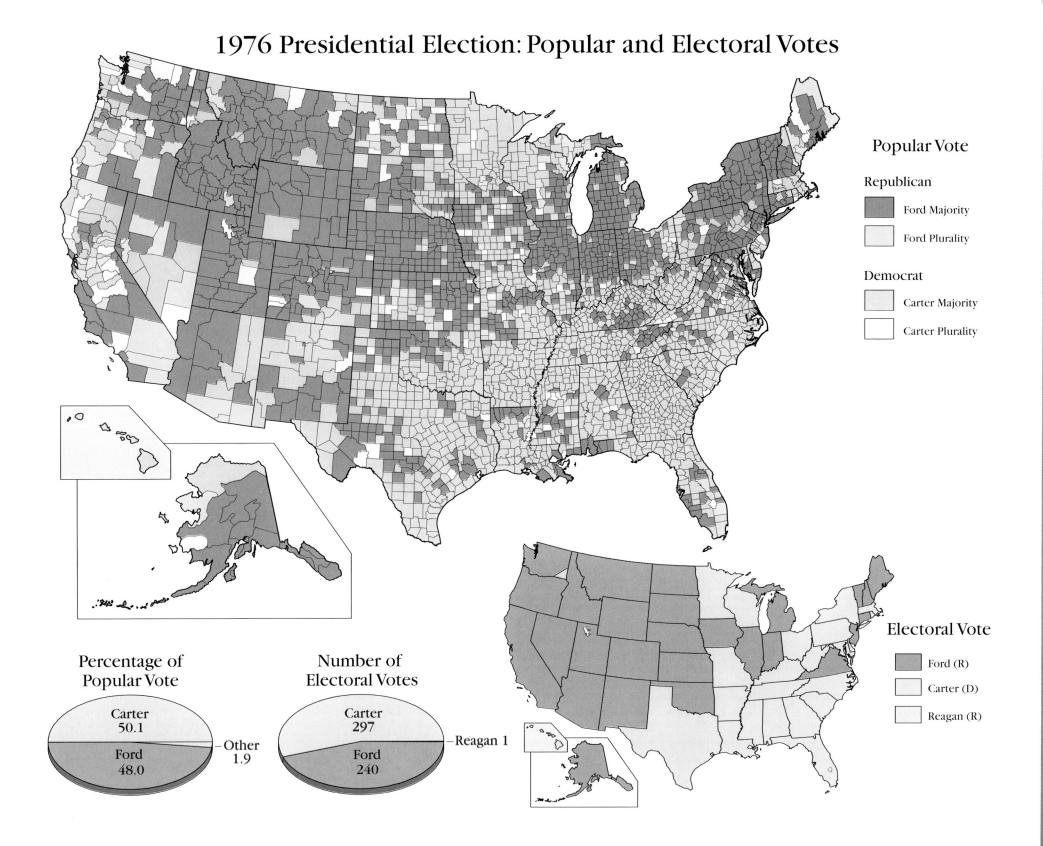

Popular Vote

Republican

Ford Majority

Ford Plurality

Democrat

Carter Majority

Carter Plurality

Electoral Vote

Ford (R)

Carter (D)

Reagan (R)

Percentage of Popular Vote

Carter 50.1

Ford 48.0

Other 1.9

Number of Electoral Votes

Carter 297

Ford 240

Reagan 1

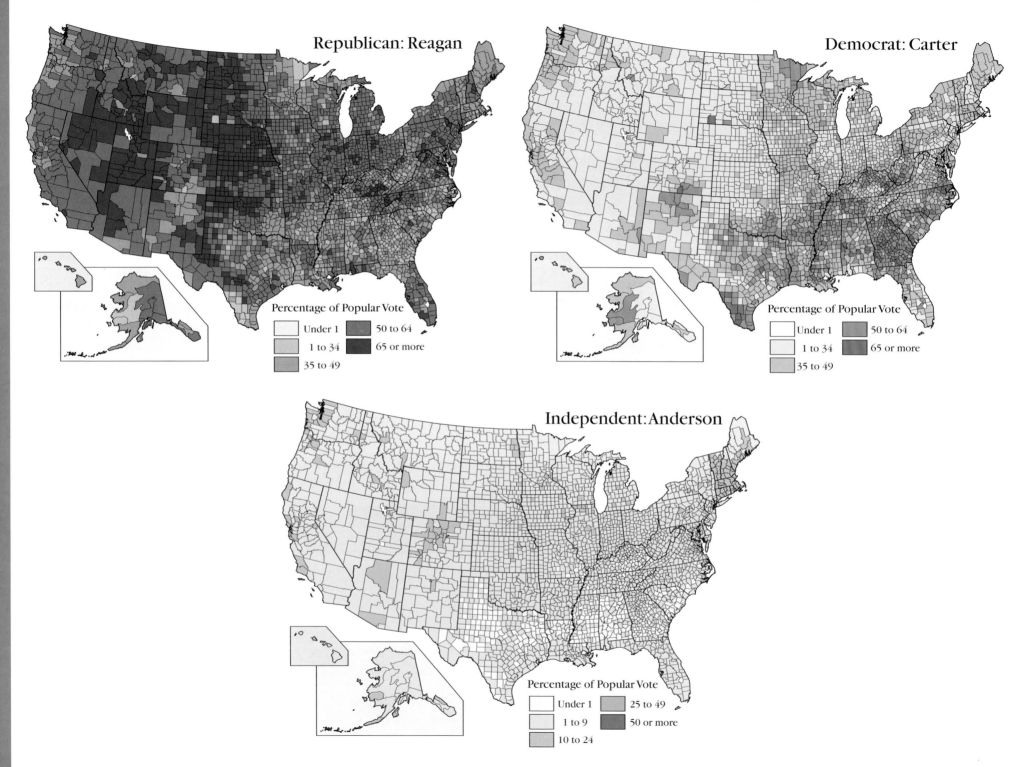

Map
49

1980 Presidential Election: Popular Support for Leading Candidates

Republican: Reagan

Democrat: Carter

Percentage of Popular Vote

Under 1
1 to 34
35 to 49
50 to 64
65 or more

Percentage of Popular Vote

Under 1
1 to 34
35 to 49
50 to 64
65 or more

Independent: Anderson

Percentage of Popular Vote

Under 1
1 to 9
10 to 24
25 to 49
50 or more

1980 Presidential Election: Popular and Electoral Votes

Map
49

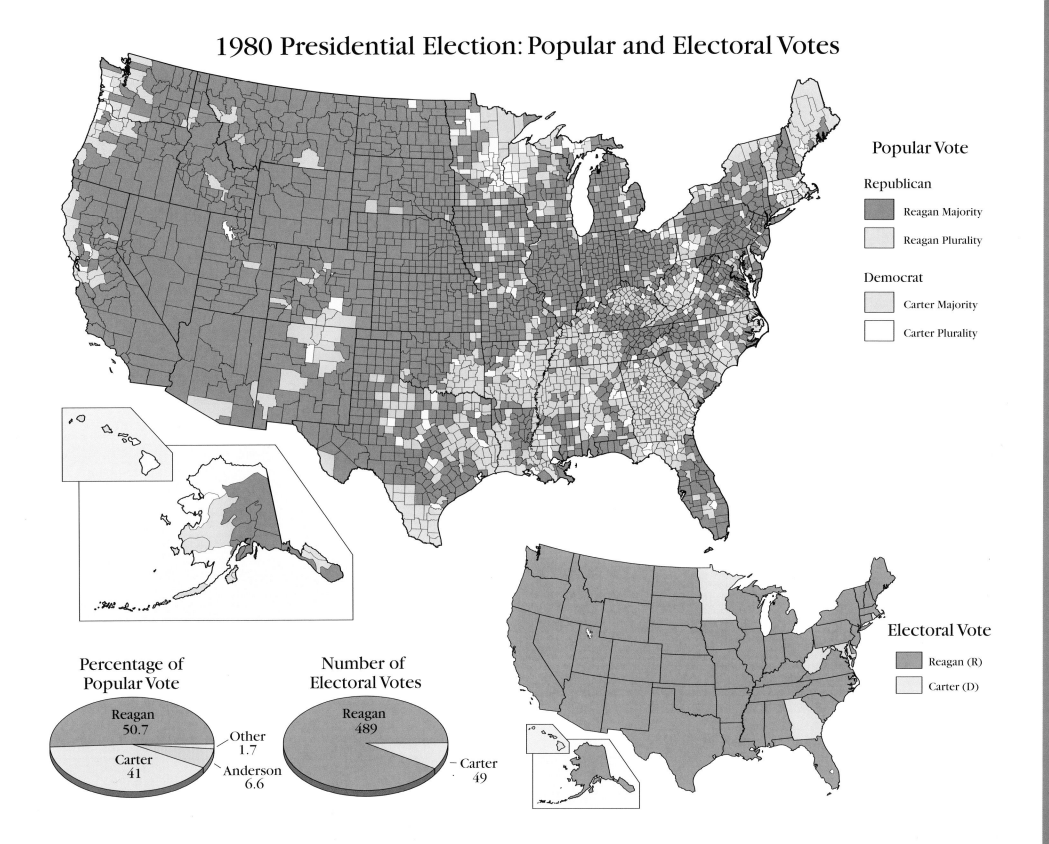

Popular Vote

Republican

Reagan Majority

Reagan Plurality

Democrat

Carter Majority

Carter Plurality

Percentage of Popular Vote

Reagan 50.7

Carter 41

Other 1.7

Anderson 6.6

Number of Electoral Votes

Reagan 489

Carter 49

Electoral Vote

Reagan (R)

Carter (D)

Map
50

1984 Presidential Election: Popular Support for Leading Candidates

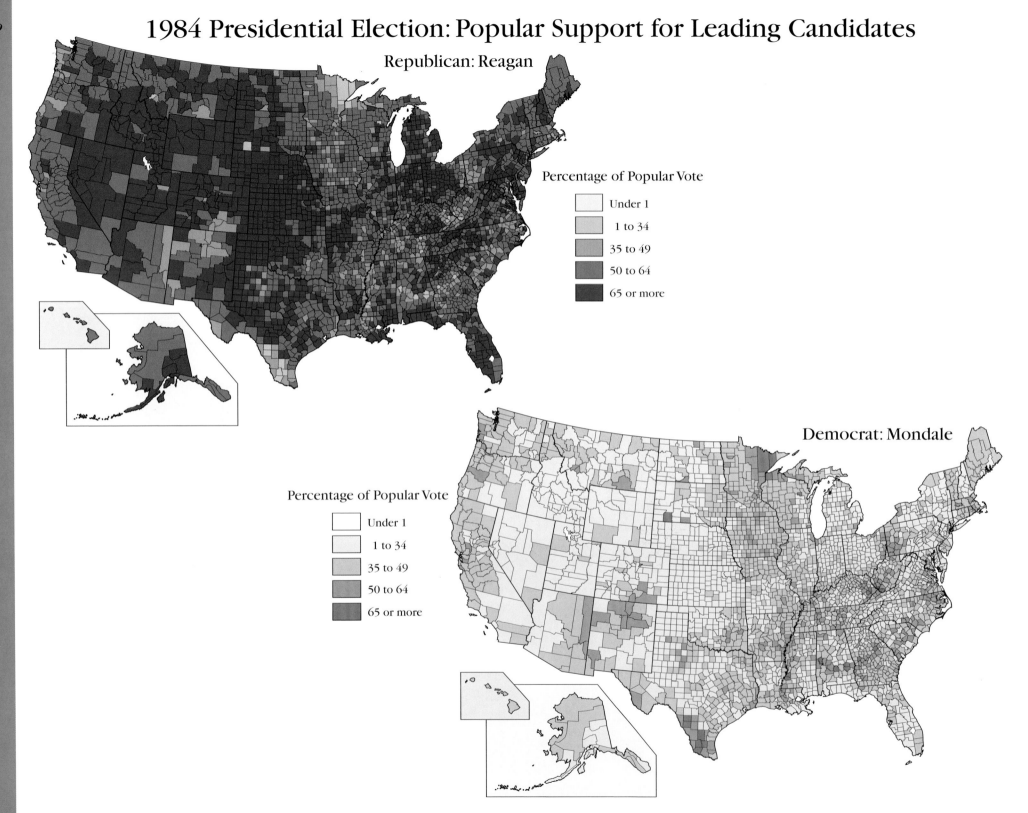

Republican: Reagan

Percentage of Popular Vote

- Under 1
- 1 to 34
- 35 to 49
- 50 to 64
- 65 or more

Democrat: Mondale

Percentage of Popular Vote

- Under 1
- 1 to 34
- 35 to 49
- 50 to 64
- 65 or more

1984 Presidential Election: Popular and Electoral Votes

Map 50

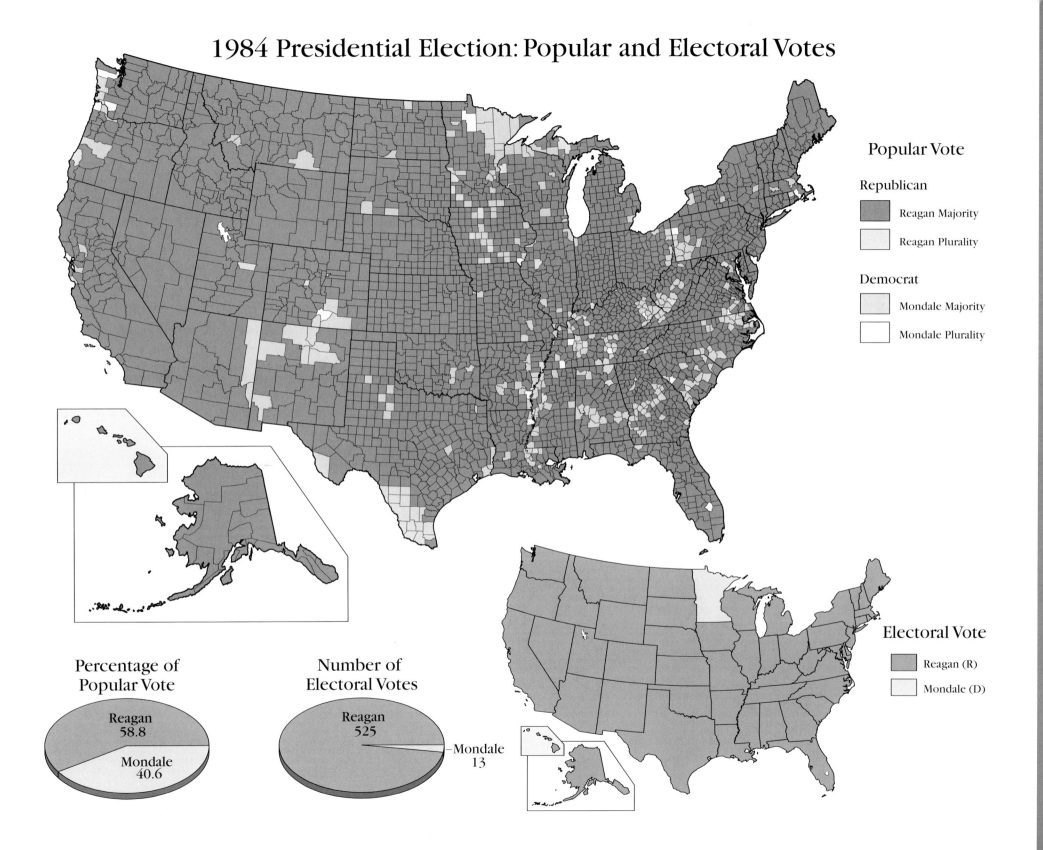

Popular Vote

Republican

Reagan Majority

Reagan Plurality

Democrat

Mondale Majority

Mondale Plurality

Electoral Vote

Reagan (R)

Mondale (D)

Percentage of Popular Vote

Reagan 58.8

Mondale 40.6

Number of Electoral Votes

Reagan 525

Mondale 13

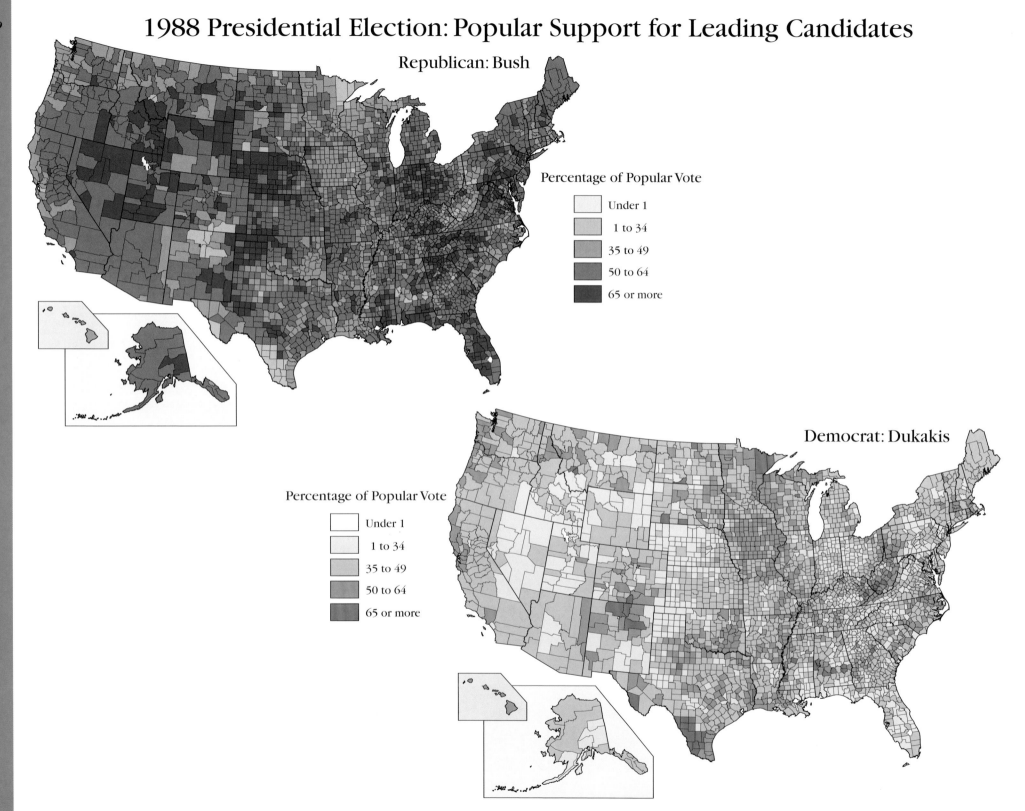

Map
51

1988 Presidential Election: Popular Support for Leading Candidates

Republican: Bush

Percentage of Popular Vote

- Under 1
- 1 to 34
- 35 to 49
- 50 to 64
- 65 or more

Democrat: Dukakis

Percentage of Popular Vote

- Under 1
- 1 to 34
- 35 to 49
- 50 to 64
- 65 or more

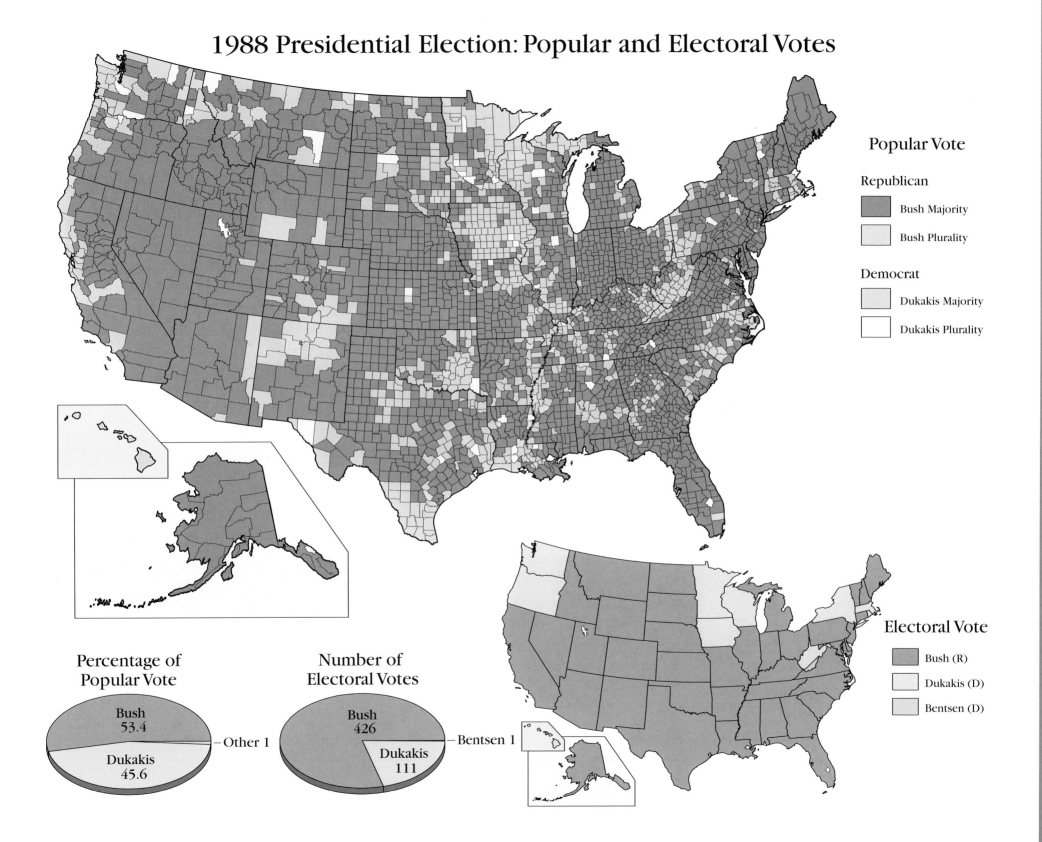

1988 Presidential Election: Popular and Electoral Votes

Map 51

Popular Vote

Republican

- Bush Majority
- Bush Plurality

Democrat

- Dukakis Majority
- Dukakis Plurality

Percentage of Popular Vote

Bush 53.4
Dukakis 45.6
— Other 1

Number of Electoral Votes

Bush 426
Dukakis 111
— Bentsen 1

Electoral Vote

- Bush (R)
- Dukakis (D)
- Bentsen (D)

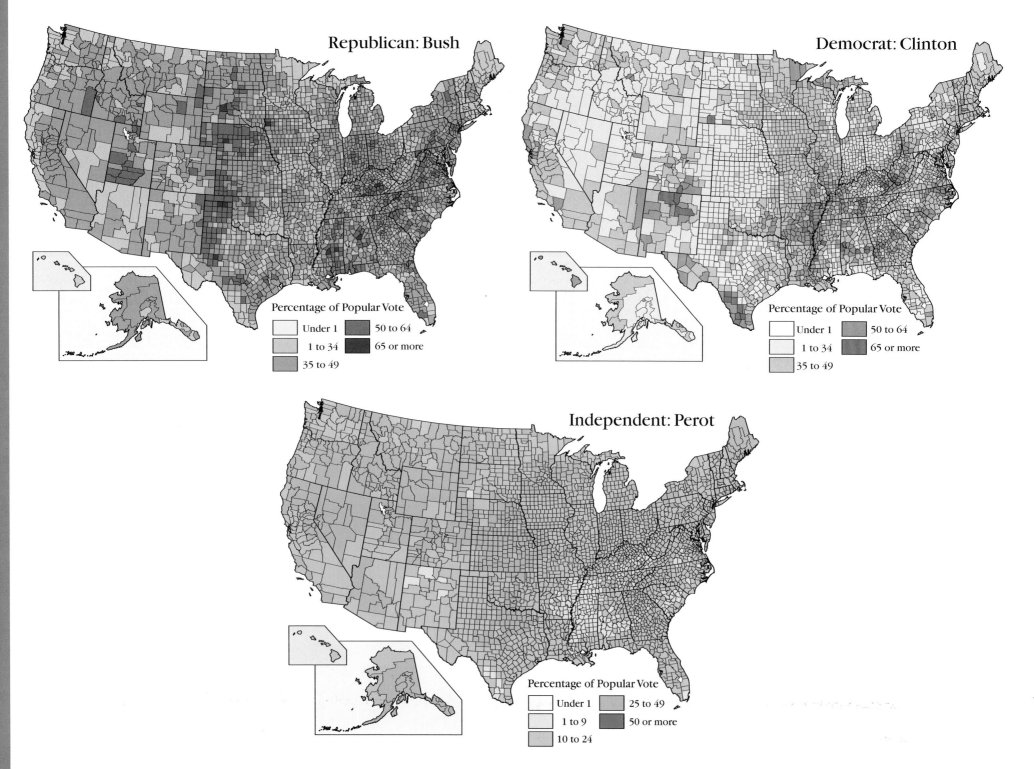

Map
52

1992 Presidential Election: Popular Support for Leading Candidates

Republican: Bush

Percentage of Popular Vote

- Under 1
- 1 to 34
- 35 to 49
- 50 to 64
- 65 or more

Democrat: Clinton

Percentage of Popular Vote

- Under 1
- 1 to 34
- 35 to 49
- 50 to 64
- 65 or more

Independent: Perot

Percentage of Popular Vote

- Under 1
- 1 to 9
- 10 to 24
- 25 to 49
- 50 or more

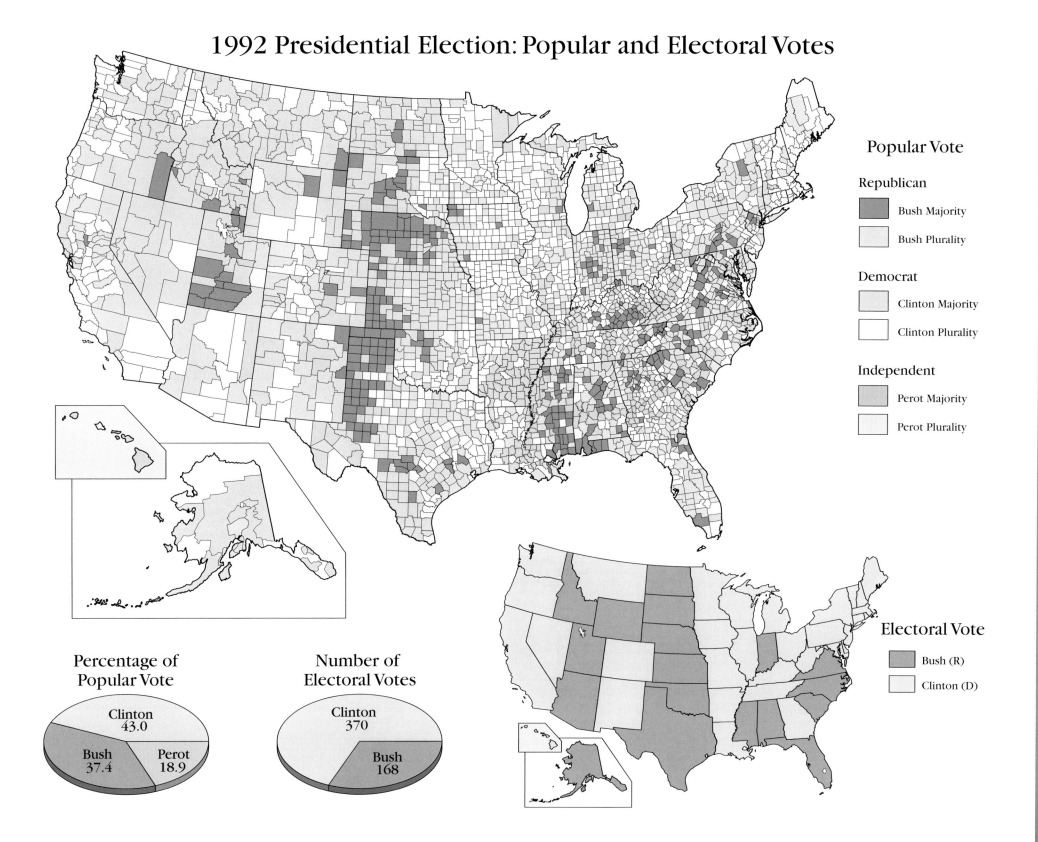

1992 Presidential Election: Popular and Electoral Votes

Map
52

Popular Vote

Republican
Bush Majority
Bush Plurality

Democrat
Clinton Majority
Clinton Plurality

Independent
Perot Majority
Perot Plurality

Electoral Vote
Bush (R)
Clinton (D)

Percentage of Popular Vote
Clinton 43.0
Bush 37.4
Perot 18.9

Number of Electoral Votes
Clinton 370
Bush 168

Map
53

1996 Presidential Election: Popular Support for Leading Candidates

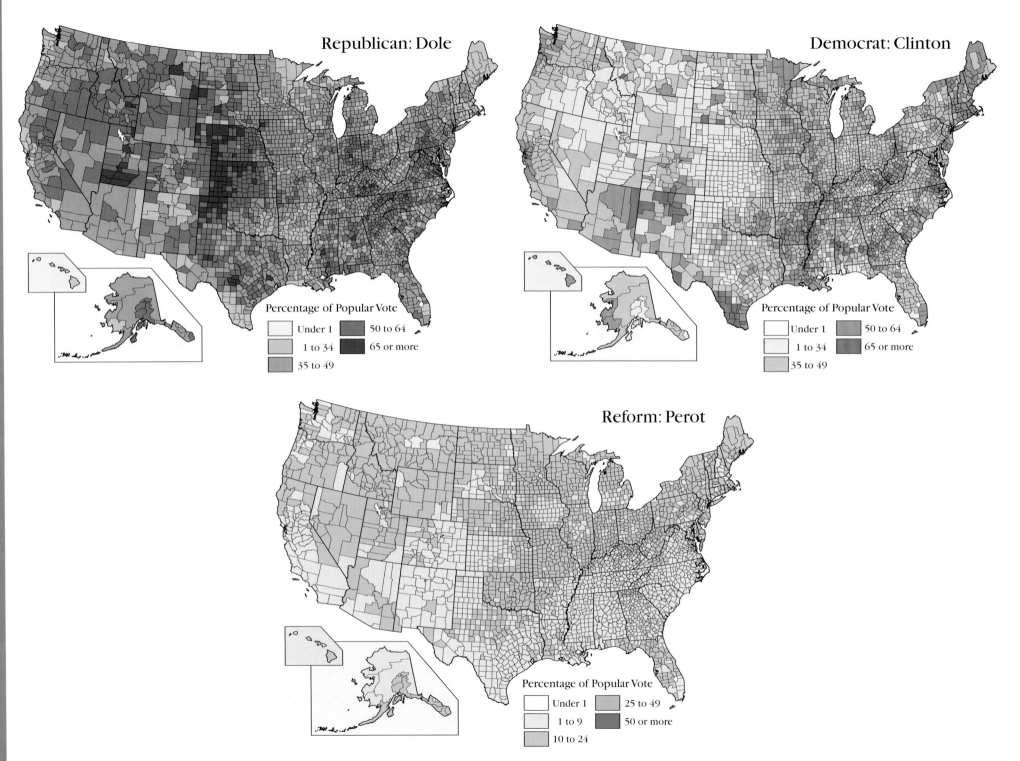

Republican: Dole

Democrat: Clinton

Reform: Perot

Percentage of Popular Vote

Under 1
1 to 34
35 to 49
50 to 64
65 or more

Percentage of Popular Vote

Under 1
1 to 34
35 to 49
50 to 64
65 or more

Percentage of Popular Vote

Under 1
1 to 9
10 to 24
25 to 49
50 or more

1996 Presidential Election: Popular and Electoral Votes

Map
53

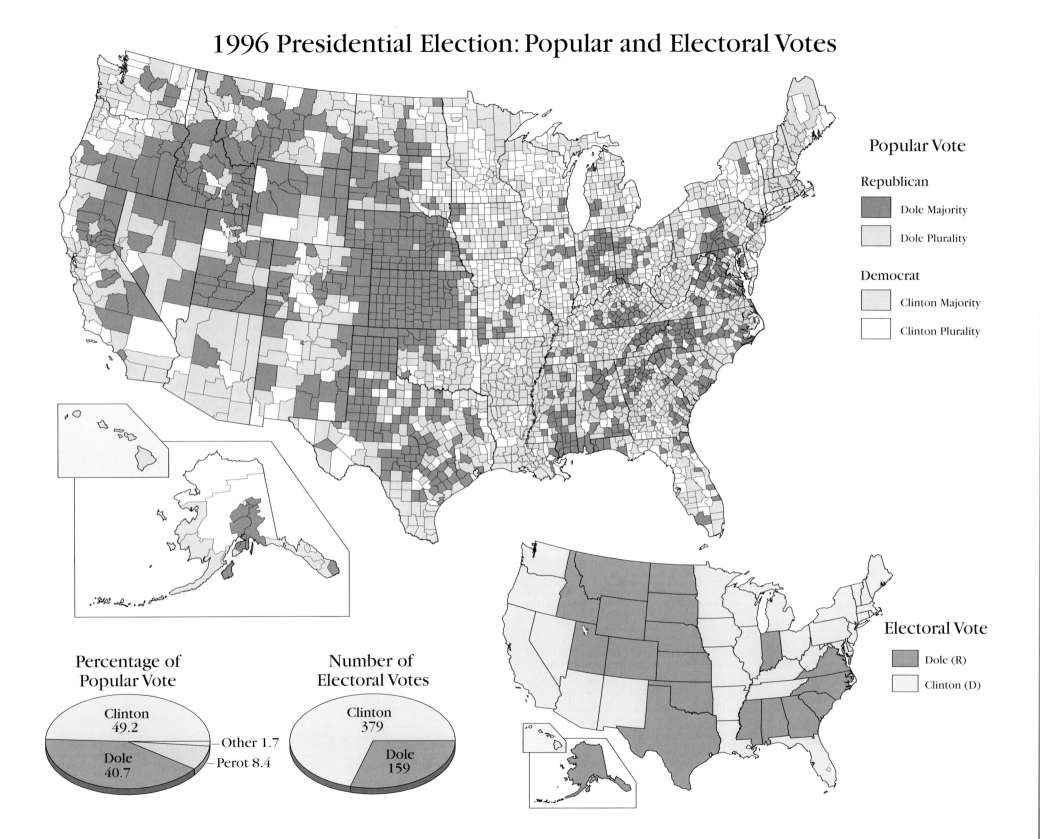

Popular Vote

Republican

Dole Majority

Dole Plurality

Democrat

Clinton Majority

Clinton Plurality

Electoral Vote

Dole (R)

Clinton (D)

Percentage of Popular Vote

Clinton 49.2

Dole 40.7

Other 1.7

Perot 8.4

Number of Electoral Votes

Clinton 379

Dole 159

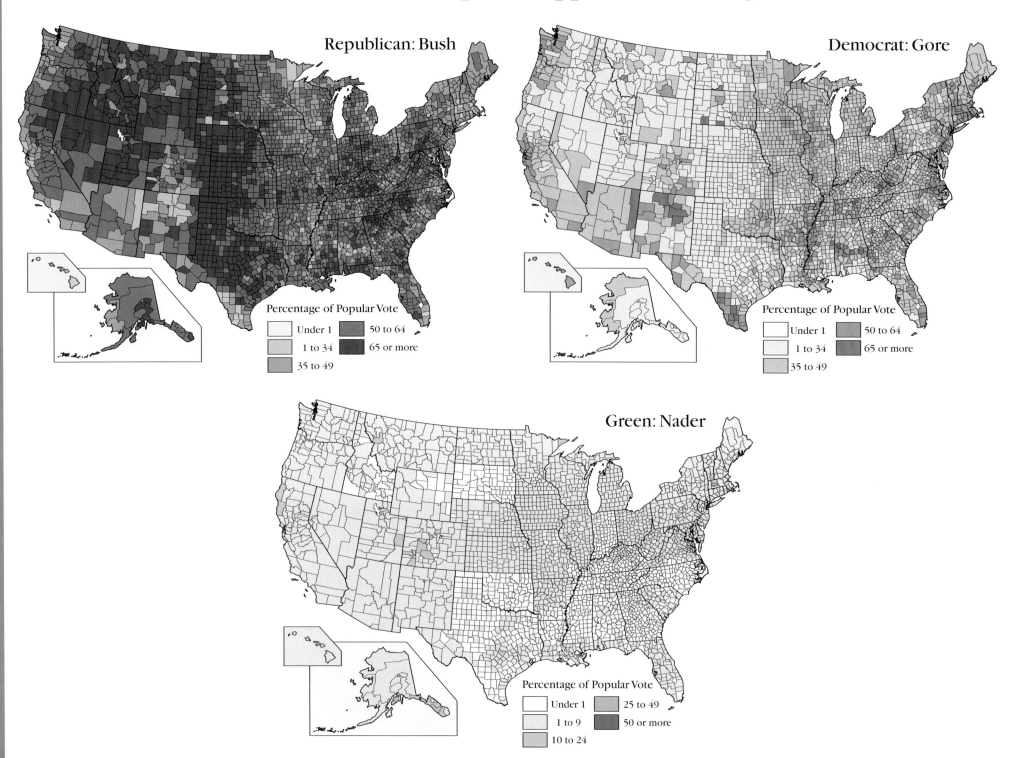

2000 Presidential Election: Popular Support for Leading Candidates

Map
54

Republican: Bush

Percentage of Popular Vote

- Under 1
- 1 to 34
- 35 to 49
- 50 to 64
- 65 or more

Democrat: Gore

Percentage of Popular Vote

- Under 1
- 1 to 34
- 35 to 49
- 50 to 64
- 65 or more

Green: Nader

Percentage of Popular Vote

- Under 1
- 1 to 9
- 10 to 24
- 25 to 49
- 50 or more

2000 Presidential Election: Popular and Electoral Votes

Map 54

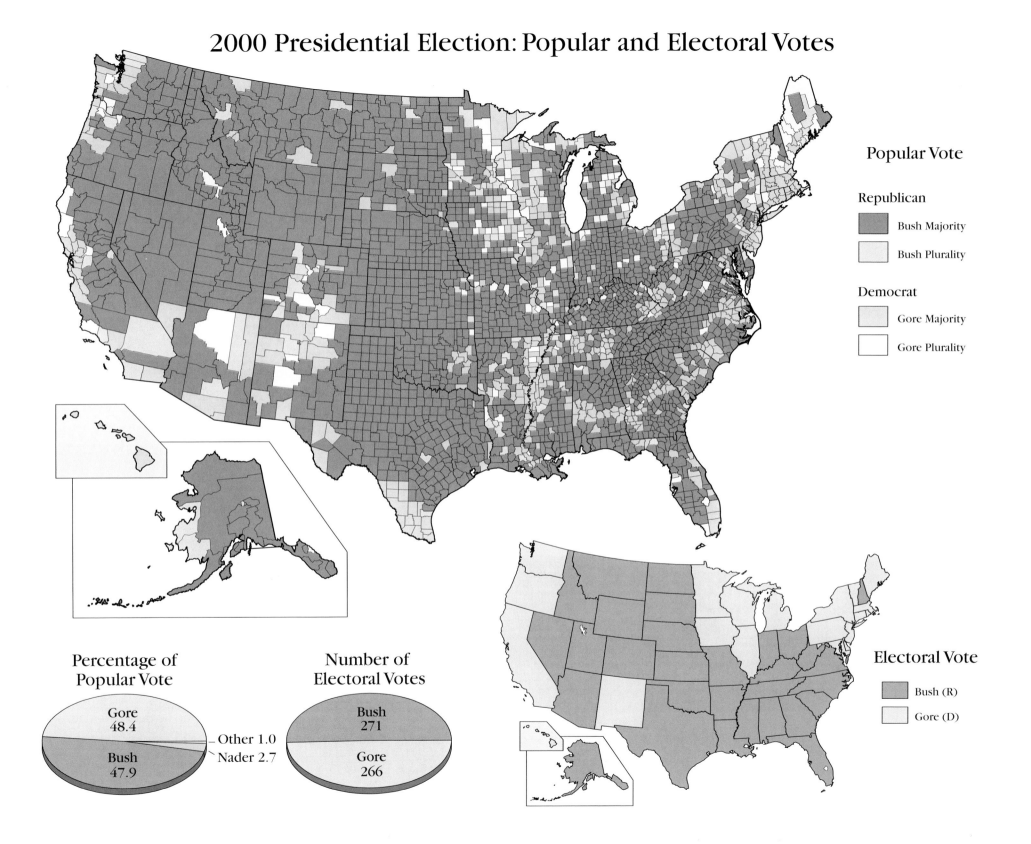

Popular Vote

Republican

Bush Majority

Bush Plurality

Democrat

Gore Majority

Gore Plurality

Percentage of
Popular Vote

Gore
48.4

Other 1.0

Nader 2.7

Bush
47.9

Number of
Electoral Votes

Bush
271

Gore
266

Electoral Vote

Bush (R)

Gore (D)

Map
55

2004 Presidential Election: Popular Support for Leading Candidates

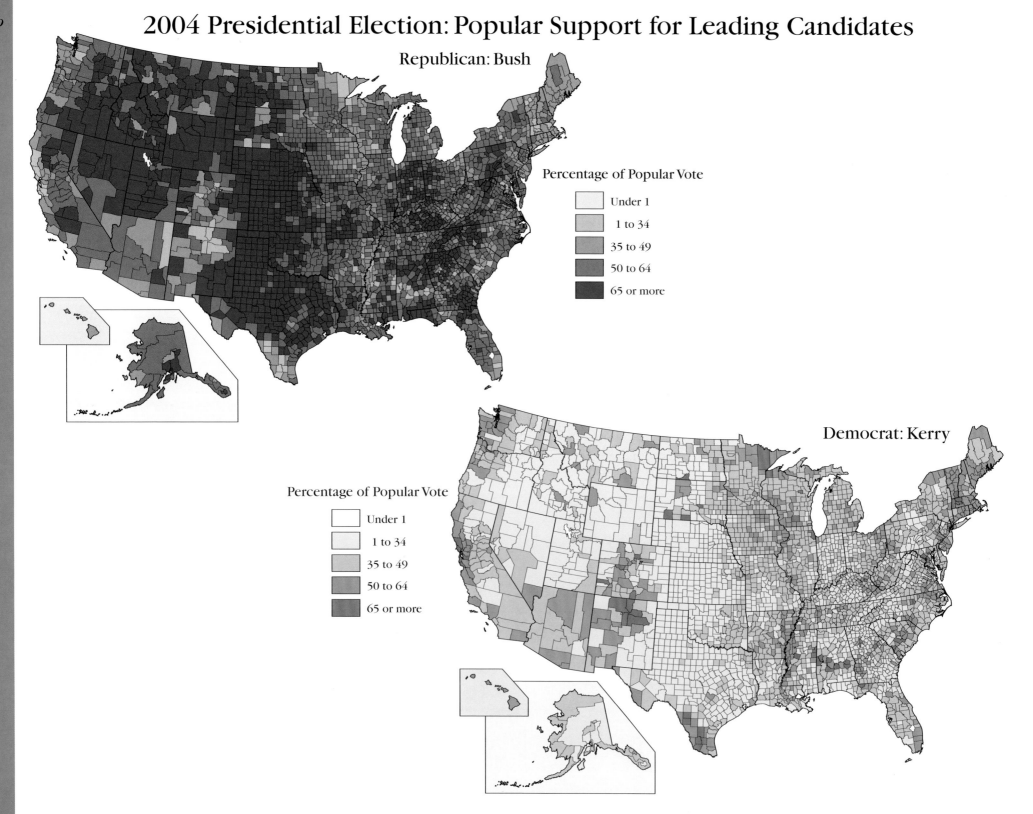

Republican: Bush

Percentage of Popular Vote

Under 1
1 to 34
35 to 49
50 to 64
65 or more

Percentage of Popular Vote

Under 1
1 to 34
35 to 49
50 to 64
65 or more

Democrat: Kerry

2004 Presidential Election: Popular and Electoral Votes

Map 55

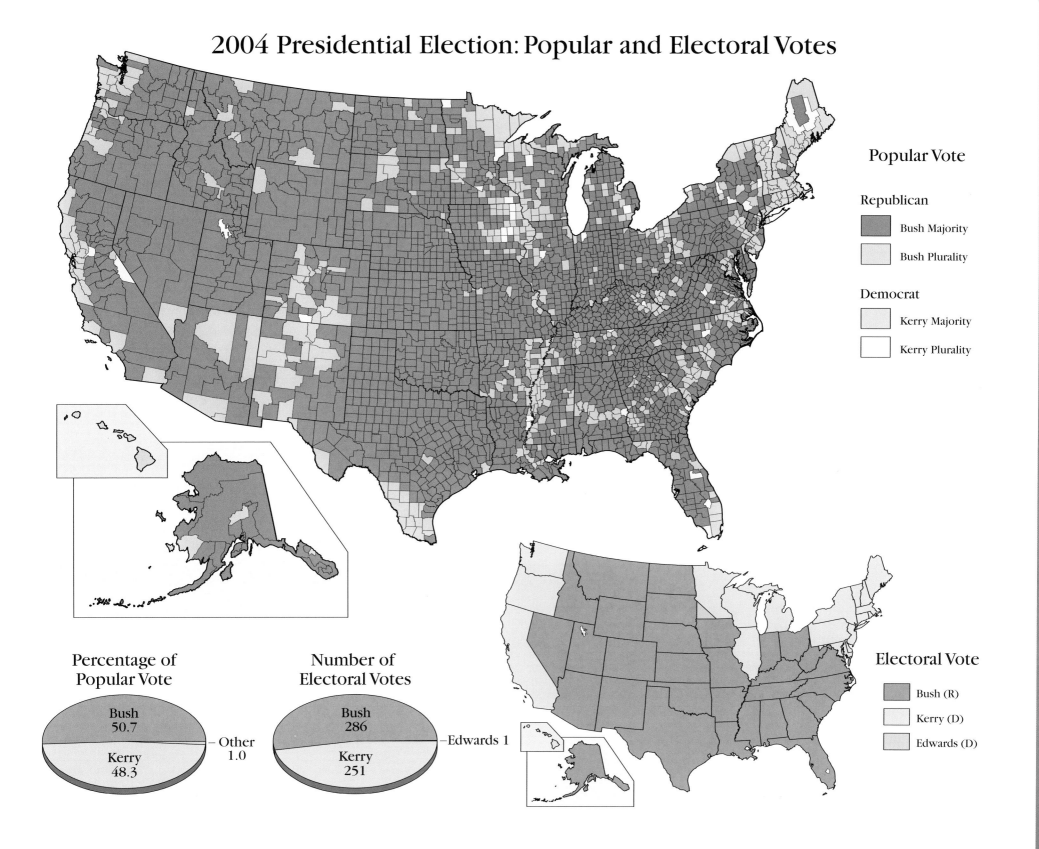

Popular Vote

Republican
- Bush Majority
- Bush Plurality

Democrat
- Kerry Majority
- Kerry Plurality

Electoral Vote
- Bush (R)
- Kerry (D)
- Edwards (D)

Percentage of Popular Vote
- Bush 50.7
- Kerry 48.3
- Other 1.0

Number of Electoral Votes
- Bush 286
- Kerry 251
- Edwards 1

1856

PRESIDENTIAL ELECTION

CANDIDATES	POPULAR VOTE PERCENTAGE	ELECTORAL COLLEGE VOTE PERCENTAGE AND (VOTE)
Democrat		
James Buchanan (Pennsylvania)	45.3	58.8 (174)
Vice Presidential Nominee: John Breckenridge (Kentucky)		
Republican		
John Fremont (California)	33.1	38.5 (114)
Vice Presidential Nominee: William Dayton (New Jersey)		
American-Whig		
Millard Fillmore (New York)	21.5	2.7 (8)
Vice Presidential Nominee: Andrew Jackson Donelson (Tennessee)		

Map 18

The presidential elections of 1856 and 1860 marked the beginning of a new electoral era in U.S. history. The Whig-Democrat era had been a nonsectional period distinguished by two national parties attempting to obtain votes nationwide and maintain the unity of their northern and southern wings. The 1856 election brought the first truly "geographical," or sectional, party with a platform addressing the concerns of only one part of the country. This party, the Republican Party, resulted from numerous political events. Slavery and its expansion into the territories were the core political issues of the day.

If one event can be considered the catalyst for renewed sectional strife prior to the 1856 election, it would probably be the Kansas-Nebraska Act of 1854. Sponsored by Democratic senator Stephen A. Douglas of Illinois, the act created the Kansas and Nebraska territories and instructed that the issue of slavery be determined by popular sovereignty of the local population. That slavery could possibly be expanded into Kansas, the more southern of the two territories, represented a direct repeal of the Missouri Compromise of 1820 and a rejection of the spirit of the Compromise of 1850. The act outraged the northern electorate. Northern

Whigs and some antislavery Democrats in Congress voted against it, but the act nonetheless passed with nearly unanimous support of southern Whigs and Democrats and their northern Democratic allies.

In Kansas, southerners and northerners launched efforts to bring settlers into the territory from their respective regions to sway the vote for establishing Kansas as a slave or free state. Migration, once a naturally occurring event, had in this instance become a geopolitical act. Antislavery zeal was at its highest in the Northeast, where the New England Emigrant Aid Company formed in Massachusetts, funded in part by industrialist Amos A. Lawrence. The company sent two groups of settlers to Kansas, where they established the settlement of Lawrence in 1854. Like western New York and the Western Reserve of Ohio, a bit of Yankee religious and political sentiment migrated west from New England, this time to the Great Plains. Southerners, many from the neighboring slave state of Missouri, also rushed to Kansas. Violence erupted, including the sacking of Lawrence in May 1856 by southern vigilantes, as the two factions struggled over the establishment of the territorial government. Several days after the attack on

Lawrence, five proslavery southern men were murdered by so-called Free State Volunteers, probably led by abolitionist John Brown. Bleeding Kansas became the focal point of the 1856 presidential campaign.

In the elections of 1854 and 1855 for the Thirty-fourth Congress (1855–1857), increasing numbers of candidates were labeled in the North as simply anti-Nebraska or pro-Nebraska rather than by political party affiliation. In February 1854, a group of Free Soilers, Conscience Whigs, and antislavery Democrats convened in Ripon, Wisconsin, to protest the impending Kansas-Nebraska Act and call for the creation of a new political party. In July 1854, the Republican Party was founded in Jackson, Michigan, with the primary tenet of resisting the expansion of slavery. By 1856 the Republicans had organized in all the northern states, and they held their first national presidential nominating convention in June of that year in Pittsburgh. In addition to all the free states being represented, delegates also arrived from the border states of Delaware, Kentucky, Maryland, and Virginia and the Kansas Territory, but none attended from the Deep South.

In a skillful move, the Republicans decided to nominate a political novice rather than a more well known and controversial ideological member of the party. They chose Californian John C. Fremont, noted western explorer and war hero, on the first ballot. Also on the first ballot, they nominated William Dayton of New Jersey for vice president. One Republican campaign slogan alluded to the recent Free Soil past, "Free Soil, Free Speech, Fremont." The core of their platform was banning slavery from all territories, opposing popular sovereignty, and admitting Kansas as a free state. Their platform did not call for the total abolition of slavery and included other planks, among them federal backing of internal improvements, such as a transcontinental railroad, an issue of historical interest to and with the support of business-oriented northern Whigs.

The collapse of the Whig Party had opened the door for the creation of not only the Republican Party, but also for the national revival and expansion of the American, or "Know-Nothing," Party. The Native American, or American, Party, had formed in the 1840s as a secret society opposed to foreigners and immigration. Because it was a secret organization, American Party members often said that they "knew nothing" when asked about their involvement in it. The party emerged on the national scene when six of its members from the cities of New York and Philadelphia, which were experiencing an influx of Irish immigrants following the Irish potato famine of the 1840s, were elected to the House for the Twenty-ninth Congress (1845–1847). With the Irish immigrants being Catholic, the movement also had a strong anti-Catholic flavor. By the mid-1850s, the revived Americans were at many times the only anti-Democrat alternative on the ballot. It had members elected to state and local government and fifty-one members to the House for the Thirty-fourth Congress (1855–1857). The American Party held their one and only

national presidential convention in February 1856 in Philadelphia. The platform was "nativist" and "America first" and called for restrictions on citizenship, immigration, and voting and office holding for immigrants already here. The delegates nominated former Whig president Millard Fillmore for president and Tennessean Andrew Jackson Donelson, the nephew of former president Andrew Jackson, for vice president. The nearly defunct Whig Party met in September and endorsed the American ticket. In almost all the states, Fillmore ran under the American banner, but there was obvious Whig ballot support in the traditional Whig states of Connecticut, Maine, Massachusetts, New Jersey, New York, Rhode Island, Vermont, and even in Virginia. Fillmore is listed as an American-Whig candidate on the *Atlas* maps because of party endorsements, ballot listings, and voter support.

The Democrats met in Cincinnati, in June 1856. Democratic president Franklin Pierce was not the convention's favorite. Sensing electoral victory over the two upstart parties, the delegates instead wanted a noncontroversial candidate. James Buchanan of Pennsylvania had served as U.S. ambassador to Britain the three previous years and thus had been overseas and out of the fray over Kansas and slavery. Sympathetic to the South, Buchanan won the nomination on the seventeenth ballot. The Democrats nominated Representative John Breckenridge of Kentucky for vice president. The Democrats' platform supported popular sovereignty, noninterference with slavery, and limited government with continued reticence toward a national bank and internal improvements. Furthermore, the Democrats derided the Know-Nothings, calling their platform offensive and un-American in its treatment of immigrants. Much of the Democrats' support in the North came from urban immigrant areas. The Democrats' opposition to the Know-Nothings during this period helped solidify the Democratic Party as a friendly home for immigrant populations. This perception continued into the 1890s and the twentieth and even the twenty-first century.

In the three-way race, the more established Democrats emerged with a popular and electoral college victory. Buchanan received 45.3 percent of the popular vote, with Republican Fremont getting 33.1 percent and American-Whig Fillmore 21.5 percent. Buchanan and Fillmore appeared on the ballot in every state, while the Republican Fremont appeared on the ballot only in the northern states; he received a scattering of votes in Delaware and Maryland. In the electoral college the Democrats won 174 votes (58.8 percent) to the Republicans' 114 (38.5 percent), with Fillmore carrying Maryland, where Fremont did not appear on the ballot, with 8 votes (2.7 percent). The electoral college was sharply divided by region. As evident on the electoral college map, the Democrat Buchanan carried all the slave states, the border states (with the exception of Maryland), and five northern states (which included the free state of California). Republican support was strictly along the far northern tier.

The popular vote map provides insight into the intrastate patterns that many times dictate the electoral college winner. Republican support was solid in the counties along the Deep North—New England, upstate New York, Michigan, and Wisconsin. Massachusetts, the former Whig bastion, supplied the largest percentage of the Republican vote, with Fremont receiving 63.6 percent of it. The American-Whig Fillmore only got 11.5 percent of the vote in Massachusetts. The Massachusetts vote, an electoral switch of immense proportions, is the classic example of the new party system emerging in 1856. A definite north-south intrastate divide is evident in five of the six states that border slave states. The popular vote map clearly shows this division in Illinois. Such a divide also occurred in Indiana, Ohio, Pennsylvania, and even in Iowa. The candidate map for the Republican Fremont illustrates the Illinois and Indiana divides even more vividly.

The candidate maps for Fillmore and Fremont also clearly show that in 1856 the Republicans were the major anti-Democrat ballot alternative in the North, while the Americans were the major ballot alternative in the South. The Democrats' victories were extensive in all the slave states, but even here Fillmore gained a scattering of support in hard-core former Whig counties and Whig subregions described and analyzed in the elections and maps from 1836 to 1852. Old political affiliations die hard, and areas like the Mississippi River valley, Kentucky, and Tennessee still held to anti-Democrat sentiments. Fillmore actually won Maryland with support of old Whig Chesapeake Bay counties. Fillmore was basically the only anti-Democrat ballot option in Maryland, with the Republican Fremont getting some support in the city of Baltimore.

The 1856 election is historic in its electoral geography, which is dramatically different from the previous presidential elections, pointing to a new, emerging political era. An even more geographically divided United States and party system would appear in the 1860 election and the final march toward Civil War.

REFERENCES: Baum, Dale. *The Civil War Party System: The Case of Massachusetts, 1848–1876.* Chapel Hill: University of North Carolina Press, 1984.

Billington, Ray Allen. *The Protestant Crusade, 1800–1860: A Study of the Origins of American Nativism.* New York: Macmillan, 1938.

Overdyke, W. Darrell. *The Know-Nothing Party in the South.* Baton Rouge: Louisiana State University Press, 1950.

1860

PRESIDENTIAL ELECTION

~

Candidates	Popular Vote Percentage	Electoral College Vote Percentage and (Vote)
Republican		
Abraham Lincoln (Illinois)	39.8	59.4 (180)
Vice Presidential Nominee: Hannibal Hamlin (Maine)		
Democrat		
Stephen Douglas (Illinois)	29.5	4.0 (12)
Vice Presidential Nominee: Herschel Johnson (Georgia)		
Southern Democrat		
John Breckenridge (Kentucky)	18.1	23.8 (72)
Vice Presidential Nominee: Joseph Lane (Oregon)		
Constitutional Union		
John Bell (Tennessee)	12.6	12.9 (39)
Vice Presidential Nominee: Edward Everett (Massachusetts)		

The presidential election of 1860—a sectional political struggle of immense proportions—is one of the most critical, complex, and geographically revealing in U.S. history. Because the electoral college system allocates electoral strength by geography of population, a unified region with a majority of the votes can prevail and force its agenda upon the rest of the nation.

Democratic president James Buchanan, in his March 1857 inaugural address, expressed his hope of unifying the nation, especially with respect to the expansion of slavery through the use of popular sovereignty. Two days later, the Supreme Court delivered the *Scott* decision putting the sectional clash over slavery on an inevitable course. Dred Scott, a slave, had sued for his freedom when his owner took him to free territory in the North. After eleven years of litigation, the Supreme Court ruled that Scott was not entitled to his freedom. The decision in effect made slavery legal in all

Map 19

of the United States and its territories. The majority of the Supreme Court justices at that time was southern and Democrat. Because the expansion of slavery into the territories had been the central issue in the preceding presidential campaigns, the *Scott* ruling held immense political consequences, not the least of which was nullifying the Missouri Compromise and the Compromise of 1850. The ruling outraged northerners, while southerners felt vindication. Political stances with respect to slavery hardened in both sections.

As the 1860 presidential nominations and campaign drew close, another incident exacerbated sectional differences. In October 1859, radical abolitionist John Brown and twenty-one of his followers seized the federal arsenal in Harper's Ferry, Virginia (now West Virginia), with the purpose of inciting a slave rebellion in the South. The government suppressed the insurrection within two days. Brown, arrested and quickly tried and found guilty of treason, was hanged in December 1859.

The North touted Brown as a hero, savior, and martyred saint, and the South reviled him as a madman and a traitor.

The Democrats, the majority party in the late 1850s, convened in Charleston, South Carolina, in April 1860 and immediately found themselves hopelessly split along sectional lines on the expansion of slavery into the territories. Southern extremists held that the *Scott* decision demanded the existence and protection of slavery in the territories, while northern Democrats argued for popular sovereignty as the party's position to maintain electoral support in the North. When popular sovereignty won the day, a sizable block of delegates, mostly from the Deep South, walked out of the convention and the party. After failing to nominate a candidate, the remaining Democrats decided to reconvene in Baltimore in June. Following much infighting, the reconvened convention nominated Sen. Stephen Douglas of Illinois for president. Douglas, a principal author of the Kansas-Nebraska Act, was closely associated with the policy of popular sovereignty. The Democratic National Committee chose Herschel Johnson of Georgia for vice president. The southern Democratic delegates who had walked out of the Charleston convention met in Baltimore later that June and nominated Vice President John Breckenridge of Kentucky for president and Sen. Joseph Lane of Oregon for vice president. The southern Democrats approved a platform similar to the regular Democratic platform, except with respect to slavery in the territories.

The Republicans met for their second presidential convention in May 1860 in Chicago. Delegates from all the northern states, six slave states, and the territories of Kansas and Nebraska attended. The Republican platform, of course, opposed expansion of slavery into the territories and derided the *Scott* decision. To appeal to antislavery northern Democrats, the Republicans also came out in support of states' rights, an unspoken repudiation of radical abolitionists. Their platform also favored homesteading, internal improvements, and a protective tariff, the latter two being nationalist economic development programs supported by former Whigs and northern manufacturing interests.

Abraham Lincoln, a Republican, had come to the nation's attention two years previously as a result of the famous Lincoln-Douglas debates during the Senate race in Illinois. Lincoln was considered a moderate and geographically appealing, as Illinois would be a crucial swing state for creating a winning northern coalition in the electoral college. In addition, Lincoln was thought to be acceptable to American Party nativists, whom Republicans wished also to attract to their coalition. Lincoln won the nomination on the third ballot and was paired with Sen. Hannibal Hamlin of Maine.

A significant bloc of anti-Democratic sentiment lingered over the South. Members of the Thirty-sixth Congress (1859–1861) included more than thirty representatives from slave states elected under American Party, Opposition, or Independent Democrat banners. In addition, a sizable number of former Whigs continued to be active in southern politics. These opposition groups were generally Unionist, and believing in the preservation of the United States at all costs, disliked the so-called extremism of the Republicans as well as of the southern Democrats. The various opposition factions met in May 1860 in Baltimore and formed the Constitutional Union Party. The party platform, only two paragraphs, defended the Constitution and called for unity and preservation of the Union. It stated that the American people had been deceived by "the political division of the country, by the creation and encouragement of geographical and sectional parties." The Constitutional Unionists nominated John Bell of Tennessee for president and Edward Everett of Massachusetts for vice president.

A simplistic view of the 1860 election is that there were really two elections: one in the North, pitting the Republican Lincoln against the northern Democrat Douglas, and one in the South, featuring the southern Democrat Breckenridge against the Constitutional Unionist Bell. The voting, however, was extremely complex. Because of the long-term organization of the Democratic Party, the "regular" Democrat Douglas appeared on the ballot or received votes in all the states. For example, in Alabama, Douglas received 13,618 votes (15.1 percent). The southern Democrat Breckinridge was on the ballot or received votes in all the states except New Jersey, New York, and Rhode Island. (In these three states, Douglas, Breckinridge, and Bell supporters formed alliances and "fusion" tickets in which they actually shared and supported one electoral list.) For example, the proslavery Breckinridge received 14,372 votes in Connecticut (19.2 percent), almost as many as the northern Democrat Douglas's 15,431 votes (20.6 percent).

The Tennessean and Constitutional Unionist Bell also appeared on the ballot or received votes in all the states except New Jersey, New York, and Rhode Island. For example, in Massachusetts, Bell received 22,331 votes (13.3 percent). The Republican Lincoln did not appear on the ballot in nine southern states, but was on the ballot or received votes in five slave states bordering on the North. He received 3,822 votes in Delaware (23.7 percent) and 17,028 votes in Missouri (10.3 percent). In the end, Lincoln received 39.8 percent of the national popular vote, Douglas 29.5 percent, Breckenridge 18.1 percent, and Bell 12.6 percent.

As the electoral college map illustrates, the unified bloc voting of all the northern free states gave Lincoln the presidency without his carrying one slave state. Through industrialization, urbanization, immigration, and dense farm settlement on fertile Midwestern agricultural soils, the North had acquired a substantial population advantage—and therefore a majority in the electoral college—over the South by the mid-nineteenth century. The final electoral college tally gave Lincoln 180 votes (59.4 percent), Breckenridge 72 (23.8 percent), Bell 39 (12.9 percent), and Douglas 12 (4 percent). The votes in the electoral college were extremely divided geographically, with Lincoln carrying all the northern states and Breckinridge the Deep South. Among the band of states separating the Deep North and Deep South, Douglas carried Missouri and took three of the seven votes on the New Jersey fusion ticket. Bell carried Virginia, Kentucky, and the old Whig bastion of Tennessee. Breckinridge carried the border states of Delaware and Maryland, but only by pluralities of 45.5 and 45.9 percent.

Analysis of the popular vote patterns of the 1860 election requires supplemental examination of the four individual candidate maps for maximum elucidation. Four distinct patterns stand out on the popular vote map. Lincoln carried almost all the counties in the Deep North, and moreover, almost all of them with an absolute majority. The northern vote, without a doubt, made the Republicans the major party in the North. Breckinridge carried the vast majority of the counties in the Deep South. The farther south, the greater proslavery, pro-Breckenridge voting tendencies became. In the border states and the upper South the voting pattern is mixed and more complex. Bell did well in many of the counties in Kentucky, Missouri, North Carolina, Tennessee, and Virginia, where many voters were proslavery but also pro-Union and anti-secession. Douglas carried very few counties nationwide. His strength was centered in southern Illinois, with some support in other Midwestern states. Because of Lincoln's strong support in the more densely populated northern farming counties, Lincoln carried critical Illinois with 50.7 percent of the vote to Douglas's 47.2 percent.

Lincoln's map shows the stark contrast of support for him in all the counties in the North and a little support or virtually none in those in the South. The Republicans overwhelmingly dominated in northern Illinois, northeastern Ohio, and Vermont, this last state giving Lincoln his largest victory of 75.7 percent of the vote. The Breckinridge map illustrates an interesting geographic anomaly—strong support for him in Pennsylvania. In that state, Breckinridge, with 37.5 percent of the vote, came in second to Lincoln, significantly outpolling the northern Democrat Douglas, who garnered only 3.5 percent. This can be explained by President James Buchanan, a Pennsylvanian, having persuaded the Pennsylvania Democratic Party to favor Breckinridge over Douglas on the ballot because of Douglas's opposition to his Kansas policies. The Douglas map shows more clearly his lack of support from Pennsylvania and other northeastern states, including areas of northeastern Ohio. Douglas's native Midwest gave him a modicum of support. Bell's map shows several clusters of Unionist support in the South. Many of these counties were in old Whig areas with commercial ties to the North, and at the time, pro-Union. Prominent among these areas are the old Whig areas in Kentucky, Tennessee, along the Mississippi River valley in Mississippi, and former Whig areas in western North Carolina and western Virginia.

The presidential election of 1860 was even more sectionally divided than the 1856 election. Although Breckinridge proclaimed that he was not a secessionist, southern agitators had warned since the mid-1850s that if the "Black Republicans" ever won the presidential election, secession would be in order. The 1860 vote for Douglas and Bell in the South indicates large unionist and anti-secessionist feelings, especially in the border states and the upper South. Nevertheless, in the month after the strictly regional Republican Party had gained control of the presidency, a secessionist convention gathered in South Carolina, and that state declared itself to no longer be part of the Union. The presidential election of 1860 represented the final straw for the South and led to civil war.

REFERENCES: Baker, Jean H. *Affairs of Party: The Political Culture of Northern Democrats in the Mid-nineteenth Century.* Ithaca, N.Y.: Cornell University Press, 1983.

Coleman, John F. *The Disruption of the Pennsylvania Democracy, 1848–1860.* Harrisburg: Pennsylvania Historical and Museum Commission, 1975.

Foner, Eric. *Free Soil, Free Labor, Free Men: The Ideology of the Republican Party before the Civil War.* New York: Oxford University Press, 1970.

1864

PRESIDENTIAL ELECTION

Candidates	Popular Vote Percentage	Electoral College Vote Percentage and (Vote)*
Republican		
Abraham Lincoln (Illinois)	55.0	90.6 (212)
Vice Presidential Nominee: Andrew Johnson (Tennessee)		
Democrat		
George McClellan (New Jersey)	45.0	9.0 (21)
Vice Presidential Nominee: George Hunt Pendleton (Ohio)		

Shortly after the November 1860 election of Abraham Lincoln as president, secession swept the South. Eleven states eventually seceded and formed the Confederate States of America. The geography of secession fervor and timing resembled the geographic intensity of support for the various candidates in the slave states in the 1860 election.

The seven Deep South states—South Carolina, Georgia, Florida, Alabama, Mississippi, Louisiana, and Texas—became the first group to secede. After months of attempting to resolve the situation, the upper southern states of Virginia, North Carolina, Tennessee, and Arkansas seceded after the call for volunteers to forcibly quell the rebellion and the firing on Fort Sumter, in Charleston in April 1861. Four border slave states—Delaware, Maryland, Kentucky, and Missouri—did not secede, but the last three experienced significant internal division, strife, and violence.

The four years of the first Lincoln administration (1861–1865) roughly coincide with the Civil War, the bloodiest conflict in U.S. history. More Americans died in the Civil War than in all other U.S. wars combined. Yet the democratic process continued. As the 1864 presidential nominations and campaign neared, the goals, conduct, and success of the war effort emerged as the central issues. In the 1860 election, the Republicans had won almost 60 percent of the seats in the House of Representatives and had gained full control of Congress after the southern secessions. The Democrats, however, made significant gains in the 1862 midterm elec-

tions to the Thirty-ninth Congress (1863–1865). After the midterms, the Republicans held 46 percent of the House and had to rely on friendly Unionist representatives from slave border states to retain control of it. With this in mind, and with the war stagnating in spring 1864, Lincoln's reelection was by no means assured.

The issue of slavery had dominated U.S. politics for decades, perhaps since the nation's founding. The 1860 Republican platform called simply for a halt to the expansion of slavery into any new territory of the United States. The issuance of the Emancipation Proclamation in September 1862 added the cause of black liberation—at least in the states under rebellion—to the war to halt the spread of slavery and preserve the Union. Emancipation and the conduct of the war created sharp divisions within the Republican Party between radical and conservative factions prior to their June 1864 convention in Baltimore. The Republicans shrewdly called the convention the National Union Party convention to attract northern "War Democrats" and others in this time of national crisis. Lincoln supporters were in full control of the conference, and he won the nomination on the first ballot. In a move to substantiate the "union" intent of the party, on the ticket convention delegates replaced abolitionist vice president Hannibal Hamlin of Maine with Andrew Johnson of Tennessee. Johnson, a former Democrat and a former slave owner, was a strong Unionist and the only senator from a seceding state who refused to leave

One Nevada elector did not vote.

Congress. In 1864 Johnson held the post of military governor of Tennessee. The 1864 Republican platform called for the eradication of slavery from the United States by way of a constitutional amendment.

The Democrats did not meet until late August 1864, in Chicago, to give themselves a chance to better gauge the course of the war. Democrats from the North, far West, and border states split into roughly two groups: "Peace Democrats," who wanted an immediate end to the war and a negotiated settlement, and "War Democrats," who supported the war but criticized its goals and general management. Peace Democrats were strongest in the Midwest and border states, and they carried the day by passing a platform plank calling for a "cessation of hostilities" and a negotiated peace. The delegates nominated New Jersey's Gen. George McClellan of Civil War fame for president and George Hunt Pendleton of Ohio for vice president. After receiving the nomination, McClellan repudiated the peace plank in the platform but rebuked the Lincoln administration by calling for a more efficient conduct of the war and adopting an anti-emancipation stance.

Battlefield success and failure played a role in the final vote. In early September 1864, Gen. William T. Sherman's troops captured and occupied Atlanta. The occupation of this key southern city and Sherman's continued march through Georgia lifted northern spirits, as did Gen. Ulysses S. Grant's progress at Petersburg, Virginia, and Gen. Philip Sheridan's successes in the valleys of Virginia. In November 1864, the electorates of twenty-five northern, border, and far western states gave Lincoln 55 percent of the popular vote and McClellan 45 percent. Although the national popular vote total indicated some support for the Democrats, Lincoln won most states by comfortable margins. Some margins were enhanced by soldier votes, which were heavily pro-Lincoln. Only in New York was the race close, with Lincoln receiving 50.5 percent of the vote. Kansas, then only recently admitted to the Union as a free state, gave Lincoln his biggest winning margin with 79.2 percent of the vote. The electoral college map illustrates the sweeping nature of the election for Lincoln, who won twenty-two of the twenty-five states participating. McClellan carried the two border states of Delaware and Kentucky and his home state of New Jersey. The final electoral vote count was Lincoln 212 (90.6 percent) and McClellan 21 (9 percent).

The popular vote map highlights a number of important patterns in the participating states. Lincoln again dominated New England and the Deep North. In the New York race, Lincoln carried most of the upstate counties, but in New York City McClellan won by more than a margin of two to one (73,709 versus 36,681). Pockets of Democratic strength remained in southern Illinois and southern Indiana and some Ohio and Pennsylvania counties.

The border states in 1864 deserve special attention. First, many southern sympathizers and Democrats had joined the Confederate army, fled south, were in hiding, or otherwise did not participate in the election. Second, some areas of these states were unable to hold elections because of intrastate guerrilla civil war and a lack of safe polling and organized government. For example, in the newly admitted state of West Virginia, the northern counties were more stable, more sympathetic to the North, and in favor of breaking away from old Virginia. Voters in these counties provided large margins of victory to Lincoln. In southern West Virginia, many of the counties did not vote, or the canvass was reported late or erratically, because of threats, intimidation, and local warfare by southern sympathizers. This was also the case in six neighboring Kentucky counties. In southern Missouri, eight southern counties did not submit election returns, but the rest of the state voted heavily for Lincoln. In Kentucky, there was widespread sympathy for Confederates, Peace Democrats, and anti-emancipation sentiment, especially in the central and western portions, which had a significant slave population. The map also shows, however, a large cluster of Republican support in southeastern Kentucky, a mountainous Appalachian area with few blacks. Here Unionist sentiment appeared after events at Fort Sumter, and locals blamed the Democratic state government for neglecting their region economically and militarily. Anti-Democratic sentiment grew when Confederate sympathizers and guerrillas killed local Unionists and destroyed property. Many parts of Appalachia exhibited strong Union sympathies, and numerous areas of mountainous South suffered years of local civil war. In Maryland, the plantation counties in the Chesapeake region voted Democrat while the more mountainous counties turned Republican. For example, in southern Saint Mary's County, the vote was Lincoln 99, McClellan 968, while in northwestern Allegany County, it was Lincoln 2,455, McClellan 1,990. Even Delaware experienced a north-south divide, with the northern county and city of Wilmington going for Lincoln, while the southern two counties, with southern-type agriculture, voted Democrat.

With the South out of the political process, the northern Republican Party had complete control of the presidency and both chambers of Congress. During this period of political dominance, other aspects of the Republican agenda in social and economic policy were passed into law, including the Homestead Act, Morrill Act (college land grant act), a tariff, and legislation friendly to industrialists and railroads. In the span of six fateful days in April 1865, Confederate general Robert E. Lee surrendered to Grant at Appomattox Courthouse, Virginia, and Lincoln was assassinated in Washington, D.C. Reconstruction of the South and the fate of African Americans replaced slavery at the top of the political agenda. With the death of Lincoln, his agenda fell into the hands of President Andrew Johnson, southerner, Democrat, and former slave owner.

REFERENCE: Baker, Jean H. *The Politics of Continuity: Maryland Political Parties from 1858–1870.* Baltimore, Md.: Johns Hopkins University Press, 1973.

1868

PRESIDENTIAL ELECTION

~

Candidates	Popular Vote Percentage	Electoral College Vote Percentage and (Vote)
Republican		
Ulysses S. Grant (Illinois)	52.7	72.8 (214)
Vice Presidential Nominee: Schulyer Colfax (Indiana)		
Democrat		
Horatio Seymour (New York)	47.3	27.2 (80)
Vice Presidential Nominee: Francis Preston Blair Jr. (Missouri)		

There was never a more trying, conflicting presidency in U.S. history than that of Andrew Johnson, who assumed the office after the assassination of Abraham Lincoln in 1865. Johnson, as a Unionist but a southern Democrat, had been placed on the Republican (Union) ticket in 1864 to attract northern Democratic votes and to suggest national solidarity. The issue of Reconstruction dominated Johnson's administration (1865–1869). Sympathetic to the South, Johnson opposed universal black suffrage, favored the restoration of white government (including unrepentant Confederates), and supported pardons for the main leaders of the rebellion. In his second inaugural address, Lincoln had included the phrase "with malice toward none, with charity toward all" as an indication of his intention to pursue a moderate policy of Reconstruction. Many members of the Republican-dominated Congress, however, were unsympathetic toward the South. They strongly supported full citizenship, including voting and other civil rights, for African Americans and were intent on making loyalty to the United States a condition for political participation. They also opposed restoration of voting and other political privileges for Confederate leaders. The clash over the conflicting presidential and congressional visions of Reconstruction topped the list of political issues between 1865 and the 1868 presidential election.

In Congress, the Republicans, who were in the majority, fell into two camps: the larger moderate faction and the smaller Radical Republican faction. The latter

Map 21

favored sweeping social and political change in the South. In the battle over Reconstruction, President Johnson vetoed a bill to establish a Freedmen's Bureau to aid and educate newly liberated African Americans. He also vetoed a proposed civil rights act that would have given voting privileges to African American men and assured all blacks equal protection under the law. These vetoes, and Johnson's general administration of Reconstruction, unified the two factions of the Republican Party in Congress. Republicans overrode many of Johnson's vetoes and passed the Reconstruction amendments to the Constitution: the Thirteenth Amendment, which formally outlawed slavery; the Fourteenth Amendment, which granted full citizenship to African Americans; and the Fifteenth Amendment, which conferred voting rights to all African American males.

In the South, the white population had viewed the Republicans before the Civil War as "Black Republicans," and radical Reconstruction confirmed their worst fears. They saw the Republicans as not only a northern sectional party, but also as simply "anti-southern." They blamed the Republicans for the physical, economic, and cultural destruction of their region and were especially scornful of northerners who moved south in an attempt to enrich themselves at the expense of the disheveled South during Reconstruction. A large majority of white southerners opposed the Republicans and therefore turned to the Democratic Party. They would vote Democratic for nearly a hundred years.

Meanwhile, newly freed African American slaves in the South viewed the Republicans and Lincoln as their liberators and saviors, and radical Reconstruction confirmed their greatest hopes. They perceived the Republican Party as the vehicle for building a new South in which they would have equal representation. African American southerners supported the Republican Party until their voting rights were denied them in the post-Reconstruction period. Most whites in the North viewed the Republicans as a moral reform party, loyal to the principles of Christian values in having conducted an honorable crusade in the Civil War to free the nation from bondage. Majorities in many Deep North counties voted Republican in the vast majority of presidential elections for the next hundred years.

Radical Republicans hostile to Johnson engineered his impeachment in the House in early 1868, filing eleven articles of impeachment against him, including the "illegal" firing of Secretary of State Edwin Stanton. In May, after a trial, the Senate acquitted Johnson by a single vote, with seven Republicans joining the Senate's Democrats in voting for acquittal. Having failed to remove Johnson from office through the impeachment process, the Republican leadership focused on preventing his reelection in 1868. Johnson's actions involving Reconstruction became central to the 1868 campaign and reflected the general differences in the postwar Democratic and Republican Parties.

The Republicans continued the long American tradition of nominating a war-hero candidate for president by selecting Gen. Ulysses S. Grant, the greatest military figure to emerge from the Civil War. Grant, an Illinois resident, received the nomination on the first ballot at the May Republican convention in Chicago. Another northerner, Speaker of the House Schuyler Colfax of Indiana, was selected as the vice presidential nominee. The Republican platform attacked Johnson and praised congressional Reconstruction. It also called for universal suffrage for all black men in the South, but left African American suffrage in the North to the states. The issue of "soft money" versus "hard money" in terms of currency policy also arose. The Republicans, increasingly being influenced by northeastern banking, industrial, and financial groups, stated in their platform that they favored a hard money policy backed by gold, a tight money supply, and low inflation.

Many in the North viewed Democrats, especially Peace Democrats, as treasonous in their actions before and during the Civil War, as racist, immoral, and, to say the least, lacking as defenders of the Union. The Democrats—as the party of Andrew Jackson, defenders of poor working-class whites in the cities and yeoman farmers in the countryside, and defenders of recent immigrants—would win some northern urban counties but lose most rural northern counties in presidential elections for the next century.

The weakened Democrats voted on and rejected a number of possible candidates at their July 1868 convention in New York City. They eventually nominated former New York governor Horatio Seymour for the presidency and former Republican general Francis P. Blair Jr. of Missouri for vice president. The Democratic platform praised the actions of President Johnson, condemned radical Reconstruction, and included the racist (and inaccurate) statement that the South had been subjected to "negro supremacy." On the other major issue of the day, the currency, the Democrats favored a soft money policy, printing more greenbacks (dollars) to induce moderate inflation, which would be helpful to poor struggling Midwestern farmers and generally all those in debt.

Grant won the 1868 election with 52.7 percent of the popular vote, and Seymour receiving a respectable 47.3 percent. As in 1864, the Democrats were somewhat competitive in the popular vote, though Grant won a majority of states by comfortable margins. This is reflected in the electoral college results, with 214 votes (72.8 percent) for Grant and 80 votes (27.2 percent) for Seymour. Florida was the only state to choose its electors by legislature. Seymour carried three northern states—his native New York, New Jersey, and Oregon—by extremely tight margins, 50.6 percent, 50.9 percent, and 50.4 percent, respectively. The Democrats prevailed by wide margins in Kentucky (74.6 percent), Maryland (67.2 percent), and Delaware (59.0 percent), three former slave border states that had not gone through Reconstruction and where most white males could vote. Georgia and Louisiana, Deep South states supposedly undergoing Reconstruction, also went to Seymour. Grant carried New England and the rest of the North, and, for the first time, the Republicans won the remaining readmitted southern states. First-time black voting in the South allowed Grant to not only carry these states, but also to register a popular vote majority. Southern black voting quickly became an important equation in national voting patterns.

The 1868 popular vote map illustrates now familiar patterns in the North. The Republican Grant carried New England and most of the northern tier of counties from upstate New York through Iowa. The Democrat Seymour carried most counties in the border states of Delaware, Kentucky, and Maryland, where most white males retained the right to vote. The Republican cluster in southeastern Kentucky held steady from the previous election (as it would for the next century). In Appalachian West Virginia, the Unionists judged the Republican Party the best place for them in the immediate postwar years. In Missouri, many former Confederates were denied the vote, but large numbers of newly enfranchised blacks cast ballots. Among those voting Republican in Missouri were majorities in the northern border counties with northern migrants and in the southwestern Ozarks, which was populated with migrants from Unionist areas of Kentucky and Tennessee. They were joined by Union veterans and Unionist German Americans in St. Louis and the "Missouri Rhineland" counties extending west from St. Louis County.

Voting patterns and politics in the 1868 South were complex. In an electoral sense, Reconstruction meant three things: the disenfranchisement of white males who had pledged allegiance to the Confederacy, the enfranchisement of black males, and the restoration of civil government at a federally prescribed pace. Some northerners went south during Reconstruction and became eligible to vote and participate there, including holding elective office in newly organizing civil governments. Native white southerners called these northerners "carpetbaggers." Some southerners cooperated with the military occupation for pragmatic reasons and on principle, took loyalty oaths, and participated in civil government. Native white southerners called these native southerners—especially those motivated by pragmatism—"scalawags." In the early stages of Reconstruction, carpetbaggers, scalawags, and black males could vote, and they voted mostly Republican. Congressional Reconstruction allowed southern white males to vote once their state had been readmitted to the Union and after they had taken an individual oath of loyalty to the Union.

Important in the analysis of the 1868 electoral geography is the effect of "electoral terrorism," that is, the use of threats, violence, and murder to influence voting results. A prime example, but not the only example, are the actions of the Ku Klux Klan. The Klan, founded in 1866 as a white supremacist organization, dedicated itself to the restoration of white government in the South. Some of its earliest activities targeted balloting, candidates, elections, and the electoral system with violence and intimidation. In Louisiana and Georgia, the only states in the South where a majority of counties supported the Democrat Seymour, the Klan and other groups intimidated hundreds, and perhaps thousands, of officeholders, candidates, carpetbaggers, scalawags, and African Americans. In Louisiana, the only counties that voted Republican were those tied to the old plantation economy of the Mississippi River valley and Red River valley, where African American numbers were too large to fully sway.

Tennessee, the only former Confederate state not to go through congressional Reconstruction, was the first to be readmitted in March 1866, after it ratified the Fourteenth Amendment. The large cluster of counties in eastern Tennessee, the home area of President Johnson, was a prominent site of Republican support. In the 1860 election, eastern Tennessee staunchly supported John Bell, the Unionist presidential candidate. This Appalachian area of Unionists and low African American population turned to the Republican Party after the Civil War and remained loyal to it for more than a century, and it could be argued, into the twenty-first century.

In the rest of the South, African American turnout helped carry the day for the Republicans. South Carolina had a majority African American population, and the counties where they were concentrated are Republican on the map. In Alabama, the string of Republican counties across the state pinpoints the heavily African American counties of the black belt. The 1868 voting patterns of African Americans in the South are interestingly similar to the voting patterns of their Whig masters in the pre–Civil War decades, in effect identifying the locations of old large-scale plantation agriculture. In Arkansas, the counties along the Mississippi River valley and Arkansas River valley are also identifiable as having large numbers of African Americans. Virginia, Mississippi, and Texas had not been readmitted to the Union in 1868 and therefore did not participate in that year's election.

In the North, voting patterns in the post–Civil War United States reflected the patterns that prevailed in the prewar period. In the South, African American voters changed the electoral geography by creating a Republican presence. With the restoration of white governments in the 1870s, African Americans would lose their constitutional voting rights, and the Republican-dominated patterns of 1868 would fade. With the restoration of blacks' civil and voting rights in the 1960s, they would vote heavily Democratic, and the geographical patterns similar to those of the 1860s and 1870s would reemerge, but in reverse in terms of party loyalty.

REFERENCES: Abbott, Richard H. *The Republican Party and the South, 1855–1877.* Chapel Hill: University of North Carolina Press, 1986.

Curry, Richard O., ed. *Radicalism, Racism, and Party Realignment: The Border States during Reconstruction.* Baltimore, Md.: Johns Hopkins Press, 1969.

1872

PRESIDENTIAL ELECTION

~

Candidates	Popular Vote Percentage	Electoral College Vote Percentage and (Vote)*
Republican		
Ulysses S. Grant (Illinois)	55.6	78.1 (286)
Vice Presidential Nominee: Henry Wilson (Massachusetts)		
Liberal Republican–Democrat		
Horace Greeley (New York)	43.8	17.2 (63)**
Vice Presidential Nominee: Benjamin Gratz Brown (Missouri)		

The 1868 election of Civil War hero Ulysses S. Grant represented a triumph of Republicanism and northern nationalism. Grant's first term (1869–1873), however, was badly blemished by nepotism, cronyism, and corruption. The corruption and mismanagement proved to be so pervasive that Grant became tainted through his denial, naivete, and, as some charge, actual malfeasance. Although deliberate wrongdoing on Grant's part was never proven, many reform-minded Republicans had serious doubts about Grant before the midpoint of his first term.

By 1872 many had begun calling for the creation of a new third party and a national presidential nominating convention. The Liberal Republican Party, begun in 1870 in Missouri, held a national convention in May 1872 in Cincinnati. The party leaders chose their name to suggest three things: they were Republicans; they were moderate Republicans, not Radical Republicans; and they were a liberal reform faction of the party ready to fight corruption at the highest levels. One of their primary goals was to create a nonpartisan, performance-based civil service commission to oversee government employees. Government workers would be

Map 22

hired based on experience, education, and accomplishment rather than political party affiliation, family ties, bribery, or patronage, as had become rampant during the first Grant administration. The Liberal Republicans also endorsed ending radical Reconstruction, extending the franchise to former Confederates, and pulling federal troops out of the South. These proposals appealed immensely to Democrats. Although many prominent Republicans joined the Liberal Republican movement, none could muster a majority at the convention. On the sixth ballot, Horace Greeley, the publisher of the *New York Tribune,* captured the nomination. Greeley, a long-time Whig and later Republican, was a well-known, reform-minded journalist who had taken sometimes-controversial stances on many issues of the day. The new third party nominated Missouri Liberal Republican governor Benjamin Gratz Brown, a former antislavery advocate and border state Unionist, as their vice presidential choice.

The Republican Party met in Philadelphia in June 1872. With large numbers of reformists having joined with the Liberal Republicans, President Grant received enthusiastic first ballot support. Because of corruption charges surrounding Vice

*The Republican-controlled Congress in 1873 refused to accept the Greeley electoral votes of Arkansas (6) and Louisiana (8) because of so-called voting irregularities resulting from Reconstruction. Congress also refused to count three Greeley votes from Georgia. In the final count, Greeley surrogates received 63 (17.2 percent) of the 366 possible electoral votes.

**Horace Greeley died after the presidential election but before the electoral college met. Because of his death, the actual Greeley vote was cast for four individuals, mainly for Democratic governor Thomas Hendricks of Indiana (42 votes), a conservative opponent of radical Reconstruction, and vice presidential candidate Benjamin Gratz Brown (18 votes). In addition, Charles J. Jenkins of Georgia received two votes, and David Davis of Illinois received one vote.

President Schulyer Colfax, especially with respect to the Crédit Mobilier scandal, the party dumped him in favor of Sen. Henry Wilson, a Radical Republican from Massachusetts. The Republican platform mentioned possible civil service reform and pledged continued party support for civil rights in all sections of the nation.

The Democrats met for a one-day convention in Baltimore in late June 1872. They previously had debated the best way to exploit the split in the dominant Republican Party, and in the end the convention voted not to present a candidate, but instead to support Greeley and the platform of the Liberal Republicans. Most Democrats thought that they stood no chance in a three-way race, but were sympathetic to ending radical Reconstruction and a strategy for defeating the Grant administration. Other Democrats, however, felt that as a national party they should always field a candidate. Because Greeley was a Republican nominated by the splinter Liberal Republican Party but receiving endorsement and most of his votes from Democrats, he is labeled in the *Atlas* as Liberal Republican–Democrat.

With the candidates selected, the campaign devolved into character assassination without any real debate over the issues of the day. The Liberal Republicans painted Grant as bungling and corrupt. Republicans portrayed Greeley as too forgiving of former Confederates, ignoring Klan violence, and simply strange with respect to such things as his forays into socialism and vegetarianism. The Republican Party, with its base in the North, felt the pressure of northern industrialists, railroaders, financiers, and bankers, who strongly supported Grant. Many moral reformists and those wishing to separate the party from industrial and financial backing were disappointed with Greeley as the choice of the Liberal Republicans and so did not enthusiastically get behind the movement.

With the continued support of Union veterans and African Americans at the polls, Grant emerged with a substantial reelection victory. Grant received 55.6 percent of the popular vote versus Greeley's 43.8 percent—the largest popular vote margin since Andrew Jackson's in 1828. The electoral college map depicts another overwhelming victory for the Republicans. All the states in the North and West went for Grant, marking the continuation of Republican dominance that would last in some places for many years. For example, Vermont voted Republican in 1856 and would continue to do so in every presidential election until 1964. In addition, the Republicans carried most of the southern states under Reconstruction. Greeley won Maryland, Kentucky, and Missouri, border states where the white male franchise was not greatly restricted. Tennessee went into the Democrats' column, where it would stay (with two exceptions) until 1952. As in 1868, Georgia also went Democratic (and would vote consistently Democratic until 1964). Newly readmitted Texas voted Democratic by a wide margin, 58.5 percent for the Liberal Republican–Democrat Greeley (and would remain in the Democratic column, with one exception, until 1952).

Greeley died on November 30, after the election but before the electoral college convened. The Greeley electoral votes were split between four individuals. Most Greeley electors supported Democratic governor Thomas Hendricks of Indiana (42 votes), a conservative opponent of radical Reconstruction, and vice presidential candidate Benjamin Gratz Brown (18 votes). In addition, Charles J. Jenkins of Georgia received two votes, and David Davis of Illinois received one vote. The Republican Congress in 1873 refused to accept the Greeley electoral votes of Arkansas (6) and Louisiana (8) because of so-called voting irregularities resulting from Reconstruction. Congress also refused to count three Greeley votes from Georgia. In the final tally Grant received 286 (78.1 percent) of a possible 366 electoral votes.

The 1872 popular vote map provides a complete national view of voting patterns after the readmittance of Virginia, Mississippi, and Texas. In general, the Republicans again won the northern tier counties. Democratic counties held steady in southern Illinois, southern Indiana, and areas of Ohio not settled by New Englanders or constituting old Whig areas. In the border states the voting again was complex. In Maryland, black counties in the south and white counties in the mountain region went Republican, but a strong Democratic vote in Baltimore city and Baltimore County gave Greeley a slim 50.3 percent victory. In West Virginia, the geographic divide was stark. Northern counties, having commercial and political ties to the North, voted Republican, while more conservative southern counties supported the Democrats. Kentucky went to Greeley, but the strong Republican area in the mountains again supported Grant. In Missouri, some German Americans and moderate Republicans may have been swayed by the home state Liberal Republican vice presidential candidacy of Gov. Brown, but in northern Missouri, near the Iowa border, and in southwestern Missouri, in the Ozarks, a majority of the popular vote went to Grant.

The vote configuration in the South is complex because of Republican, African American, scalawag, and carpetbagger voting. In Tennessee, Republicans made a strong showing in the Unionist counties of the mountain region. In the Deep South, the pattern usually illustrates Republican support where African American majorities lived. In Virginia, mountain counties with few African Americans gave majorities to Greeley, while the old plantation areas of the Tidewater, with their large African American populations, supported Grant. A similar coastal-plantation-versus-mountain difference also holds for North Carolina. In certain states, such as reconstructed Virginia, South Carolina, and Mississippi, the white vote remained restricted. In hundreds of counties in the South, African Americans constituted the majority of the population. In the 1870 census, South Carolina, Mississippi, and Louisiana had the highest percentages of African American population in the nation, 58.9, 53.7, and 50.1 percent, respectively, and the county voting patterns reflect this. In Arkansas, Louisiana, and Mississippi, the African American voting pattern is clearly evident along the old plantation regions of the Mississippi, Red, and Arkansas River valleys. The black belt counties of Alabama and eastern Mississippi are also discernible, as they had been in 1868.

Newly readmitted Texas produced an interesting cluster of Republican counties in the midst of this Democratic state. Many of these southeastern counties had a large Africa American presence, primarily in cotton plantation areas near the coast. In addition, counties to the east of Austin and to the west of San Antonio had been settled by German Americans, many of whom opposed slavery and took a pro-Union position before and during the Civil War. In the first postwar congressional election, German American Edward Degener of San Antonio was elected as a Republican in the Fourth District. Although the Reconstruction Republican Party in Texas was largely black, the German vote contributed to the postwar voting pattern. This Republican cluster held until the 1900 presidential election. It slowly diminished as African Americans were denied the vote, but German Americans continued to support Republicans. The German American counties of Texas remain predominantly Republican.

In the far West, Oregon, California, and Nevada went Republican by comfortable margins in 1872. The Willamette Valley of western Oregon was the terminus of the Oregon Trail and the most heavily populated area of the state. Many of the original settlers came from the North. Although Lincoln won a plurality in Oregon in 1860, the state had a strong Democratic element until 1872, when Oregon voted Republican (and continued to do so in every election until 1912, when the Republicans split over two candidates). California also had a strong Democratic Party in the 1850s, but Lincoln won a plurality in 1860 (and the state voted Republican in every election except for three from 1860 until 1932). Nevada had

had a strong Republican state party since its statehood (and with one exception a Republican won in every presidential election from 1864 until it split with the party over the silver issue in 1892). In general, the far western states had a strong northern presence, but they generally followed the national trends, which as they came into political maturity was a time of Republican Party domination in national politics. Because of the eclectic nature, origin, and timing of settlement in the early far western states, specific patterns of habitation and related voting are less discernible there than in the nation's earliest settled areas.

In 1872 the Democratic Party was extremely weak following the loss of its southern base during and immediately after the Civil War. In addition, the Republicans dominated in the North. The Democrats did not nominate a candidate in 1872, choosing instead to support the third-party Liberal Republicans. This is the only time in the history of the Democratic and Republican Parties that such an event has occurred. The Republican dominance in northern counties and most state legislatures made it a powerful force for all who wished to be part of political life and civil society. During the second Grant administration, however, continued corruption, economic depression, and the emergence of former Confederate white male voting power in the South converged to bring more balance to national electoral politics.

REFERENCES: Baum, Dale. *The Shattering of Texas Unionism*. Baton Rouge: Louisiana State University Press, 1998.

Casdorph, Paul. *A History of the Republican Party in Texas, 1865–1965*. Austin, Texas: Pemberton Press, 1965.

Jordan, Terry G. *German Seed in Texas Soil*. Austin: University of Texas Press, 1966.

1876

PRESIDENTIAL ELECTION

Candidates	Popular Vote Percentage	Electoral College Vote Percentage and (Vote)
Republican		
Rutherford B. Hayes (Ohio)	48.0	50.1 (185)
Vice Presidential Nominee: William Wheeler (New York)		
Democrat		
Samuel J. Tilden (New York)	51.0	49.9 (184)
Vice Presidential Nominee: Thomas Hendricks (Indiana)		

President Ulysses S. Grant had been reelected under a cloud of corruption in 1872, and his second administration (1873–1877) brought with it even more scandal and incompetence. Furthermore, the Republican Party came under additional pressure in 1873 with a severe depression brought on by irrational exuberance in railroad investing. The Panic of 1873 had resulted in bank failures, a cascading business collapse, and high unemployment. The public's response to the panic helped the Democratic Party take control of the House of Representatives in the 1874 midterm elections, the first time since 1856. The Democrats, with only 88 seats (30.1 percent) in the Forty-third Congress (1873–1875), increased their representation to 182 seats (62.1 percent) in the Forty-fourth Congress (1875-1877). The Democrats won virtually all of the congressional districts in the border states and made huge gains in the southern states as Reconstruction came to a close. Although Republicans passed such laws as the Ku Klux Klan Act and other legislation to protect blacks in the South in 1871 and 1872, legislation also passed that backed away from Reconstruction, such as the 1872 law allowing all but the highest-ranking Confederate officials to run for public office. By the mid-1870s, Republicans, no longer in the majority in the House, backpedaled on radical Reconstruction to placate skittish northern voters. This backtracking and the normal process of Reconstruction led to the Democratic takeover of state after state in the South,

Map 23

because the re-enfranchised white population became the majority of voters in all but South Carolina, Mississippi, and Louisiana.

The Republicans and the Democrats felt pressure with respect to government corruption and Reconstruction at their 1876 national conventions. The Republicans met first, in June, in Cincinnati. Their platform called for continuing the tariff, hard money fiscal policy, and civil service reform. After an initial deadlock, the Republicans nominated reform-minded Ohio governor Rutherford B. Hayes on the seventh ballot. Another northerner, William Wheeler, a member of the House of Representatives from New York, received the vice presidential nomination. The more conciliatory Republican platform and general party demeanor tried in part to appeal to the moderate Liberal Republicans who had bolted in 1870 and 1872. Most did opt to return to the party rather than support the Democrats.

The Democrats met later that June in St. Louis with the strategy to run an anti-Grant, pro-reform campaign. Its prominent reformist, New York governor Samuel J. Tilden, had taken on and defeated Tammany Hall, the infamous Boss Tweed operation, and other corrupt enterprises in his state. Tilden won the presidential nomination on the first ballot. The Democratic choice for vice president, Thomas Hendricks of Indiana, had received the majority of the 1872 Democratic electoral vote following Horace Greeley's death. While the Republicans slowly backtracked from radical Reconstruction, the Democrats advocated its termination, including restoration of the vote to all former Confederates, the removal of all federal troops from the South, and the establishment of "home rule" (white) government.

With Tilden and Hayes in agreement on civil service reform and somewhat in agreement on the currency question, the campaign in the North and the border states focused on personal attacks, the economy, and corruption in the Grant administration. In the South, the campaign centered on whites' hatred of Reconstruction, Republicans and Republican black (and white) voters, and reestablishment of white Democratic Party rule. Electoral violence by the Ku Klux Klan continued in the South. By the 1876 presidential election, Reconstruction governments remained in control of South Carolina, Florida, and Louisiana. In Mississippi, with a 53.7 percent African American population, physical violence, along with economic, political, social, and psychological intimidation, had already led to a white takeover.

One of the closest and perhaps most disputed presidential elections took place on November 7, 1876. The Democrat Tilden won 50.97 percent of the popular vote to the Republican Hayes's 47.95 percent. Almost 1 percent of the national vote went to the Greenback Party, an organization that displayed remarkable strength in the Midwestern farm belt, winning, for example, 6.3 percent of the vote in Kansas. The Greenbackers opposed the Republicans' hard money policy, which the Democrats had basically accepted. With Tilden having received more popular votes than Hayes, many observers expected that the electoral college vote would confirm the Democrat as the next president. As the electoral college map illustrates, Tilden carried four important northern states, including his home state of New York and neighboring New Jersey and Connecticut. In Indiana, the home of vice presidential candidate Hendricks, the Tilden-Hendricks ticket mustered a plurality victory of 49.5 percent, with the Greenbackers denying them the majority by garnering 2.2 percent. Tilden carried all the border states—Delaware, Maryland, West Virginia, Kentucky, and Missouri. In the South, states that were fully reconstructed and had had white government restored, voted solidly Democratic. The return of the South to the Democratic column made the Democrats once again nationally competitive, especially when they managed to hold the border states and carry a few key northern states. This pattern of regional competitiveness resembled the prewar 1856 presidential election and would continue until the 1940s.

In the 1876 election, the electoral college results hinged on the three states that continued to be governed by Reconstruction governments—South Carolina, Florida, and Louisiana. If these states were to fall into the Republican column, Hayes would have an electoral college majority and take the White House. The vote count in these states was razor thin. Democrats accused the Reconstruction governments of stuffing the ballot boxes, double-counting black votes, and generally tampering with the official results. The Republicans countered that voter

intimidation and violence had led many voters to stay at home and had resulted in so many other "voting irregularities" that the entire vote in each state should be reexamined thoroughly. Each of the three Reconstruction states sent two certificates of ascertainment of electoral college votes to Congress—one for Tilden and one for Hayes. The Democrat-controlled House and Republican-controlled Senate, of course, disagreed on which slate of electors to certify for each state. After weeks of vigorous debate, Congress formed an electoral commission to examine the evidence and to review the electoral procedures followed in each of the three states in question. The fifteen-member commission consisted of seven Democrats and seven Republicans and one allegedly independent Supreme Court justice. The independent member, a Republican, voted in favor of the Hayes electors in each case. In secret meetings, the Democrats, led by southerners, agreed to accept the commission's decision if the Republicans would agree to end Reconstruction and withdraw the last of the federal troops from the South. The commission's ultimate decision was made public on March 2, 1877, two days before the constitutionally mandated date for the presidential inauguration. The final 1876 electoral college vote as tallied in Congress gave Hayes 185 votes (50.1 percent) and Tilden 184 votes (49.9 percent).

The 1876 popular vote map reflects a number of remarkable geographic differences from the 1872 map. In the South, the number of counties with Republican majorities dropped precipitously as "home rule" replaced Reconstruction governance. In Mississippi in 1872, for example, the Republicans carried a majority of the counties, but in 1876 Republicans carried only a few counties, mainly along the Mississippi River, where black majorities were extremely large. The only large pockets of Republican support left in the South were found in South Carolina and Louisiana, both with Reconstruction governments, and along the Mississippi, Red, and Arkansas River valleys. These pockets of black Republican support would slowly fade and almost completely disappear by the 1890s as Jim Crow laws severely restricted African American political participation. The only large areas of white Republican support remaining in the eleven former Confederate states were in the Unionist area of eastern Tennessee and some German American counties in Texas. The border states gave the Democrats a clean sweep, with southeastern Kentucky, the Ozarks of southern Missouri, and farming areas of northern Missouri retaining some Republican clusters.

In the North, the Democrats claimed numerous counties in southern Illinois, Indiana, Ohio, and Pennsylvania. The Democrats' spread in Ohio did not touch the old Western Reserve area in the northeast; its historic eighteenth-century boundaries are almost exactly outlined in the 1876 popular vote map. The Republicans remained strong in the northern tier states, including in Michigan, Minnesota, and Wisconsin and in Maine, New Hampshire, and Vermont. Large areas of Republican dominance appeared in other parts of New England, in northern Illinois, and in Iowa, Kansas and Nebraska.

The presidential election of 1876 is analogous to the election pitting the Democrat Al Gore against the Republican George W. Bush in 2000. As in 2000, the 1876 election was disputed, and the candidate with the most popular votes failed to secure an electoral college majority. The election of 1876 effectively ended Reconstruction in the South, and the end of Reconstruction effectively ended statewide Republican competitiveness in the South for well into the twentieth cen-

tury. Beginning with the 1880 presidential election (with the exception of Tennessee in 1920), none of the eleven former Confederate States of America would again vote Republican until 1928.

REFERENCES: McKinney, Gordon B. *Southern Mountain Republicans, 1865–1900.* Chapel Hill: University of North Carolina Press, 1978.

Unger, Irwin. *The Greenback Era: A Social and Political History of American Finance, 1865–1879.* Princeton, N.J.: Princeton University Press, 1964.

1880

PRESIDENTIAL ELECTION

Candidates	Popular Vote Percentage	Electoral College Vote Percentage and (Vote)
Republican		
James A. Garfield (Ohio)	48.3	58.0 (214)
Vice Presidential Nominee: Chester A. Arthur (New York)		
Democrat		
Winfield Scott Hancock (Pennsylvania)	47.9	42.0 (155)
Vice Presidential Nominee: William H. English (Indiana)		
Greenback		
James B. Weaver (Iowa)	3.3	0 (0)
Vice Presidential Nominee: B. J. Chambers (Texas)		

The election of 1880 was the first to be held after the completion of Reconstruction. Republican president Rutherford B. Hayes, elected in the disputed election of 1876, had pursued a policy of moderate reform. During the 1876 campaign, Hayes had announced his intention to serve only one term, and he kept his promise, despite his popularity among the Republican rank and file. Thus the Republican nomination for 1880 was wide open.

Many Republicans supported Hayes's predecessor, former president Ulysses S. Grant, who expressed interest in running for an unprecedented third term and did nothing to discourage his friends and supporters from promoting his candidacy. Some Republican administrators, however, opposed Grant, whose administration had been marked by cronyism, corruption, and scandal. Many of these leaders supported Sen. James G. Blaine of Maine and Secretary of the Treasury John Sherman of Ohio. The Republican national convention, meeting in Chicago, was deadlocked among supporters of Blaine, Grant, and Sherman. Rep. James Garfield of Ohio gave a major speech in support of Sherman, but eventually the delegates selected Garfield as a compromise candidate on the thirty-sixth ballot. Although Garfield

had served as a major general in the Civil War and nine terms in the House of Representatives, he was little known nationally. The Republicans chose Chester A. Arthur, the collector of the Port of New York and a Grant supporter, as their vice presidential nominee to appease the defeated Grant forces.

Hoping to capture the White House for the first time in twenty-four years, the Democrats considered numerous candidates, including Samuel Tilden, who had lost the 1876 election to Hayes. At the party's national convention in St. Louis, delegates eventually settled on Pennsylvanian Winfield Scott Hancock, who had served as a major general in the Civil War. After the war, Hancock had become active in Reconstruction and was respected in the South for his leniency toward former Confederates. The Democrats chose former representative William English of Indiana as Hancock's running mate. Thus, both parties selected "balanced" tickets, with one candidate from the Mid-Atlantic states and the other from the Great Lakes region. Both major parties would sustain this trend of geographic balance between the Mid-Atlantic and Great Lakes regions until after World War II.

The fall campaign focused more on personalities and images than on issues. The tariff was the only major issue dividing the two parties, with Republicans supporting a high protective tariff and the Democrats opposing it. Republicans in the North "waved the bloody shirt" and attacked Hancock and the Democrats as being disloyal to the Union. Democrats hammered Republicans for incompetence and corruption. In the end, in absolute numbers, the popular vote was one of the closest in U.S. history, with Garfield (48.3 percent) outpolling Hancock (47.9 percent) by less than 35,000 votes. A substantial portion of the difference involved approximately 30,000 votes cast. Most of the remaining portion (3.3 percent) of the vote went to James B. Weaver of the Greenback, or National, Party. The Greenback movement had emerged in the mid-1870s as a reaction to the gold standard and tight monetary policy of the Republicans and their eastern banking supporters. The Greenbacks favored paper money—greenbacks—and the moderate inflation such a policy would promote. The movement began among midwestern and Great Plains farmers struggling with debt. As the Greenback candidate map illustrates, most of Weaver's support came from these regions, with double-digit support in Texas (11.7 percent) and Iowa (10 percent). The electoral college results were more decisive than the close popular vote, with Garfield winning a majority of 214 electoral votes to Hancock's 155.

The election of 1880 presaged most of the elections over the next sixty years. The country remained sharply polarized, with the South solidly Democratic and the North solidly Republican, but the states in between—especially New York, New Jersey, Ohio, Indiana, and Illinois—were more evenly divided between the two parties. These states' status as key battlegrounds in 1880 and subsequent elections influenced both parties to nominate candidates for high public office from them throughout the late nineteenth and early twentieth centuries.

With Reconstruction complete, local Democratic politicians firmly controlled the South. Hancock won the electoral votes of every state in the South, a Democratic trend that would continue unbroken until 1920. He also carried New Jersey and the border states of Delaware, Maryland, Kentucky, and Missouri as well as West Virginia, despite the Mountain State having opposed secession and being admitted to the Union in its own right during the Civil War. Hancock also received most of the electoral votes of California and won Nevada. He failed, however, to carry his home state of Pennsylvania, which cost him the election.

Although Hancock won a majority of counties in the South, Garfield took a large pocket of counties in the Appalachian regions of southeastern Kentucky and Tennessee, where many residents had opposed secession. (The Republicans dominate many areas of Appalachia to this day.) Garfield also won in several parishes of southern Louisiana and the area around Galveston, at the time the largest city in Texas and a major port of entry for immigrants. He also won areas such as the Mississippi River valley counties of northwestern Mississippi and southeastern Arkansas, where large numbers of former slaves voted prior to the enactment and enforcement of Jim Crow laws. Elsewhere in the South, most counties went to Hancock, except for several in western Virginia, which went to the "Readjuster" faction rather than to the regular Democratic electoral slate.

Garfield, meanwhile, won a large majority of counties north of the Mason-Dixon Line, especially in rural areas. In New York, for example, Hancock took most cities, including New York City, but lost in the countryside and therefore lost the state's electoral votes. Garfield won most of New England, including every county in Vermont and Massachusetts, except for Suffolk County (home to the city of Boston and many Irish Americans and other immigrants). In the Midwest, the electorate remained divided along ethnic and sectional lines. Garfield's native Western Reserve of Ohio and other areas settled by Yankees and Republican-leaning immigrants voted heavily Republican. Southern Illinois and southern Indiana and areas settled by southerners or by Democratic-leaning immigrants tended toward the Democrats. Hancock carried most counties in Nevada and many of those in Oregon and California, but the electoral votes of these sparsely populated states were insufficient to affect the national outcome in the electoral college.

The first post-Reconstruction election represents a harbinger of elections for the next two decades featuring an electorate divided along ethnic and sectional lines. Economic matters and the issue of governmental reform were two of the most important considerations in 1880 and would remain so for the rest of the nineteenth century.

REFERENCE: Ackerman, Kenneth D. *The Dark Horse: The Surprise Election and Political Murder of James A. Garfield.* New York: Carlton and Graf, 2003.

1884

PRESIDENTIAL ELECTION

Candidates	Popular Vote Percentage	Electoral College Vote Percentage and (Vote)
Democrat		
Grover Cleveland (New York) *Vice Presidential Nominee:* Thomas Hendricks (Indiana)	48.5	54.6 (219)
Republican		
James G. Blaine (Maine) *Vice Presidential Nominee:* John Logan (Illinois)	48.2	45.4 (182)

On July 2, 1881, Charles Guiteau, a disappointed office seeker, shot Republican president James Garfield in Washington, D.C. Garfield fought for his life for ten weeks, but his physicians ultimately proved unsuccessful in treating his wounds. Garfield died on September 19, and Vice President Chester A. Arthur assumed the presidency. The assassination of Garfield brought renewed attention to the issue of replacing the old "spoils" system of filling government jobs. Calls for civil service reform received a boost given that Guiteau had been denied a government position before shooting Garfield and because Arthur had been associated with corrupt politicians in New York City before becoming vice president. Arthur would in 1883 support and sign the Pendleton Act, a sweeping civil service reform bill.

Arthur proved to be generally popular, and he might have been nominated for a full term had he actively sought the Republican nomination. He did not do so, however, and many Republican leaders felt disinclined to encourage him to run. Although unknown to many people at the time, Arthur suffered from Bright's disease, a serious illness affecting the kidneys. Arthur died in 1886, less than two years after leaving office. With Arthur out of the running, the Republicans turned to former senator James G. Blaine of Maine at their national convention in Chicago. Blaine, who had also served as Speaker of the House of Representatives and briefly as secretary of state, had been seriously considered for the party's nomination in

Map 25

1876 and 1880. The Republicans selected Sen. John Logan of Illinois as his running mate.

Meanwhile, the Democrats considered Samuel Tilden and Winfield Scott Hancock, who had narrowly lost the elections of 1876 and 1880, respectively. Meeting in Chicago, the Democratic national convention declined to renominate either Tilden or Hancock. Instead, the delegates turned to Gov. Grover Cleveland of New York. Cleveland had been elected mayor of Buffalo and governor of New York on a reform-oriented, anti-corruption platform. The Democrats chose Sen. Thomas Hendricks of Indiana, who had been a potential presidential candidate also, to run for vice president.

Both sides launched vitriolic campaigns, and each charged the other with corruption. A Boston bookkeeper, James Mulligan, had discovered letters written by Blaine to various railroad companies implying that he would use his influence in Congress to support legislation of interest to them in exchange for money. Although the charges associated with the Mulligan letters were never proven, the taint of corruption remained. Some Republican supporters of reform, disgusted with the association of the party's presidential nominee with such charges, supported Cleveland. These reformers became known as Mugwumps. Meanwhile, it came to light that Cleveland had admitted and accepted responsibility for fathering an illegitimate child, an act that his opponents did not hesitate to use against him.

The 1884 election hinged on the outcome in New York state, which Cleveland carried by only about 1,000 votes. A few days before the election, Blaine had attended a meeting of Protestant clergy in New York. One clergyman remarked, "We are Republicans, and do not propose to leave our party and identify ourselves with the party whose antecedents have been rum, Romanism, and rebellion." That evening, Blaine dined at Delmonico's famous restaurant in New York City with many of the nation's richest and most powerful business leaders. Flyers and cartoons showing Blaine consorting with tycoons, including John D. Rockefeller, Henry Morgan, and Cornelius Vanderbilt, circulated widely, especially among Roman Catholics, many of whom were offended by Blaine's refusal to disavow the anti-Catholic slur associated with the "rum, Romanism, and rebellion" comment. The Roman Catholic community in New York City and other cities with large Catholic immigrant populations turned out strongly for Cleveland. The damage associated with these events likely cost Blaine New York's electoral votes and therefore the election.

The election of 1884 marked the return of the Democratic Party to national power for the first time in the post–Civil War period. Like many other elections of the late nineteenth century, it was a close one. Cleveland (48.5 percent) outpolled Blaine (48.2 percent) by only about 26,000 popular votes and won the electoral college vote by a margin of 219 to 182. Cleveland received the electoral votes of the entire South and the border states along with the northern states of Indiana (home of vice presidential candidate Hendricks), New Jersey, New York, and Connecticut. Blaine won the rest of the country, including most of New England, Pennsylvania, Ohio, Illinois, the upper Midwest, and the West. Cleveland's 1,000-vote margin—a 48.3 percent plurality—in New York thus proved decisive. The presence on the ballot of a Prohibition Party candidate, John St. John of Kansas, also contributed to Blaine's defeat. St. John won 25,000 votes in New York (2.1 percent). Given that many Prohibition voters were of New England ancestry and took a highly moralistic approach to politics, it is likely that many of St. John's votes would have gone to Blaine had the Prohibition Party not been on the ballot. St. John's vote also exceeded Cleveland's margin over Blaine in neighboring Connecticut and New Jersey. Benjamin Franklin Butler, a Union general in the Civil War and former member of the House, received approximately 175,000 votes as the candidate of the Greenback and Anti-Monopoly Parties. His strongest showings were in his native Massachusetts (13.7 percent) and Maryland (11.5 percent).

The popular vote patterns were highly sectionalized, making them very much consistent with most other late nineteenth-century presidential elections. Cleveland won a large majority of the counties in the South. By 1884 Reconstruction had faded into history, and local Democratic leaders had regained control of political activity throughout much of the region. Many people in counties in the Appalachian hill country of eastern Tennessee and Kentucky had opposed secession, opposed the Democratic takeover of local politics, and supported national Republicans. This pattern persisted well into the twentieth century. Elsewhere, most of the rest of the South supported the Democratic ticket.

The states along the northern tier, meanwhile, sat firmly in the Republican camp. Blaine swept northern New England, including his home state of Maine, and won most counties in upstate New York, although he lost the state's electoral votes because of his defeat in New York City. Throughout the northern half of the United States, a large majority of rural counties favored Blaine. Most of the counties that supported Cleveland were urban or had substantial immigrant or Catholic populations. The increasingly populous West also gave Blaine a substantial amount of support. Within the next decade, however, western farmers and ranchers would become increasingly dissatisfied with the close association between the Republican Grand Old Party and eastern-based corporate interests.

REFERENCE: Summers, Mark W. *Rum, Romanism, and Rebellion: The Making of a President, 1884.* Chapel Hill: University of North Carolina Press, 2000.

1888

PRESIDENTIAL ELECTION

Candidates	Popular Vote Percentage	Electoral College Vote Percentage and (Vote)
Republican		
Benjamin Harrison (Indiana)	47.8	58.1 (233)
Vice Presidential Nominee: Levi Morton (New York)		
Democrat		
Grover Cleveland (New York)	48.6	41.9 (168)
Vice Presidential Nominee: Allen G. Thurman (Ohio)		
Prohibition		
Clinton B. Fisk (New Jersey)	2.2	0 (0)
Vice Presidential Nominee: John A. Brooks (Missouri)		

As in previous elections, the tariff was a major issue in the campaign of 1888. In December 1887, Democratic president Grover Cleveland had sent a message to Congress proposing a substantial tariff reduction, which was anathema to northeastern industrial interests. At the time, the British were actively promoting free trade throughout the world, and supporters of free trade were therefore labeled as pro-British, and by implication, anti-Irish. Associating Cleveland with the Union Jack allowed Republican campaigners to make inroads into traditionally Democratic strongholds in Irish-American areas.

The Democratic national convention in St. Louis renominated Cleveland by acclamation. Vice President Thomas Hendricks had died in 1885, and the Democrats selected former senator Allen G. Thurman of Ohio as Cleveland's running mate despite his being seventy-five years old. Thurman's age became an issue because Cleveland adhered to the tradition of the time that presidential candidates refrain from campaigning, instead delegating that responsibility to the vice presidential nominee.

Map 26

Meanwhile, the Republicans selected as their presidential nominee Indiana's Benjamin Harrison, the grandson of former president William Henry Harrison who had served as a U.S. senator from 1881 to 1887. Harrison easily outpolled former secretary of the Treasury John Sherman and other candidates at the party's Chicago convention. Levi Morton, a New York financier who had served as a member of the House and as U.S. ambassador to France, received the vice presidential nomination.

Shortly before the election, a Republican partisan using the pseudonym Charles Murchison wrote a letter to the British ambassador to the United States in which he claimed to be a British-born U.S. citizen and asked the ambassador for advice on whom he should vote for. The ambassador replied that Cleveland would be the better choice from Britain's perspective. The fictitious letter, including the ambassador's response, circulated widely, especially in Irish American communities, where anti-British sentiment fueled by Cleveland's support of British free trade policy was considerable. On election day, Irish Americans' lack of support may well have cost Cleveland the electoral votes of New York and therefore the election.

Harrison ousted Cleveland, as the electorate denied a sitting president reelection for the first time since 1840. With the exception of the disputed 1876 election, the 1888 election also marked the first time since all the states had begun selecting their presidential electors by popular balloting that the candidate who won a plurality of the national popular vote did not win an electoral college majority and thus the presidency.

As the popular vote map illustrates, the outcome of the 1888 election mirrors the geographical pattern of polarization evident in 1880 and 1884. Cleveland swept the entire South, along with the border states of Delaware, Maryland, West Virginia, Kentucky, and Missouri. He also won New Jersey and Connecticut. He, however, lost his home state of New York. The victorious Harrison swept all the remaining states along the northern tier from New England through the Midwest to the Pacific Coast.

A highly sectionalized pattern is also evident in the electoral college returns. Cleveland's popular vote margins were highest in the Deep South, where he won more than 70 percent of the vote in South Carolina, Georgia, Mississippi, and Louisiana, winning a large majority of their counties. Pockets of Republican support were found in the old Unionist areas of Appalachia and Tidewater Virginia and counties in the Mississippi River valley, areas with such a large African American presence that the states had been unable to totally disenfranchise black males.

Harrison won his largest majorities in the northernmost areas, including northern New England, upstate New York, and northern parts of Michigan, Wisconsin, and Minnesota. In Ohio, Indiana, and Illinois, ethnic and settlement heritage once again proved key to election outcomes. For example, the Western Reserve of northeastern Ohio, which had been settled by New Englanders, remained heavily Republican and would continue to be Republican-dominated until the New Deal. Many parts of southern and western Ohio and southern Indiana and southern Illinois, however, had been settled by migrants from Virginia and Kentucky, and majorities in these counties continued to support the Democrats. The same pattern prevailed in Ohio and neighboring Great Lakes states until the Great Depression of the 1930s.

The Prohibition Party appeared on the ballot in many states, receiving votes in all but one. The party had been convening since 1872 and in 1888 received more than 2 percent of the national vote for the first time. The party addressed a number of issues in its platform, but its primary concern was, of course, prohibition of the "manufacture, importation, exportation, transportation and sale of alcoholic beverages." Prohibition would become a persistent issue in U.S. politics in the late nineteenth and early twentieth centuries, culminating in the Eighteenth Amendment in 1919 and its repeal in 1933. The map for Prohibition candidate Clinton B. Fisk shows some strength throughout the North and even parts of the South, with the midwestern states of Minnesota (5.8 percent), Nebraska (4.7 percent), and Michigan (4.4 percent) providing him the largest portion of the vote. In New York state, the Prohibition vote was large enough that the Harrison ticket won with only a plurality rather than a majority of the popular vote.

Although a majority of counties in the upper Midwest and the West supported Harrison, it was becoming evident that increasing numbers of western and midwestern farmers were growing dissatisfied with the Republicans' high tariffs, tight monetary policy, and corporate influence. During Harrison's term, these opponents would coalesce into a third party whose activities would have a considerable influence on the direction of U.S. politics into the twentieth century.

REFERENCE: Calhoun, Charles W. *Benjamin Harrison*. New York: Henry Holt, 2005.

1892

PRESIDENTIAL ELECTION

~

Candidates	Popular Vote Percentage	Electoral College Vote Percentage and (Vote)
Democrat		
Grover Cleveland (New York)	46.1	62.4 (277)
Vice Presidential Nominee: Adlai Stevenson (Illinois)		
Republican		
Benjamin Harrison (Indiana)	43.0	32.7 (145)
Vice Presidential Nominee: Whitelaw Reid (New York)		
Populist		
James B. Weaver (Iowa)	8.5	4.9 (22)
Vice Presidential Nominee: James G. Field (Virginia)		
Prohibition		
John Bidwell (California)	2.2	0 (0)
Vice Presidential Nominee: James B. Canfield (Texas)		

Map 27

During Republican president Benjamin Harrison's administration (1889–1893), dissatisfaction among economically stressed farmers increased sharply, especially in the Midwest and the West. Strong support among disaffected farmers resulted in Democratic victories throughout the Midwest in the 1890 midterm elections, in which the Democrats gained control of both Houses of Congress for the first time since the Civil War. Farther west, disaffected farmers and miners airing political grievances formed the Populist, or People's, Party, which elected eight members to Congress in 1890. One of the several reform issues that the Populists advocated was increased coinage of silver, a proposal popular in the South and West because an increased money supply and the accompanying inflation would benefit indebted farmers.

Some Republican leaders regarded Harrison as cold, standoffish, and unwilling to listen to advice, so they wanted to replace him on the 1892 ticket. A number of delegates supported James G. Blaine, who had narrowly lost the 1884 election to Cleveland. Blaine had served as Harrison's secretary of state, but had broken with the president and resigned. The Republicans also considered Ohio representative William McKinley. Blaine refused to campaign actively for the nomination, which went to Harrison on the first ballot at the national convention in Minneapolis. The delegates dropped Vice President Levi Morton, replacing him with Whitelaw Reid, the editor of the *New York Tribune* and a former U.S. ambassador to France.

The Democrats, meanwhile, renominated Cleveland on the first ballot at their national convention, in Chicago, and selected Adlai Stevenson of Illinois as his running mate. (Stevenson's grandson and namesake would be the Democratic standard-bearer in 1952 and 1956.) Cleveland thus became the first person to receive three consecutive nominations from a major party. (Thus far only Cleveland,

Henry Clay, William Jennings Bryan, Franklin Delano Roosevelt, and Richard Nixon have been nominated as major-party candidates for president three or more times. Only Cleveland and Roosevelt received three consecutive nominations.) Cleveland's opposition to free silver attracted northeastern business leaders, who were increasingly sympathetic toward his candidacy.

Neither major party endorsed the Populist platform of free silver. With little attention paid them by the major parties, the Populists selected Gen. James B. Weaver, a former U.S. representative from Iowa and the 1880 Greenback candidate, as their presidential candidate. In addition, the Prohibition Party nominated John Bidwell of California for the presidency. Neither major-party candidate campaigned actively in the fall of 1888. Harrison's wife, Caroline Scott Harrison, suffered from a serious illness and died two weeks before the election, and Cleveland, out of respect for his opponent, refused to campaign actively during Harrison's bereavement.

In 1892 the voters decisively turned Harrison out of office, and for the first time a former president reclaimed the White House after having lost an earlier reelection bid. Cleveland was the first (and so far the only) president to serve nonconsecutive terms. He won the popular vote by a margin of 46.1 percent to 43 percent. Weaver received 8.5 percent of the popular vote, with most of the remainder (2.2 percent) going to Bidwell. Cleveland's victory in the electoral college was even more decisive, outpolling Harrison by a margin of 277 votes to 145, with 22 going to Weaver. Cleveland swept the South and the border states, and he also won California, Connecticut, and New Jersey. He became the first Democrat to win Illinois and Wisconsin since before the Civil War and the creation of the Republican Party. He also took Harrison's home state of Indiana.

Harrison won the electoral votes of most of the northern states, including those of northern New England, Pennsylvania, Ohio, and Michigan. He also found success in most of the newly admitted northern tier western states. The Populist Weaver made significant inroads in the increasingly disaffected agricultural and mining Great Plains and West, winning the electoral votes of Kansas, Colorado, Idaho, and Nevada. He also won individual electoral votes in North Dakota and Oregon.

The popular vote map shows a continuation of the sectional pattern that had emerged in the 1880s, but also highlights the Populists' inroads, especially in the upper Midwest and the West. Weaver won his greatest majorities in the silver-mining states of Nevada (66.8 percent), Colorado (57.1 percent), and Idaho (54.2 percent). The region with the second best show of support for Weaver was the Great Plains, where distressed farmers who had settled agriculturally marginal lands faced difficulties in competing with midwestern farmers, who had settled in areas of higher rainfall (and who generally remained loyal to the Republicans or switched to the Democrats rather than to the more radical Populists in 1892). Although gaining pluralities in many southern counties, the Populists had hoped to make even greater inroads but had failed to do so in part because conservative southern Democratic leaders enacted Jim Crow laws to limit African American and poor white access to the ballot box. Dozens of African Americans had been elected to the House and Senate during the years after the Civil War. (The last of them, Sen. George White of North Carolina, left office in 1900, and Congress would remain all white until 1929.) East of the Mississippi River, the traditional sectional pattern prevailed, with Cleveland dominating the South and border states, Harrison winning pluralities or majorities throughout the northern states, but the Democrats making substantial gains in many midwestern agricultural counties.

The 1892 election was the first in which Populism played a major role in the electoral outcome. Four years later, the Populists would merge with the Democrats, ushering in a new era in U.S. politics that would last well into the twentieth century.

REFERENCE: Brodsky, Alyn. *Grover Cleveland: A Study in Character.* New York: St. Martin's Press, 2000.

1896

PRESIDENTIAL ELECTION

~

Candidates	Popular Vote Percentage	Electoral College Vote Percentage and (Vote)
Republican		
William McKinley (Ohio)	51.0	60.6 (271)
Vice Presidential Nominee: Garret Hobart (New Jersey)		
Democrat		
William Jennings Bryan (Nebraska)	46.7	39.4 (176)
Vice Presidential Nominee: Arthur Sewall (Maine)		

Map 28

The vote of 1896 was a watershed election. Since the end of Reconstruction, the electorate had been sectionally divided, with the Republicans dominating the North and the Democrats controlling the South. A few Mid-Atlantic and Great Lakes states in between had decided the closely contested elections of 1880, 1884, 1888, and 1892. During the 1880s and 1890s, dissatisfaction among Western farmers over economic conditions continued to increase, with many blaming northeastern industrial interests and an unsympathetic federal government for their economic problems. By 1896 the Populist movement had grown to the point that the Populist presidential nominee would also become the nominee of the Democratic Party.

During the three previous elections, the Democrats had put forth Grover Cleveland as their presidential candidate, and he had won in 1884, lost in 1888, and won again in 1892. Soon after Cleveland's second inauguration in March 1893, the country experienced one of its worst economic downturns. Many banks failed, some 15,000 companies went out of business, and thousands of people lost their jobs. Because the Democrats controlled the White House as well as Congress, many blamed them for the panic, high tariffs, and poor financial policy. Meanwhile, the Sherman Silver Purchase Act of 1890 had tied the value of the dollar to silver and to gold, with the value of both fixed at a 16:1 ratio. Miners in the West were producing silver in large quantities, but the act in effect made silver more valuable

despite its lessening scarcity. It also contributed to inflation, thereby enabling indebted midwestern and southern farmers to repay loans with cheaper dollars. Eastern financial interests, however, demanded repeal of the act and a return to the traditional gold standard. Thus many westerners favored and many easterners opposed the free coinage of silver.

Free coinage of silver was an important component of the platform of the Populist, or People's, Party, which had become prominent in U.S. politics in the early 1890s. Populist candidate James B. Weaver had won the electoral votes of four western states in 1892. During the depression of the 1890s, Populist ideas grew in popularity among voters, and the party increased its vote in the midterm elections of 1894, gaining seats in both chambers of Congress. In addition to advocating the free coinage of silver, the Populists also argued against the concentration of power in the hands of large industrial corporations, supported the labor movement, favored continued civil service reform, and argued for major reforms in the political process, including use of the secret ballot, initiative and referendum, and the election of U.S. senators by popular vote rather than indirectly by state legislatures.

The Democratic national convention, meeting in Chicago, found delegates divided between supporters and opponents of Populist monetary policy. Cleveland favored a return to the gold standard, but a majority of the delegates from the South and the West favored free coinage of silver and repudiated the president's tight monetary policies. William Jennings Bryan, a representative from Nebraska and a renowned orator, electrified the audience with his "Cross of Gold" speech. It brought Bryan national attention, and the pro-silver majority of delegates nominated the "Boy Orator of the Platte," a thirty-six-year-old, for the presidency. To shore up support among disaffected and more conservative eastern Democrats, the convention selected Arthur Sewall of Maine as the party's vice presidential nominee. Sewall, a wealthy shipbuilder, industrialist, and member of the Democratic National Committee, had never held elective office.

The Democrats' selection of Bryan put the Populist Party in a dilemma. Should it endorse Bryan's nomination or should it nominate another candidate? Meeting in St. Louis in July, the party decided to endorse Bryan's nomination but declined to support Sewall. Instead, it selected Tom Watson of Georgia as the party's vice presidential nominee. A majority of Republican national convention delegates, also meeting in St. Louis, opposed the Populist platform and favored a higher tariff and hard money policy. The delegates selected Gov. William McKinley of Ohio as their party's presidential nominee. A former representative, McKinley had received serious consideration for his party's nomination in 1888 and 1892. Continuing the Republican tradition of an East-Midwest balance, the delegates selected New Jersey's Garret Hobart, a long-time member of the party's national committee, as McKinley's running mate. In contrast to the Democratic plank, the Republican platform emphasized the gold standard and a high protective tariff, which favored financial institutions and growing industries located mainly in the emerging northeastern manufacturing belt.

The competing economic visions of the Republican and the Democratic/Populist fusion candidates dominated the 1896 election campaign. Dispensing with tradition, Bryan traveled throughout the country to campaign in support of his election. Bryan and the Democrats hoped to unite disaffected farmers in the South and West and to make inroads among industrial workers in the Northeast. By 1896 the depression associated with the Panic of 1893 had receded, and Bryan found many easterners unreceptive to his message. On election day, Bryan's hopes went unrealized, as McKinley won the election convincingly. He received more than 7 million popular votes—the largest amount to that time—and won the electoral college by a margin of 271 votes to 176. Although Bryan won more popular votes than any previous losing candidate, his defeat was nonetheless decisive.

The maps of the popular and electoral votes show the high degree of geographic polarization of the 1896 election. McKinley won by sweeping the traditional Republican base of densely populated northern and midwestern states. Connecticut, New York, New Jersey, and Indiana, all of which had been closely contested in previous elections, voted decisively Republican. McKinley also won California, Oregon, and the border states of Kentucky, West Virginia, Maryland, and Delaware. Bryan swept the Democratic South and took many of the new western states that had generally supported Republican nominees, including the silver mining states of Colorado, Idaho, and Nevada. His impressive popular vote margin in these new, thinly populated states was not, however, sufficient for him to overcome McKinley's lead in the large electoral vote–rich industrial states of the North. The Northeast versus South and West split is also evident from the returns. As the popular vote map shows, McKinley carried a large majority of counties north of the Mason-Dixon Line and east of the Mississippi River. Bryan, meanwhile, won most of the South and most counties in the West, especially those that had supported the Populist Weaver four years earlier.

The contrasts between the 1896 election and the election of 2004 are enlightening. In both cases, one party dominated the Northeast and Pacific Coast and the other the South and interior West. The Republicans won both elections, but the geographies are reversed: the conservative, corporate-oriented Republican McKinley defeated the Democrat Bryan in 1896 by sweeping the Northeast, whereas the conservative, corporate-oriented Republican George W. Bush defeated the Democrat John Kerry in 2004 by sweeping the South and the West.

McKinley's victory, and Bryan's defeat, would shape U.S. politics for years to come. The Republican victory reinforced the Grand Old Party as the nation's majority party at the end of the nineteenth century. Only one Democrat, Woodrow Wilson, would capture the White House during the next eight elections. The Panic of 1893 led to a Republican takeover of the House and Senate in the 1894 midterm elections. Some consider the 1894 congressional elections and the 1896 presidential election to be the beginning of a new party era that would last until the early 1930s. Yet, ironically, most of the ideas advocated by the Populists, including corporate and civil service reform and the direct election of U.S. senators, would become law by the 1920s.

REFERENCE: Glad, Paul W. *McKinley, Bryan and the People*. Philadelphia: Lippincott, 1964.

1900

PRESIDENTIAL ELECTION

~

Candidates	Popular Vote Percentage	Electoral College Vote Percentage and (Vote)
Republican		
William McKinley (Ohio)	51.7	65.3 (292)
Vice Presidential Nominee: Theodore Roosevelt (New York)		
Democrat		
William Jennings Bryan (Nebraska)	45.5	34.7 (155)
Vice Presidential Nominee: Adlai Stevenson (Illinois)		

Map 29

In 1898, during Republican president William McKinley's first administration (1897–1901), the United States became a colonial power by virtue of winning the Spanish-American War. That year, it took control of Cuba, Puerto Rico, and the Philippines and annexed the Hawaiian Islands. Thus, for the first time, the United States ruled over an overseas colonial empire. In addition, the U.S. economy had recovered and was stronger in 1900 than it had been in the mid-1890s.

The Republicans and the nation, not surprisingly, credited McKinley and his administration for sound monetary policies and the nation's newfound prosperity as well as for success on the battlefield. Meeting in Philadelphia, the delegates to the Republican national convention renominated McKinley by acclamation. Vice President Garret Hobart had died in 1899, so the delegates selected Gov. Theodore Roosevelt of New York as the party's vice presidential nominee. Roosevelt was well known throughout the country as a leader of the Rough Riders, who won the battle of San Juan Hill in Cuba during the Spanish-American War. He was also a reformer whose progressive policies irritated some conservative Republican regulars, who liked the idea of his moving from the important post of New York governor to the obscurity of the vice presidency.

The Democrats, meanwhile, renominated William Jennings Bryan of Nebraska as their presidential candidate at their convention in Kansas City. Bryan, who had lost to McKinley in 1896, remained a nationally known and charismatic figure. The convention delegates considered several possible vice presidential nominees before settling on Illinois's Adlai Stevenson, who had served as vice president during Grover Cleveland's second term (1893–1897).

The 1900 election campaign lacked the fire and drama of the 1896 contest. Republicans, employing the slogan "Four More Years of the Full Dinner Pail," emphasized the return to prosperity and the success of the United States in becoming a colonial power. Bryan again focused on populist values, but the economic upturn blunted the appeal of these populist views among many voters. The economic good times, in addition, negated the impact of Bryan's support of free silver, an issue that had resonated more fully during hard times, as in 1896. The isolationist Bryan also raised questions about the appropriateness of the United States—itself a former colony—joining the ranks of the colonial powers. Bryan's arguments appealed particularly to midwesterners of German and Scandinavian ancestry, but a majority of Americans had supported the war effort against Spain and some regarded Bryan's questioning of U.S. imperialism as inappropriate, if not unpatriotic.

McKinley convincingly defeated his opponent, winning 51.7 percent of the popular vote to Bryan's 45.5 percent. The rest of the vote was scattered among several minor-party candidates. McKinley won an electoral college majority of 292 votes to 155, bettering his showing of four years earlier. As in 1896, he swept the

Northeast and Midwest. He also won several states in the Great Plains and Rocky Mountain regions that had supported Bryan four years earlier, including South Dakota, Nebraska, Kansas, Wyoming, and Washington. Bryan swept the South along with the silver-producing states of Montana, Idaho, Nevada, and Colorado. He also won Kentucky, which McKinley had taken four years earlier, but his victories in these states were not nearly enough for an electoral college victory.

The map of the popular vote somewhat parallels that of 1896. Nearly all of the counties in the Northeast went to McKinley, while most counties in the South favored Bryan. The major difference between the two elections can be found in the Great Plains and Rocky Mountain states, where McKinley won areas that Bryan had captured four years earlier, including Bryan's home state of Nebraska (50.5 per-

cent). As a supporter of the unlimited coinage of silver, Bryan was naturally popular in silver-mining counties throughout the Rocky Mountain states, for example, Montana, Idaho, Nevada, and Colorado. Across the West, however, the 1900 election results made clear the Populist tide's retreat.

The first election of the twentieth century represented a reprise of the monumental election of 1896. An assassin's bullet would change the course of history less than a year later, and the elevation of Theodore Roosevelt to the presidency would have far-reaching consequences for U.S. politics and public policy.

REFERENCE: Kazin, Michael. *A Godly Hero: The Life of William Jennings Bryan.* New York: Knopf, 2006.

1904

PRESIDENTIAL ELECTION

CANDIDATES	POPULAR VOTE PERCENTAGE	ELECTORAL COLLEGE VOTE PERCENTAGE AND (VOTE)
Republican		
Theodore Roosevelt (New York)	56.4	70.6 (336)
Vice Presidential Nominee: Charles Fairbanks (Indiana)		
Democrat		
Alton B. Parker (New York)	37.6	29.5 (140)
Vice Presidential Nominee: Henry G. Davis (West Virginia)		
Socialist		
Eugene V. Debs (Indiana)	3.0	0 (0)
Vice Presidential Nominee: Benjamin Hanford (New York)		

Map 30

Economic prosperity and U.S. military success in the Spanish-American War of 1898 marked Republican president William McKinley's successful first term (1897–1901) and led to his comfortable reelection in 1900 with Theodore Roosevelt, then governor of New York, as his running mate. On September 6, 1901, McKinley attended the Pan-American Exposition in Buffalo, New York, where Leon Czolgosz, an anarchist known in the radical community for violent tendencies, shot him. McKinley lingered for eight days while physicians attempted to treat his wounds, but he died on September 14. Roosevelt succeeded him at the age of forty-two, becoming the youngest person to serve as president. He quickly became popular with Americans, who were captivated by his youth and vigor and by his young family. After taking office, Roosevelt moved the country in a progressive direction relative to the more conservative actions of McKinley. He supported reforms that the Populists had advocated in the 1890s and in essence co-opted these issues from the Populists and Democrats. Rank-and-file voters welcomed his "trust-busting" reforms limiting the power of big business. Roosevelt also supported government regulation of railroads and conservation of natural resources.

Some conservative Republicans mistrusted Roosevelt's progressive measures. Ohio senator Mark Hanna, who had been McKinley's close friend and mentor, made plans to challenge Roosevelt for the Republican Party nomination, but he died in February 1904. Any thought of a conservative challenge to Roosevelt passed away with him. Delegates to the Republican national convention in Chicago nominated Roosevelt by acclamation. Delegates chose Indiana senator Charles Fairbanks, a representative of the conservative wing of the party, to run for vice president.

In 1896 and 1900 the Democrats had nominated William Jennings Bryan, who had run on a populist and free-silver platform but had lost twice to McKinley. In 1904 a majority of delegates to the Democratic national convention in St. Louis favored moving the party in a more conservative direction, abandoning their previous support for free silver. These delegates likely reasoned that the progressive Roosevelt would be particularly popular in the West, where free silver remained an especially popular issue. Rather than try to defeat Roosevelt in the West, they thought that they would have a better chance of ousting him by winning over conservative easterners, trying to create an electoral college majority by combining votes in the East and in the solidly Democratic South.

The delegates selected Alton B. Parker, the chief justice of the New York Court of Appeals, to run against Roosevelt. Unlike Bryan, Parker opposed free silver and supported the gold standard. Parker, however, had never held elective office and was little known to ordinary voters. Former West Virginia senator Henry G. Davis became Parker's running mate. At the age of eighty, Davis was the oldest major-party national candidate in history. (His nephew John W. Davis would become the Democrats' presidential nominee in 1924.)

The lackluster fall campaign ended in a Republican landslide. The Democrats' emphasis on the gold standard aroused little enthusiasm, while the Republicans successfully framed the election as a referendum on Roosevelt's popular policies and his colorful personality. The voters handed Roosevelt the Grand Old Party's largest election victory since Reconstruction. He won 56.4 percent of the popular vote to Parker's 37.6 percent, with the remaining 6 percent going to third-party candidates. Socialist Eugene V. Debs received 3 percent of the vote nationwide, with his strongest support in the West, especially in California (8.9 percent), Montana (8.9 percent), and Oregon (8.3 percent). Many of these votes came from mining regions.

Roosevelt's victory in the electoral college was even more resounding, as he won by a margin of 336 votes to 140. As the electoral vote map indicates, all of Parker's electoral votes came from the South: the eleven states of the Old Confederacy and the border states of Maryland and Kentucky. Roosevelt won the remaining thirty-two states. His popular vote margins were more than two to one in most states along the northern tier and in the Midwest, including Maine, Michigan, Minnesota, Wyoming, and Washington.

The popular vote map shows the extreme sectional contrast of the 1904 election. Roosevelt carried the large majority of the counties outside the South. For example, he carried every county in Washington, Oregon, Idaho, Kansas, and Nebraska, as well as in Minnesota, Michigan, and the New England states. In the Midwest, he lost a few traditionally Democratic counties to the little-known Parker. As had been the case since the Civil War, these counties were primarily places with populations dominated by descendants of southern immigrants or by members of such ethnic groups as German Catholics, who were traditionally supportive of the Democrats. Parker won a large majority of southern counties, with the pro-Republican African American vote now made negligible by Jim Crow laws restricting access to the ballot box. Roosevelt won majorities in those parts of the South with a long tradition of Republican support, including Appalachia, the Ozarks of Arkansas and Missouri, and some German American counties in Texas.

The map in Missouri reflects long-standing sectional divisions in the Show Me State. Here Roosevelt ran strongest in the antislavery, Unionist Ozark region in the southwestern part of the state. Parker's strongest area was the Little Dixie region of north-central Missouri. This area had been settled prior to the Civil War by southerners from Tennessee and Mississippi moving north and west along the Missouri River. This pattern is typical of the electoral breakdown of Missouri between the Civil War and World War II and illustrates the long-standing influence of ethnic and sectional divisions within Missouri, as well as in other states.

The 1904 Republican landslide represented a national endorsement of President Roosevelt's progressive policies. Progressives in both parties would dominate U.S. presidential politics for the next sixteen years, until the country took a sharp conservative turn after World War I.

REFERENCE: Morris, Edmund. *Theodore Rex*. New York: Random House, 2001.

1908

PRESIDENTIAL ELECTION

Candidates	Popular Vote Percentage	Electoral College Vote Percentage and (Vote)
Republican		
William Howard Taft (Ohio)	51.6	66.5 (321)
Vice Presidential Nominee: James Sherman (New York)		
Democrat		
William Jennings Bryan (Nebraska)	43.0	33.5 (162)
Vice Presidential Nominee: John Kern (Indiana)		
Socialist		
Eugene V. Debs (Indiana)	2.8	0 (0)
Vice Presidential Nominee: Benjamin Hanford (New York)		

Map 31

resident Theodore Roosevelt remained highly popular throughout his first full term (1905–1909), after having been elected in his own right in 1904. Although he was only forty-nine years old in 1908, Roosevelt followed long-standing tradition and declined to run for a second full term. He advocated his secretary of war, William Howard Taft of Ohio, as his successor.

Some of the delegates to the Republican national convention in Chicago supported other candidates, including House Speaker Joseph Cannon of Illinois, Gov. Charles Evans Hughes of New York (who would be the party's 1916 nominee), and Sen. Robert LaFollette of Wisconsin. Because of Roosevelt's support, however, the delegates selected Taft on the first ballot and chose James Sherman, a long-time representative from upstate New York, as Taft's running mate. As in many other elections, the Republicans thus selected a ticket consisting of one candidate from the Mid-Atlantic states and one from Ohio, Indiana, or Illinois.

With Roosevelt out of the race, some Democrats hoped that their party could capture the White House for the first time since 1892. Convening in Denver, the party selected William Jennings Bryan of Nebraska as its candidate for the third time. Bryan had lost to William McKinley in 1896 and again in 1900. John Kern, a former state representative and unsuccessful gubernatorial candidate from Indiana, won the vice presidential nomination.

During the campaign, Taft and Bryan both took progressive positions on major issues. Taft pledged to carry forward Roosevelt's reformist policies. Bryan had run earlier as a strong advocate of free silver, but by 1908 the issue had lost salience with most voters. Instead, Bryan focused on opposition to what he called "government by privilege," hoping to secure the support of labor and small farmers and to paint Taft as a tool of big business. His efforts failed, however, and Taft easily defeated him, giving the Republicans their fourth consecutive presidential victory. Taft won 51.6 percent of the popular vote compared to 43 percent for Bryan, with the remainder going to third-party candidates. Once again Socialist Eugene V. Debs placed highest among the third-party candidates with 2.8 percent of the popular vote. As in his first run for the presidency in 1904, Debs received his highest percentages of the vote in the West and other mining regions, with Nevada and

Montana (both with 8.6 percent of the state vote) leading the way. Taft won a decisive electoral college victory by a margin of 321 votes to 162.

Both the electoral college and the popular vote maps illustrate a high degree of geographic polarization. Bryan won the electoral votes of the South, including the Old Confederacy and the border states of Maryland, Kentucky, and Oklahoma. He also captured his home state of Nebraska and the silver-producing states of Colorado and Nevada, where his long-time support of free silver continued to resonate with voters. Taft won the remaining states, many by substantial margins. These sectional differences are also clearly evident at the county level. Taft swept New England, carrying every county in Maine, Vermont, and Massachusetts by margins of more than two to one. He won every county in Michigan and nearly all of the counties of Wisconsin and Minnesota. Bryan carried several upper Midwest counties with large German Catholic populations, including Stearns County (St. Cloud), Minnesota, and Dubuque County, Iowa. Taft carried all of Washington and Oregon and most of California. Even Cook County (Chicago), Illinois, Wayne County (Detroit), Michigan, and Allegheny County (Pittsburgh), Pennsylvania—large industrial centers with considerable Democratic-leaning Eastern European immigrant populations—went Republican.

Like most Democratic candidates between the Civil War and World War II, Bryan ran well in the South but poorly elsewhere. He lost only Appalachia and a few Hispanic strongholds in southern Texas while otherwise sweeping the South. As opposed to Alton Parker, who supported the gold standard four years earlier, Bryan again made inroads in the West. He won a majority of counties in his home state of Nebraska, where he won a statewide plurality (49.1 percent). The Colorado map is especially revealing. Bryan won the mining-oriented counties in the western half of the state. His margins in these counties and in the city of Denver were large enough for him to win the state's electoral votes despite Taft carrying all of the agricultural counties east of the Front Range. Bryan similarly swept silver-producing Nevada.

The newly admitted state of Oklahoma was divided on the basis of sectionalism. The southern and eastern portions of the state, which had been settled primarily by natives of the South, went to Bryan, whereas northern and western Oklahoma, many of whose residents came originally from Illinois, Iowa, and Kansas, supported Taft.

The 1908 election, like that of 1904, can be seen as a validation of Roosevelt and his reform efforts. Four years later, however, a split between progressives and conservatives within the Republican ranks would propel a Democrat into the White House for the first time in two decades.

REFERENCE: Bromley, Michael. *William Howard Taft and the First Motoring Presidency, 1909–1913.* New York: McFarland and Company, 2003.

1912

PRESIDENTIAL ELECTION

~

Candidates	Popular Vote Percentage	Electoral College Vote Percentage and (Vote)
Democrat		
Woodrow Wilson (New Jersey)	41.8	81.9 (435)
Vice Presidential Nominee: Thomas Marshall (Indiana)		
Progressive		
Theodore Roosevelt (New York)	27.4	16.6 (88)
Vice Presidential Nominee: Hiram Johnson (California)		
Republican		
William Howard Taft (Ohio)	23.2	1.5 (8)*
Vice Presidential Nominee: James Sherman (New York)		
Socialist		
Eugene V. Debs (Indiana)	6.0	0 (0)
Vice Presidential Nominee: Emil Seidel (Wisconsin)		

Map 32

Republican William Howard Taft, who had served as secretary of war under Theodore Roosevelt from 1904 to 1908, had easily won the 1908 election with Roosevelt's support. Shortly after leaving office, Roosevelt embarked on a year-long African safari, followed by an extended visit to Europe. Upon returning to the United States, he was dismayed to find that Taft had moved away from his progressive policies in favor of charting a much more conservative course. Roosevelt resolved to challenge Taft for the 1912 Republican nomination and entered several presidential primaries, outpolling Taft in all but one. At that time, however, most convention delegates were selected by local party leaders, who tended to favor Taft's conservative approach. Thus the majority of delegates to the Republican national convention in Chicago were Taft supporters. They renominated Taft along with Vice President James Sherman of New York. Sherman died a week before the election, and the Republican National Committee selected Nicholas Murray Butler, the president of Columbia University in New York, to replace him on the ticket.

After Taft's renomination, Roosevelt asked his progressive supporters to walk out of the Chicago convention, arguing that Taft's conservative approach did not represent the views of the majority of Republican voters throughout the country. The Roosevelt supporters reconvened and endorsed Roosevelt's bid for the presidency under the banner of the Progressive Party. They selected California senator Hiram Johnson, a long-time leader of the Republicans' progressive wing, to run for vice president. After accepting the Progressive nomination, Roosevelt told reporters that he felt "as fit as a bull moose," after which "Bull Moose" became the nickname of Roosevelt's third-party candidacy.

The Democrats sensed that the split between the Progressives and the more conservative regular Republicans afforded them an opportunity to take the presi-

Republican vice presidential nominee James Sherman died before the election, and the Republican vice presidential electoral votes went to Nicholas Murray Butler of New York.

dency. They seriously considered several candidates at the party's convention in Baltimore, including Nebraskan William Jennings Bryan, who had been the Democrats' nominee in 1896, 1900, and 1908, and Missouri's James Beauchamp "Champ" Clark, the Speaker of the House of Representatives. After forty-six ballots, the deadlocked convention turned to Gov. Woodrow Wilson of New Jersey as a compromise presidential candidate. Prior to his election as governor, Wilson had been the president of Princeton University. Gov. Thomas Marshall of Indiana was selected as Wilson's running mate. For the only time in U.S. history, three men who at one point would occupy the Oval Office squared off against each other in a presidential election.

During the fall campaign, Wilson successfully steered a middle course between the progressive Roosevelt and the conservative Taft. In the election of 1912, the Democrats captured the White House for the first time since 1892, with Wilson winning almost 42 percent of the popular vote, compared to 27 percent for Roosevelt and 23 percent for Taft. Nearly 8 percent of the voters cast ballots for other candidates, including more than 900,000 (6 percent) for the Socialist Eugene V. Debs.

Wilson indeed benefited from the split between the progressive and conservative elements of the Republican Party in winning the election. He won in the electoral college by an overwhelming margin, garnering 435 votes compared with 88 for Roosevelt and 8 for Taft. Wilson held pluralities in states in all regions of the country. Following the pattern set by other Democrats in the late nineteenth and early twentieth centuries, the Virginia-born Wilson, who had spent much of his childhood in Georgia, swept the South. He won absolute majorities in most of the states of the Old Confederacy, including more than three-quarters of the popular vote in South Carolina, Georgia, Mississippi, and Louisiana. He also took advantage of the Republican split to capture the electoral votes with pluralities in New York (41.3 percent), Ohio (41 percent), Indiana (43.1 percent), and Wisconsin (41.1 percent) as well as his home state of New Jersey (41.2 percent). He won a majority of states west of the Mississippi, and all by a plurality with the exception of Texas. Illinois is a classic example of the possible ramifications of a third party in the winner-take-all U.S. electoral college system. Wilson won all twenty-nine of Illinois's electoral votes with only 35.3 percent of the vote to Roosevelt's 33.7 percent and Taft's 22.1 percent.

Roosevelt ran best in the traditionally Republican northern tier of states, capturing the electoral votes of Pennsylvania, Michigan, Minnesota, South Dakota (where Taft did not appear on the ballot and Roosevelt was endorsed by state Republican leaders), Washington, and California. Taft captured only Utah and Vermont, giving the latter the distinction of being the only state to go Republican in every election up to that time since the Republican Party's founding in 1856.

Vermont would remain in the Republican column in every succeeding election until 1964.

The popular vote pattern at the county level illustrates how Wilson was able to take advantage of the Republicans' split. In fact, the 1912 map is the only one that illustrates the vast majority of counties having a plurality winner rather than a majority winner. Wilson's greatest strength was in the Deep South, where he won a majority of the popular vote in many counties. Outside of the South, Wilson carried many of the counties in his home state of New Jersey, Indiana, Ohio, and southern Illinois but without winning absolute majorities. Wilson also did well in the old mining strongholds in the West. Of note, he carried all but one county in Nevada, every county in newly admitted Arizona, and all of Idaho with the exception of the agricultural, Mormon-dominated southeastern portion of the state, which supported Taft.

With slightly more than a quarter of the popular vote, Roosevelt failed to come close to capturing the presidency, but he had the best showing for a third-party candidate since the Democrat-Republican party era began in 1856. Indeed, no third-party candidate since 1912 has come in second in either popular or electoral votes. Roosevelt ran strongest in rural counties in the northern states from Pennsylvania westward to the progressive upper Midwest to the Dakotas. He won a majority of counties in Pennsylvania, Michigan, Minnesota, and northern portions of Illinois and Iowa. He also took many of the traditionally Republican counties of northern New England and the Appalachians.

Taft's support was limited primarily to areas in and around Vermont and Utah, the two states that he carried. In the Northeast, Taft won pluralities in most of Vermont, western Massachusetts, northern Connecticut, and rural upstate New York. He also carried the Mormon-culture region of Utah and Idaho and Hispanic-dominated areas of Texas and newly admitted New Mexico. The Great Plains region split among the three candidates. In Oklahoma, for example, the conservative Taft carried numerous counties north and west of Oklahoma City, whereas the Socialist Debs ran well in eastern and southern counties. (Roosevelt did not appear on the ballot in Oklahoma.) Debs exceeded 10 percent of the popular vote in seven western states, and he won pluralities in a few rural counties in Minnesota, North Dakota, and Kansas.

The Democrats won the White House in 1912 by taking advantage of an ideological split in the Republican ranks, but President Wilson, in seeking reelection four years later, would face a united Republican Party and find himself hard pressed to remain in the White House.

REFERENCE: Chace, James. *1912: Wilson, Roosevelt, Taft and Debs: The Election That Changed the Country.* New York: Simon and Schuster, 2004.

1916

PRESIDENTIAL ELECTION

CANDIDATES	POPULAR VOTE PERCENTAGE	ELECTORAL COLLEGE VOTE PERCENTAGE AND (VOTE)
Democrat		
Woodrow Wilson (New Jersey)	49.2	52.2 (277)
Vice Presidential Nominee: Thomas Marshall (Indiana)		
Republican		
Charles Evans Hughes (New York)	46.1	47.8 (254)
Vice Presidential Nominee: Charles Fairbanks (Indiana)		
Socialist		
Allan L. Benson (New York)	3.2	0 (0)
Vice Presidential Nominee: George R. Kirkpatrick (New Jersey)		

President Woodrow Wilson, the first Democrat elected in the twentieth century, took the oath of office in 1913. In 1914 *Map 33* Archduke Franz Ferdinand of Austria was assassinated in Sarajevo, and Europe plunged into World War I, with Britain and France and their allies fighting the Central Powers, including Austria-Hungary and Germany. The United States remained neutral and attempted to continue trade with both sides. Many Americans supported the Allies against the Central Powers, especially after a German submarine fired upon and sank the *Lusitania,* a British ocean liner, off the coast of Ireland in May 1915. Nearly 1,200 passengers, including many Americans, lost their lives in the attack, which the Germans justified on the grounds that they believed that the ship was carrying munitions to Britain. The sinking of the *Lusitania* galvanized public opinion in the United States against the Germans, although many Americans of German ancestry quietly supported the Central Powers. Nevertheless, Wilson maintained U.S. neutrality throughout his first term, and his supporters adopted the slogan "He Kept Us Out of War" in promoting his reelection. Wilson and Vice President Thomas Marshall of Indiana were renominated by acclamation at the Democratic national convention in St. Louis.

In 1912 the Republicans had been badly split between regular Republicans, who supported President William Howard Taft, and a progressive faction, which had broken away and supported former president Theodore Roosevelt as a third-party candidate. Republican leaders anxiously sought to reunite the two factions of the party. Delegates to the Republican national convention in Chicago selected Charles Evans Hughes, an associate justice of the U.S. Supreme Court and former governor of New York, as their presidential nominee. Hughes, a moderate, was supported by the progressive faction as well as the conservative faction within the party. As Hughes's running mate, the Republicans nominated Indianan Charles Fairbanks, who had served as vice president under Roosevelt (1905–1909). Some Progressives attempted to maintain a viable party and build upon the success that they had had under Roosevelt in 1912. A Progressive national convention formally offered Roosevelt its nomination, but he declined to run and instead supported Hughes.

The war played a central role in the fall campaign. Hughes criticized the Wilson administration for allegedly being insufficiently prepared in the event of being drawn into the conflict. This position proved popular in the Northeast, where pro-British sentiment was strongest. Wilson emphasized his work in keeping the United States neutral and his support of labor. The election would be the closest since the 1880s, and not until 1960 would the electorate again be so evenly divided. Voters reelected Wilson by a margin of approximately 600,000 popular votes out of 18.5 million cast and an electoral college majority of 277 votes to 254.

Wilson won by dominating the South and the West, while Hughes dominated the Northeast. In this sense, Wilson succeeded in doing what William Jennings Bryan twenty years earlier had tried unsuccessfully to do—unite the sectional interests of the South and West against the northeastern industrial core. Wilson carried the entire South, and with the exception of Iowa, Minnesota, South Dakota, and Oregon, all of the states west of the Mississippi River. He also won Ohio (51 percent) and New Hampshire (49.1 percent, with votes for Socialist nominee Allan Benson allowing only a plurality victory). The key to Wilson's victory was California, which he carried by some 3,800 popular votes (46.6 percent for Wilson, with votes for the Socialist and Prohibition parties combining for 7.1 percent of the vote). The switch of either Ohio or California in 1916 would have given the Republicans victory in the electoral college.

The polarization between the Northeast and the South and West is evident on the popular vote map. Wilson swept the South, as he had done four years earlier. With the African American vote almost completely eliminated, he won almost every county in the Deep South, carrying most of them by large margins. Only in central Appalachia—an old Civil War Unionist region generally carried by Republicans—did Hughes win significant numbers of counties in the South. Hughes also won traditionally Republican strongholds in New England, the Mid-Atlantic states, and the Midwest. He carried every county in Vermont and nearly every county in upstate New York. He also won much of Michigan, northern Illinois, and Iowa. Hughes also took many of the counties along the Pacific Coast, although Wilson had enough support to win plurality victories and the electoral votes of California and Washington. Wilson captured the Rocky Mountain region with impressive margins, winning all but one county in Montana, all but one in Colorado, and all but two in Wyoming. Of note, he won Utah easily even though he had lost it decisively in 1912. Wilson also maintained strength in the Great Plains states, where his emphasis on neutrality may have helped him win support among voters in this often isolationist region.

Wilson's emphasis on keeping the country out of the war appeared to be important to his reelection. Less than a year after his second inauguration, however, the United States would enter World War I. This conflict and the implications of the peace agreements flowing from it would have significant implications for the presidency four years later and throughout the 1920s.

REFERENCE: Nordholt, J. W. Schulte. *Woodrow Wilson: A Life for World Peace.* Berkeley: University of California Press, 1991.

1920

PRESIDENTIAL ELECTION

Candidates	Popular Vote Percentage	Electoral College Vote Percentage and (Vote)
Republican		
Warren G. Harding (Ohio)	60.3	76.1 (404)
Vice Presidential Nominee: Calvin Coolidge (Massachusetts)		
Democrat		
James M. Cox (Ohio)	34.1	23.9 (127)
Vice Presidential Nominee: Franklin D. Roosevelt (New York)		
Socialist		
Eugene V. Debs (Indiana)	3.4	0 (0)
Vice Presidential Nominee: Seymour Stedman (Ohio)		

Map 34

Democratic president Woodrow Wilson had narrowly won reelection in 1916, in part because he campaigned on the slogan "He Kept Us Out of War." In 1917, however, the United States entered World War I on the side of the Allies. U.S. military strength and industrial might turned the tide of war in favor of the Allies, and on November 11, 1918, Germany signed an armistice ending the conflict.

Shortly after the armistice, Wilson traveled to France to participate in the peace conference that resulted in the Treaty of Versailles. While there, he promulgated his Fourteen Points, including the right of self-determination for minority populations throughout Europe. In addition, Wilson advocated the establishment of the League of Nations. Many Americans, however, opposed the league. Several prominent isolationist Republican senators, led by Massachusetts' Henry Cabot Lodge, demanded reservations that would have prevented the subordination of U.S. decision-making authority to the league. After Wilson refused to support these reservations, the Senate rejected the treaty, despite Wilson's strong support.

After returning from Europe, Wilson embarked on a cross-country tour to generate public support for the league. Shortly after returning to Washington, he suffered a severe stroke on October 2, 1919. The seriousness of Wilson's condition was concealed from journalists and the public, and Wilson remained incapacitated for the remainder of his term. The Democratic national convention, meeting in San Francisco, considered nominating Secretary of the Treasury William McAdoo or Attorney General Mitchell Palmer for the presidency before selecting Gov. James Cox of Ohio on the forty-fourth ballot. Delegates then selected Franklin D. Roosevelt of New York as his running mate. A distant cousin of former president Theodore Roosevelt, Franklin Roosevelt brought a famous name as well as an East-Midwest geographic balance to the Democratic ticket.

Meanwhile, the Republican national convention, held in Chicago, considered several potential nominees, including Gen. Leonard Wood, Sen. Hiram Johnson of California, and Gov. Frank Lowden of Illinois. The convention remained deadlocked after several ballots. Party leaders, meeting late at night in a "smoke-filled room," finally selected Sen. Warren G. Harding of Ohio as the presidential nominee. They proposed Sen. Irvine Lenroot of Wisconsin as Harding's running mate, but conventioneers rebelled and selected Massachusetts governor Calvin Coolidge, who was best known for his efforts to break a strike by Boston police a year earlier, as the party's vice presidential nominee. The election became, in effect, a referendum on the League of Nations. Cox supported the league, while Harding did not take a public position. Harding instead called for a return to pre–World War I "normalcy," thus attracting the support of traditional Republican voters, voters who opposed the League, and those skeptical of the United States' increased international role. In 1920 voters overwhelmingly elected Harding, returning the White House to Republican control after the eight-year Democratic administration of Wilson. Harding easily defeated Cox, winning more than 60 percent of the popular vote and in the electoral college garnering 404 votes to 127.

In taking Tennessee, with 51.2 percent of the popular vote, Harding became the first Republican to win a southern electoral vote since Reconstruction. He lost Kentucky to Cox by only 4,000 popular votes and won nearly 44 percent of the popular vote in North Carolina. The North went solidly for Harding, who won 78 percent of the popular vote in North Dakota, 76 percent in Vermont, and 71 percent in Minnesota, Iowa, and Wisconsin. Cox won electoral votes only in the Democratic Solid South.

The Republican dominance of the North and the Democratic dominance of the South are evident from the popular vote map. Harding won nearly all of New England, the upper Midwest, and the Pacific Northwest. He carried every county in northern New England, upstate New York, Wisconsin, Minnesota, North Dakota, Idaho, Washington, and Oregon. In the Midwest, he lost only the traditionally Democratic counties of the "Little Dixie" region of east-central Missouri, an area that had been settled by migrants from the South. Harding also carried the traditionally Republican counties of Appalachia in eastern Kentucky, eastern Tennessee, western North Carolina, and western Virginia. Cox won most of the remaining southern counties by overwhelming margins, but his lack of significant support outside the Old Confederacy cost him the election. Even large industrial northern cities with large immigrant populations that tended to vote Democratic did not support him. The 1920 voting pattern is somewhat similar to those from 1896 to 1908, before the Republicans split in 1912. In this sense, the 1920 election represents a return to normalcy with respect to sectional party support.

The Nineteenth Amendment, which gave women the right to vote in federal elections, had been adopted in 1919, and thus women voted in their first presidential election in 1920. The overall number of popular votes increased dramatically, from about 18.5 million in 1916 to more than 26.7 million in 1920. Public opinion polls and voting patterns showed little difference in voting habits between men and women. Not until the 1980s would a "gender gap," in which women would prove to be more likely than men to support Democratic presidential candidates, become evident in U.S. politics.

REFERENCE: Dean, John W. *Warren G. Harding.* New York: Times Books, 2004.

1924
PRESIDENTIAL ELECTION

~

Candidates	Popular Vote Percentage	Electoral College Vote Percentage and (Vote)
Republican		
Calvin Coolidge (Massachusetts)	54.0	71.9 (382)
Vice Presidential Nominee: Charles G. Dawes (Illinois)		
Democrat		
John W. Davis (West Virginia)	28.8	25.6 (136)
Vice Presidential Nominee: Charles W. Bryan (Nebraska)		
Progressive		
Robert LaFollette (Wisconsin)	16.6	2.5 (13)
Vice Presidential Nominee: Burton K. Wheeler (Montana)		

Map 35

Republican president Warren G. Harding had been elected in a landslide in 1920 on a platform of a return to "normalcy" following World War I. The Harding administration, however, soon became enmeshed in scandal. Secretary of the Interior Albert B. Fall was indicted for accepting bribes in return for leasing valuable oil reserves at Teapot Dome, Wyoming, to cronies without competitive bidding. Other members of the administration faced charges of corruption as well, shaking the public's confidence.

During the summer of 1923, Harding embarked on a long western journey, including a visit to Alaska. On his way back to Washington, he became ill and died in San Francisco on August 2, 1923. Vice President Calvin Coolidge succeeded Harding. Known for his integrity, Coolidge fired corrupt officeholders and replaced them with honest people, removing the taint of scandal from the Republican Party. Meanwhile, the economy had gone into a recession in 1922 and early 1923, but by 1924 it was entering a boom that would last for the remainder of the decade. The Republican national convention, meeting in Cleveland, nominated Coolidge for a full term by acclamation. They selected Charles G. Dawes of Illinois, the director of the Bureau of the Budget, as his running mate.

The Republicans' decision had been an easy one, but the Democrats faced a much more difficult road in choosing their party's nominee. Several prominent candidates vied for the nomination. The leading contenders included Californian William McAdoo, the former secretary of the Treasury and son-in-law of Woodrow Wilson. Gov. Alfred E. Smith of New York was also a major candidate, while many southerners supported Sen. Oscar W. Underwood of Alabama. The Democratic national convention, held in New York, deadlocked between McAdoo and Smith. One of the issues dividing the Democrats was Prohibition. The Eighteenth Amendment, prohibiting the manufacture and sale of alcoholic beverages, had been added to the Constitution in 1919. McAdoo favored continuing Prohibition and had strong support in the South and West. Smith, who favored repealing the Eighteenth Amendment, was supported by most delegates from the Northeast and urban areas. The convention lasted two weeks, and delegates cast 103 ballots before agreeing on a compromise candidate—John W. Davis, a former solicitor general under President Woodrow Wilson and former representative from West Virginia who had also served as ambassador to the United Kingdom. The convention chose Nebraska governor Charles W. Bryan, the brother of William Jennings Bryan, as Davis's running mate.

Some liberals in the Midwest and West expressed unhappiness with the conservative leanings of both major-party tickets. Wisconsin Republican Robert LaFollette, a leading Senate liberal, ran as a third-party candidate, reviving the Progressive Party, which had been formed by supporters of Theodore Roosevelt in 1912 but had fallen apart after Roosevelt died in 1919. LaFollette selected a Democratic colleague, Sen. Burton Wheeler of Montana, as his running mate. LaFollette and the Progressives campaigned for business regulation, the abolition of child labor, nationalization of railroads, and government control of natural resources. Many former supporters of Theodore Roosevelt's 1912 Bull Moose campaign supported him, as did farmers and labor organizations, former Populists, and some progressive Democrats and Socialists. For the first time since 1896, a Socialist candidate did not appear on the presidential ballot.

The outcome of the election was never in doubt. Employing the slogan "Keep Cool with Coolidge," the Republicans emphasized the country's prosperity. Coolidge cruised to an easy victory with 54 percent of the popular vote and 382 electoral votes. As is evident on the electoral college map, Davis won the electoral votes of the South, taking the Old Confederacy along with the border state of Oklahoma. LaFollette carried only his native Wisconsin. Coolidge swept the rest of the country, including the entire Northeast and the entire West. He also won the usually Democratic border states of Delaware, Maryland, West Virginia, Kentucky, and Missouri.

The popular vote map equally illustrates the sectional distribution of votes. Davis ran well only in the reliably Democratic sections of the Old South, though he lost many of the counties in central Appalachia and a few German American areas in Texas. Outside the South, Davis won only a small minority of counties. Most of those in which he ran reasonably well were in the Midwest and dominated by German Catholics or other ethnic groups who had long been reliable sources of votes for Democrats. Coolidge swept his native New England, New York, and Pennsylvania. In fact, Coolidge won New York City, becoming the only Republican in the twentieth century to achieve this feat.

In the Midwest and the West, the Progressive LaFollette, rather than the conservative Democrat Davis, emerged as Coolidge's chief rival in several states and many counties. In fact, Davis's percentage of the popular vote in 1924 was the lowest of any Democrat in the twentieth century. In California, for example, Coolidge won with 733,250 popular votes, but LaFollette came in second, with 424,649, far ahead of Davis's 105,514. LaFollette also came in second statewide in North Dakota (45.2 percent), Minnesota (42.3 percent), South Dakota (37 percent), and Iowa (28.1 percent). In the West, he finished second, including in Montana (37.8 percent), Washington (35.8 percent), Idaho (35.8 percent), and Oregon (24.5 percent). As the LaFollette map illustrates, he especially did well from Wisconsin westward along the northern tier to the Pacific Coast, including in California and Nevada. Throughout these states, LaFollette won pluralities or majorities in a number of counties, and he ran second to Coolidge in many others. He did particularly well in those counties oriented toward mining or agriculture that had supported Populist ideas and candidates in the 1880s and 1890s. LaFollette received double-digit support in twenty-six of the forty-eight states.

The 1924 election proved to be a resounding victory for the Republicans. Since then, only two other Republicans—Richard Nixon and Ronald Reagan—have won as easily and decisively as Coolidge did in attaining a full term in the White House.

·

REFERENCE: Sobel, Robert. *Coolidge: An American Enigma.* Washington, D.C.: Regnery Publishing, 1998.

1928

PRESIDENTIAL ELECTION

~

Candidates	Popular Vote Percentage	Electoral College Vote Percentage and (Vote)
Republican		
Herbert Hoover (California)	58.2	83.6 (444)
Vice Presidential Nominee: Charles Curtis (Kansas)		
Democrat		
Alfred E. Smith (New York)	40.8	16.4 (87)
Vice Presidential Nominee: Joseph T. Robinson (Arkansas)		

The U.S. economy boomed throughout much of the 1920s, and Republican president Calvin Coolidge remained popular. In August 1927, however, Coolidge announced, "I do not choose to run for President in 1928." Herbert Hoover, who had served as secretary of commerce under Coolidge and his predecessor, Warren G. Harding, became the front-runner for the party's nomination and encountered little opposition. At the Republican national convention, in Kansas City, delegates nominated Hoover for the presidency and selected Sen. Charles Curtis of Kansas as his vice presidential running mate. The Republican platform gave the GOP credit for continued prosperity, expressed support for continued Prohibition, and pledged to continue the policies of the Coolidge administration.

In 1924 the Democrats had been deadlocked between the "drys"—rural southern and midwestern natives who supported continuing Prohibition—and the "wets"—urban residents and most immigrants who favored repealing the Eighteenth Amendment. They had selected John W. Davis as a compromise candidate, and he had lost decisively to Coolidge. In 1928 the wets held a majority and their favorite, Gov. Alfred E. Smith of New York, won the Democratic nomination on the first ballot at their national convention, in Houston. Smith was the first Roman Catholic to be nominated for president on a major-party ticket. To balance the ticket politically and geographically, and to placate rural opposition to Smith,

Map 36

the Democrats selected Sen. Joseph Robinson of Arkansas as their vice presidential nominee. In contrast to Smith, who was born and raised in New York City, Robinson was a southerner, a Protestant, and a dry. Robinson was also the first candidate from a former Confederate state to be nominated by the Democrats for national office since the Civil War.

Expecting the continuing prosperity of the Roaring Twenties, the Republicans called for "a chicken in every pot and a car in every garage." Moreover, some Americans expressed concern about the prospect of a Roman Catholic in the White House. Opposition to Smith on religious grounds was especially strong in rural parts of the South. In 1928 the Republicans won their third consecutive election by a comfortable margin, with Hoover defeating Smith in a popular and electoral landslide. Hoover received more than 58 percent of the popular vote and won in the electoral college by a margin of 444 votes to 87. With 444 electoral votes, his electoral vote tally surpassed that of both Harding and Coolidge. Hoover became the first Republican to win a significant number of southern states, with Tennessee (55.5 percent) and for the first time since Reconstruction Florida (57.1 percent), North Carolina (54.9 percent), Virginia (53.9 percent), and Texas (51.7 percent) moving into the Republican column. Smith won only the Deep South states of South Carolina, Georgia, Alabama, Mississippi, and Louisiana; Robinson's native Arkansas; and Massachusetts and Rhode Island, which had large Roman Catholic populations.

The popular vote map illustrates an overwhelming Republican victory in good economic times. As in the 1920 and 1924 elections, the Republicans won the vast majority of counties along the entire northern tier, from New England to the Pacific Coast. In addition, Republican majorities held steady in the southwestern states. The southern states that the Republicans carried exhibited clear intrastate sectional divisions. In Tennessee, Republican growth expanded from the Appalachian counties, but the western portion remained Democratic. In Florida, the northern counties, with ties and traditions of the Old South, remained Democratic, while South Florida switched to the Republicans. In Texas, the cotton-growing areas in the east voted Democratic, while the Great Plains section of the state supported the GOP. To some extent, Texas represented a microcosm of the United States in 1928, with the issues of Prohibition and racial and religious prejudice playing an important role in the electoral outcome.

The prosperity of the Roaring Twenties ensured Republican retention of the White House in 1928. Less than a year after Hoover took office, however, the country would become mired in the worst economic depression in U.S. history, and the Republicans would be swept out of office for twenty years.

REFERENCE: Brown, Norman. *Hood, Bonnet, and Little Brown Jug: Texas Politics, 1921–1928.* College Station: Texas A&M University Press, 1984.

1932
PRESIDENTIAL ELECTION

Candidates	Popular Vote Percentage	Electoral College Vote Percentage and (Vote)
Democrat		
Franklin D. Roosevelt (New York)	57.4	88.9 (472)
Vice Presidential Nominee: John Nance Garner (Texas)		
Republican		
Herbert Hoover (California)	39.6	11.1 (59)
Vice Presidential Nominee: Charles Curtis (Kansas)		
Socialist		
Norman M. Thomas (New York)	2.2	0 (0)
Vice Presidential Nominee: James H. Maurer (Pennsylvania)		

Map 37

The stock market crash of October 1929 abruptly ended several years of prosperity and ushered the United States into the Great Depression. The Republican-sponsored Smoot-Hawley Tariff resulted in the curtailing of foreign trade, reducing exports and increasing already high unemployment rates. By 1932 nearly 13 million American adults were out of work, and millions more were underemployed. As during previous economic downturns, many in the electorate blamed the party in power for failing to resolve the economic misery, in this case, Hoover and the Republican administration. Nevertheless, Republicans meeting at their national convention in Chicago, renominated Hoover and Vice President Charles Curtis with little opposition. The Republicans campaigned on a platform of continued high tariffs and reduced federal expenditures.

Given the state of the economy, many Democrats felt confident that their party would take the White House for the first time in twelve years. Also holding their national convention in Chicago, Democrats chose among several candidates for their party's nomination. Franklin D. Roosevelt, their 1920 vice presidential nomi-

nee and the governor of New York, emerged as the favorite. Others seriously considered included House Speaker John Nance Garner of Texas, Gov. Albert Ritchie of Maryland, and former New York governor Alfred E. Smith, the unsuccessful Democratic nominee in 1928. The convention deadlocked through three ballots, but on the fourth Roosevelt won the support of the critical Texas and California delegations. The delegates then selected Garner, who had served in the House for thirty years, as Roosevelt's running mate in recognition of this support and to balance the ticket geographically.

After securing the nomination, Roosevelt made the dramatic gesture of flying to Chicago from his home in Albany, New York, to accept the nomination in person. Candidates previously had been expected to stay away from the convention and wait to be formally "notified" of their selections by official delegations of party leaders at a later date. The Democratic platform called for reduced tariffs, increased federal intervention to reduce the effects of the depression, and extensive financial and banking reform. In his acceptance speech, Roosevelt called for a "New Deal" for the forgotten American that involved expanding direct federal efforts to combat the depression. Hoover opposed such efforts and felt that the business community could be relied upon to solve the nation's economic problems.

Roosevelt defeated Hoover in a landslide. The results surprised few people. Roosevelt won more than 57 percent of the popular vote and a huge majority of votes—88.9 percent—in the electoral college. Hoover won only Maine, New Hampshire, Vermont, Connecticut, Pennsylvania, and Delaware, with Roosevelt carrying the remaining forty-two states, many by large margins. Roosevelt captured large majorities of the popular vote in the South and became the first Democrat to win a popular vote majority in Minnesota (59.9 percent) and in Wisconsin (63.5 percent). He also won by impressive margins in the usually Republican northwestern states, including Idaho (58.7 percent), Oregon (58 percent), and Washington (57.5 percent). From a nationwide perspective, Hoover ran roughly even with Roosevelt in the Northeast (except for in large cities), but the Democrat trounced his opponent elsewhere.

The county-level results on the popular vote map clearly illustrate the overwhelming nature of the Democratic victory. Roosevelt won most counties in the South, many with very large majorities. Every county in Texas, Louisiana, Mississippi, Alabama, and South Carolina went Democratic. In the region as a whole, Roosevelt lost to Hoover only in the traditionally Republican counties of eastern Tennessee and southeastern Kentucky. Roosevelt also won a large majority of counties west of the Mississippi River, sweeping most of those in the drought-stricken Great Plains states along with almost every county in Washington, Oregon, California, Idaho, and Montana. One of the important notable aspects of the 1932 election is the realignment of northern urban industrial counties toward the Democrats. Part of this realignment represented the solidification of immigrant groups within the Democratic Party, movement of blacks from the GOP to the Democratic column, and the shift of industrial union, working-class whites to the Democrats. This realignment was particularly important in places such as Cook County (Chicago), Illinois; Wayne County (Detroit), Michigan; and Allegheny County (Pittsburgh), Pennsylvania, as these areas would become pivotal in swinging the electoral outcomes of their states in the next fifty years.

Hoover carried significant numbers of counties only in the northeastern quadrant of the country, from Pennsylvania northward and eastward. He won most of the counties in Pennsylvania and New York state, losing the electoral votes of the latter because of Roosevelt's strength in New York City. He also took most counties in New England and some rural counties in the traditionally Republican strongholds of Michigan, the Western Reserve of Ohio, and northern Illinois.

By ousting Hoover, Roosevelt became only the third Democrat to take the White House since the Civil War. Voters expressed a strong desire for a new approach to combating the Great Depression. Shortly after taking office, Roosevelt instituted the New Deal, the series of reforms that would prove to be popular with the electorate and would keep him in office for the rest of his life. In addition to winning the presidency, the Democrats captured both chambers of Congress in 1932. They would hold a majority of seats in the House of Representatives for fifty-eight of the next sixty-two years. The 1932 election was a political revolution of immense proportions and ushered in a new Democrat-dominated political party era. Until the 1960s, a coalition of the northern urban poor and working class and southern rural poor and working class would form the base of the Democratic Party. The 1932 presidential election would be the first of five consecutive Democratic victories.

REFERENCE: Schlesinger, Arthur M., Jr. *The Crisis of the Old Order, 1919–1933.* Boston: Houghton Mifflin, 2003.

1936

PRESIDENTIAL ELECTION

Candidates	Popular Vote Percentage	Electoral College Vote Percentage and (Vote)
Democrat		
Franklin D. Roosevelt (New York)	60.8	98.5 (523)
Vice Presidential Nominee: John Nance Garner (Texas)		
Republican		
Alfred Landon (Kansas)	36.5	1.5 (8)
Vice Presidential Nominee: Frank Knox (Illinois)		

*I*n 1932 Democratic challenger Franklin D. Roosevelt had ousted his Republican predecessor, Republican Herbert Hoover, by promising Americans a "New Deal" to help them recover from the worst economic depression in U.S. history. After taking office on March 4, 1933, Roosevelt told Americans that "the only thing we have to fear is fear itself." He called for unprecedented government intervention in the economy, blaming the problems associated with the depression on corporate greed.

A heavily Democratic Congress enacted most of the sweeping reforms Roosevelt proposed, including the creation of Social Security, the Tennessee Valley Authority, and the Federal Deposit Insurance Corporation and the establishment of farm price supports and other measures intended to ensure monetary stability, create employment, and alleviate suffering. These reforms resulted in unprecedented federal involvement in the U.S. economy. Although the Supreme Court declared unconstitutional some of the laws enacting these measures, Roosevelt's charisma, optimism, and his novel approach to dealing with the depression proved popular among voters across the country. Roosevelt was the first U.S. president to consistently take advantage of radio to spread his message, using his famous "fireside chats" to deliver eloquent reassurances to the nation about the state of the country and ongoing efforts to improve it. Economic conditions in 1936 remained poor, but

Map 38

many Americans felt that the economy had turned the corner and that prosperity lay ahead.

Roosevelt stood as the clear favorite in 1936, and the Democratic national convention, held in Philadelphia, renominated him and Vice President John Nance Garner without opposition. The delegates also approved a significant amendment of convention rules making a simple majority, rather than a two-thirds majority, the threshold for a nomination. The intent was to prevent protracted deadlocks, as had occurred in 1924 and at earlier conventions.

Few prominent Republicans actively sought the GOP's nomination. Former president Herbert Hoover, who had lost in 1932 in a landslide, remained anathema to many Americans and to party leaders. Popular former president Calvin Coolidge and Sen. William Borah of Idaho had died. With few alternatives, the Republican national convention, meeting in Cleveland, selected Gov. Alfred Landon of Kansas. Landon was one of the few prominent Republican officeholders to remain in office during the Democratic landslide and was known as a progressive Republican. The delegates chose Frank Knox, the publisher of the *Chicago Daily News* and a long-time Republican activist, as their vice presidential candidate. Knox had been a Progressive supporter of Theodore Roosevelt in 1912. The Republican platform accepted the need for government intervention to address the depression and argued for curtailing the power of big business, but it criticized the New Deal approach to addressing the situation as corrupt and inefficient.

The fall campaign was uneventful. The Democrats successfully framed the election as a referendum on the New Deal, and few were surprised when Roosevelt won reelection by a landslide, one of the biggest in U.S. history. Roosevelt captured more than 60 percent of the popular vote—the highest percentage by a Democratic presidential nominee to that time. (It has been exceeded only by Lyndon Johnson's landslide victory in 1964.) Roosevelt carried forty-six of the forty-eight states, losing only Maine and Vermont to Landon.

The popular vote map illustrates dramatically the magnitude of Roosevelt's win. As in 1932, the Republicans carried significant numbers of counties only in the northeastern quadrant of the country. Landon won most counties in northern New England and most of upstate New York. Indeed, Roosevelt lost upstate New York in all four of his presidential campaigns, winning the Empire State by virtue of his large margins in New York City. Landon also carried traditionally Republican areas, such as the central Appalachians, parts of Michigan, northern Illinois, and the Ozarks of southwestern Missouri. He also won numerous counties in his home state of Kansas, although Roosevelt won the state's electoral votes (with 53.7 percent of the popular vote). Roosevelt carried the large majority of counties elsewhere, sweeping the South and most of the West. His considerable popularity among industrial workers and farmers, who gave him credit for addressing the problems of the Great Depression, was key to his reelection.

REFERENCE: Burns, James McGregor. *Roosevelt: The Lion and the Fox, 1882–1940.* New York: Harcourt, 1957.

1940

PRESIDENTIAL ELECTION

Candidates	Popular Vote Percentage	Electoral College Vote Percentage and (Vote)
Democrat		
Franklin D. Roosevelt (New York)	54.7	84.6 (449)
Vice Presidential Nominee: Henry Wallace (Iowa)		
Republican		
Wendell Willkie (New York)	44.8	16.0 (82)
Vice Presidential Nominee: Charles McNary (Oregon)		

Democratic president Franklin D. Roosevelt's efforts to combat the Great Depression of the early 1930s had proved to be popular with voters, and he had coasted to an easy reelection victory in 1936. The depression dragged on throughout the decade, however, and the international situation worsened. In 1939 Germany invaded Poland, setting World War II in motion. The United States remained officially neutral, although Roosevelt quietly supported Great Britain and its allies against Germany and the Axis Powers. The international situation became even more dire in early 1940 when France surrendered to Germany. Many observers expected the Germans to next invade Britain and thereby complete their conquest of Western Europe.

Both parties took the war into consideration in making their nominations for the 1940 election. Since the days of George Washington, presidents had voluntarily left office after two terms. Most observers expected Roosevelt, who had been elected in 1932 and 1936, to follow suit. Several prominent Democrats, notably Vice President John Nance Garner of Texas and Postmaster General James Farley of New York, had expressed interest in the Democratic nomination. In light of the worsening international situation, however, many Democrats urged Roosevelt to break tradition and run for a third term. Shortly before the Democratic national convention met in Chicago, Roosevelt let it be known that he would "accept a draft" from the delegates rather than retire. Roosevelt easily outpolled Garner and Farley to receive the nomination on the first ballot.

Map 39

The Democrats then addressed the issue of who should receive the party's vice presidential nomination. Roosevelt and Garner had had a falling out, and by 1940 the two men barely spoke to each other. The Democrats removed Garner from the ticket at Roosevelt's insistence and replaced him with Secretary of Agriculture Henry Wallace of Iowa. Wallace, a former Republican and Progressive, was expected to shore up support among midwestern farmers but was distrusted and opposed by many southern conservatives.

The Republicans mounted a spirited campaign for their party's nomination. The Democrats had held large majorities in Congress and a majority of governorships throughout the 1930s. Many previous Republican leaders had died, retired, or were no longer active politically. Party leaders did not give serious thought to renominating Herbert Hoover or Alfred Landon, who had lost by landslides to Roosevelt in 1932 and 1936, respectively. Instead, they looked carefully at new faces. At first, the leading contenders included Sens. Robert Taft of Ohio and Arthur Vandenberg of Michigan and New York City district attorney Thomas Dewey. At the Republican national convention in Philadelphia, however, Wendell Willkie, a New York financier originally from Indiana, emerged as a dark-horse candidate. Willkie, a former Democrat who had been a delegate to the 1932 Democratic national convention, had only recently switched parties. His supporters crowded the galleries at the convention shouting "We Want Willkie," and eventually the convention selected him on the sixth ballot. Sen. Charles McNary of Oregon got the vice presidential nomination.

Like Roosevelt, Willkie was an internationalist. He criticized the Roosevelt administration for lack of preparedness in case of war and also argued that New Deal programs had not been successful in combating the depression. Roosevelt announced plans to step up the nation's military preparedness during the campaign, and he framed the election in terms of a choice between increased prosperity under his administration relative to the depths of the Depression under his Republican predecessor, Herbert Hoover.

Roosevelt won a solid victory, although Willkie fared far better at the polls than had Hoover and Landon in the two previous elections. Roosevelt won nearly 55 percent of the popular vote and the electoral college by a margin of 449 votes to 82. In 1936 Roosevelt had won forty-six of the forty-eight states, losing only Maine and Vermont to Landon. Willkie carried these states in 1940 and also won his native Indiana, Michigan, Colorado, and the traditionally Republican farm-oriented states of North Dakota, South Dakota, Nebraska, Kansas, and Iowa (Wallace's home state). Roosevelt won the remaining thirty-eight states, including the entire South, all of the states west of the Rocky Mountains, and the remainder of the Northeast. Urban support in Chicago, Cleveland, and Cincinnati helped him secure the electoral votes of Ohio (52.2 percent) and Illinois (51 percent).

The popular vote map of the 1940 election reveals not only the sectional divide in the electorate, but also the extent to which Roosevelt's popularity declined in normally Republican rural northern areas during his second term. Roosevelt swept the South (as he did in all four of his successful presidential campaigns). He won large majorities throughout the region, losing only some of the traditionally Republican counties of Appalachia. He also won a large majority of counties in the Rocky Mountain and Pacific states. Willkie won most of New England and a large majority of counties in Michigan, Ohio, Indiana, and Illinois. The Republicans' shift away from Roosevelt was especially pronounced in the Great Plains. Whereas Roosevelt had won almost every county in Nebraska and Kansas in 1936, in 1940 he lost almost all of them. Willkie won 100 of Kansas's 105 counties (56.9 percent) and all but 7 of the 93 counties of Nebraska (57.2 percent). Since 1940, the four northern Great Plains states of North Dakota, South Dakota, Nebraska, and Kansas have voted Republican in every presidential election, except for the 1964 Lyndon Johnson landslide.

Despite slippage in the farm belt, Roosevelt won a comfortable reelection to a third term in light of a worsening international situation. Within a year after Roosevelt's third term began, the Japanese would attack Pearl Harbor, Hawaii, and the United States would become fully involved in the world's greatest armed conflict.

REFERENCE: Peters, Charles. *Five Days in Philadelphia: The Amazing "We Want Willkie" Convention of 1940 and How It Freed FDR to Save the Western World*. New York: Perseus, 2005.

1944

PRESIDENTIAL ELECTION

Candidates	Popular Vote Percentage	Electoral College Vote Percentage and (Vote)
Democrat		
Franklin D. Roosevelt (New York)	53.4	81.4 (432)
Vice Presidential Nominee: Harry S Truman (Missouri)		
Republican		
Thomas Dewey (New York)	45.9	18.6 (99)
Vice Presidential Nominee: John W. Bricker (Ohio)		

In 1940 the Democrat Franklin D. Roosevelt had become the first man to be elected president three times, winning his third term with World War II raging across Europe and Asia. Less than a year after Roosevelt's inauguration in 1941, the Japanese bombed Pearl Harbor, Hawaii, on December 7. The day that would "live in infamy" galvanized U.S. public opinion against the Axis Powers. The following day, the United States declared war on Japan, and a few days later it declared war against its Axis allies, Germany and Italy.

Before the United States entered World War II, the Axis Powers had gained control of most of continental Europe and much of East Asia. In 1942 Japan invaded the Aleutian Islands of Alaska and seized Attu and Kiska. It was the first and so far the only time that U.S. territory has been occupied by a foreign power during wartime. The addition of U.S. military forces to the conflict eventually turned the tide in favor of the Allies. By 1944 Italy had surrendered. On June 6, D-Day, Allied troops landed at Normandy and began to reclaim Nazi-held portions of continental Europe. In the Pacific, the United States and its allies gradually reclaimed Japanese-held islands and mainland territories in Southeast Asia. As election day approached, it became clear that the Allies would likely win the war, although no one knew how much longer the war would last or how many additional casualties would be suffered.

The progress of the war effort formed the backdrop to the presidential election of 1944. With the war continuing and victory at hand, Roosevelt decided to run for

Map 40

a fourth term to secure victory and to put his stamp on the postwar world. Close observers noted, however, that the president's health had begun to fail. These concerns led some of Roosevelt's advisors to urge him to remove vice president Henry Wallace, who was considered too far to the left, from the Democratic ticket. At the Democratic national convention in Chicago, the Democrats selected Missouri senator Harry S Truman, a solid supporter of Roosevelt's policies, as their vice presidential candidate. As a candidate from a border state, a World War I veteran, and a one-time farmer, Truman was expected to increase support for the national ticket in the South and Midwest.

The Republicans also held their national convention in Chicago in 1944. They seriously considered several candidates, including 1940 nominee Wendell Willkie and Gov. Harold Stassen of Minnesota, for the nomination. Both belonged to the progressive wing of the Republican Party. The convention, however, ultimately selected Gov. Thomas Dewey of New York as the presidential nominee. Dewey had initially made a name for himself as a "gang-busting" district attorney in New York City prior to being elected governor in 1942. To balance the ticket ideologically and geographically, the delegates picked Sen. John W. Bricker of Ohio as Dewey's running mate. Willkie declined to endorse Dewey's nomination and instead supported Roosevelt, but he died unexpectedly in October before the election.

With the war in full swing and millions of soldiers in service overseas, the campaign attracted relatively little attention. Democrats framed it around Roosevelt's continuing popularity and the success of the war effort. The Republicans pushed the issue of conversion from a wartime to a peacetime economy, arguing that government regulation should be decreased and that the size of government should be reduced once the war came to a close. On election day, voters gave Roosevelt his fourth straight victory with a popular vote margin of 53 percent to 46 percent. His 25 million popular votes represented the lowest percentage of his career, but it was no doubt depressed by large numbers of servicemen, who strongly supported the president, being unable to cast absentee ballots because of wartime.

Roosevelt won the electoral college by a margin of 432 votes to 99. The distribution of electoral votes resembled that of 1940. Indeed, only five of the forty-eight states switched parties from 1940 to 1944: Ohio, Wisconsin, and Wyoming were Democratic in 1940 and Republican in 1944, while Indiana and Michigan shifted from Republican in 1940 to Democratic in 1944. Roosevelt swept the South, the Far West, the Mid-Atlantic states, and most of New England. Dewey won only Maine, Vermont, Ohio, Indiana, and several states in and near the northern Great Plains.

The popular vote map of the 1944 election is also quite similar to the map of 1940. Roosevelt swept the South and won a majority of counties in the Far West. He lost most rural counties in the Northeast and Midwest, but his margins in large cities, such as New York City, Detroit, and Chicago, remained sufficient for him to carry the electoral votes of New York (52.3 percent), Illinois (51.5 percent), and Michigan (50.2 percent). Dewey ran well in the Great Plains, as Willkie had done four years earlier.

The coalition of votes in the South and the big cities ensured that Roosevelt would be reelected to the presidency for a fourth time. This "Roosevelt coalition" would dominate the Democratic Party for another generation after Roosevelt's death, which occurred in April 1945, less than three months into his fourth term.

REFERENCE: Ferrell, Robert E. *The Dying President: Franklin D. Roosevelt, 1944–1945.* Columbia: University of Missouri Press, 1998.

1948

PRESIDENTIAL ELECTION

~

CANDIDATES	POPULAR VOTE PERCENTAGE	ELECTORAL COLLEGE VOTE PERCENTAGE AND (VOTE)
Democrat		
Harry S Truman (Missouri)	49.6	57.1 (303)
Vice Presidential Nominee: Alben Barkley (Kentucky)		
Republican		
Thomas Dewey (New York)	45.1	35.6 (189)
Vice Presidential Nominee: Earl Warren (California)		
States' Rights Democrat ("Dixiecrat")		
Strom Thurmond (South Carolina)	2.4	7.3 (39)
Vice Presidential Nominee: Fielding Wright (Mississippi)		
Progressive		
Henry Wallace (Iowa)	2.4	0 (0)
Vice Presidential Nominee: Glen Taylor (Idaho)		

Ailing Democratic president Franklin D. Roosevelt died on April 12, 1945. Harry S Truman, his vice president and a former senator from Missouri, assumed the presidency with victory in sight over Germany and Japan in World War II. Germany surrendered in May, and after the United States detonated atomic bombs over Hiroshima and Nagasaki, the Japanese surrendered in August.

During his first term, Truman devoted much of his attention to the conversion from a wartime economy to peacetime. Following up on Roosevelt's initiative, Truman spearheaded efforts to create the United Nations. He also had to deal with the Soviet Union's efforts to control Eastern Europe. In 1946, in a speech in Truman's home state, former British prime minister Winston Churchill declared that "an iron curtain" had descended across Europe. By 1948 the cold war was in full swing. Truman promoted the Marshall Plan, which provided significant

Map 41

amounts of U.S. aid to rebuild the shattered economies of Western Europe.

Truman also had to deal with the rapid demobilization of millions of soldiers and sailors as they returned home and reentered civilian life. Organized labor became restive, staging numerous strikes and work stoppages. In 1947 Congress passed the controversial Taft-Hartley Labor Act, overriding Truman's veto. The act expanded federal control over labor disputes and allowed the government to impose an eighty-day "cooling-off" period if a strike was deemed perilous to national security or the nation's economic well-being.

As the 1948 election approached, Truman's popularity was low. The Republicans had won control of both houses of Congress in 1946, and many Republicans believed that they could take the White House in 1948 for the first time in twenty years. The Republicans held their national convention in Philadelphia and renominated their 1944 standard-bearer, Gov. Thomas Dewey of New York. Dewey had run a respectable race against the popular Roosevelt during wartime four years earlier and was favored to defeat Truman. As Dewey's running mate, the Republicans chose Gov. Earl Warren of California.

Meanwhile, the Democrats were split between left and right wings of the party. Roosevelt had appointed his former vice president, Henry Wallace, as secretary of commerce after Truman succeeded Wallace as vice president. Wallace opposed Truman's strong stand against Soviet expansion, so Truman fired him in 1947. In 1948 Wallace ran as a third-party candidate for the Progressive Party, opposing the cold war and the Marshall Plan. Democratic senator Glen Taylor of Idaho became his running mate. Many observers expected Wallace to lure away Truman's more liberal supporters. Some leading Democrats proposed replacing Truman with Gen. Dwight D. Eisenhower or Supreme Court justice William Douglas, but both declined overtures from party leaders. No real alternative to a Truman candidacy existed.

The Democrats held their national convention in Philadelphia. A narrow majority of the delegates supported a strong pro–civil rights plank in the party platform proposed by Mayor Hubert H. Humphrey of Minneapolis, Minnesota, and other northern liberals. Some southern delegates opposed to this plank walked out of the convention and later reconvened under the States' Rights banner and nominated Gov. Strom Thurmond of South Carolina for president, with Gov. Fielding Wright of Mississippi running for vice president. This "Dixiecrat" ticket was expected to win the support of conservative southern Democrats, further imperiling Truman's chances of capturing the electoral college.

Despite the walkout, the Democrats renominated Truman by acclamation and selected Sen. Alben Barkley of Kentucky as his running mate. Public opinion polls showed Truman running well behind Dewey, but Truman mounted a vigorous campaign, barnstorming the country by railroad, speaking to thousands of people at "whistle stops" from coast to coast. Truman criticized the Republican "do-nothing" 80th Congress and defended his veto of the Taft-Hartley Act. He also compared the prosperity of the 1940s to the dire depths of the Great Depression, which he blamed on Republicans. Most public opinion pollsters completed their surveys several weeks before the election and therefore missed the shift toward the Democrats late in the campaign.

Truman pulled off one of the biggest upsets in U.S. political history, defeating Dewey by a margin of 49.6 percent of the popular vote to 45.1 percent. Thurmond and Wallace each received 2.4 percent of the popular vote. In the electoral college, Truman defeated Dewey with 303 votes to 189. South Carolina, Alabama, Mississippi, and Louisiana gave Thurmond a total of 39 electoral votes. Truman

captured the rest of the South and most of the western states. His narrow margins in Illinois (50.1 percent), Ohio (49.5 percent), and California (47.6 percent, a plurality win because the Progressive Wallace took 4.7 percent of the popular vote) proved crucial to his victory nationwide. He also won his home state of Missouri, along with Iowa, Wisconsin, and Minnesota. Dewey carried his home state of New York and most of the Northeast, along with Indiana, Michigan, and the four northern Great Plains states. In the South, Truman lost those counties in South Carolina, Alabama, Mississippi, and Louisiana where local Democratic Party organizations endorsed Thurmond. He did especially well across Texas and Oklahoma and in rural eastern Virginia and North Carolina, which had long been Democratic strongholds. Truman's strength in the farming areas of the Midwest was critical to his victory. He carried a majority of counties in Iowa, Wisconsin, and Minnesota.

Dewey, like most Republican nominees in the late nineteenth and early twentieth centuries, won most rural counties in the Northeast. The far West split fairly evenly between Truman and Dewey. The West had been reliably Democratic since the days of William Jennings Bryan, but the 1948 election demonstrates the extent to which these traditional Democratic ties had loosened. Beginning in 1952 (with the exception of 1964), the West would become reliably Republican, a pattern that would continue until the Democrats established their dominance in the Pacific Coast subregion in the 1990s.

The two third-party candidates, Thurmond and Wallace, proved to be much less successful than their supporters had hoped. Thurmond won majorities in most of the counties in the four states that he carried. Elsewhere, he won pluralities in only a few scattered counties. In Georgia, for example, the state Democratic Party endorsed the Truman-Barkley ticket, and Thurmond outpolled Truman in only a few rural counties. The 1948 election extended Georgia's record of voting for the national Democratic ticket in every election since 1868. This pattern would continue until 1968.

Wallace had hoped for significant support among labor union members, African Americans, and left-wing progressives. In general, however, the Roosevelt Democratic coalition put together in the late 1920s and early 1930s held fast. Wallace's strongest areas were large central cities, such as New York, but he did not win enough support in these places to affect the electoral outcome. The Wallace map shows areas of some support in the North and West similar to the Progressive areas earlier in the century.

REFERENCE: McCullough, David. *Truman*. New York: Simon and Schuster, 1993.

1952

PRESIDENTIAL ELECTION

~

CANDIDATES	POPULAR VOTE PERCENTAGE	ELECTORAL COLLEGE VOTE PERCENTAGE AND (VOTE)
Republican		
Dwight D. Eisenhower (New York)	55.1	83.2 (442)
Vice Presidential Nominee: Richard M. Nixon (California)		
Democrat		
Adlai Stevenson (Illinois)	44.4	16.8 (89)
Vice Presidential Nominee: John J. Sparkman (Alabama)		

In 1948 Democratic president Harry Truman had defeated his Republican challenger, Thomas Dewey, to win a full term in his own right after having assumed the presidency upon the death of Franklin D. Roosevelt in 1945. Entering his second term, Truman faced a host of problems on the home front as well as abroad.

The economy was sputtering, and tensions between organized labor and big business ran high. Overseas, the United States became involved in the first major armed skirmish of the cold war. Communists backed by the Soviet Union had consolidated control over China, the world's most populous country, in 1948 and 1949. Chinese-backed communist forces invaded Korea, and in 1950 the Korean War began in earnest as UN forces, led by the United States, defended against communist aggression in the southern part of the Korean peninsula. Gen. Douglas MacArthur, the commander of the UN forces, proposed that U.S. troops invade China. When MacArthur ignored Truman's order to keep U.S. troops below the 38th parallel in southern Korea, Truman relieved MacArthur of his command. The firing of the popular MacArthur reduced Truman's already low approval ratings, and early in 1952 Truman announced that he would not run for another term.

For only the third time since 1900, the name of an incumbent president would not appear on the ballot. The other occurrences involved the seriously ill Woodrow Wilson, whose poor health precluded his running for a third term in 1920, and

 Map 42

Calvin Coolidge, who in 1928 had announced that he "did not choose to run." In 1951 the Twenty-second Amendment was adopted, formally limiting future presidents to two full terms. Since its enactment, voters have chosen between non-incumbents in 1968, 1988, and 2000.

The Republicans sensed victory after a twenty-year absence from the Oval Office. Yet the Grand Old Party was split between a conservative, isolationist faction and a liberal, internationalist wing. Their 1944 and 1948 candidate, Thomas Dewey, and the 1940 Republican nominee, Wendell Willkie, were members of the liberal wing of the party. In 1952 the conservative wing favored Ohio senator Robert Taft, the son of former president William Howard Taft, for the presidential nomination. The internationalist wing supported Gen. Dwight D. Eisenhower, who had been supreme commander of the Allied forces in Europe during World War II and had later served as commander of North Atlantic Treaty Organization (NATO) forces and as president of Columbia University. In 1948 both parties had tried unsuccessfully to persuade Eisenhower to run on their tickets. In 1952, however, Eisenhower declared that he had always been a Republican and made himself available for the GOP nomination.

Though a strong internationalist, on domestic issues Eisenhower held conservative views, which his supporters felt were close to those of the mainstream of the American electorate. A divided Republican national convention met in

Philadelphia and by a narrow margin selected Eisenhower over Taft as their presidential nominee. For the vice presidency, the delegates selected California senator Richard M. Nixon, who was at the time best known for his role in exposing State Department official Alger Hiss as a former communist. Nixon was selected to balance the ticket geographically. His conservative credentials served to placate the Taft wing of the party, though he was also an internationalist.

The Democrats, meanwhile, set about identifying a potential successor to Truman. They seriously considered several candidates, including Tennessee senator Estes Kefauver, who had defeated Truman in an early primary before Truman's withdrawal. They also looked at Gov. Averell Harriman of New York and Sen. Richard Russell of Georgia. A number of party leaders supported Illinois governor Adlai Stevenson, whose grandfather had served as vice president from 1893 to 1897 under Grover Cleveland. Stevenson defeated Kefauver on the third ballot to clinch the nomination. The 1952 national conventions would be the last in which a major-party convention would take more than one ballot to select its nominee. The Democrats selected Sen. John Sparkman of Alabama as Stevenson's running mate.

During the campaign, the candidates and their supporters focused on the Korean War, the expansion of communism in China, and domestic issues. Eisenhower criticized the Democrats for poor management of the international situation and resolved to "go to Korea" to end the fighting. The 1952 campaign was notable for an incident involving Nixon, who had received undeclared gifts from wealthy supporters. Some Republicans advocated removing him from the Republican ticket, but Nixon defended himself in his famous "Checkers" speech and remained in the race.

The Republicans regained control of the White House with Eisenhower defeating Stevenson by comfortable majorities in the popular balloting and the electoral college. Eisenhower's decisive victory extended the American tradition of electing war heroes—among them Andrew Jackson, Zachary Taylor, and Ulysses Grant—despite their lack of political experience. Eisenhower won the popular vote by a margin of 55.1 percent to 44.4 percent and the electoral college with 442 votes to Stevenson's 89. Stevenson carried seven former Confederate states and the border states of West Virginia and Kentucky. Eisenhower won the electoral votes of the former Confederate states of Virginia (56.3 percent), Florida (55 percent), Texas (53.1 percent), and Tennessee (50 percent), and he won every state in the Northeast, Midwest, and West.

The popular vote map illustrates the broad base of Eisenhower's support. Stevenson ran well in the Deep South, especially in Georgia, Alabama, and Mississippi, but Eisenhower ran well in the tidewater portion of South Carolina and in central Appalachia, west Texas, and northern Oklahoma. In Florida, solid Democratic support held steady in the northern counties, but migrants from the Republican North were beginning to politically change the central and southern parts of the state. Eisenhower carried Dallas, Houston, and San Antonio, presaging growing Republican strength in the rapidly growing suburban and metropolitan areas of the South. Outside the South, Eisenhower held majorities in a large plurality of counties.

Stevenson won only a few counties in the Northeast. He prevailed by substantial margins in large cities, such as Boston, New York, and Pittsburgh, but his support there was easily offset by strong voting in rural and rapidly growing suburban areas for the Republicans. The farm states also solidly backed Eisenhower. The West continued its steady movement toward the Republicans; only a handful of primarily small and rural counties west of the Rocky Mountains gave popular vote majorities to Stevenson.

The 1952 election is noteworthy not only for the Republicans' return to the White House for the first time in twenty years, but also for its signaling of long-term electoral movements, including the growth of Republican strength in the South and the West.

REFERENCE: Ambrose, Stephen. *Eisenhower.* New York: Touchstone Books, 1991.

1956

PRESIDENTIAL ELECTION

Candidates	Popular Vote Percentage	Electoral College Vote Percentage and (Vote)
Republican		
Dwight D. Eisenhower (Pennsylvania)	57. 4	86.1 (457)
Vice Presidential Nominee: Richard M. Nixon (California)		
Democrat		
Adlai Stevenson (Illinois)	42.0	13.7 (73)*
Vice Presidential Nominee: Estes Kefauver (Tennessee)		

Map 43

Dwight D. Eisenhower's election in 1952 put Republicans in control of the White House for the first time in twenty years. Eisenhower proved to be a popular president, making good on his pledge to end the Korean War by signing an armistice during his first year in office. The economy went into a recession early in his first term but by 1956 was moving toward a sustained recovery. As the 1956 election approached, Eisenhower's health became a concern for many voters. He had suffered a heart attack in 1955, and many assumed that he would not run for a second term. Eisenhower's health improved, however, and in February 1956 he announced his intention to run for reelection. Meeting in San Francisco, the Republican national convention renominated Eisenhower by acclamation. A few Republicans argued for removing Vice President Richard Nixon from the ticket, but Nixon received the nomination with only token opposition.

The Democratic national convention, meeting in Chicago, for the second time selected Adlai Stevenson of Illinois as the Democratic presidential candidate. Stevenson had battled with Sen. Estes Kefauver of Tennessee in several primary elections, but the convention chose Stevenson on the first ballot. In an unprecedented move, Stevenson did not recommend a running mate; instead, he allowed the convention to select one. Kefauver, Sen. John F. Kennedy of Massachusetts, and

Sen. Albert Gore of Tennessee (the father of the 2000 Democratic nominee) stood as the three leading contenders. Kefauver defeated Kennedy, his nearest challenger, to take the vice presidential nomination.

The fall campaign was uneventful. Stevenson called for an increase in social programs and a reduction in military spending, but these issues made little headway among moderate voters, who tended to support the popular president. In October 1956, Soviet troops entered Budapest, Hungary, to crush an anti-communist rebellion. Many saw the Hungarian crisis as justifying the need to maintain military spending levels and a "get-tough" policy against the Soviet Union.

Few expected Stevenson to defeat Eisenhower, and as predicted the president won easily, winning the popular vote by a margin of 57 percent to 42 percent and the electoral college by a margin of 457 votes to 73 votes. Stevenson won seven states in the South, and Eisenhower swept the rest of the country. The electoral college map was largely a rerun of 1952, with only four states changing hands: Missouri shifted to the Democrats, while Louisiana, West Virginia, and Kentucky went Republican.

The popular vote map resembles the one of 1952. Stevenson's strength was concentrated in the South. In South Carolina, a slate of unpledged electors opposed to civil rights legislation carried most counties in the southern and central part of the

One Alabama elector refused to vote for Stevenson and instead cast his ballot for Walter B. Jones, an Alabama judge.

124

state, but the regular Democratic slate, with support in the "upcountry" areas, secured the state's electoral votes with a 45.4 percent plurality victory. A similar pattern prevailed in Mississippi. All in all, the anti–civil rights slate carried 29.5 percent of the vote in South Carolina, 17.3 percent in Mississippi, 7.2 percent in Louisiana, and 4.1 percent in Alabama. Eisenhower continued to make inroads into the South, doing especially well in urban and suburban areas. Not only did he carry Dallas and Houston as in 1952, but he also won Shelby County (Memphis), Tennessee, Mobile County (Mobile), Alabama, and the independent city of Richmond, Virginia. Some southern states continued to exhibit strong intrastate differences in party preference, such as west versus Appalachian Tennessee, Tidewater versus Appalachian North Carolina, and northern versus southern Florida.

Outside the South, Eisenhower won a large majority of the counties. The biggest slippage in his support took place in farm states, where many farmers were unhappy with his conservative secretary of agriculture, Ezra Taft Benson. Stevenson ran ten to fifteen points ahead of his 1952 performance in many farm belt counties, although this increase in support remained insufficient to win electoral college votes. Additional support in rural Missouri, however, was important to Stevenson's narrowly capturing the electoral votes of the Show Me State (50.1 percent). Missouri has not cast its electoral votes for a losing candidate since 1956.

REFERENCE: Damms, Richard V. *The Eisenhower Presidency.* New York: Longman, 2002.

1960

PRESIDENTIAL ELECTION

~

Candidates	Popular Vote Percentage	Electoral College Vote Percentage and (Vote)
Democrat		
John F. Kennedy (Massachusetts)	49.7	56.4 (303)
Vice Presidential Nominee: Lyndon B. Johnson (Texas)		
Republican		
Richard M. Nixon (California)	49.5	40.8 (219)
Vice Presidential Nominee: Henry Cabot Lodge (Massachusetts)		

In 1951 ratification of the Twenty-second Amendment limited presidents to serving two full terms. For the first time since 1928, in 1960 political leaders and voters knew well in advance that the popular incumbent, Dwight D. Eisenhower, would not stand for reelection.

A recession in 1957 and 1958 marked Eisenhower's second term. Unemployment reached its highest level since before World War II. Meanwhile, the Soviet Union launched its Sputnik satellite in 1957, raising concerns that the United States was falling behind the Soviets in military and space technology. Perhaps in response to these issues, the Democrats picked up forty-nine seats in the House of Representatives and sixteen seats in the Senate in the 1958 midterm elections. Many of these new seats were located in traditionally Republican farming and suburban areas in the North. These gains made many Democrats optimistic that their party could regain the White House after eight years of Republican rule.

Several prominent Democratic senators—including John F. Kennedy of Massachusetts, Lyndon B. Johnson of Texas, Hubert Humphrey of Minnesota, and Stuart Symington of Missouri—competed for the Democratic nomination. Johnson, Symington, and former Illinois governor Adlai Stevenson, who had lost to Eisenhower in 1952 and 1956 but remained interested in running a third time, sat out the primaries. They hoped that none of the other candidates would register a majority of delegates on the first ballot at the Democratic convention, leading a divided party to turn

Map 44

to one of them. Kennedy had been a World War II veteran and war hero, but some Democratic Party leaders expressed concern about his youth— he was only forty-three years old—and his Roman Catholic faith. Alfred E. Smith, the only Roman Catholic previously nominated for the presidency, had lost some southern states in part because of anti-Catholic sentiment in 1928. Kennedy defeated Humphrey in the primaries in Wisconsin, adjacent to Humphrey's home state of Minnesota, and in rural Protestant West Virginia, knocking Humphrey out of the race and giving him a plurality of delegates at the convention.

At the Democratic national convention, held in Los Angeles, delegates nominated Kennedy on the first ballot. Kennedy then selected Johnson as his running mate. Although Johnson's selection surprised many observers, Kennedy followed the tradition of geographically balancing the ticket. He also hoped that Johnson's southern background would shore up support for the Democratic ticket in the South, particularly in Johnson's native Texas.

With Eisenhower ineligible for a third term, the role of heir apparent for the Republicans went to Vice President Richard Nixon. Some liberal northern Republicans had hoped that New York governor Nelson Rockefeller, one of a few prominent Republicans to withstand the Democratic sweep in the 1958 midterms, would seek the presidency. After considering the possibility, in early 1960 Rockefeller decided not to seek the nomination. Meanwhile, some conservative Republicans backed Arizona senator Barry Goldwater, who never mounted a significant campaign. At the Republican national convention in Chicago, delegates selected Nixon as their presidential candidate in a near-unanimous first ballot. Nixon chose Henry Cabot Lodge, a former senator from Massachusetts, as his vice presidential running mate. In accepting the nomination, Nixon promised to campaign in all fifty states, including newly admitted Alaska and Hawaii. This promise may have sealed Nixon's electoral fate, because keeping this promise forced Nixon to expend valuable time campaigning in small, sparsely populated states with few electoral votes.

Throughout the fall, public opinion polls showed the candidates running neck and neck. For the first time, the major-party candidates participated in nationally televised debates. Polls of television viewers indicated that the telegenic Kennedy performed well in the debates, easing fears among some voters about his youth and inexperience.

As predicted, the election turned out to be one of the closest in U.S. history. Kennedy won a plurality of the popular vote by a margin of only about 112,000 of nearly 69 million votes cast. He won more decisively in the electoral college by a margin of 303 votes to 219. (Fourteen unpledged electors in Mississippi and Alabama and one Republican elector from Oklahoma cast their electoral college ballots for Sen. Harry F. Byrd of Virginia.) Kennedy achieved his electoral college victory by winning large northeastern industrial states along with several states in the South. He prevailed decisively in New York and Michigan and by impressive margins won his native Massachusetts and neighboring Connecticut and Rhode Island, which had large Roman Catholic populations. He narrowly won Illinois with 49.98 percent of the popular vote to Nixon's 49.80 percent. Some Republicans attributed Kennedy's success in Illinois to vote fraud in Chicago. Johnson's presence on the ticket helped Kennedy carry Texas (50.5 percent) and several other southern states. Nixon carried his native California and did well in the West and Great Plains, his strongest regions of support. Although the Republicans won several states in New England, the Midwest, and the South, losses of key northern states to the Democrats cost them the election.

The popular vote map shows that Kennedy won the electoral votes of many large northeastern states despite losing a majority of their counties. In New York, for example, Kennedy outpolled Nixon by nearly 400,000 popular votes, but he won only twelve of the state's sixty-two counties. Kennedy's large margin in New York City and other urban areas thus outweighed Nixon's strengths in rural parts of the Empire State. A similar pattern emerged in Illinois, where Kennedy won only nine of the state's one hundred two counties, but won a statewide plurality by amassing a large margin in Cook County, including in Chicago. Even in his native New England, Kennedy lost more than half the region's counties. He easily won Massachusetts, Connecticut, and Rhode Island but lost the less urbanized states of Maine, New Hampshire, and Vermont to Nixon. Demography likely helped the

Democrats in the Northeast as well. Democratic-leaning labor union members in the 1930s tended to have larger families than did Republican-leaning management officials, and by 1960 many of these children were old enough to vote. Following their parents' lead in the voting booth, they cast their ballots for the Democrats.

The once Democratic "solid South" continued to erode, as it had in 1952 and 1956. Republicans made substantial gains, although Kennedy managed to win a majority of counties there. In response to growing civil rights sentiment within the national Democratic Party, local party officials in Louisiana and Mississippi placed slates of unpledged electors on the ballot. In Mississippi, the unpledged slate outpolled the Kennedy Democrats as well as the Republicans. Alabama divided between counties supporting Kennedy and those supporting the unpledged electors. Because these electors represent the regular Democratic slate in Alabama, they are presented on the popular vote map as Democrats. The unpledged electors in Mississippi and Alabama, however, eventually cast their electoral votes for Byrd.

Nixon won several southern states, including Virginia, Tennessee, and Florida. All of these states produced a reverse of the urban-rural pattern in the North. The Republicans did best in urban and suburban areas, which generally included the fastest-growing metropolitan areas in these states and were where many northern migrants had settled. The Kennedy-Johnson ticket won the Lone Star State by about 50,000 popular votes but lost the state's largest and fastest-growing metropolitan areas, Houston and Dallas. Thus the 1960 election presaged ongoing Republican gains in rapidly growing areas of the South in future elections.

A large majority of counties in the Midwest and in the Great Plains gave popular-vote majorities to Nixon, but Kennedy carried numerous heavily Catholic counties, including Stearns County (St. Cloud), Minnesota, Dubuque County (Dubuque), Iowa, and Ellis County (Hays), Kansas. Nixon narrowly took California (50.1 percent) while losing Los Angeles, San Francisco, and the Central Valley, a region whose population included high numbers of Great Depression migrants from the South and the southern Plains. He won rapidly growing suburban counties, such as Orange and Santa Clara, along with the San Diego metropolitan area, which compensated for his losses elsewhere in the Golden State.

Thus the Democrats succeeded in holding together their fragile coalition between the rural South and the urban Northeast in winning the 1960 election. Trends were, however, evident in foreshadowing increasing levels of Republican strength in future elections, especially the development of Republican support in more conservative, urbanized, and affluent portions of the South. Since Kennedy's election, all three Democratic presidents have had southern roots and connected with enough southern voters to win their states in the electoral college.

REFERENCE: White, Theodore H. *The Making of the President, 1960.* New York: Atheneum Publishers, 1961.

1964

PRESIDENTIAL ELECTION

~

Candidates	Popular Vote Percentage	Electoral College Vote Percentage and (Vote)
Democrat		
Lyndon B. Johnson (Texas)	61.0	90.3 (486)
Vice Presidential Nominee: Hubert H. Humphrey (Minnesota)		
Republican		
Barry Goldwater (Arizona)	38.5	9.7 (52)
Vice Presidential Nominee: William Miller (New York)		

Map 45

ee Harvey Oswald assassinated Democratic president John F. Kennedy in Dallas on November 22, 1963, and Vice President Lyndon Johnson assumed the presidency. Johnson pledged to carry out Kennedy's agenda, including support for a strong civil rights bill. At the Democratic national convention in Atlantic City, New Jersey, delegates nominated Johnson to run for a full term by acclamation. Johnson selected a liberal, pro–civil rights northerner, Sen. Hubert Humphrey of Minnesota, as his running mate.

Johnson's standing in public opinion polls remained high throughout the spring and summer of 1964. Regardless, several Republicans competed actively for the Grand Old Party's nomination, including Arizona senator Barry Goldwater, a leading conservative, and New York governor Nelson Rockefeller, a leader of the liberal faction of the party. Many Republican voters also supported former vice president Richard Nixon and former senator Henry Cabot Lodge, the two members of the party's 1960 ticket.

The California primary was critical, with Goldwater defeating Rockefeller by a narrow margin. Goldwater's opposition to civil rights legislation and New Deal social programs concerned some of the more liberal and moderate Republicans. After Rockefeller withdrew his name from consideration, Gov. William Scranton of Pennsylvania entered the race in an effort to move the party in a more moderate direction. Goldwater, however, received the nomination on the first ballot at the

Republican national convention in San Francisco. He selected William Miller, a representative from upstate New York and the chair of the national Republican Party, as his running mate. Miller was the first Roman Catholic selected as a national candidate by the Republicans. In contrast to the situation in 1960, Miller's faith would have little effect on the election.

Johnson maintained a steady lead in public opinion surveys through the fall of 1964. He emphasized his predecessor's legacy and pointed to his success in getting Congress to pass Kennedy's legislative program, including the landmark Civil Rights Act of 1964. The Democrats portrayed Goldwater as an extremist and a zealot whose election could result in nuclear conflict with the Soviet Union. Goldwater, meanwhile, argued against the increasing concentration of federal power and in favor of cutting various spending programs. He had opposed the Civil Rights Act on the grounds that it represented an unnecessary federal intrusion on state authority.

Johnson won easily with 61 percent of the popular vote—the largest landslide since Franklin D. Roosevelt's first reelection in 1936. Goldwater carried only South Carolina, Georgia, Alabama, Mississippi, and Louisiana along with his native Arizona. Johnson won the remaining forty-four states along with the District of Columbia, which voted in a presidential election for the first time following ratification of the Twenty-third Amendment to the Constitution in 1961.

President Johnson not only won a decisive majority in the electoral college, but he also garnered large popular vote margins in many parts of the North that had long been dominated by the Republicans. Johnson became the first Democrat to carry Vermont (66.3 percent) since 1852. Not only did he win the Green Mountain State's electoral votes, but he won a popular-vote majority in every county in Vermont as well as all but one county in the other five New England states. Whereas Kennedy had won only twelve of New York's sixty-two counties, Johnson won all of them. In Illinois, Kennedy had taken only nine of one hundred two counties; Johnson carried eighty. Johnson similarly won all but three counties in Pennsylvania, all but three in Michigan, and all but four in Ohio. He also carried many of the counties in the rural Midwest and Great Plains states that Kennedy had lost four years earlier. For example, he won ninety-two of Iowa's ninety-nine counties and forty-five of North Dakota's fifty-three counties. This change in northern voting patterns represented a historic precedent.

In contrast, Johnson did less well in the South than had Kennedy. The 1964 election was the last in which large numbers of African Americans in the South would be disenfranchised. Many white southerners, unhappy with the Civil Rights Act and the national Democratic Party, turned to Goldwater, who had voted against the measure as a senator. With African American turnout in the Deep South miniscule, Goldwater won majorities in five Deep South states. The geographical pattern of the Goldwater vote is an excellent indicator of the extent of white opposition to the Civil Rights Act in that region, extending into northern and central Florida and northern Louisiana. The Republican victory in the South represented a precursor of future trends. Since Reconstruction, no Republican had carried South Carolina, Georgia, Alabama, or Mississippi, so Goldwater's success in these states also established a historic precedent, in southern voting patterns. Since 1964, only two Democratic candidates—Jimmy Carter of Georgia and Bill Clinton of Arkansas— have collected electoral votes in these states. Johnson fared better in states along the margins of the Deep South, carrying his native Texas easily along with Virginia, North Carolina, Tennessee, Florida, and Arkansas. In the West, Johnson made inroads into traditionally Republican counties in Montana, Colorado, Washington, and Oregon.

Johnson and the Democrats dominated the 1964 election by retaining much of the traditional Democratic Party base, with the exception of the Deep South. Their success in labeling Goldwater as an extreme conservative helped them to sweep traditionally Republican regions in the North. Many of these areas, including New England and parts of the upper Midwest, would move into the Democratic column over the next four decades. Although Goldwater's campaign was unsuccessful, his nomination presaged the rise of Republican strength in the Sunbelt, a phenomenon with important consequences for U.S. politics for the remainder of the twentieth century.

REFERENCE: White, Theodore H. *The Making of the President, 1964.* New York: Atheneum Publishers, 1966.

1968
PRESIDENTIAL ELECTION

CANDIDATES	POPULAR VOTE PERCENTAGE	ELECTORAL COLLEGE VOTE PERCENTAGE AND (VOTE)
Republican		
Richard M. Nixon (California)	43.4	55.9 (301)
Vice Presidential Nominee: Spiro T. Agnew (Maryland)		
Democrat		
Hubert H. Humphrey (Minnesota)	42.7	35.5 (191)
Vice Presidential Nominee: Edmund Muskie (Maine)		
American Independent		
George Wallace (Alabama)	13.5	8.6 (46)
Vice Presidential Nominee: Curtis LeMay (Ohio)		

Democrat Lyndon B. Johnson had won the presidency in a landslide in 1964. Following the election, Johnson initiated several landmark domestic policy initiatives, including the Medicare program and the War on Poverty. Even more important for future elections, he helped enact the Voting Rights Act of 1965. The act required that the federal government guarantee African Americans and other minority group members the franchise. At the same time, the United States had become increasingly involved in an undeclared war in Vietnam. Many Republicans and conservative Democrats accused the Johnson administration of not doing enough to ensure military victory, while many on the left, particularly in the Democratic Party, argued that the United States should disengage from Vietnam. This debate between "hawks" and "doves" dominated the tumultuous and bitterly contested election of 1968.

In late 1967, Minnesota senator Eugene McCarthy, an opponent of Johnson's Vietnam policy, announced that he would challenge the sitting president for the Democratic Party's 1968 nomination. After McCarthy almost defeated Johnson in the New Hampshire primary, New York senator Robert Kennedy, brother of former

Map 46

president John F. Kennedy, also entered the Democratic race. Under such pressure, Johnson announced on March 31 that he would not seek reelection. Vice President Hubert Humphrey then announced his candidacy for the nomination. Four days later, tensions further increased with the assassination of Dr. Martin Luther King Jr., the prominent civil rights activist and Nobel Peace Prize winner.

Kennedy and McCarthy battled in several primaries, while Humphrey declined to participate in them, choosing instead to concentrate on securing support from delegates not selected through primary elections. After narrowly defeating McCarthy in the crucial California primary in June, Kennedy was assassinated at a victory celebration in Los Angeles. Tensions remained high throughout the summer. The Democratic national convention met in Chicago and was marred by violent antiwar protests and riots. Delegates gave the nomination to Humphrey on the first ballot. He selected another northerner, Sen. Edmund Muskie of Maine, as his running mate.

The Republicans also held a spirited contest to determine their nominee. Former vice president Richard Nixon had entered and won several primaries. Many in the liberal wing of the party again supported Gov. Nelson Rockefeller of New York, while conservatives favored Gov. Ronald Reagan of California. Nixon, who tried to steer a middle path between the liberals and the conservatives and avoid making controversial statements on the Vietnam issue, fended off these challenges. At the Republican national convention, in Miami Beach, delegates selected Nixon on the first ballot. He chose Gov. Spiro T. Agnew of Maryland as his running mate.

Meanwhile, former governor George Wallace of Alabama entered the race as a third-party candidate. Wallace, well known for his opposition to integration during the civil rights movement of the early 1960s, had unsuccessfully challenged Johnson in several presidential primaries in 1964. In 1968 Wallace claimed that there was not "a dime's worth of difference" between the two major parties. He argued for "law and order" and for states' rights and announced his candidacy as the leader of the American Independent Party. During the fall campaign, he selected retired Air Force general Curtis LeMay as his running mate.

Nixon began the fall campaign with a substantial lead in public opinion polls, with Humphrey, whose support among antiwar Democrats remained lukewarm, trailing. Wallace enjoyed substantial support among white southerners, and he made efforts to increase support among working-class voters outside the South. Although few expected Wallace to win the election, some of his supporters hoped that he would garner enough backing to deny both Nixon and Humphrey a majority and send the election to the House of Representatives. As election day approached, some Wallace supporters had second thoughts, in part because he was well behind in the polls. Wallace's support began to decline. A few weeks before the election, Humphrey announced his opposition to any further escalation of the war. With growing support among antiwar activists, Humphrey began to climb in the polls, and shortly before the election some pollsters pronounced the election too close to call.

Nixon emerged with a plurality of popular votes and a solid electoral college majority of 301 votes as opposed to 191 for Humphrey and 46 for Wallace. He won the entire West with the exceptions of Washington and Hawaii. Beginning in 1968, the West, especially the interior West, would strongly support the Republicans. In the Midwest, Nixon lost Michigan and Humphrey's home state of Minnesota but won the electoral votes of Illinois (with a 47.1 percent plurality versus 8.5 percent for Wallace) and Ohio (with a 45.2 percent plurality and 11.8 percent for Wallace); he had lost the former in 1960. The convention thus continued to stand that no Republican had won the presidency without carrying Ohio. In the South, Wallace won Georgia, Alabama, Mississippi, Louisiana, and Arkansas, but Nixon took the rest of the region, excluding Texas. It was the first time since the Civil War that only one southern state had supported the Democratic ticket. Humphrey won most of the electoral votes of the Northeast but could not overcome Nixon's lead in the South, Midwest, and West.

At the county level, as the popular vote map indicates, Nixon and Humphrey divided the Northeast, where Wallace had little support. Humphrey, like Johnson in 1964 and John Kennedy in 1960, swept Massachusetts, Rhode Island, and Connecticut and won most counties in Maine, the home state of vice presidential nominee Muskie. In New York and Pennsylvania, Nixon captured majorities in most counties, though Humphrey won both states' electoral votes courtesy of large majorities in urban areas. Humphrey captured majorities in only six of New York's sixty-two counties, but these included the four largest boroughs of New York City along with Albany and Erie Counties, containing the cities of Albany and Buffalo, respectively. Humphrey's margin in these urban counties provided him with the state's electoral votes (49.8 percent) despite Nixon majorities in forty-eight of New York's counties and pluralities in six others.

A similar pattern prevailed in the Great Lakes region. In a pattern reminiscent of the 1960 election, Nixon outpolled Humphrey in seventy-three of Ohio's eighty-eight counties and ninety of Illinois's one hundred two counties. Humphrey's large margin in Wayne County (Detroit) enabled him to carry Michigan (with a 48.2 percent plurality and 10 percent for Wallace) despite Nixon carrying most of the Lower Peninsula. Only in Michigan's Upper Peninsula, central and northern Minnesota, and northern Wisconsin did Humphrey find considerable rural support in the Midwest. Humphrey also carried a large swath of counties in the steel and coal-mining country of eastern Ohio, western Pennsylvania, West Virginia, and eastern Kentucky.

The 1968 presidential election was the first after the enactment of the Voting Rights Act. With federal officials guaranteeing minority voters access to the ballot box, turnout increased dramatically among African Americans. A large majority of African Americans supported Humphrey and the Democrats, recognizing Democratic support of civil rights legislation and social programs that had begun during the New Deal and continued under the Johnson administration. The Democrats won majorities or pluralities in many southern counties with large African American populations, including Fulton County (Atlanta), Georgia, and Orleans Parish (New Orleans), Louisiana. Heavily Latino counties in southern Texas, northern New Mexico, and southern Colorado also strongly supported Humphrey. Wallace carried portions of the Deep South, for example, sweeping rural Georgia (though losing Atlanta to Humphrey and several suburban Atlanta counties to Nixon). Wallace did best among poorer whites in the rural South, while Nixon found success among upscale, more urbanized whites. The vote pattern for Wallace resembles that for Goldwater in 1964, including support from northern Florida counties. Nixon did better in other areas of the South, including Unionist areas of Appalachia dating back to the Civil War and central and south Florida.

Nixon won majorities in counties across the West, the Great Plains, and the rural Midwest. For example, he captured a majority in ninety-eight of Kansas's one hundred five counties and a plurality in six others, losing only in Wyandotte County (Kansas City) with its substantial African American population. In Nebraska, Humphrey won only Seward County, which had a large Czech American Catholic population. Humphrey, like other Democrats since the New Deal, ran well in mining communities, such as Butte, Montana, and Native American reservations. On the West Coast, Nixon took his native Southern California but lost most of the San Francisco Bay area along with Portland and Seattle (which would remain in the Democratic column into the twenty-first century).

In 1968 Nixon succeeded in putting together an electoral college majority by balancing conservative and liberal opposition, making significant inroads in the South, and holding the Republican areas of the Midwest and the West.

Reference: White, Theodore H. *The Making of the President, 1968.* New York: Atheneum Publishers, 1969.

1972
PRESIDENTIAL ELECTION

Candidates	Popular Vote Percentage	Electoral College Vote Percentage and (Vote)*
Republican		
Richard M. Nixon (California)	60.7	96.7 (520)
Vice Presidential Nominee: Spiro T. Agnew (Maryland)		
Democrat		
George McGovern (South Dakota)	37.5	3.2 (17)
Vice Presidential Nominee: R. Sargent Shriver (Maryland)		

Map 47

In 1968 the Republican Richard M. Nixon had been elected with 43 percent of the popular vote in a three-way race. During his first term (1969–1973), Nixon tried to steer a middle path between liberals and conservatives. Prominent leaders on both fronts, however, resented some of his policies. Liberals who wanted the United States to disengage from the war in Vietnam immediately opposed Nixon's refusal to do so. On the other hand, some conservatives felt that Nixon had moved too far to the left by recognizing China, pursuing a policy of détente with the Soviet Union, and establishing such programs as the Environmental Protection Agency. Despite these concerns, Nixon faced no serious opposition to renomination. At the Republican national convention in Miami Beach, delegates renominated Nixon and Vice President Spiro T. Agnew by acclamation.

The Democrats, who controlled both houses of Congress, had increased their majorities slightly in the House and the Senate in the 1970 midterm elections. Several Democrats competed in primary elections during the spring of 1972. Maine senator Edmund Muskie, who had been the party's vice presidential nominee in 1968, was the early front-runner in the polls. Minnesota senator Hubert Humphrey, a former vice president and the 1968 Democratic presidential nominee, also sought the nomination. South Dakota senator George McGovern, a leading liberal and

antiwar activist, and Alabama governor George Wallace, who had returned to the Democratic Party after running as an independent four years earlier, also competed for the nomination.

Muskie lost to McGovern in the opening primary in New Hampshire and soon withdrew from the race. McGovern won several other primaries in the Northeast and his native upper Midwest. Wallace ran well among white southerners and also tried to drum up support among conservative Democrats in other areas. As Wallace campaigned in Maryland, however, a would-be assassin shot him, leaving him paralyzed. Wallace subsequently withdrew from the race, and none of McGovern's rivals could build enough momentum to stop him. Delegates nominated McGovern on the first ballot at the Democratic national convention, in Miami Beach.

McGovern selected Sen. Thomas Eagleton of Missouri as his running mate. A few weeks after the nomination, the media revealed that Eagleton had undergone shock treatment for depression several years earlier. McGovern initially defended his choice but later asked Eagleton to resign from the ticket. He then selected R. Sargent Shriver, a brother-in-law of the late president John F. Kennedy, to replace him. McGovern's indecision about the Eagleton nomination stalled his campaign. Although few doubted McGovern's sincerity on the war issue, many voters expressed

One Nixon elector in Virginia voted for Libertarian John Hospers for president.

133

doubts about his liberal domestic policy proposals. His reversal on the Eagleton issue also induced some voters to regard McGovern as indecisive and vacillating. Nixon maintained a comfortable lead in opinion polls throughout the fall campaign.

Nixon won the election in a landslide with a popular vote margin rivaling that of Lyndon B. Johnson eight years earlier. Once again, the American electorate voted against the extreme wing of one of the major parties. Nixon carried forty-nine of the fifty states in the electoral college, losing only Massachusetts and the District of Columbia. As the popular vote map indicates, Nixon won a majority of popular votes in a vast majority of counties throughout the United States, carrying more than 80 percent of the nation's counties. Nixon not only did well in rural counties, but was also especially strong in suburban and exurban areas. McGovern carried a number of central cities while losing by large margins in their suburbs. For example, he won New York City, Detroit, and San Francisco while losing decisively these cities' suburbs.

The 1972 election is the first in which a Republican carried all eleven former Confederate states in the electoral college. On the national level, the election represented the completion of the realignment of the South from the Democratic column to the Republicans'. The long ideological struggle within the Republican Party in the twentieth century seemingly was won by the right wing with the nominations of Goldwater in 1964 and then those of Ronald Reagan in 1980 and 1984. The ideological struggle in the Democratic Party between northern urban liberals and southern rural conservatives appears to have been won by the left wing with the nominations of Kennedy in 1960, McGovern in 1972, and then Mondale in 1984 and Dukakis in 1988. The general Democratic support of civil rights legislation in the 1960s, feminism, and other social trends in the 1970s and perceived lack of support of the military in the 1980s ran counter to traditional southern values of the time and helped spark this geographical realignment in U.S. politics. White southerners have historically always voted for the most conservative party. The

Democrats' electoral victories when they nominated southerners in 1976, 1992, and 1996 would represent deviations in the general trend of the late twentieth and early twenty-first centuries.

Outside metropolitan areas, McGovern did best in a few counties with populations dominated by minority group members. In the South, Nixon carried a large majority of the counties, but McGovern carried counties with large African American populations, for example, in the black belt region of central Alabama and Georgia and several Mexican American–dominated counties in south Texas. The enactment of the Twenty-sixth Amendment in 1971 gave persons between eighteen and twenty-one the right to vote. McGovern did well in college communities, such as Johnson County, Iowa (Iowa City and the University of Iowa) and Washtenaw County, Michigan (Ann Arbor and the University of Michigan).

Although the 1972 election was not close, the patterns produced by it would persist through the remainder of the twentieth century. The concentration of Democratic strength in large cities, minority communities, college towns, and certain farming, mining, and manufacturing areas would continue into the early twenty-first century. Republican strength, although considerable throughout the country, concentrated in suburban areas, in the traditional Republican heartlands in the Great Plains, and in certain portions of Appalachia and the interior West. The Republicans continued to gain strength in the South, especially in suburban and non-minority rural areas. In fact, the 1972 election map is similar to the Republican victories of 1984, 2000, and 2004. Although Republicans continued to gain strength in these areas, domestic scandal largely ignored during the 1972 campaign would result in a cataclysmic reversal in U.S. electoral politics four years later.

REFERENCE: White, Theodore H. *The Making of the President, 1972.* New York: Atheneum Publishers, 1973.

1976

PRESIDENTIAL ELECTION

Candidates	Popular Vote Percentage	Electoral College Vote Percentage and (Vote)*
Democrat		
Jimmy Carter (Georgia)	50.1	55.2 (297)
Vice Presidential Nominee: Walter Mondale (Minnesota)		
Republican		
Gerald R. Ford (Michigan)	48.0	44.6 (240)
Vice Presidential Nominee: Robert Dole (Kansas)		

In 1972 Republican president Richard M. Nixon had won reelection by one of the largest margins in U.S. history. After his second term began, however, his administration began to unravel as the Watergate scandal unfolded. In the fall of 1973, Vice President Spiro T. Agnew admitted to having accepted bribes while serving as governor of Maryland prior to his election as vice president in 1968. He pleaded no contest to the charges and resigned. The Twenty-fifth Amendment, which had been passed in 1967, empowered the president to appoint a new vice president with majority confirmation of both Houses of Congress. Nixon selected Michigan representative Gerald R. Ford, the minority leader of the House. Although considered a conservative, Ford was respected by the leaders of both parties for his integrity, forthrightness, and honesty. He was easily confirmed.

Meanwhile, Congress continued to investigate charges against several of Nixon's aides and associates stemming from revelations uncovered following break-ins at Democratic National Committee headquarters in Washington's Watergate complex in 1972. The trail eventually led back to Nixon's White House, after which some congressional leaders began to call for Nixon's impeachment. In July 1974, the House Judiciary Committee voted to impeach Nixon. By this point, it had become clear that the president would likely be impeached by the House and convicted in a Senate trial. Facing the likelihood of his involuntary removal from office, Nixon

Map 48

resigned on August 9, 1974. Ford was sworn in to succeed him. Shortly after taking office, Ford selected Gov. Nelson Rockefeller of New York as vice president.

A month after taking office, Ford pardoned Nixon. The decision proved controversial, leading some critics to charge that Ford had agreed to a deal to exonerate the disgraced former president. In addition to political controversy, the economy, which had gone into a recession in 1973, continued to perform poorly in 1974 and 1975. Regardless, Ford announced that he would run for a full term as president in 1976. Ford, however, faced strong opposition within his own party. Former California governor Ronald Reagan, whom party conservatives strongly supported, ran against Ford and nearly wrested the nomination from him. Ford's selection of the liberal Rockefeller as vice president in December 1974 had angered many conservative Republicans. Well before the campaign for the nomination had begun in earnest, Ford announced that Rockefeller would not run for a full term on the Republican ticket. After Ford narrowly defeated Reagan to secure the nomination at the Republican national convention in Kansas City, he selected Sen. Robert Dole of Kansas as his vice presidential running mate.

The Watergate scandal and the economy's weak performance left many Democrats feeling confident about regaining the White House in 1976. Several

One Republican elector from the state of Washington voted for former California governor Ronald Reagan.

prominent Democrats competed for their party's nomination. Two of the leading contenders included Minnesota senator Hubert Humphrey, the 1968 nominee, and former Alabama governor George Wallace. Others included Sens. Henry Jackson of Washington and Frank Church of Idaho, Gov. Jerry Brown of California, Rep. Morris Udall of Arizona, and former governor Jimmy Carter of Georgia. The little-known Carter emphasized his honesty and pledged always to tell the truth, presenting a sharp contrast to the scandals that had brought down the Nixon administration. With strong African American support, the moderate Carter defeated the conservative Wallace in several southern primaries. Furthermore, Carter demonstrated surprising strength and outpolled his liberal opponents in several northern states to clinch the nomination. Before the Democratic national convention in New York, Carter selected Minnesota senator Walter Mondale, a liberal protégé of former vice president Hubert Humphrey, as his running mate.

The 1976 election was one of the closest of the twentieth century. Although Carter enjoyed a substantial lead in early public opinion polls, as the campaign wore on Ford began to narrow the gap. Carter held on to win, however, with a tiny majority of the popular vote and an electoral college majority of 297 votes to 240. Carter, who became the first major-party nominee and president from the Deep South since before the Civil War, swept the South and won much of the Northeast. From the Great Plains westward, Ford won the electoral votes of every state except for Texas and Hawaii.

In capturing the West, Ford won the vast majority of counties in the central Great Plains and the interior West, with the exception of mining-dominated areas and counties with large Native American and Latino populations. Although his popular vote margin in the states along the Pacific Coast was narrower than that farther east, Ford's margin in Orange, San Diego, Santa Barbara, San Mateo, and other inland and suburban counties outweighed Carter's margins in central cities, including San Francisco, Los Angeles, and Alameda Counties (the latter including Oakland and Berkeley). In the end, Ford carried California and all of its forty-five electoral votes with a 49.35 percent popular vote plurality.

Carter won a large majority of the counties in the South. He swept African American–majority counties in South Carolina, Alabama, Mississippi, and other states, extending a Democratic trend that would continue into the twenty-first century. Unlike the northern liberal George McGovern in 1972, Carter ran well throughout the region. He won all 159 counties of his native Georgia, all but 3 counties in neighboring South Carolina, and all but 3 in Arkansas. Many of the counties that Carter lost to Ford were suburban (for example, Collin and Montgomery Counties in Texas, Jefferson Parish in Louisiana, and Shelby County in Alabama) or contained large military installations (for example, several counties along the Gulf Coast in western Florida, Alabama, and Mississippi). These areas with major military installations would remain bulwarks of Republican support into the twenty-first century. In the end, many southerners demonstrated regional pride and supported the Southern Baptist Carter after years of scandal in Washington.

In the Northeast, Ford won a majority of counties but lost most of the region's electoral votes. Urban support for Carter outweighed Ford's majorities in the smaller rural counties. Only in the historically progressive upper midwestern states of Iowa, Minnesota, and Wisconsin did significant numbers of rural counties support Carter. Ford won his native Michigan easily and most of the northern counties in neighboring northern Ohio, Indiana, and Illinois with the exception of Cook County (Chicago). Carter's majorities in New York City, Philadelphia, Pittsburgh, and Cleveland allowed him to carry these states, despite losing a majority of counties in New York state, Pennsylvania, and Ohio. The Ohio results are emblematic of the national results, with Carter carrying the state by a razor-thin 48.9 percent plurality over Ford's 48.7 percent. Given the Watergate scandal and a lagging economy, the Republicans ran surprisingly well and came quite close to retaining their grip on the White House.

REFERENCE: Brady, David W., and Craig Volden. *Revolving Gridlock: Politics and Policy from Jimmy Carter to George W. Bush.* Boulder, Colo.: Westview Press, 2006.

1980

PRESIDENTIAL ELECTION

Candidates	Popular Vote Percentage	Electoral College Vote Percentage and (Vote)
Republican		
Ronald Reagan (California)	50.7	90.9 (489)
Vice Presidential Nominee: George H. W. Bush (Texas)		
Democrat		
Jimmy Carter (Georgia)	41.0	9.1 (49)
Vice Presidential Nominee: Walter Mondale (Minnesota)		
Independent		
John B. Anderson (Illinois)	6.6	0 (0)
Vice Presidential Nominee: Patrick Lucey (Wisconsin)		

After the 1976 election, Democratic president Jimmy Carter faced a variety of problems. The economy stagnated, and the country suffered under high levels of unemployment and double-digit inflation. The Organization of the Petroleum Exporting Countries (OPEC) had implemented policies resulting in substantial increases in energy costs that further weakened the U.S. economy. In late 1979 during the Iranian Revolution, a group of Iranians seized the U.S. embassy in Tehran, capturing fifty-three Americans. This crisis and a failed attempt to rescue the hostages enforced perceptions among many Americans of Carter as a weak, indecisive, and ineffective president.

Many liberals in Carter's party criticized him for taking too moderate a course. Massachusetts senator Edward Kennedy, the brother of the late president John F. Kennedy and the late senator Robert F. Kennedy, challenged Carter for the 1980 Democratic nomination. Although Kennedy defeated Carter in several primaries, Carter won a majority of the contests. The Democratic national convention, held in New York, split between supporters of Carter and Kennedy, but delegates ultimately renominated Carter and Vice President Walter Mondale.

 Map 49

Former California governor Ronald Reagan had narrowly lost the 1976 Republican nomination to President Gerald R. Ford, and he remained popular among conservative Republicans. Reagan positioned himself as an early front-runner in 1980, but several others also sought the nomination. The hopefuls included George H. W. Bush, a former Texas representative and former U.S. ambassador to the United Nations. Reagan defeated Bush in the New Hampshire primary and repeated his performance in several southern primaries. Reagan clinched the nomination, and then selected Bush as his running mate at the Republican national convention in Detroit. After Reagan's nomination, John B. Anderson, a liberal Republican representative from Illinois who had challenged Reagan for the nomination, decided to run as an Independent. He selected former Wisconsin governor Patrick Lucey, a Democrat, as his running mate.

. Public opinion polls showed Carter and Reagan running evenly until shortly before the election, when Reagan pulled away. Reagan went on to defeat Carter by decisive margins in the popular and electoral college votes; for the second straight election, voters replaced the incumbent with the challenger from the opposing party. Reagan won slightly more than 50 percent of the popular vote, with 41 percent for Carter and nearly 7 percent for Anderson. Reagan's margin in the electoral college, however, was much more significant. Carter won only Rhode Island, Maryland, the District of Columbia, West Virginia, Georgia, Minnesota, and Hawaii. He lost the remaining forty-four states to Reagan, whose electoral college majority totaled 489 votes to Carter's 49.

The Republicans registered substantial gains throughout the country relative to 1976, while levels of Democratic support tended to decline. Many of the voters who had supported Carter in 1976 but turned to Reagan in 1980 were socially conservative suburban residents and blue-collar workers, many of whom lived in suburban and exurban areas of the Midwest and the South. These so-called Reagan Democrats would constitute an important group of swing voters throughout the 1980s and 1990s.

As the first Deep South native to be nominated and elected president by a major party since before the Civil War, Carter had carried a large plurality of counties throughout the South in 1976. He, however, won only his native Georgia in 1980, losing the rest of southern electoral vote to the more conservative Reagan. Carter did, however, win many of the counties in the South. For example, he carried 146 of Georgia's 159 counties, but significantly lost most of the suburban counties surrounding Atlanta. Elsewhere in the region, Reagan lost north Florida but won most of central and south Florida, including Dade County (Miami), where conservative Cuban Americans turned out in large numbers for him. Reagan also did well in the suburbs of Houston, Dallas, New Orleans, Birmingham, and other southern cities. He swept traditionally Republican counties in the Appalachians and the Ozarks. Many white southerners felt that the conservative westerner Reagan better exemplified their values and political opinions than did the southerner Carter.

In the Northeast, Reagan managed plurality victories in liberal Massachusetts (41.9 percent) and New York (46.7 percent) because of a strong Anderson turnout. In New York, Carter carried only Albany, Buffalo, New York City, and Rochester, losing the rest of the state to Reagan. In Maryland, Carter won the state's electoral votes despite winning majorities only in Baltimore City and Prince George's County, both of which were home to large African American populations, and pluralities in two rural counties. Reagan won by pluralities or extremely narrow mar-

gins in Pennsylvania, Ohio, Michigan, and Illinois despite losing Philadelphia, Pittsburgh, Cleveland, Detroit, and Chicago to Carter, who lost decisively in the suburbs of these and other large cities and in rural areas.

The West proved to be a Republican stronghold. In the interior West, Reagan won every county in Wyoming, Utah, Idaho, and Nevada. Carter won only a small scattering of the region's counties. These included counties with Latino majorities in northern New Mexico and southern Colorado, Native American reservations in South Dakota, and a few mining-oriented and university communities. Carter took Hawaii, which had only supported a Republican in the Nixon landslide of 1972. He, however, lost Honolulu County, the site of the city of Honolulu and a large military population.

Anderson, with 6.6 percent of the popular vote, failed to win a plurality in a county. The geography of the Anderson vote concentrated along the northern edge of the nation and included counties in New England, in the historically progressive upper Midwest, and along the Pacific Northwest coast. Statewide, he received nearly 10 percent of the vote in Iowa and in Minnesota. His highest county-level percentages (above 15 percent) were found in university and upscale communities, such as Aspen, Colorado, and Nantucket, Massachusetts. Examples of other such counties include Story and Johnson Counties in Iowa (Iowa State and the University of Iowa, respectively), Washtenaw County, Michigan (Ann Arbor and the University of Michigan), and Douglas County, Kansas (Lawrence and the University of Kansas). As the popular vote map illustrates, Anderson's presence on the ballot meant, however, that neither Reagan nor Carter won majorities in many of the counties that comprised his areas of strength. In several states, Anderson's support meant that the major-party leader took a state's electoral votes with only a plurality of the popular vote.

Throughout the country, Reagan held on to the Republican base established in previous elections, including the rural Great Plains and Appalachia, outer suburbs, the interior West, and military base communities that had been trending Republican since the Vietnam War. He ousted Carter by also cutting into the support of traditionally Democratic areas, especially in the South and Midwest.

REFERENCE: Busch, Andrew. *Reagan's Victory: The Presidential Election of 1980 and the Rise of the Right.* Lawrence: University Press of Kansas, 2005.

1984

PRESIDENTIAL ELECTION

Candidates	Popular Vote Percentage	Electoral College Vote Percentage and (Vote)
Republican		
Ronald Reagan (California)	58.8	97.6 (525)
Vice Presidential Nominee: George H. W. Bush (Texas)		
Democrat		
Walter Mondale (Minnesota)	40.6	2.4 (13)
Vice Presidential Nominee: Geraldine Ferraro (New York)		

Map 50

The U.S. economy had gone into a recession in 1981 and 1982, but by 1984 it had recovered, providing Republican president Ronald Reagan with high approval ratings. Many people who had long supported Democratic nominees—including white southerners, northern blue-collar workers, and persons of continental European ancestry in the cities, suburbs, and towns of the Northeast and Midwest—greatly admired Reagan. His support among these "Reagan Democrats" proved to be critical to his election victories, as well as to the victory of his successor, Vice President George H. W. Bush, four years later. Delegates to the 1984 Republican national convention, in Dallas, renominated Reagan and Bush by acclamation. Former vice president Walter Mondale of Minnesota, Sen. Gary Hart of Colorado, and civil rights leader Rev. Jesse Jackson emerged as the three leading candidates for the Democratic nomination. Mondale received the approval of the Democratic national convention, meeting in San Francisco, and selected Rep. Geraldine Ferraro of New York as his running mate. Ferraro was the first (and so far the only) woman to be nominated for vice president on a major-party ticket.

Reagan held a comfortable lead in public opinion polls throughout the fall campaign. The pollsters' predictions of a decisive Reagan victory proved to be accurate. In one of the biggest landslides in U.S. history, Reagan took 58.8 percent of the popular vote and in the electoral college won by a margin of 525 votes to 13. The incumbent Reagan captured forty-nine of the fifty states, losing only Mondale's native Minnesota and the District of Columbia. The magnitude of the Reagan victory is evident on the popular vote map. Reagan carried nearly 90 percent of the approximately 3,100 counties. He swept the Great Plains, the Rocky Mountain states, and the interior West, the Gulf Coast, and the traditionally Republican central Appalachian region. Reagan also swept the suburbs across the country. In many parts of the nation, Mondale won in central cities, but Reagan prevailed in their suburban areas. For example, Mondale took Fulton County, Georgia, home to the city of Atlanta, but Reagan won the surrounding suburbs. This trend is significant given that voter turnouts in the suburbs tend to be considerably higher than those in central cities and because the suburbs were growing (and continue to grow) much more rapidly than inner city areas. Similar situations can be seen in many other metropolitan areas, including Philadelphia, Chicago, Detroit, Kansas City, and Denver.

Many of the 320 counties—slightly more than 10 percent of the nation's total—won by Mondale contained large ethnic minority populations. These included rural majority African American counties in the deltas of Mississippi and Arkansas, eastern North Carolina, and the black belt of Alabama and Mississippi, which had stood out as a distinctive electoral area since before the Civil War. Mondale also did well in majority Latino counties in southern Texas and northern New Mexico, and he carried many majority Native American counties and reservations across the West. Mondale also won portions of the rust belt, including poor coal-mining counties in eastern Kentucky and West Virginia and steel-producing areas of eastern Ohio and western Pennsylvania. He also took the mining-oriented Mesabi Range of Minnesota. All of these places had been hit hard by the decline of U.S. heavy industry, which was moving with increasing rapidity to locations outside the United States. Mondale also carried counties containing academic communities, such as Johnson County (Iowa City), Iowa, Dane County (Madison), Wisconsin, and Lane County (Eugene), Oregon. Throughout the country, a large majority of the counties carried by Mondale in 1984 have since been carried by Democratic nominees.

The 1984 election was the Republicans' biggest triumph in the party's history. Reagan swept the Republican heartland, and helped by Reagan Democrats, also carried substantial numbers of ordinarily Democratic counties. The 1984 election remains a high-water mark for the GOP, which would win three of the next five elections but nonetheless fail to approach the broad level of national support that Reagan generated.

REFERENCE: Cannon, Lou. *President Reagan: The Role of a Lifetime.* New York: Perseus Books, 1991.

1988

PRESIDENTIAL ELECTION

~

Candidates	Popular Vote Percentage	Electoral College Vote Percentage and (Vote)
Republican		
George H. W. Bush (Texas)	53.4	79.2 (426)
Vice Presidential Nominee: Dan Quayle (Indiana)		
Democrat		
Michael S. Dukakis (Massachusetts)	45.6	20.6 (111)*
Vice Presidential Nominee: Lloyd Bentsen (Texas)		

Map 51

Republican incumbent Ronald Reagan maintained a high level of popularity throughout his second term (1985–1989), despite concerns about his advancing age and mental capacities and the Iran-contra scandal, which involved shipping arms to Iran in exchange for money that was then funneled illegally to contra forces in Nicaragua. Because the Twenty-second Amendment made the highly popular Reagan ineligible to run for a third term, Vice President George H. W. Bush became the early favorite for the 1988 Republican nomination. Some Republican conservatives, however, regarded Bush as a representative of the eastern liberal Establishment. Despite his long-time residence in Texas, Bush's New England background and Yale education fed this distrust. Several Republicans challenged Bush for the Republican nomination, including Kansas senator Robert Dole, the 1976 Republican vice presidential nominee, and Rev. Pat Robertson, a religious broadcaster from Virginia. Dole won the Iowa precinct caucuses, the first in the nation, with Robertson coming in second. Bush came back to win the New Hampshire primary and swept several southern primaries shortly thereafter. Before the Republican national convention, held in New Orleans, Bush selected conservative senator Dan Quayle of Indiana as his running mate. Some Republicans questioned the choice of Quayle, who was inexperienced and came from a safely Republican state. Quayle was the first "baby boomer" to be nominated for high office on a major-party ticket.

Several Democrats competed for their party's nomination. Early primaries revealed a split between former Massachusetts governor Michael Dukakis, Sen. Paul Simon of Illinois, Rep. Richard Gephardt of Missouri, Sen. Al Gore of Tennessee, and civil rights leader Rev. Jesse Jackson, the last of whom had competed for the party's nomination in 1984. Each won several primaries or caucuses, but Dukakis emerged as the nominee after winning crucial primaries in Florida and Texas. At the Democratic national convention in Atlanta, delegates nominated Dukakis along with his running mate, Sen. Lloyd Bentsen of Texas.

Dukakis began the fall campaign with a lead in public opinion polls, but Bush eventually moved ahead, as voters responded to aggressive Republican campaign tactics. The GOP sought to portray Dukakis and the Democrats as excessively liberal, eager to raise taxes, and soft on crime and criminals, while presenting Bush, despite the impression of his not being a true conservative, as Reagan's heir. Bush became the first sitting vice president to be elected president in his own right since Martin Van Buren succeeded Andrew Jackson in 1836. He captured slightly more than 53 percent of the popular vote, but nevertheless won forty of the fifty states in the electoral college, handing the GOP its third consecutive victory.

Bush lost only three states in the Northeast, the upper Midwest, and the Pacific Coast, respectively, along with West Virginia and the District of Columbia to

One Democratic elector from West Virginia voted for Bentsen for president and Dukakis for vice president.

Dukakis. As illustrated by the popular vote map, the geographic pattern in 1988 resembles those of 1980 and 1984. Bush's support in many places, however, was weaker than that of Reagan. Some counties in the upper Midwest and the Great Plains gave Bush as much as 20 percent less of the vote than they had Reagan four years earlier. In fact, Iowa went Democratic for the first time since 1964 and ranked second among the fifty states in its total Democratic percentage (54.7 percent). Bush did better in the Rocky Mountain states and the interior West, where he won most of the counties, except for those with large minority populations or mining-oriented communities. In the Pacific Northwest, Dukakis won most of the counties along the coast. He won counties containing large cities, including King County (Seattle), Washington, Multnomah County (Portland), Oregon, and San Francisco County, California. He also did well in coastal rural counties, among them Mendocino, California, and Coos, Oregon, which featured a blend of progressive politics among migrants and depressed resource-based economies affecting long-established residents. Bush did better farther inland in rural agricultural and ranching counties, winning eastern Washington and Oregon as well as most of California's Central Valley and the outer suburbs of Los Angeles.

Like Reagan in 1980 and 1984, Bush swept the South, winning a large majority of the counties. Many of the counties won by Dukakis contained large African American populations, including areas in eastern North Carolina and South Carolina, central Alabama, and northwestern Mississippi. Bush and Dukakis ran evenly in the Northeast. The Democrat won most counties with central cities, among them Boston, New York, Baltimore, Cleveland, and Detroit, by large majorities. Bush did far better in the suburbs, repeating the 1980 and 1984 Republican patterns. Most rural counties in upstate New York and northern New England voted Republican.

As in 1980 and 1984, the South and the Reagan Democrats across the country determined the outcome of the 1988 presidential election. Although Bush's popularity never matched that of his predecessor, he held on to the Republican base and made sufficiently strong inroads into historically Democratic territory to ensure a comfortable victory.

REFERENCE: Germond, Jack W., and Jules Witcover. *Whose Broad Stripes and Bright Stars: The Trivial Pursuit of the Presidency, 1988.* New York: Warner Books, 1989.

1992

PRESIDENTIAL ELECTION

CANDIDATES	POPULAR VOTE PERCENTAGE	ELECTORAL COLLEGE VOTE PERCENTAGE AND (VOTE)
Democrat		
Bill Clinton (Arkansas)	43.0	68.8 (370)
Vice Presidential Nominee: Al Gore (Tennessee)		
Republican		
George H. W. Bush (Texas)	37.4	31.2 (168)
Vice Presidential Nominee: Dan Quayle (Indiana)		
Independent		
Ross Perot (Texas)	18.9	0 (0)
Vice Presidential Nominee: James Stockdale (Illinois)		

*I*n 1989, during the administration of George H. W. Bush, the communist governments of the Soviet satellites in Eastern Europe collapsed. Two years later the Soviet Union itself fell, bringing an end to the cold war. In 1991 the United States took the lead in organizing a multinational effort under the auspices of the United Nations to repel Iraqi forces from Kuwait, which they had invaded in August 1990. Bush's foreign policy successes led to the public giving him high approval ratings, and as late as the fall of 1991 few believed that he could be defeated in the next election. The U.S. economy, however, went into a recession, which in concert with the perception that Bush and the Republican Party cared little for the concerns of ordinary poor and middle-class Americans gave the Democrats an issue to exploit.

Bush faced no significant opposition to renomination, and delegates at the Republican national convention, in Houston, selected him and Vice President Dan Quayle by acclamation. The Democrats, however, waged a spirited contest for their party's nomination. Several prominent party members, including Tennessee senator Al Gore, New Jersey senator Bill Bradley, and New York governor Mario Cuomo

Map 52

declined to seek the nomination. Those who did seek the position included Iowa senator Tom Harkin, Nebraska senator Bob Kerrey, and Massachusetts senator Paul Tsongas, along with Bill Clinton, who had served as governor of Arkansas for twelve years but was little known to the public outside his home state. Clinton lost the New Hampshire primary to Tsongas but later won on "Super Tuesday," when several southern states hold primaries simultaneously in hopes of increasing the South's influence on the selection of the Democratic Party's nominee. This momentum carried Clinton to the nomination. Shortly before the Democratic national convention met in New York, Clinton chose Gore, who had run unsuccessfully for the 1988 nomination, as his running mate. In doing so, Clinton selected a candidate from a neighboring southern state, thus breaking with the tradition of geographically balancing the ticket with the vice presidential nominee.

Meanwhile, business executive Ross Perot announced his intention to run for the presidency as an independent candidate. Promising to "clean up the mess" in Washington, Perot briefly took the lead in a three-way race in spring public opinion polls. He curiously dropped out of the running during the summer, but then resumed campaigning in the fall. Perot chose as his running mate retired admiral James Stockdale. Clinton held the lead over both Bush and Perot in public opinion polls throughout the fall campaign.

Clinton became the first Democrat since Jimmy Carter in 1976 to win a presidential election, while Bush became the third incumbent president in five elections to fall in defeat. Clinton took 43 percent of the popular vote to Bush's slightly more than 37 percent and almost 19 percent for Perot. Although he won only a plurality of the popular vote, Clinton prevailed with a solid majority in the electoral college. He swept the Northeast and Midwest (except for Vice President Quayle's Indiana) and divided the South with Bush. The Democratic ticket carried the home states of the two candidates and the border states of Delaware, Maryland, West Virginia, Kentucky, and Missouri. In the West, Clinton carried Oregon, Washington, and Hawaii, which had supported Michael Dukakis in 1988. He also won the states of California, Nevada, Colorado, and Montana, none of which had given their electoral votes to a Democrat since Lyndon B. Johnson's 1964 landslide. President Bush carried all of the Great Plains states and four states in the interior West.

As illustrated by the popular vote map, Clinton's strongholds in the West included minority-dominated areas, such as Native American reservations and Latino-dominated counties in south Texas and northern New Mexico. These counties had supported Democratic nominees throughout the 1960s, 1970s, and 1980s. Despite two strong opponents, Clinton won absolute majorities in counties containing the West's large central cities, including San Francisco and Los Angeles Counties, California; Denver County, Colorado; King County (Seattle), Washington; and Multnomah County (Portland), Oregon. In Nevada, Clinton carried only Clark County (Las Vegas) and one other small county, but he won the state's electoral votes despite finishing third to Bush and Perot in the popular vote of the state's remaining counties combined. Clinton did much better than his Democratic predecessors had in suburban communities in the West, capturing many suburban counties around the region's larger cities.

In the South, Clinton won absolute majorities in most counties in his native Arkansas along with many in Gore's native state of Tennessee. He also won most majority–African American counties in Georgia, Alabama, Mississippi, and other states, usually by absolute majorities. He won the central cities of Atlanta, New Orleans, and Memphis, but was less successful in their suburbs. Clinton won many northeastern and other counties as well, including the labor union–oriented coal, iron, and steel communities of West Virginia, western Pennsylvania, and eastern Ohio. He swept the large cities of the Northeast and won much of non-urban New

England, including every county in Vermont, which went Democratic (46.1 percent) for only the second time since the Civil War. (Perot received 22.8 percent of the popular vote in Vermont.)

Meanwhile, Bush did well in traditionally Republican areas, including the Gulf Coast, counties in the South outside of the black belt, parts of Appalachia (including southeast Kentucky), the Great Plains states, and the interior West. Suburbs tended to support the Republicans, although many suburban-based Reagan Democrats, worried about the weak economy, turned to Clinton. Nevertheless, the central city–suburban distinction remained evident in metropolitan areas, such as Milwaukee, Chicago, New Orleans, and Atlanta.

Third-party candidate Perot's 19 percent of the popular vote represented the best showing for a third-party candidate since Theodore Roosevelt won 27.4 percent in 1912. As the Perot map suggests, his strongest areas of support were his native Texas, the Great Plains and Rocky Mountain states, and northern New England. On a statewide percentage basis, the top five Perot supporters were Maine (30.4 percent), Alaska (28.4 percent), Utah (27.3 percent), Idaho (27.1 percent), and Kansas (27.0 percent). Perot generally did poorest in the South, with Tennessee (10.1 percent) and Mississippi (8.7 percent) giving him his lowest percentages. He finished second to Clinton in Maine and second to Bush in Utah. Although some Republicans blamed Perot for siphoning enough votes from Bush to cost the incumbent the election, this interpretation is suspect given that the Republicans won most of Perot's strongest states. As the popular vote map shows, Perot won pluralities in a few rural counties in Maine, Kansas, Texas, Colorado, and northern California. One effect of the strong Perot vote is that most counties were won by a plurality rather than a majority as in most elections.

The 1992 Democratic ticket of two moderate southerners restored the Democrats to power and reinforced the electoral importance of the South and of the conservative and moderate Reagan Democrats. It also presaged trends that would become even more important after Clinton left office, including an increasingly sharp divide between large central cities and exurbs and between urban and rural areas. The 1992 election also revealed strong Republican support in the Great Plains states and continued emerging Republican strength in the South and interior West after the Reagan years. This split and these trends would be crucial in determining the 2000 and 2004 presidential elections.

REFERENCES: Goldman, Peter, et al. *Quest for the Presidency, 1992*. College Station: Texas A&M University Press, 1994.

Pomper, Gerald M., et al. *The Election of 1992: Reports and Interpretations*. Chatham, N.J.: Chatham House Publishers, 1993.

1996

PRESIDENTIAL ELECTION

~

CANDIDATES	POPULAR VOTE PERCENTAGE	ELECTORAL COLLEGE VOTE PERCENTAGE AND (VOTE)
Democrat		
Bill Clinton (Arkansas)	49.2	70.4 (379)
Vice Presidential Nominee: Al Gore (Tennessee)		
Republican		
Bob Dole (Kansas)	40.7	29.6 (159)
Vice Presidential Nominee: Jack Kemp (Virginia)		
Reform		
Ross Perot (Texas)	8.4	0 (0)
Vice Presidential Nominee: Pat Choate (Washington, D.C.)		

Map 53

Democratic president Bill Clinton's administration experienced a variety of problems after the 1993 inauguration, including a sluggish economy and an unsuccessful attempt to implement national health insurance. In the midterm elections of November 1994, voters had rebuked the administration by electing Republican majorities to both houses of Congress for the first time since 1952.

The new Republican majority in Congress pursued a strongly conservative legislative agenda and painted Clinton 'as a free-spending liberal. The economy, however, began to gather steam in 1994 and 1995. Late in 1995, the Republican Congress and the administration failed to reach agreement on the federal budget, forcing a shutdown of a variety of government services for a few weeks in late 1995 and early 1996. This shutdown led some voters to perceive the Republicans as mean-spirited and insensitive to the needs of ordinary persons. Many voters blamed the situation on the Republicans' partisanship and antigovernment philosophy. These developments increased the Democrats' optimism about Clinton's chances for reelection. Delegates to the Democratic national convention in Chicago renominated Clinton and Vice President Al Gore by acclamation.

Several Republicans competed actively for the right to run against Clinton in the general election, with Robert Dole of Kansas emerging as the early favorite. Dole, a World War II veteran, had served for nearly thirty years as a senator from the Sunflower State, including several years as majority leader, before resigning from the Senate to make his run for the presidency. He had been the Republicans' vice presidential nominee in 1976. Other contenders included conservative political commentator Pat Buchanan, former governor Lamar Alexander of Tennessee, Sen. Richard Lugar of Indiana, and publishing executive Steve Forbes. Buchanan narrowly defeated Dole and Alexander in the New Hampshire primary, but Dole defeated Buchanan in the critical South Carolina primary, in which trade policy had been an issue. South Carolina had the largest direct European investment per capita of any state, and Dole emphasized the importance of international trade while painting Buchanan as an isolationist. Running well in other southern and midwestern primaries, Dole soon clinched the nomination. He selected Jack Kemp, a former representative from upstate New York and secretary of housing and urban development under President George H. W. Bush, as his running mate before the Republican national convention met in San Diego.

145

Ross Perot announced that he would run in his second consecutive election and received the nomination of the Reform Party. He chose economist Pat Choate as his running mate, but his campaign failed to attract the attention that it had four years earlier, in part because of the increasing strength of the national economy.

The fall campaign generated little excitement. Clinton maintained a steady lead in public opinion polls and won decisively on election day, becoming the first Democrat since Franklin D. Roosevelt to win election to two full terms. He defeated Dole by comfortable margins in the popular vote and the electoral college. Perot's impact as a third-party candidate was much less than it had been four years earlier.

The electoral college results were similar to those of 1992, with forty-five of the fifty states supporting the same party in both elections. Clinton won by pluralities in Florida (48.0 percent) and Arizona (46.5 percent), both of which he had lost in 1992. These states were home to substantial numbers of elderly voters who may have been concerned about possible Republican support for cutbacks in Social Security. Dole, however, defeated Clinton in Georgia, Colorado, and Montana, all of which Clinton had won in 1992. The electoral votes of the remaining states were the same as in 1992. Arkansas and Tennessee, the home states of the Democratic candidates, again supported the Democrats, as did the border states of Delaware, Maryland, West Virginia, Kentucky, and Missouri.

The popular vote margins in many states resembled those of 1992. Dole, however, won much larger margins than Bush had four years earlier in more rural states, especially in the Great Plains, Rocky Mountains, and interior West. Dole's higher margins in these areas resulted in part from Perot's weaker showing and the increasing polarization of the electorate between urban Democrats and rural Republicans.

Clinton swept large central cities throughout the country, including Los Angeles, San Francisco, Denver, Chicago, New York, and Boston. He, however, lost many suburban and exurban areas to Dole. Outside major metropolitan areas, Clinton did best in minority-dominated areas and in the Northeast and Midwest. He won most rural counties in the progressive midwestern states of Iowa, Wisconsin, Minnesota, and Michigan as well as nearly all of New England and New York. Dole swept most counties in the Great Plains, Rocky Mountains, and interior West. Perot's impact on the outcome of the election was negligible. He received 8.4 percent of the vote nationwide, and unlike in 1992, carried no counties. He did win enough votes to deny the major-party candidates majorities in some counties, especially in the upper Midwest and the interior West, though far fewer than in 1992. Maine gave Perot his best showing in 1996 (14.2 percent, down from 30.4. percent in 1992), and Tennessee and South Carolina represented his worst showing (both at 5.6 percent).

The southern composition of the Democratic ticket and the booming economy in 1996 masked considerable divisions within the electorate between urban and rural, coastal and interior, and liberal and conservative. These differences reflected the increasing polarization of fundamental values among the American electorate that became especially evident in 2000 and 2004.

REFERENCES: Dover, E. D. *The Presidential Election of 1996: Clinton's Incumbency and Television.* Westport, Conn.: Greenwood Press, 1998.

Pomper, Gerald M., et al. *The Election of 1996: Reports and Interpretations.* Chatham, N.J.: Chatham House Publishers, 1997.

2000

PRESIDENTIAL ELECTION

CANDIDATES	POPULAR VOTE PERCENTAGE	ELECTORAL COLLEGE VOTE PERCENTAGE AND (VOTE)*
Republican		
George W. Bush (Texas)	47.9	50.4 (271)
Vice Presidential Nominee: Richard Cheney (Wyoming)		
Democratic		
Al Gore (Tennessee)	48.4	49.4 (266)
Vice Presidential Nominee: Joseph Lieberman (Connecticut)		
Green		
Ralph Nader (Connecticut)	2.7	0 (0)
Vice Presidential Nominee: Winona LaDuke (Minnesota)		

Map 54

The Republican-controlled House of Representatives impeached Democratic president Bill Clinton in late 1998 for allegedly lying under oath in a civil deposition, but the Senate acquitted him early in 1999. As Clinton neared the end of his second term, his popularity ratings among voters remained high. Ineligible to run for a third term, Clinton supported his vice president, Al Gore of Tennessee, to succeed him. Sen. Bill Bradley of New Jersey contested the nomination, but Gore won a majority of primaries and clinched the Democratic nomination well in advance of the Democratic national convention, which was held in Los Angeles. Gore selected Sen. Joseph Lieberman of Connecticut as his running mate, making Lieberman the first Jewish candidate to be nominated by a major party for high office.

The major contenders for the Republican nomination were Governor George W. Bush of Texas, the son of former president George H. W. Bush, and Sen. John McCain of Arizona. McCain defeated the younger Bush in the New Hampshire primary, but Bush beat McCain in South Carolina and shortly thereafter in several Super Tuesday southern primaries. McCain subsequently withdrew from the race, and delegates at the Republican national convention in Philadelphia nominated Bush by acclamation. Bush selected Richard Cheney, a former representative from Wyoming and secretary of defense in his father's administration, as his running mate. Two third-party candidates also contested the presidency. Long-time consumer activist and liberal Ralph Nader ran as the nominee of the Green Party, while on the conservative side of the spectrum, political commentator Pat Buchanan received the nomination from the Reform Party. Buchanan's campaign drew little support from conservatives, however, most of whom supported Bush.

The campaign was closely and bitterly fought, and public opinion polls throughout the fall had the two major-party nominees running a close race. The 2000 election would be one of the closest in U.S. history. Bush defeated Gore in the electoral college, although Gore won a plurality of approximately 540,000 popular votes. Bush became only the fourth president—the others being Benjamin Harrison (1888), Rutherford Hayes (1876), and John Quincy Adams (1824)—to win the presidency with an electoral college majority but not a plurality of the popular vote.

One Democratic elector from the District of Columbia declined to cast an electoral ballot to protest the District's lack of congressional representation.

Bush's electoral college victory hinged on the outcome in Florida, where the vote was closely contested. After a recount, the state-certified results gave Bush a plurality by 537 votes (48.85 percent of the popular vote to 48.84 percent for Gore). Democrats sued to overturn the results. Five weeks after the election, however, the U.S. Supreme Court confirmed the original results, giving Bush Florida's twenty-five electoral votes that he needed to win the election. Many Gore supporters blamed Nader for their candidate's defeat. Nader received more than 97,000 popular votes in Florida, many of which might have gone to Gore had Nader's name not been on the ballot. Nader's popular vote total in New Hampshire, which Bush narrowly won, also exceeded Bush's margin of victory in the Granite State. Overall, Nader collected more than 2,880,000 votes, or 2.7 percent of the popular vote. Buchanan, the other third-party candidate, won less than one-half of 1 percent of the total vote.

The electoral vote pattern illustrates the level of geographic polarization that had been developing for two decades. Bush swept the entire South. His victories in Gore's native Tennessee, Clinton's home state of Arkansas, Kentucky, and West Virginia were critical to the national outcome; had Gore won any of these states, he would have won the election regardless of the outcome in Florida. Heavily Democratic West Virginia had gone Republican only twice since 1956, but concerns about Gore's environmentalism and possible policies on coal mining as well as his support for federal control of firearms put Bush over the top. Bush also swept the Great Plains and Rocky Mountain states and the interior West along with Alaska, Indiana, Ohio, and New Hampshire. This coalition was barely enough to overcome Gore's electoral votes in the more heavily populated Northeast, upper Midwest, and Pacific Coast states.

The county-level results confirmed this polarization and that urban areas had become more Democratic and rural areas more Republican. Bush won majorities in about 85 percent of the counties despite Gore winning a nationwide plurality of the popular vote. Gore won central city counties, such as Suffolk County (Boston), Massachusetts; Fulton County (Atlanta), Georgia; Wayne County (Detroit), Michigan; San Francisco and Los Angeles Counties, California; and the five bor-

oughs comprising New York City. He won these and many other urban counties with large majorities. Bush, however, did far better in the suburbs and exurban areas surrounding these cities, for example, including those surrounding Atlanta, Chicago, and Los Angeles.

Outside major metropolitan areas, Gore did well in New England, poor counties in central Appalachia, and the progressive upper Midwest. Following a three-decade trend, Gore also carried many minority-dominated rural counties across the country, such as the southern black belt, Hispanic border counties, and Native American reservations. Academic and university communities, such as Ann Arbor, Madison, Iowa City, and Eugene, strongly backed Gore.

As the Bush map indicates, he generated high percentages of support in the Great Plains and interior West. In general, the counties Bush carried reported an overall population growth rate of 14 percent during the 1990s, whereas counties carried by Gore grew by only 5 percent during the same period. Much of the growth associated with Bush supporters took place in suburban and exurban areas, along with regions of the Sunbelt and the West. In the early twenty-first century, these places continued to grow at much faster rates than central cities and the Northeast in general.

The 2000 election was one of the closest and more controversial elections in the history of the United States. A highly polarized electorate delivered a narrow and disputed victory to the Republicans, and division on the basis of race, class, and location grew.

REFERENCES: Dover, E. D. *The Disputed Presidential Election of 2000: A History and Reference Guide.* Westport, Conn.: Greenwood Press, 2003.

Steed, Robert, and Laurence W. Moreland. *The 2000 Presidential Election in the South: Partisanship and Southern Party Systems in the 21st Century.* Westport, Conn.: Praeger, 2002.

Wayne, Stephen J., and Clyde Wilcox, eds. *The Election of the Century and What It Tells Us about the Future of American Politics.* Armonk, N.Y.: M. E. Sharpe, 2002.

2004

PRESIDENTIAL ELECTION

Candidates	Popular Vote Percentage	Electoral College Vote Percentage and (Vote)*
Republican		
George W. Bush (Texas)	50.7	53.2 (286)
Vice Presidential Nominee: Richard Cheney (Wyoming)		
Democratic		
John Kerry (Massachusetts)	48.3	46.7 (251)
Vice-Presidential Nominee: John Edwards (North Carolina)		

Map 55

ight months after Republican president George W. Bush took office following the disputed 2000 election, nineteen members of al-Qaida hijacked four commercial aircraft on September 11, 2001, and crashed two of them into the World Trade Center towers in New York City and one into the Pentagon outside Washington, D.C. A fourth hijacked plane crashed in rural Pennsylvania after passengers on board fought for control of the aircraft. Nearly 3,000 people died in the day's attacks.

The events of September 11 would play a central role in U.S. politics for the remainder of Bush's first term (2001–2005). In October 2001, the U.S. military invaded Afghanistan, whose hard-line Taliban regime continued to harbor al-Qaida and the organization's leader, Osama bin Laden. American forces quickly deposed the Taliban and initiated efforts to establish a new government and promote democracy in Afghanistan.

In the January 2002 State of the Union address, Bush referred to Iraq, Iran, and North Korea as an "axis of evil," accusing the leaders of these countries of abetting terrorists and developing weapons of mass destruction (WMD). In 2003 Bush ordered the military invasion of Iraq, whose leader, Saddam Hussein, Bush and others in his administration had accused of attempting to develop WMD and of harboring and having connections to terrorists, including al-Qaida. U.S.-led forces

quickly toppled Hussein's government, but over the next eighteen months, more than a thousand U.S. troops would be killed in skirmishes and battles with insurgent Iraqi forces and members of al-Qaida in Iraq, a group of primarily foreign fighters led by Abu Musab Zarqawi, who had entered into an alliance with bin Laden's network after the U.S. invasion. Most Republicans supported the war, as did some Democrats. Many other Democrats, however, were skeptical of Bush's policy, and opposition to it intensified as the war and occupation appeared to bog down and as it became clear that Iraq did not, despite administration assertions, possess weapons of mass destruction or have ties to al-Qaida.

The Republican national convention, meeting in New York City, renominated Bush and Vice President Richard Cheney by acclamation. Given opposition to the war and a sluggish economy, many Democrats felt that their party had a chance to defeat Bush in 2004. Democratic strategists recalled that the party had won a plurality of the popular vote four years earlier. Anticipating possible success, several prominent Democrats contested the party's nomination. Four of the early front-runners were Rep. Richard Gephardt of Missouri, former governor Howard Dean of Vermont, and Sens. John Kerry of Massachusetts and John Edwards of North Carolina. Gephardt had the support of labor union members and some old-line Democrats, while Dean generated strong grassroots support among opponents of

One Minnesota Kerry elector voted for John Edwards for president.

Bush's Iraq policy. Edwards ran a populist-style campaign, emphasizing economic issues and the differences between the "haves" and "have-nots." During the Iowa precinct caucuses, Kerry narrowly defeated Edwards (who made a point of refusing to run negative advertising), with Dean and Gephardt trailing. Gephardt soon withdrew from the race, and some Dean supporters turned to Kerry as the more experienced candidate. Kerry won in his neighboring state of New Hampshire and in most other contested primaries outside the South. After clinching the nomination, Kerry selected Edwards, his chief rival for the nomination, as his running mate. Ralph Nader ran again, though this time as an independent candidate.

The 2004 popular vote was comparable to the outcome four years earlier, though Bush's share of it increased slightly, giving him a slim majority. The electoral college results were similar to 2000's as well. Only three states switched parties. New Hampshire went Democratic (50.2 percent), and Iowa (49.9 plurality for Bush) and New Mexico (49.8 plurality for Bush), in the Democratic column in 2000, both supported Bush in 2004. Nader received only a little more than one-third of 1 percent of the national vote.

Ohio proved to be the pivotal state in the election. During the campaign, Kerry had pointed out that Ohio had lost more than 200,000 jobs during Bush's administration, thus attempting to lay the blame on Bush's economic policies. Bush stressed his conduct of the war in Iraq and his administration's "war on terror" as well as cultural and moral values. On election day, Bush won Ohio (50.8 percent) by approximately 120,000 votes, ensuring a majority in the electoral college. He carried seventy-two of the state's eighty-eight counties, losing the other sixteen to Kerry. Kerry won the counties containing many of the state's rust belt industrial communities, including Akron, Cleveland, Toledo, and Youngstown. The counties carried by Kerry averaged 350,000 in population and had lost a net total of 20,000 persons between 2000 and 2003. On the other hand, the average size of a Bush county in Ohio was 82,000 persons and had grown by a collective total of 100,000 people between 2000 and 2003. The results in Ohio mirrored a nationwide pattern in which rapidly growing areas, particularly in suburbs and exurban communities, supported Republican nominees.

Elsewhere, the 2004 election was equally reminiscent of the 2000 election. Bush was especially strong in rural areas of the Great Plains and interior West, winning every county in Utah and Oklahoma. His strong margins in Kansas City and St. Louis were critical to victory in Missouri (53.2 percent). Kerry, like his recent Democratic predecessors, did best in large central cities, among ethnic minority voters, and in academic communities. He won a majority of counties along the Pacific Coast, as well as in New England and the Northeast and various areas of the rust belt. Across the country, however, Republican strength in the suburbs and rural areas offset or outweighed Kerry's large margins in central cities. On average, Republican counties continued to grow more rapidly than Democratic counties, a trend that will no doubt be critical in 2008 and beyond.

REFERENCE: Ceaser, James W., and Andrew E. Busch. *Red over Blue: The 2004 Elections and American Politics.* Lanham, Md.: Rowman and Littlefield, 2005.

BIBLIOGRAPHY

Abbott, Richard H. *The Republican Party and the South, 1855–1877*. Chapel Hill: University of North Carolina Press, 1986.

ABC-CLIO Information Services. *The American Electorate: A Historical Bibliography*. Santa Barbara, Calif.: ABC-CLIO, 1984.

Ackerman, Kenneth D. *The Dark Horse: The Surprise Election and Political Murder of James A. Garfield*. New York: Carlton and Graf, 2003.

Adobe Systems. Adobe Illustrator CS2. San Jose, Calif.: Adobe Systems Inc., 2005.

Agnew, John A. *The United States in the World-Economy: A Regional Geography*. New York: Cambridge University Press, 1987.

Alexander, Thomas B. *Sectional Stress and Party Strength*. Nashville, Tenn.: Vanderbilt University Press, 1967.

Ambler, Charles Henry. *Sectionalism in Virginia from 1776 to 1861*. New York: Russell and Russell, 1964.

Ambrose, Stephen. *Eisenhower*. New York: Touchstone Books, 1991.

Anderson, Hattie Mabel. *The Social and Economic Bases of the Rise of the Jackson Group in Missouri, 1815–1828: A Study in Frontier Democracy*. Columbia: Missouri Historical Review, 1940.

Andrews, J. Cutler. "The Antimasonic Movement in Western Pennsylvania." *Western Pennsylvania Historical Magazine,* December 1935, 255–266.

Androit, John L. *Population Abstract of the United States*. McLean, Va.: Androit Associates, 1983.

Archer, J. Clark, and Fred M. Shelley. *American Electoral Mosaics*. Washington, D.C.: Association of American Geographers, 1986.

Archer, J. Clark, and Peter J. Taylor. *Section and Party: A Political Geography of American Presidential Elections, From Andrew Jackson to Ronald Reagan*. New York: Research Studies Press, 1981.

Archer, J. Clark, Stephen J. Lavin, Kenneth C. Martis, and Fred M. Shelley. *Atlas of American Politics, 1960–2000*. Washington, D.C.: CQ Press, 2002.

Archer, J. Clark, Fred M. Shelley, Peter J. Taylor, and Ellen R. White. "The Geography of U.S. Presidential Elections." *Scientific American,* July 1988, 18–25.

Asher, Herbert B. *Presidential Elections and American Politics: Voters, Candidates, and Campaigns since 1952*. Homewood, Ill.: Dorsey Press, 1984.

Baker, Jean H. *Affairs of Party: The Political Culture of Northern Democrats in the Mid-nineteenth Century*. Ithaca, N.Y.: Cornell University Press, 1983.

———. *The Politics of Continuity: Maryland Political Parties from 1858–1870*. Baltimore, Md.: Johns Hopkins University Press, 1973.

Barone, Michael. *Our Country: The Shaping of America from Roosevelt to Reagan*. New York: Free Press, 1990.

Baum, Dale. *The Civil War Party System: The Case of Massachusetts, 1848–1876*. Chapel Hill: University of North Carolina Press, 1984.

———. *The Shattering of Texas Unionism*. Baton Rouge: Louisiana State University Press, 1998.

Beard, Charles A., and Mary R. Beard. *The Rise of American Civilization*. New York: Macmillan, 1937.

Bensel, Richard F. *Sectionalism and American Political Development*. Madison: University of Wisconsin Press, 1984.

Berger, Mark L. *The Revolution in the New York Party System, 1840–1860*. Port Washington, N.Y.: Kennikat Press, 1973.

Bergeron, Paul H. *Antebellum Politics in Tennessee*. Lexington: University Press of Kentucky, 1982.

Bernhard, Winfred E. A., ed. *Political Parties in American History*. Vol. 1, *1789–1828*. New York: Putnam, 1973.

Berry, Brian J. L. *Long-Wave Rhythms in Economic Development and Political Behavior*. Baltimore, Md.: Johns Hopkins University Press, 1991.

Billington, Ray Allen. *Frederick Jackson Turner: Historian, Scholar, Teacher*. New York: Oxford University Press, 1973.

———. *The Protestant Crusade, 1800–1860, A Study of the Origins of American Nativism*. New York: Macmillan, 1938.

———. *Westward Expansion: A History of the American Frontier*. New York: Macmillan, 1982.

Black, Earl, and Merle Black. *The Vital South: How Presidents Are Elected*. Cambridge: Harvard University Press, 1992.

Blais, Andre, Loius Assicottee, and Antonie Yoshinaka. "Deciding Who Has the Right to Vote: A Comparative Analysis of Election Laws." *Electoral Studies* 20 (2001): 41–62.

Block, Robert H. "Frederick Jackson Turner and American Geography." *Annals of the Association of American Geographers* 70 (March 1980): 31–42.

Blue, Frederick J. *The Free Soilers: The Party Politics, 1848–1854*. Urbana: University of Illinois Press, 1973.

Boller, Paul F., Jr. *Presidential Campaigns*. New York: Oxford University Press, 2004.

Bonadio, Felice A. *North of Reconstruction: Ohio Politics, 1865–1870*. New York: New York University Press, 1970.

————, ed. *Political Parties in American History.* Vol. 2, *1828–1890.* New York: Putnam, 1974.

Borden, Morton. *Parties and Politics in the Early Republic, 1789–1815.* New York: Thomas Crowell Company, 1967.

Brady, David W. *Critical Elections and Congressional Policymaking.* Palo Alto, Calif.: Stanford University Press, 1988.

Brady, David W., and Craig Volden. *Revolving Gridlock: Politics and Policy from Jimmy Carter to George W. Bush.* Boulder, Colo.: Westview Press, 2006.

Brewer, Cynthia A., and Mark A. Harrower. ColorBrewer. www.ColorBrewer.org.

Brewer, Cynthia A., Geoffrey W. Hatchard, and Mark A. Harrower. "ColorBrewer in Print: A Catalog of Color Schemes for Maps." *Cartography and Geographic Information Science,* January 2003, 5–32.

Brodsky, Alyn. *Grover Cleveland: A Study in Character.* New York: St. Martin's Press, 2000.

Bromley, Michael. *William Howard Taft and the First Motoring Presidency, 1909–1913.* New York: McFarland and Company, 2003.

Broussard, James H. *The Southern Federalists, 1800–1816.* Baton Rouge: Louisiana State University Press, 1978.

Brown, Norman. *Hood, Bonnet, and Little Brown Jug: Texas Politics, 1921–1928.* College Station: Texas A&M University Press, 1984.

Brown, Ralph H. *Historical Geography of the United States.* New York: Harcourt, Brace and World, 1948.

Brunn, Stanley D. *Geography and Politics in America.* New York: Harper and Row, 1974.

Burdick, Eugene, and Arthur J. Brodbeck, eds. *American Voting Behavior.* Glencoe, Ill.: Free Press, 1959.

Burnham, Walter Dean. *Critical Elections and the Mainsprings of American Politics.* New York: Norton, 1970.

————. *Presidential Ballots, 1836–1892.* Baltimore, Md.: Johns Hopkins Press, 1955.

Burns, James McGregor. *Roosevelt: The Lion and the Fox, 1882–1940.* New York: Harcourt, 1957.

Busch, Andrew. *Reagan's Victory: The Presidential Election of 1980 and the Rise of the Right.* Lawrence: University Press of Kansas, 2005.

Calhoun, Charles W. *Benjamin Harrison.* New York: Henry Holt, 2005.

Campbell, Angus, Philip E. Converse, Warren E. Miller, and Donald E. Stokes. *The American Voter.* New York: Wiley, 1960.

————. *Elections and the Political Order.* New York: Wiley, 1966.

Campbell, Bruce A., and Richard J. Trilling, eds. *Realignment in American Politics: Toward a Theory.* Austin: University of Texas Press, 1980.

Cannon, Lou. *President Reagan: The Role of a Lifetime.* New York: Perseus Books, 1991.

Cappon, Lester J. "The Historical Map in American Atlases." *Annals of the Association of American Geographers* 69 (1979):622–634.

Casdorph, Paul D. *History of the Republican Party in Texas, 1865–1965.* Austin, Texas: Pemberton Press, 1965.

Cayton, Andrew R. L. *The Frontier Republic: Ideology and Politics in the Ohio Country, 1780–1825.* Kent, Ohio: Kent State University Press, 1986.

Ceaser, James W. *Presidential Selection: Theory and Development.* Princeton. N.J.: Princeton University Press, 1979.

Ceaser, James W., and Andrew E. Busch. *Red over Blue: The 2004 Elections and American Politics.* New York: Rowman and Littlefield, 2005.

Chace, James. *1912: Wilson, Roosevelt, Taft and Debs: The Election That Changed the Country.* New York: Simon and Schuster, 2004.

Chambers, William Nisbet. *The Democrats in American Politics: A Short History of a Popular Political Party.* New York: Van Nostrand, 1972.

————. *Political Parties in a New Nation: The American Experience, 1776–1809.* New York: Oxford University Press, 1963.

————, ed. *The First Party System: Federalists and Republicans.* New York: Wiley, 1972.

Chambers, William Nisbet, and Walter Dean Burnham, eds. *The American Party System: Stages of Political Development.* New York: Oxford University Press, 1975.

Chang, Kang-tsung. *Introduction to Geographic Information Systems.* Boston: McGraw Hill, 2004.

Channing, Edward. *The Jeffersonian System, 1801–1811.* New York: Harper and Brothers, 1906.

Chase, James S. *Emergence of the Presidential Nominating Convention, 1789–1832.* Urbana: University of Illinois Press, 1973.

The Chicago Daily News Almanac and Year-Book. Chicago: Chicago Daily News, various years.

Chrisman, Nicholas. *Exploring Geographic Information Systems.* New York: Wiley, 2002.

Clark, Charles Branch. "Politics in Maryland during the Civil War." *Maryland Historical Magazine,* June 1944, 149–161.

Clarke, Keith C. *Getting Started with Geographic Information Systems.* Upper Saddle River, N.J.: Prentice Hall, 2001.

Claude, Richard P. *The Supreme Court and the Electoral Process.* Baltimore, Md.: Johns Hopkins Press, 1970.

Clubb, Jerome M. "Historical Politics: American Elections, 1824–1970." *Social Science Research Council Items,* December 1971, 46–50.

Clubb, Jerome M., William H. Flanigan, and Nancy H. Zingale. *Partisan Realignment: Voters, Parties and Government in American History.* Beverly Hills, Calif.: Sage, 1980.

Cohen, Saul Bernard. *Geopolitics of the World System.* New York: Rowman and Littlefield, 2003.

Cole, Donald B. *Jacksonian Democracy in New Hampshire, 1800–1851.* Cambridge, Mass.: Harvard University Press, 1970.

Coleman, John F. *The Disruption of the Pennsylvania Democracy, 1848–1860.* Harrisburg: Historical and Museum Commission, 1975.

Congressional Quarterly's Guide to U.S. Elections. Washington, D.C.: CQ Press, 2001.

Connolly, Michael J. *Capitalism, Politics and Railroads in Jacksonian New England.* Columbia: University of Missouri Press, 2003.

Costantini, Edmond, John R. Owens, and Louis F. Weschler. *California Politics and Parties.* New York: Macmillan, 1970.

Cox, Kevin R. *Political Geography: Territory, State and Society.* Malden, Mass.: Blackwell, 2002.

Cunningham, Noble E. *The Presidency of James Monroe.* Lawrence: University Press of Kansas, 1996.

Curry, Richard O., ed. *Radicalism, Racism, and Party Realignment: The Border States during Reconstruction.* Baltimore, Md.: Johns Hopkins Press, 1969.

Damms, Richard V. *The Eisenhower Presidency.* New York: Longman, 2002.

Dauer, Manning J. *The Adams Federalists.* Baltimore, Md.: Johns Hopkins Press, 1953.

David, Paul Theodore. *Party Strength in the United States, 1872–1970.* Charlottesville: University of Virginia Press, 1972.

Dean, John W. *Warren G. Harding.* New York: Times Books, 2004.

Delmatier, Royce D., Clarence F. McIntosh, and Earl G. Waters, eds. *The Rumble of California Politics, 1848–1970.* New York: Wiley, 1970.

Denboer, Gordon, Lucy Trumbull Brown, Alfred Lindsay, and Charles D. Hagermann, eds. *The Documentary History of the First Federal Elections.* Madison: University of Wisconsin Press, 1989.

Dent, Borden D. *Cartography: Thematic Map Design.* New York: McGraw Hill, 1999.

DiClerico, Robert E. *Voting in America: A Reference Handbook.* Santa Barbara, Calif.: ABC-CLIO, 2004.

Dikshit, Ramesh Dutta, ed. *Developments in Political Geography: A Century of Progress.* Thousand Oaks, Calif.: Sage, 1997.

Dover, E. D. *The Disputed Presidential Election of 2000: A History and Reference Guide.* Westport, Conn.: Greenwood Press, 2003.

———. *The Presidential Election of 1996: Clinton's Incumbency and Television.* Westport, Conn.: Greenwood Press, 1998.

Dubin, Michael J. *United States Congressional Elections, 1788–1997: The Official Results of the 1st through 105th Congresses.* Jefferson, N.C.: McFarland, 1998.

———. *United States Presidential Elections, 1788–1860: The Official Results by County and State.* Jefferson, N.C.: McFarland, 2002.

Duverger, Maurice. *Political Parties: Their Organization and Activity in the Modern State.* New York: Wiley, 1962.

Earle, Carville. Historical United States County Boundary Files, 1790–1970 [AtlasGRAPHICS agf format digital data]. Geoscience Publications, Department of Geography and Anthropology, Louisiana State University, Baton Rouge, 1991 and 1996.

Elazar, Daniel J. *American Federalism: A View from the States.* New York: Harper and Row, 1984.

———. *The American Mosaic: The Impact of Space, Time and Culture on American Politics.* Boulder, Colo.: Westview Press, 1994.

Ershkowitz, Herbert. "The Election of 1824 in New Jersey." *Proceedings of the New Jersey Historical Society* 84 (April 1966): 113–132.

Ettlinger, Adrian B. AniMap Plus: County Boundary Historical Atlas, Version 2.51. Alamo, Calif.: Gold Bug, 2002.

Evitts, William J. *A Matter of Allegiances: Maryland from 1850 to 1861.* Baltimore, Md.: John Hopkins University Press, 1974.

Fee, Walter R. *The Transition from Aristocracy to Democracy in New Jersey, 1789–1829.* Somerville, N.Y.: Somerset Press, 1933.

Fenton, John H. *Politics in the Border States: A Study of the Patterns of Political Organization, and Political Change, Common to the Border States—Maryland, West Virginia, Kentucky, and Missouri.* New Orleans: Hauser Press, 1957.

Ferling, John E. *Adams vs. Jefferson: The Tumultuous Election of 1800.* New York: Oxford University Press, 2004.

Ferrell, Robert E. *The Dying President: Franklin D. Roosevelt, 1944–1945.* Columbia: University of Missouri Press, 1998.

Fisher, Ronald M. *National Geographic Historical Atlas of the United States.* Washington, D.C.: National Geographic Society, 2004.

Flanigan, William H., and Nancy H. Zingale. *Political Behavior of the American Electorate.* Boston: Allyn and Bacon, 1979.

Foner, Eric. *Free Soil, Free Labor, Free Men: The Ideology of the Republican Party before the Civil War.* New York: Oxford University Press, 1970.

Gaither, Gerald H. *Blacks and the Populist Revolt: Ballots and Bigotry in the "New South."* University: University of Alabama Press, 1977.

Gannett, Henry. *Boundaries of the United States and of the Several States and Territories, With an Outline of the History of All Important Changes of Territory.* U.S. Geological Survey Bulletin no. 171. Washington, D.C.: Government Printing Office, 1900.

Garreau, Joel. *The Nine Nations of North America.* Boston: Houghton Mifflin, 1981.

Garrett, Wilbur E., ed. *Historical Atlas of the United States.* Centennial edition. Washington, D.C.: National Geographic Society, 1988.

Germond, Jack W., and Jules Witcover. *Whose Broad Stripes and Bright Stars: The Trivial Pursuit of the Presidency, 1988.* New York: Warner Books, 1989.

Gieske, Millard L. *Minnesota Farmer-Laborism: The Third Party Alternative.* Minneapolis: University of Minnesota Press, 1979.

Glad, Paul W. *McKinley, Bryan, and the People.* Philadelphia: Lippincott, 1964.

Glassner, Martin Ira. *Political Geography.* New York: J. Wiley, 1996.

Goldman, Peter, et al. *Quest for the Presidency, 1992.* College Station: Texas A&M University Press, 1994.

Goodman, Paul, ed. *The Federalists vs. the Jeffersonian Republicans.* New York: Holt, Rinehart and Winston, 1967.

Goss, John. *The Mapping of North America: Three Centuries of Map-making, 1500–1860.* Secaucus, N.J.: Wellfleet, 1990.

Gregg, Gary L. *Securing Democracy: Why We Have an Electoral College.* Wilmington, Del.: ISI Books, 2001.

Grim, Ronald E. *Historical Geography of the United States: A Guide to Information Sources.* Detroit: Gale Research, 1982.

Grossman, Lawrence. *Democratic Party and the Negro: Northern and National Politics, 1868–92.* Urbana: University of Illinois Press, 1976.

Haller, Mark H. "The Rise of the Jackson Party in Maryland, 1820–1829." *Journal of Southern History* 28 (August 1962): 307–326.

Hammond, Jabez D. *The History of Political Parties in the State of New York.* Cooperstown, N.Y.: H. and E. Phinney, 1844.

Hart, Roger L. *Redeemers, Bourbons, and Populists: Tennessee, 1870–1896*. Baton Rouge: Louisiana State University Press, 1975.

Hasen, Richard L. *The Supreme Court and Election Law*. New York: New York University Press, 2003.

Havel, James T. *U.S. Presidential Candidates and the Elections: A Bibliographical and Historical Guide*. New York: Macmillan Library Reference USA, 1996.

Hewes, Fletcher W. *Citizen's Atlas of American Politics, 1789–1888*. New York: Charles Scribner's Sons, 1888.

Hewes, Fletcher W., and Henry Gannett. *Scribner's Statistical Atlas of the United States, Showing by Graphic Methods Their Present Condition and Their Political, Social and Industrial Development*. New York: Charles Scribner's Sons, 1883.

Hicks, John Donald. *The Populist Revolt: A History of the Farmers' Alliance and the People's Party*. Minneapolis: University of Minnesota Press, 1931.

Higginbotham, Sanford W. *The Keystone in the Democratic Arch: Pennsylvania Politics, 1800–1816*. Harrisburg: Pennsylvania Historical and Museum Commission, 1952.

Hilliard, Sam B. *Atlas of Antebellum Southern Agriculture*. Baton Rouge: Louisiana State University Press, 1984.

———. "Indian Land Cessions." *Annals of the Association of American Geographers* 62 (June 1972). Map supplement no. 16.

Hoadley, John F. "The Emergence of Political Parties in Congress, 1789–1803." *American Political Science Review* 74 (September 1980): 757–779.

———. *Origins of American Political Parties, 1789–1803*. Lexington: University Press of Kentucky, 1986.

Hofstadter, Richard. *The Idea of a Party System: The Rise of Legitimate Opposition in the United States, 1780–1840*. Berkeley: University of California Press, 1969.

Holt, Michael F. "A Time of Uncertainty: The Civil War and America's Two-Party System." Robert Fortenbaugh Memorial Lecture, Gettysburg College, Gettysburg, Penn., 2003.

———. *The Rise and Fall of the American Whig Party: Jacksonian Politics and the Onset of the Civil War*. New York: Oxford University Press, 1999.

Hood, James Larry. "For the Union: Kentucky's Unconditional Unionist Congressman and the Development of the Republican Party in Kentucky, 1863–1865." *Register of the Kentucky Historical Society* 76 (July 1978): 197–215.

Howe, Daniel Walker. *The Political Culture of the American Whigs*. Chicago: University of Chicago Press, 1979.

Hudson, John C. *Across This Land: A Regional Geography of the United States and Canada*. Baltimore, Md.: Johns Hopkins University Press, 2002.

Inter-University Consortium for Political and Social Research. Electoral Data for Counties in the United States: Presidential and Congressional Races, 1840–1972 [Computer file]. ICPSR 8611. Ann Arbor, Mich., 1986.

———. General Election Data for the United States, 1950–1990 [Computer file]. ICPSR 0013. Ann Arbor, Mich. Updated June 6, 1995.

———. United States Historical Election Returns, 1788–1823 [Computer file]. ICPSR 79. Ann Arbor, Mich. Updated February 16, 1992.

———. United States Historical Election Returns, 1824–1968 [Computer file]. ICPSR 001. Ann Arbor, Mich. Updated April 26, 1999.

Jack, Theodore H. *Sectionalism and Party Politics in Alabama, 1819–1842*. Menasha, Wis.: George Banta Publishing, 1919.

Jensen, Merrill, and Robert A. Becker, eds. *The Documentary History of the First Federal Elections, 1788–1790*. 4 vols. Madison: University of Wisconsin Press, 1976–1984.

———. *Regionalism in America*. Madison: University of Wisconsin Press, 1951.

Johnson, David Alan. *Founding the Far West: California, Oregon, and Nevada, 1840–1890*. Berkeley: University of California Press, 1992.

Johnston, Ronald J., Fred M. Shelley, and Peter J. Taylor, eds. *Developments in Electoral Geography*. New York: Routledge, 1990.

Jordan, Terry G. *German Seed in Texas Soil*. Austin: University of Texas Press, 1966.

Kazin, Michael. *A Godly Hero: The Life of William Jennings Bryan*. New York: Knopf, 2006.

Keech, William R. *Winner Take All*. New York: Holmes and Meier, 1978.

Kelley, Robert. *The Cultural Pattern in American Politics: The First Century*. New York: Alfred A. Knopf, 1979.

Key, V. O., Jr. *Politics, Parties and Pressure Groups*. New York: Thomas Y. Crowell, 1964.

———. *The Responsible Electorate: Rationality in Presidential Voting, 1936–1960*. Cambridge, Mass.: Belknap Press, 1966.

———. *Southern Politics in State and Nation*. New York: Alfred A. Knopf and Random House, 1949.

Kincaid, John, ed. *Political Culture, Public Policy and the American States*. Philadelphia: Institute for the Study of Human Issues, 1982.

Klein, Philip S. *Pennsylvania Politics, 1817–1832*. Philadelphia: University of Pennsylvania, 1940.

Kleppner, Paul. *Continuity and Change in Electoral Politics, 1893–1928*. New York: Greenwood Press, 1987.

———. *The Cross of Culture: A Social Analysis of Midwestern Politics, 1850–1900*. New York: Free Press, 1970.

———. *The Third Electoral System, 1853–1892: Parties, Voters and Political Cultures*. Chapel Hill: University of North Carolina Press, 1979.

———. *Who Voted? The Dynamics of Electoral Turnout, 1870–1980*. New York: Praeger, 1982.

Kleppner, Paul, Walter Dean Burnham, Ronald P. Formisano, Samuel P. Hays, Richard Jenson, and William G. Shade. *The Evolution of American Electoral Systems*. Westport, Conn.: Greenwood Press, 1981.

Kousser, J. Morgan. *The Shaping of Southern Politics: Suffrage Restriction and the Establishment of the One-Party South, 1880–1910*. New Haven, Conn.: Yale University Press, 1974.

Kruman, Marc W. *Parties and Politics in North Carolina, 1836–1865*. Baton Rouge: Louisiana State University Press, 1983.

Kurtz, Stephen G. *The Presidency of John Adams: The Collapse of Federalism, 1795–1800*. Philadelphia: University of Pennsylvania Press, 1957.

Ladd, Everett Carll, and Charles D. Hadley. *Transformations of the American Party System: Political Coalitions from the New Deal to the 1970s*. New York: Norton, 1978.

Laughlin, Sceva Bright. "Missouri Politics during the Civil War." *Missouri Historical Review* 24 (October 1929): 87–113.

Lee, Susan Previant, and Peter Passell. *A New Economic View of American History.* New York: Norton, 1979.

Libby, Orin Grant. *The Geographical Distribution of the Vote of the Thirteen States on the Federal Constitution, 1787–8.* New York: Burt Franklin, 1969.

Lipset, Seymour Martin. *The First New Nation: The United States in Historical and Comparative Perspective.* Garden City, N.Y.: Anchor Books, 1963.

———, ed. *Politics and the Social Sciences.* New York: Oxford University Press, 1969.

Lipset, Seymour Martin, and Stein Rokkan. *Party Systems and Voter Alignments.* New York: Free Press, 1967.

Long, John H. "Atlas of Historical County Boundaries." *Journal of American History* 81 (1994/95): 1859–1863.

———. "A Case Study in Utilizing Computer Technology: The Atlas of Historical County Boundaries." *Perspectives: American Historical Association Newsletter,* March 1992, 16–17.

Longley, Lawrence D., and Neal R. Peirce. *The Electoral College Primer, 2000.* New Haven, Conn.: Yale University Press, 1999.

Lowenstein, Daniel Hayes. *Election Law: Cases and Materials.* Durham, N.C.: Carolina Academic Press, 1995.

Loy, William G., and Stuart Allan. *Atlas of Oregon.* Eugene: University of Oregon Press, 2001.

Lubell, Samuel. *The Future of American Politics.* New York: Harper and Row, 1965.

Maisel, L. Sandy. *Parties and Elections in America: The Electoral Process.* New York: McGraw Hill, 1993.

Markusen, Ann R. *Regions: The Economics and Politics of Territory.* Totowa, N.J.: Rowman and Littlefield, 1987.

Martis, Kenneth C. *The Historical Atlas of Political Parties in the United States Congress, 1789–1989.* New York: Macmillan, 1989.

———. *The Historical Atlas of the Congresses of the Confederate States of America, 1861–1865.* New York: Simon and Schuster, 1994.

———. *The Historical Atlas of the United States Congressional Districts, 1789–1983.* New York: Macmillan, 1982.

Martis, Kenneth C., and Gregory A. Elmes. *The Historical Atlas of State Power in Congress, 1790–1990.* Washington, D.C.: Congressional Quarterly, 1993.

Mayer, George H. *The Republican Party, 1854–1966.* New York: Oxford University Press, 1967.

Mazmanian, Daniel A. *Third Parties in Presidential Elections.* Washington, D.C.: Brookings Institution, 1974.

McCandless, Perry. *A History of Missouri, 1820 to 1860.* 2 vols. Columbia: University of Missouri Press, 1972.

McCormick, Richard P. *The History of Voting in New Jersey.* New Brunswick, N.J.: Rutgers University Press, 1953.

———. *The Second American Party System: Party Formation in the Jacksonian Era.* New York: W. W. Norton, 1973.

McCullough, David. *Truman.* New York: Simon and Schuster, 1993.

McKinney, Gordon B. *Southern Mountain Republicans, 1865–1900.* Chapel Hill: University of North Carolina Press, 1978.

Meinig, Donald William. *The Shaping of America: A Geographical Perspective on 500 Years of History.* Vol. 1, *Atlantic America, 1492–1800.* New Haven, Conn.: Yale University Press, 1986.

———. *The Shaping of America: A Geographical Perspective on 500 Years of History.* Vol. 2, *Continental America, 1800–1867.* New Haven, Conn.: Yale University Press, 1993.

Mering, John Vollmer. *The Whig Party in Missouri.* Columbia: University of Missouri Press, 1967.

Merriam, Charles Edward, and Harold Foote Gosnell. *The American Party System: An Introduction to the Study of Political Parties in the United States.* New York: Macmillan, 1949.

Mitchell, William C. *The American Polity: A Social and Cultural Interpretation.* New York: Free Press, 1970.

Monmonier, Mark. *Bushmanders and Bullwinkles: How Politicians Manipulate Electronic Maps and Census Data to Win Elections.* Chicago: University of Chicago Press, 2001.

———. *Mapping It Out: Expository Cartography for the Humanities and Social Sciences.* Chicago: University of Chicago Press, 1993.

Moon, Henry Lee. *Balance of Power: The Negro Vote.* Garden City, New York: Doubleday, 1948.

Morrill, Richard L. *Political Redistricting and Geographic Theory.* Washington, D.C.: Association of American Geographers, 1981.

Morris, Edmund. *Theodore Rex.* New York: Random House, 2001.

Morris, John D. "The New York State Whigs, 1835–1842: A Study of Political Organization." Ph.D. diss., University of Rochester, 1970.

Morse, Jarvis Means. *A Neglected Period of Connecticut's History, 1818–1850.* New Haven, Conn.: Yale University Press, 1933.

Moulton, Gary E., ed. *The Atlas of the Lewis and Clark Expedition.* 8 vols. Lincoln: University of Nebraska Press, 1983–1996.

Muehrcke, Phillip C., and Juliana O. Muehrcke. *Map Use: Reading, Analysis, Interpretation.* Madison, Wis.: JP Publications, 1998.

Munroe, John A. *Federalist Delaware, 1775–1815.* New Brunswick, N.J.: Rutgers University Press, 1954.

Murphy, Paul L. *Political Parties in American History, 1890–Present.* New York: Putnam, 1974.

National Archives and Records Administration, Office of the Federal Register. "The 2004 Presidential Election: Provisions of the United States Code." 2004, www.archives.gov/federal-register/electoral-college/2004/04electionbrochure.pdf (accessed September 1, 2005).

———. "Historical Election Results, 1789–2004: Presidential Elections." Various dates, www.archives.gov/federal-register/electoral-college/votes (accessed September 3, 2005).

Nie, Norman H., Sidney Verba, and John R. Petrocik. *The Changing American Voter.* Cambridge, Mass.: Harvard University Press, 1979.

Nordholt, J. W. Schulte. *Woodrow Wilson: A Life for World Peace.* Berkeley: University of California Press, 1991.

Norton, Clarence Clifford. *The Democratic Party in Ante-bellum North Carolina, 1835–1861.* Chapel Hill: University of North Carolina Press, 1930.

Overdyke, W. Darrell. *The Know-Nothing Party in the South.* Baton Rouge: Louisiana State University Press, 1950.

Pacione, Michael, ed. *Progress in Political Geography.* Dover, N.H.: Croom Helm, 1985.

Paullin, Charles O., and John K. Wright, eds. *Atlas of the Historical Geography of the United States.* New York: American Geographical Society; Washington, D.C.: Carnegie Institution, 1932.

Peirce, Neal R., and Lawrence D. Longley. *The People's President: The Electoral College in American History and the Direct Vote Alternative.* New Haven, Conn.: Yale University Press, 1981.

Pennock, J. Roland. *Democratic Political Theory.* Princeton: Princeton University Press, 1979.

Perman, Michael. *The Road to Redemption: Southern Politics, 1869–1879.* Chapel Hill: University of North Carolina Press, 1984.

Peters, Charles. *Five Days in Philadelphia: The Amazing "We Want Willkie" Convention of 1940 and How It Freed FDR to Save the Western World.* New York: Perseus Books, 2005.

Petersen, Svend. *A Statistical History of the American Presidential Elections.* New York: Frederick Ungar, 1963.

Phillips, Kevin P. *The Emerging Republican Majority.* New Rochelle, N.Y.: Arlington House, 1969.

Polakoff, Keith Ian. *Political Parties in American History.* New York: Wiley, 1981.

Polsby, Nelson W., and Aaron B. Wildavsky. *Presidential Elections: Strategies and Structures of American Politics.* Chatham, N.J.: Chatham House, 1996.

Pomper, Gerald M. *Elections in America: Control and Influence in Democratic Politics.* New York: Dodd, Mead and Co., 1968.

———. *Voters' Choice: Varieties of American Electoral Behavior.* New York: Dodd, Mead and Co., 1975.

Pomper, Gerald M., et al. *The Election of 1992: Reports and Interpretations.* Chatham, N.J.: Chatham House, 1993.

———. *The Election of 1996: Reports and Interpretations.* Chatham, N.J.: Chatham House, 1997.

Porter, Kirk H., and Donald Bruce Johnson, comps. *National Party Platforms, 1840–1972.* Urbana: University of Illinois Press, 1973.

Presidential Elections, 1789–1996. Washington, D.C.: CQ Press, 1997.

Prucha, Francis Paul. *Atlas of American Indian Affairs.* Lincoln: University of Nebraska Press, 1990.

———. *The Great Father.* Lincoln: University of Nebraska Press, 1984.

Rafferty, Milton D. *Historical Atlas of Missouri.* Norman: University of Oklahoma Press, 1982.

Rayback, Joseph G. *Free Soil: The Election of 1848.* Lexington: University Press of Kentucky, 1970.

Reichley, A. James, ed. *Elections American Style.* Washington, D.C.: Brookings Institution, 1987.

Risjord, Norman K. *Chesapeake Politics, 1781–1800.* New York: Columbia University Press, 1965.

———. *The Old Republicans: Southern Conservatism in the Age of Jefferson.* New York: Columbia University Press, 1965.

Robinson, Arthur H., Joel L. Morrison, Phillip C. Muehrcke, Jon A. Kimmerling, and Stephen C. Guptill. *Elements of Cartography.* New York: Wiley, 1995.

Robinson, Edgar Eugene. *The Presidential Vote, 1896–1932.* Palo Alto, Calif.: Stanford University Press, 1934. Reprint, New York: Octagon Books, 1970.

Rose, Lisle A. *Prologue to Democracy: The Federalists in the South, 1789–1800.* Lexington: University of Kentucky Press, 1968.

Roseboom, Eugene H., and Alfred E. Eckes. *A History of Presidential Elections, from George Washington to Jimmy Carter.* New York: Macmillan, 1979.

Rosenstone, Stephen J., Roy L. Behr, Edward H. Lazarus. *Third Parties in America: Citizen Response to Major Party Failure.* Princeton, N.J.: Princeton University Press, 1984.

Rowles, Ruth A., and Kenneth C. Martis. "Mapping Congress: Developing a Geographic Understanding of American Political History." *Prologue: Journal of the National Archives* 16 (Spring 1984): 5–21.

Rubel, David. *Mr. President: The Human Side of America's Chief Executives.* Alexandria, Va.: Time-Life Books, 1998.

Rusk, Jerrold G. *A Statistical History of the American Electorate.* Washington, D.C.: CQ Press, 2001.

Sale, Kirkpatrick. *Power Shift: The Rise of the Southern Rim and Its Challenge to the Eastern Establishment.* New York: Random House Vintage, 1975.

SAS Institute. *SAS/STAT User's Guide.* Cary, N.C.: SAS Institute, 1999.

Sayre, Wallace Stanley, and Judith H. Parris. *Voting for President: The Electoral College and the American Political System.* Washington, D.C.: Brookings Institution, 1970.

Scammon, Richard M. *America at the Polls: The Vote for President, 1920–1964.* Pittsburgh: University of Pittsburgh Press, 1965.

Scammon, Richard M., et al. *America Votes.* Washington, D.C.: CQ Press, various years.

Schattschneider, E. E. *The Semisovereign People: A Realist's View of Democracy in America.* New York: Holt, Rinehart and Winston, 1960.

Schlesinger, Arthur M., Jr. *The Crisis of the Old Order, 1919–1933.* Boston: Houghton Mifflin, 1957.

———. *The Cycles of American History.* Boston: Houghton Mifflin, 1986.

———. *History of American Presidential Elections, 1789–1968.* New York: Chelsea House, 1971.

Sellers, Charles Grier, Jr. *James K. Polk: Jacksonian, 1795–1843.* Princeton, N.J.: Princeton University Press, 1957.

Semple, Ellen Churchill. *American History and Its Geographic Conditions.* Boston: Houghton Mifflin, 1903.

Shafer, Byron E., ed. *The End of Realignment? Interpreting American Electoral Eras.* Madison: University of Wisconsin Press, 1991.

Shafer, Byron E., and Richard Johnston. *The End of Southern Exceptionalism: Class, Race, and Partisan Change in the Postwar South.* Cambridge, Mass.: Harvard University Press, 2006.

Sharkansky, Ira. *Regionalism in American Politics.* Indianapolis, Ind.: Bobbs-Merrill, 1970.

Shelley, Fred M., and J. Clark Archer. "Sectionalism and Presidential Politics in America." *Journal of Interdisciplinary History* 20 (1989): 227–255.

———. "Some Geographical Aspects of the 1992 American Presidential Election." *Political Geography* 13 (1994): 137–159.

Shelley, Fred M., J. Clark Archer, and Ellen R. White. "Rednecks and Quiche Eaters: A Cartographic Analysis of Recent Third Party Electoral Campaigns." *Journal of Geography* 83 (January–February 1984): 7–12.

Shelley, Fred M., J. Clark Archer, Fiona M. Davidson, and Stanley D. Brunn. *Political Geography of the United States.* New York: Guilford, 1996.

Silbey, Joel H. *A Respectable Minority: The Democratic Party in the Civil War Era, 1860–1868.* New York: Norton, 1977.

———. *Martin Van Buren and the Emergence of American Popular Politics.* Lanham, Md.: Rowman and Littlefield, 2002.

———. *The Shrine of Party.* Pittsburgh: University of Pittsburgh Press, 1967.

Silbey, Joel H., Allan G. Bogue, and William H. Flanigan, eds. *The History of American Electoral Behavior.* Princeton, N.J.: Princeton University Press, 1978.

Simms, Henry H. *The Rise of the Whigs in Virginia, 1824–1840.* Richmond, Va.: William Byrd Press, 1929.

Simpson, Brooks D. *Reconstruction Presidents.* Lawrence: University Press of Kansas, 1998.

Snyder, Charles McCool. *The Jacksonian Heritage: Pennsylvania Politics, 1833–1848.* Harrisburg: Pennsylvania Historical and Museum Commission, 1958.

Sobel, Robert. *Coolidge: An American Enigma.* Washington, D.C.: Regnery Publishing, 1998.

SPSS Inc. SPSS Base 12.0 User's Guide. Chicago: SPSS Inc., 2003.

Stanley, Harold W., and Richard G. Niemi. *Vital Statistics on American Politics, 1999–2000.* Washington, D.C.: CQ Press, 2000.

Stanwood, Edward. *A History of the Presidency.* Boston: Houghton Mifflin, 1924.

Steed, Robert, and Laurence W. Moreland. *The 2000 Presidential Election in the South: Partisanship and Southern Party Systems in the 21st Century.* Westport, Conn.: Praeger, 2002.

Steiner, Michael, and Clarence Mondale. *Region and Regionalism in the United States: A Source Book for the Humanities and Social Sciences.* New York: Garland, 1988.

Strategic Mapping Inc. Atlas*GIS Version 2.0. Santa Clara, Calif.: Strategic Mapping Inc., 1990.

———. Atlas*GIS Version 2.1. Santa Clara, Calif.: Strategic Mapping Inc., 1992.

———. Atlas*GRAPHICS. Santa Clara, Calif.: Strategic Mapping Inc., 1988.

Summary of the Proceedings of a Convention of Republican Delegates. Albany, N.Y.: Packard and Van Benthuysen, 1832.

Summers, Mark W. *Rum, Romanism, and Rebellion: The Making of a President, 1884.* Chapel Hill: University of North Carolina Press, 2000.

Sundquist, James L. *Dynamics of the Party System: Realignment of Political Parties in the United States.* Washington, D.C.: Brookings Institution, 1983.

Taylor, Peter J., and Colin Flint. *Political Geography: World-Economy, Nation-State, and Locality.* New York: Prentice-Hall, Longman, 2000.

Taylor, Peter J., and Ronald J. Johnston. *The Geography of Elections.* New York: Holmes and Meier, 1979.

Thorndale, William, and William Dollarhide. *Map Guide to the U.S. Federal Censuses, 1790–1920.* Baltimore, Md.: Genealogical Publishing, 1987.

Thrower, Norman J. W. *Maps and Civilization: Cartography in Culture and Society.* Chicago: University of Chicago Press, 1996.

Tindall, George Brown, ed. *A Populist Reader: Selections from the Works of American Populist Leaders.* Gloucester, Mass.: Peter Smith, 1976.

Tinkcom, Harry Marlin. *The Republicans and Federalists in Pennsylvania, 1790–1801.* Harrisburg: Pennsylvania Historical and Museum Commission, 1950.

Tribune Almanac. New York: New York Tribune, 1841–1914.

Tufte, Edward R. *The Visual Display of Quantitative Information.* Cheshire, Conn.: Graphics Press, 1983.

Turner, Frederick Jackson. *The Frontier in American History.* New York: Holt, 1920.

———. Papers. Henry E. Huntington Library, San Marino, Calif.

———. *The Significance of Sections in American History.* New York: Holt, 1932.

———. "The Significance of the Section in American History." *Wisconsin Magazine of History,* March 1925, 225–280.

———. *The United States, 1830–1850.* Gloucester, Mass.: Peter Smith, 1958.

U.S. Census Bureau. *Census of Population.* Washington, D.C.: Government Printing Office, various years.

———. *Historical Statistics of the United States, Colonial Times to 1970.* Washington, D.C.: U.S. Census Bureau, 1975.

———. *Population of States and Counties of the United States, 1790 to 1990* (for Microcomputers). NTIS order no. PB96-500525. National Technical Information Service, Springfield, Va., February 1996.

———. "Significant Changes to Counties and County Equivalent Entities: 1970–Present." Various years, www.census.gov (accessed September 11, 2005).

———. USA Counties on CD-ROM [machine-readable data files]. Washington, D.C.: U.S. Census Bureau, 1999.

———. *Statistical Abstract of the United States.* Washington, D.C.: U.S. Government Printing Office, various years.

U.S. Census Bureau, Geography Division. "1990 County and County Equivalent Areas (co99_d90-shp.zip)." Various dates, www.census.gov (accessed April 23, 2003).

———. "2000 County and County Equivalent Areas (co99_d00_shp.zip)." Various dates, www.census.gov (accessed April 23, 2003).

U.S. Federal Election Commission. "Federal Elections: Election Results for the U.S. President, the U.S. Senate and the U.S. House of Representatives." Various dates, www.fec.gov (accessed September 1, 2005).

U.S. Geological Survey. *Electing the President, 1789–1988.* Reston, Va.: U.S. Geological Survey, 1989.

———. *Maps of an Emerging Nation: The United States of America 1775–1987.* Reston, Va.: U.S. Geological Survey, 1987.

U.S. House of Representatives, Office of the Clerk. "Statistics of the Congressional and Presidential Election." Various years, http://clerk.house.gov/members/electionInfo/elections.html (accessed September 5, 2005).

U.S. Census Office. *Statistical Atlas of the United States Based Upon the Results of the Ninth Census 1870*. Washington, D.C.: Department of the Interior, Census Office, 1874.

Unger, Irwin. *The Greenback Era: A Social and Political History of American Finance, 1865–1879*. Princeton, N.J.: Princeton University Press, 1964.

Van Zandt, Franklin K. *Boundaries of the United States and the Several States*. U.S. Geological Survey Professional Paper no. 909. Washington, D.C.: Government Printing Office, 1976.

Wattenberg, Martin P. *Where Have All the Voters Gone?* Cambridge, Mass.: Harvard University Press, 2002.

Wayne, Stephen J. *The Road to the White House, 1992: The Politics of Presidential Elections*. New York: St. Martin's Press, 1992.

Wayne, Stephen J., and Clyde Wilcox, eds. *The Election of the Century, and What It Tells Us about the Future of American Politics*. Armonk, N.Y.: M. E. Sharpe, 2002.

Weisberger, Bernard A. *America Afire: Jefferson, Adams, and the Revolutionary Election of 1800*. New York: HarperCollins, 2000.

White, Richard. *The Roots of Dependency*. Lincoln: University of Nebraska Press, 1984.

White, Theodore H. *America in Search of Itself: The Making of the President, 1956–1980*. New York: Harper and Row, 1982.

———. *The Making of the President, 1960*. New York: Atheneum Publishers, 1961.

———. *The Making of the President, 1964*. New York: Atheneum Publishers, 1965.

———. *The Making of the President, 1968*. New York: Atheneum Publishers, 1969.

———. *The Making of the President, 1972*. New York: Atheneum Publishers, 1973.

Whittlesey, Derwent. *The Earth and the State: A Study of Political Geography*. New York: Holt, 1939.

Wishart, David J. *An Unspeakable Sadness*. Lincoln: University of Nebraska Press, 1996.

The World Almanac and Book of Facts. New York: New York World, various years.

Zagarri, Rosemarie. *The Politics of Size: Representation in the United States, 1776–1850*. Ithaca, N.Y.: Cornell University Press, 1987.

Zelinsky, Wilbur. *Exploring the Beloved Country: Geographic Forays into American Society and Culture*. Iowa City: University of Iowa Press, 1994.

———. *Nation into State: The Shifting Symbolic Foundations of American Nationalism*. Chapel Hill: University of North Carolina Press, 1988.

———. *The Cultural Geography of the United States*. Englewood Cliffs, N.J.: Prentice-Hall, 1992.

INDEX